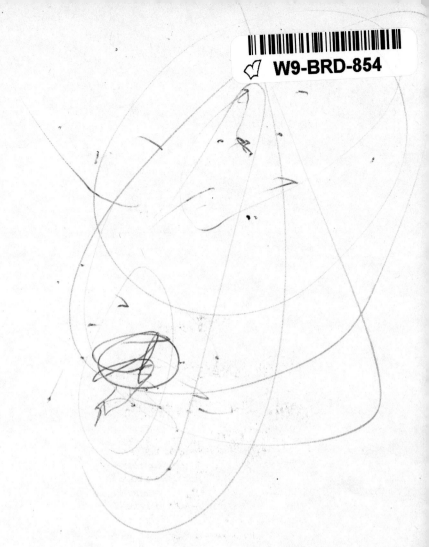

ESSAYS IN THE SOCIOLOGY OF PERCEPTION

ESSAYS IN THE SOCIOLOGY OF PERCEPTION

edited by
MARY DOUGLAS
Avalon Professor of the Humanities
Northwestern University

Routledge & Kegan Paul
London, Boston and Henley
Published in co-operation with the Russell Sage Foundation

First published in 1982
by Routledge & Kegan Paul Ltd
39 Store Street,
London WC1E 7DD,
9 Park Street,
Boston, Mass. 02108, USA and
Broadway House,
Newtown Road,
Henley-on-Thames,
Oxon RG9 1EN
Printed in Great Britain by
Robert Hartnoll Ltd
Bodmin, Cornwall

ISBN 0-7100-0881-3

CONTENTS

CONTRIBUTORS

David Ostrander
Anthropologist, Russell Sage Foundation, New York

Michael Thompson
Research Scholar, The International Institute for Applied Systems
Analysis, Laxenburg, Austria. Anthropologist

James Hampton
Lecturer in Psychology, Department of Social Science and Humanities,
The City University, London

Celia Bloor
Science Studies Unit, University of Edinburgh. Sociologist

David Bloor
Science Studies Unit, University of Edinburgh. Philosopher

George Gaskell
Lecturer in Social Psychology, Department of Social Psychology,
London School of Economics

George A. Kelly
Humanities Center, The Johns Hopkins University
Professor Kelly is also Fellow of the New York Institute for the
Humanities

Katrina C.D. McLeod
Research Associate, East Asian Legal Studies, Harvard Law School,
and Special Humanities Fellow, Committee on Social Thought, University
of Chicago

Don Handelman
Associate Professor, Department of Sociology and Anthropology, The
Hebrew University of Jerusalem

Martin Rudwick
Visiting Research Fellow in the Social History of Science, Science
Studies Unit, University of Edinburgh

Steve Rayner
Research Associate, Russell Sage Foundation, New York

Dennis E. Owen
Department of Religion, College of Arts and Sciences, University of
Florida

INTRODUCTION TO GRID/GROUP ANALYSIS
Mary Douglas

Anything whatsoever that is perceived at all must pass by perceptual controls. In the sifting process something is admitted, something rejected and something supplemented to make the event cognizable. The process is largely cultural. A cultural bias puts moral problems under a particular light. Once shaped, the individual choices come catalogued according to the structuring of consciousness, which is far from being a private affair. This book is an attempt to systematize the cultural constraints. The method of exploration derives from anthropology, though very few of the contributors are anthropologists.

I broached the idea in 'Natural Symbols' (1970), which was only an impressionistic account of cultural controls upon consciousness drawn from anthropologically reported examples from all over the world. I tried to refine and to systematize it in 'Cultural Bias' (1978). In this new volume of essays, various contributors unfold the possibilities of the method, each applying it to a different field. The book divides into three sections. The first four essays directly address problems in the method. The second part consists of comparative studies in history and the history of ideas. The last part comes into close focus on selected case histories showing in detail how the method can be used for better insight. We can say that this book is an argument between the authors, and at the same time a book about kinds of argumentation. It starts from plausible assumptions about the sociological effects of arguments going on in social gatherings of all kinds. In families, in churches, in boardrooms, in sports committees, there are discussions of what should be done, and allocations of responsibility. Such argumentation defines social categories. Its outcomes are enforcements or suspensions of rules. The method tried out is devised to trace these arguments to the fundamental assumptions about the universe which they invoke; its objective is to discover how alternative visions of society are selected and sustained. Its first simplifying assumption is that the infinite array of social interactions can be sorted and classified into a few grand classes. The object is not to come up with something original but gently to push what is known into an explicit typology that captures the wisdom of a hundred years of sociology, anthropology and psychology. Then we can hope to ask new questions.

A famous social psychologist, when I mentioned the word typology, shrank in dismay. He sought to defend methodological purity against my concern to make sense of the larger scene. Typologies, he said, allow anything to be fitted into their boxes; they become an over-powerful interpretative tool. Wondering how one is even to make the smallest progress without developing any typology, I could have quoted from Katrina McLeod the Confucian rebuke to those who shirk their obligations in the name of purity. If the methodologically pure psychologist had also read her chapter below, he might have had to confess that he would prefer to be ranked with the 'pure, clean, mixed with nothing; still, unified and unchanging; limpid and inactive'. If we eschew explicit typologies which can be criticized and improved, we may stay in a celestial harmony and escape from having to deal with the relation between mind and society, but the cost of our private purity is to expose the whole domain to undeclared, implicit typologies. Either way, behaviour is going to be fitted into boxes. Take, for example, the common attempt to explain religious movements in terms of relative deprivation. The implied typology of more deprived and less deprived stalks un-challenged in the textbooks for lack of more explicit schemes with better explanatory power. Implicit typologies are also allowed at deeper levels of disagreement, as, for example, between the possibility of an economic determinist explanation of behaviour and an alternative, which (since the term ideational is aesthetically impossible) one can call the free will or voluntaristic set of explanations. Convinced economic determinists treat values and beliefs as epiphenomena, secondary to and dependent on the pattern of economic constraints; their opponents rightly do not wish to see the realm of the spirit and the source of values and thought relegated to a dependent role. A systematic cultural analysis can save the sense in both camps by bringing the implicit typology of explanations to the light of day. The analysis of the relations between individual judgments and perceived economic pressures clearly needs to be improved. The sociologist who focuses only on the outcome of long historical arguments is tempted to adopt the local perception of economic pressures. Yet opportunities depend to some extent upon how they are perceived at the time. Sociology should not naively accept the natives' theories and believe in ghostly vengeance or in the power of a gift to harm the ungenerous recipient. Yet to judge local economic pressures post hoc by the solutions contemporaries thought fit to adopt is to make an error of that type. We do not have to accept the native version of the controlling powers in the universe. We should not adopt a simple economic determinism, judging the pressures by their observed effects. Between the costs and rewards that our ancestors measured and their resulting action there lay the mediating screen of their own perceptions of what their options were. A way of estimating the local perceptual bias would help to resolve the struggle between economic determinists and the free will camp. Grid/group analysis does this by reducing social variation to only a few grand types, each of which generates necessarily its own self-sustaining perceptual blinkers. The fewness of the types is the encouraging simplification. It saves the cherished assumptions of the free will camp by starting from the apparently free argumentation that allocates responsibility as if it were a real power to be exercised. Beyond that start, this form of analysis does not promote any view of the reality of the freedom of wills. It merely notes that the assumption that persons can be held to account is necessary for interpreting the social argumentation about roles and responsibilities. Consequently, the effective ability to hold others to account must be treated as a necessary assumption for analysing the intellectual strategies in the clash of will that gives rise to society. This approach further protects the favourite tenets of the free will camp by not needing to assume any restrictions upon the individual's freedom of choice. Just because we describe the package of ideas and values that are going to surround anyone once a pattern of social relations is chosen, we do not offer any theory about personal scope for liking or evading the local cultural bias. We only say that this choice between a few social patterns is inevitably a choice between a few kinds of cultural bias. We know nothing in advance that would stop a person who finds the cultural bias uncongenial from choosing another set of social relations - otherwise revolutions would never erupt. The cost-benefit analysis of economic and political power patterns are the factors which lie beyond the scope of this approach. We can only identify what might seem attractive or repulsive about the way of life, seen from a particular standpoint.

The typology can be described as follows. We consider the various minimum forms of commitment to life in society postulated by political theory: the commitment not to interfere with each other, the commitment to mutual protection, other commitments to a larger social unit than the individual, and we decide to start with the possibility of owning or not owning allegiance to a group. For the sake of following this commitment through to all its implications we construct a dimension for group membership. Rules of admission to a group can be strong or weak, making it more or less exclusive; the life-support a group gives to its members can be complete, or partial. For any social context we can recognize appropriate measures of group commitment, whether to ancient lineage, to a learned profession or to a regiment or a church. Once our scheme has incorporated a means of measuring the possible strength of allegiance to a group, the next possibility concerns the extent of regulation, whether within or without membership of a group. For this the possibilities should run from maximum regulation to maximum freedom, the military regiment with its prescribed behaviour and rigid timetabling, contrasted at the other end with the free life, uncommitted, unregulated. If you were to ask people in modern industrial society how they would choose between these polar alternatives many would opt for freedom and against regulation and yet many others are happy and secure in the traditions of army life.

Two dimensions of control over the individual: group commitment, grid control, every remaining form of regulation; combined, these two dimensions give four extreme visions of social life. Each of these essays in first draft had a summary of the grid/group method and the same diagram. To reduce repetition I have been advised to cut out the account of the method of each essay as well as the diagram. It falls upon me to make a clear statement here that will

allow this volume to stand independently of earlier publications and
to be read as a whole. Figure 1 presents four possible social
environments in which an individual may be found, according to this
classification. David Ostrander has suggested the mnemonic titles
for each square. Square A (low grid, low group) allows options for

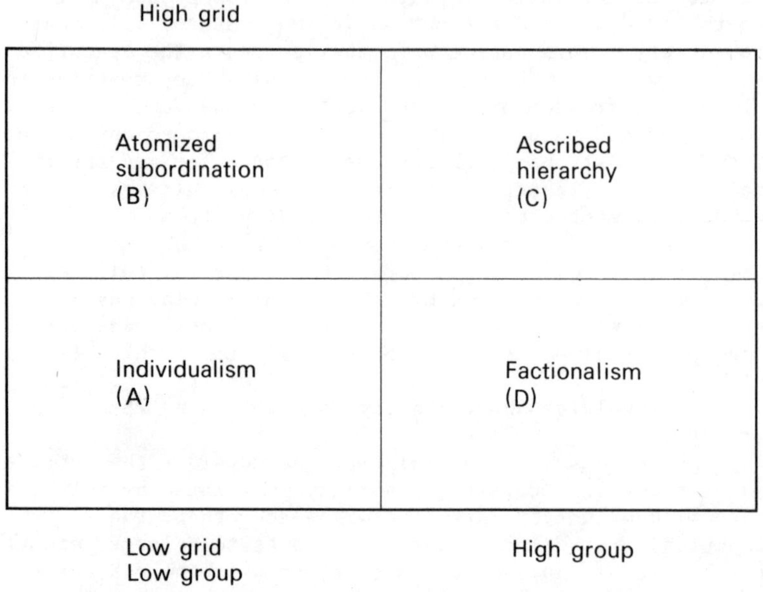

High grid

Atomized subordination (B)	Ascribed hierarchy (C)
Individualism (A)	Factionalism (D)

Low grid
Low group   High group

FIGURE 1

negotiating contracts or choosing allies and in consequence it also
allows for individual mobility up and down whatever the current
scale of prestige and influence. Square B (high grid, low group) is
the environment which ascribes closely the way an individual may
behave. In any complex society some categories of people are going
to find themselves relegated here to do as they are told, without
the protection and privileges of group membership. Square C is the
environment of large institutions where loyalty is rewarded and
hierarchy respected: an individual knows his place in a world that
is securely bounded and stratified. Finally, square D is defined by
the terms of the analysis as a form of society in which only the
external group boundary is clear: by definition all other statuses
are ambiguous and open to negotiation. The two-dimensional diagram
presents a set of limits within which the individual can move around.
Personally, I believe the limits are real, that it is not possible
to stay in two parts of the diagram at once, and that the moral
justifications which people give for what they want to do are the
hard edges of social change. If they wish for change, they will
adopt different justifications, if they wish for continuity, they
will call upon those principles which uphold the present order. In
a serious sense, the grid/group dimensions are exhaustive of certain
possibilities. In another sense, since they are abstractions,
suggestions for systematic comparison which can be adapted to whatever

level of operations is relevant, they apply to all kinds of social
relations, wherever people apply penalties and rewards.

The reason for focusing upon the social context defined in this
way is that each pattern of rewards and punishments moulds the
individual's behaviour. He will fail to make any sense of his
surroundings unless he can find some principles to guide him to
behave in the sanctioned ways and be used for judging others and
justifying himself to others. This is a social-accounting approach
to culture; it selects out of the total cultural field those
beliefs and values which are derivable as justifications for
action and which I regard as constituting an implicit cosmology.
(Douglas 1978: 6)

Throughout this volume we have all used the term cosmology to
include the ultimate justifying ideas which tend to be invoked as if
part of the natural order and yet which, since we distinguish four
kinds of cosmology, are evidently not at all natural but strictly
a product of social interaction.

All the arguments taking place in families, churches and sports
clubs are about whether the institution shall draw its group boundary
closer, or relax it, apply its rules more strictly, create more rules
or relax them all. We draw a square: we indicate increases in group
strength along the base line, and increases in the grid of other
regulations on the vertical line. We divide the whole into four
parts giving increasingly high scores for group from left to right,
increasingly high scores for grid from bottom to top. We assume that
the arguments around boardrooms and dining tables are about whether
the social unit should be pushed more to the right, more to the left,
further up or further down the diagram. We assume that for the
people who are arguing something is at stake and that the outcome
matters. As we harken to the discussion we hear appeals to morality,
normative ideas and self-justification, appeals to nature - and
finally appeals to heaven. God may be invoked, and curses uttered
before a rift, or blessings for a truce. The task of this analytic
exercise is to catch the moral bias which arises from each particular
corner position which has been taken.

The argument here presented is that amid apparent short-term
shifts of opinion there are certain social choices which have long-
run effects because they afford tangible rewards and enlist intellectually convincing moral arguments. People who have banded together
under a certain rubric or constitution will tend to coerce one
another increasingly to develop the full implications of that style
of life, or go to all the trouble of mustering support for an
alternative rubric or constitution. Whatever else may be changing,
the four extreme grid/group positions on the diagram are liable to
be stable types, steadily recruiting members to their way of life
which is at the same time inevitably a way of thought. This is the
strong assumption which justifies exploring the particular method
of analysis. If the infinite array of social types were flexibly
transformable one into another, the task of analysis would be
impossible and not worth the effort. But I claim that four
distinctive types (Michael Thompson argues five) are continually
present, inexorably drawing individuals into their ambit, delivering
to their recruits the choice of thinking alike or suffering the
penalties of failure and ostracism. If this claim is in the least

plausible, then the implications must be analysed. The students of social choice who examine the principles of individual choice and conflict of rights have no way of considering the effect of institutional forms upon moral perception. Yet something about institutional forms is generated by elementary choices and the resultant institutions incorporate judgments which reciprocally influence further perceptions of choice. Once any one of those elementary choices has been made, it entails a package of intricately related preferences and secondary moral judgments. Decisions to stiffen the conditions of entry inevitably result in strengthening social compartments, just as the alternative decision to waive admission requirements results in free flows of people and free flows of wealth. Decisions to delegate result in hierarchy; decisions to separate result in fission. But strong insulating boundaries, once set up, control flows of information that might undermine authority, so the very insulations sustain the boundary system by restricting knowledge. Conversely, to open small gates on control densitizes the control centres to flood warnings. Hierarchy once installed develops self-reinforcing moral arguments that enable more unequal steps in status to be tolerated. Fission breeds. If the swirling movements of individual choices were entirely haphazard, all institutions would long ago have become more and more alike. There would be no scope for recognizable typology. Yet one of the claims in favour of this form of analysis is that in any period or place the four extreme types in the corners of the grid/group diagram are recognizable, with their particular rules and justifying cosmologies.

As I see it, three corners exert a magnetic pull away from the middle; individualists extolling a culture of individualism tend to become more and more uncommitted to each other and more committed to the exciting gamble for big prizes. Egalitarian idealists committed to a sectarian culture strongly walled against the exterior, become more and more enraged against the outside society and more jealous of each other. The supportive framework and intellectual coherence of a hierarchical and compartmentalized society nurses the mind in cogent metaphysical speculations vulnerable to disorder and independence. According to this theory religious history does not have to find explanations for sectarianism (square D), nor secularism (square A), nor for hierarchical priesthoods (square C): each of these three corners seduces people who start to use the arguments that establish the type of society capable of being lived upon its coherent sustaining base. The fourth corner, the fully regulated individuals unaffiliated to any group, is plentifully inhabited in any complex society, but not necessarily by people who have chosen to be there. The groups (to the right of the diagram) expel and downgrade dissenters; the competition of individualists (bottom left of the diagram) pushes those who are weak into the more regulated areas where their options are restricted and they end by doing what they are told. The wish not to be forced up grid when the competition gets too hot attracts individualists towards factionalism. Those who are forced up grid have least power to perceive alternatives. The situation of being closely controlled and insulated from free social intercourse stabilizes a perception of having no options. Their passive view inevitably will be validated by history: however much outnumbering their controllers, afterwards they will seem to have had no choice against superior force. But in accepting that verdict, do not forget that a sense of helplessness is an effect of the condition of being closely regulated.

Here is the place for a note about what this analysis can do. It can expose the normally invisible screen through which culture lets options be perceived. It means that most values and beliefs can be analysed as part of society instead of as a separate cultural sphere. The endless argumentation about rules of admission, penalties and remission ends by filling all the gaps in the conception of the cosmos. Theories of the nature of man and his place in the universe are developed to justify the arguments maintained. There is nothing natural about the perception of nature; nature is heavily loaded with political bias. In so far as there is a consensus about the best kind of society to live in, there is agreement too about the kind of cosmos that the society is found in and consensus about the good life and right behaviour. This does not mean that an individual's values are not freely his own. It does not substitute sociological for economic determinism. As a theory it has very little to say about people's choices between social forms; it does not pre-empt any psychological theory of choice, or psychological theory about personality types that might do well in one social environment and be unhappy in another. It does not say what economic rewards will be strong enough to induce people to change sides in the argumentation and begin to adapt their social environment to a more open individualistic style, nor, conversely, what economic depression will be long and strong enough to deaden initiative and penalize individualism. All that and more has to be filled in for any particular historical case. But what the theory does mean is that the number of cultural packages among which people choose when they settle for any particular kind of social environment is limited. When one chooses how one wants to be dealt with and how to deal with others, it is just as well to be clear as to what else may be unintentionally chosen. Each inhabitable part of the grid/group diagram has got its own miseries and compensations. The theory predicts or explains which intellectual strategies are useful for survival in a particular pattern of social relations, and, facing the other way, it indicates which kinds of cosmology and theoretical style.

Some of the contributors met at a conference which was supported by the Russell Sage Foundation organized by David Ostrander in April 1978. Others had met at an earlier conference supported by the Social Science Research Council of Great Britain in 1976. Others know each other not at all or only by correspondence. The use of the same technical terms and the repeated appearance of the same diagram may give the impression of a private debate. I should hasten to dispel any sense of a small clique of friends in conversation or of players engrossed in a game. The range of subjects discussed and the sheer unlikelihood of such specialists ever coming across each other in their respective departments or learned journals should suggest something of their haphazard and open recruitment.

David Ostrander's chapter is a straightforward attempt to set a historical context. Exploring the properties of the diagram, he distinguishes a stable mainstream thrust in any complex society

between top right and bottom left of the diagram. In the top right
are the formal controls, the representatives of group unity and group
decisions. The equivalent of any priestly hierarchy is here. If
all the decision-making members of society were located behind the
barriers which constitute inner compartments and hierarchical layering,
they will have a problem of communicating with the outside and so of
getting information and adapting to new external conditions. Some
important functions can be discharged by entrepreneurial brokers of
information who are not full members of the central group but who are
trusted representatives, honoured for their successes in pioneering
work or delicate negotiations with outsiders. The stable diagonal,
as David Ostrander calls it, is comprised of two categories, both
involved in exerting large-scale influence. By contrast, the other
two segments, top left, highly regulated without privileges of
membership in any controlling group, and bottom right, small groups
formed in disagreement with and withdrawal from the larger society,
are both categories continually recruited by rejects or withdrawals
from the main stream. This is a helpful start to tracing the other
properties of the model.

   Any learned discipline can provide an illustration. At any one
time its members will comprise some installed in the citadels of
tradition. They are capable of distinguishing who is a true scholar,
a worthy member of the profession. Within its boundaries they are
capable of grading everyone; anyone outside the boundaries is
unclassifiable except as an outsider. The senior of these mainstream
traditionalists award the prizes and medals but they cannot in
honesty always honour the most loyal of their own kind, much as they
would like to. Inevitably sometimes new innovative work has to be
recognized and the prize-winners are often among the other half of
the stable diagonal. These will be individualist scholars, interdisciplinary in affiliation, working in the interstices of
compartmentalized learning. By their energy and brains they drive
the subject forward to new applications. These two kinds of
scholars would constitute the two segments of the stable diagonal.
Then there will be small groups of protestors, and large categories
of isolated workers who rarely get any prizes. Anyone reading this
who mentally reviews his own profession can recognize the social
characteristics of the four types upon which basis cultural analysis
reveals four kinds of cognitive bias, whatever the discipline may be.

BIBLIOGRAPHY

DOUGLAS, Mary (1978), 'Cultural Bias', London, Royal Anthropological
Institute, occasional paper no.35.

Part One

PERSPECTIVES ON METHOD

INTRODUCTION
Mary Douglas

David Ostrander organized the original conference in 1978. He wrote for it an introductory paper which aimed to introduce grid/group analysis by contrast with famous attempts to typologize social experience. Ingenious and clear, perhaps he oversimplified the great nineteenth-century sociological types and present-day theoretical contrasts. But he succeeds in his mission, which was to lay to rest the nagging sense of familiarity, 'where have I heard this before? How does it differ from what I have heard before?' He sets the effort of this book in a historical context and introduces his persuasive insights on one-dimensional and two-dimensional typologies.

Then follows Michael Thompson's bold improvement and solution to many of the problems which will later be encountered. He asks tricky questions which will be in the following essays: can two cosmologies co-exist in the same social context? How does sudden conversion take place? Where to place the hermit recluse? James Hampton feels that several problems which I would have tried to treat by closer control of focus could be solved by adding a third dimension of 'activity'. The hermit would have the same grid/group position as the individualist entrepreneur, but he would lie at the extreme of the social activity dimension and the entrepreneur at the other. Pusillanimously, I prefer to leave the hermit off the map of social controls, crediting him with full escape. But see how Michael Thompson accommodates him comfortably at a zero centre of his three-dimensional cube, the third dimension measuring the possibilities of exerting power. He uses the third dimension to construct a model which could look like a plane surface laid over an unevenly-carved-out cube. It has four stable plateaux at the same four corners of the two-dimensional diagram, but he locates them at different levels in the third dimension. The impossibility or probability of sliding from one to another could be calculated if certain specified information were given. The distribution of power accounts for the pressures and barriers to change. In the middle of the cube he finds a fifth stable habitable region: it is the hermit's cell, away from power, alone, yet a model and enticement to those in society.

I have a difficulty, common to non-numerates, in finding two dimensions rather much to handle consistently. The thought of a third boggles me. My instinct is to squeeze as much information as I can out of two. However, these suggestions are intriguing. Michael Thompson uses the methods of typology and the geometry of catastrophe to explain his development of the theory. He uses the description of cusp catastrophe as a powerful metaphor which could be turned into a set of measures for predicting sudden change. He shows that on some places on the undulating surface presented on his cube two cosmologies may be held in suspense. In any particular dilemma each may be equally appropriate, but overlapping alternatives are available as justifying resources to individuals in moral predicaments. Only at his central zero does the option to choose remain continually open. He shows what deliberate action people have to exert to keep their social relations just poised like that, with no exits closed. It is a precarious balance and at any time pressures to slide down the slope or to climb up may shift individuals out of that calm shelter. Then they will perforce choose the appropriate cosmological scheme which makes sense for where they now are. His main argument for the third dimension is that it accommodates the cases of societies which cannot be fitted into any of the four positions which I have suggested. One of the special values of this book is that Michael Thompson illustrates the limitations of a two-dimensional model by working out how to turn it into a three-dimensional one.

In the next chapter James Hampton describes how he conducted and analysed two small surveys in London in 1976. Scoffers had told us that as one descended the grid scale, as first described, one would automatically be slithering towards stronger group. James Hampton demonstrated the two constructed dimensions of grid and group to be really independent. This was a major advance. But unfortunately our samples did not include representatives of very strong group measures. The small differences between rather weak group membership do not show up anything noteworthy. The main interest of James Hampton's work lies in the questions he raises about objectivity, psychology and mismatch between predicted cosmology and social context. He remarks that it seems to be possible for a person to occupy different positions on the map according to social context. Responses to his questionnaires showed that someone might be in a free individualist environment at work and in a compartmentalized and regulated environment at home. At first, I rejected this possibility. If someone could behave as if in a high-group context in the afternoon and a low-group context in the morning, or change his grid/group score between Tuesdays and Saturdays it seemed to undermine the whole value of the method. But reflection on his results made me modify my view. If one knows anyone who works in an intensely competitive business, where no holds are barred, the weakest goes to the wall, great prizes to the swift and so on, one has seen why such a person might try to get his home life working like clockwork so that in every detail it could be absolutely relied upon not to distract from the office jungle. Then such a person would indeed be creating two totally different contexts. Even more than his family life, his office might reflect tight regulative controls that he has imposed. The people subordinate to him are up-grid, the equals he negotiates with are his world of low-grid individualists.

As new illustrative material came in for this volume, the proper

uses of this method received necessary refinement. If we are talking
about grid/group values comparatively, we must compare like with like
as far as possible. Then the homes of businessmen in a given country
could be compared and we could ask how they deal with domestic matters
when under severely competitive business pressure. We could compare
the women in their domestic or work scenes. We could not justifiably
jump from the work to the home as if the scale of operations or the
economic or social values were the same. The art of the method is to
be very delicate in matching the cases compared, usually sticking to
similar ethnographic materials. We will see how Martin Rudwick
compares geologists with geologists, Michael Thompson compares
Sherpas with other Sherpas, David Bloor compares mathematicians with
each other, Celia Bloor compares young post-doctoral industrial
scientists. The richest results come when the ceteris paribus rule
is most carefully protected. James Hampton's airing of this particular problem leads to a hypothesis: the more hotly competitive the
society of individualists, the more those in the front ranks of
competition will tend to regulate their followers, driving them up-
grid. So we would expect women, cripples and children to be strongly
regulated in a strongly competitive society, expressed public sentiments to the contrary notwithstanding. There are two answers to
James Hampton's query whether multiple cosmologies may not be lodged
in one person's head. The first answer is to be very careful,
minutely precise about maintaining the same scale of comparisons,
both in the social and cosmological parts of the investigation. The
second answer is yes, obviously a person can behave in any one day
as an autocrat at the breakfast table and meek as a lamb at the
office; but by tracing such cases we can discover further patterns
of different parts of the diagram.

James Hampton's other question about how to achieve objectivity
in an investigation is partly answered in the later paper he wrote
jointly with George Gaskell on styles in accounting. His remarks
about individuals launched somehow into a new part of the diagram
and facing problems of conversion or dissonance with their fellows
point to desirable collaboration with psychologists.

James Hampton also fears that the majority of people surveyed
will fall in 'some central grey area of eclectic, loosely integrated
cosmologies'. Again, I have my simple faith in the instrument's
capacity to be made precise. It only works where the role structure
can be clearly identified. In modern industrial society it works
well within distinctive professional classes, when objectives and
fields of interest can be clearly shown to vary on grid/group
criteria.

The most accessible of the attempts to apply grid/group analysis
to the sociology of knowledge is Celia Bloor's analysis of her
interviews of young industrial scientists. The problems which she
and her husband surmounted when they tried to allocate grid/group
scores, on social experience and theoretical bias, to the interview
records help us to understand how this method can be used. Their
sensitive illustrations of how an industrial scientist is likely to
think of his measurements and theories if he is situated in one
social environment or another are suggestive. More than anything
else in the book they raise the question for social psychology:
did these types select their social niches or did they, in one year,
adapt so thoroughly as to suggest a perfect match?

ONE- AND TWO-DIMENSIONAL MODELS OF THE DISTRIBUTION OF BELIEFS
David Ostrander

SOCIAL ENVIRONMENTS AS BASES OF COMPARISON

One requirement for a classificatory approach to the analysis of
symbolic behavior is the elimination of 'societies' as the units of
comparison in favor of the social environments of individuals. This
follows from two rather obvious, yet frequently ignored, facts
concerning the social and symbolic orders. First, societies do not
symbolize - people do. Whenever we treat a society as a single
analytic unit, we are quick to ascribe to it a unified, disembodied
symbolic order which describes it, justifies it, and prescribes
behavioral norms to keep it running smoothly. But the symbolic
order exists and articulates with the social order only through the
minds and actions of individuals operating for their own purposes
within the confines of their own social environments.

Second, even the simplest of societies has a variety of social
environments. Societies must adapt to a multitude of particular
material and social conditions, thus producing a congeries of social
environments, each of which may generate different symbolic associations. This makes classification of societies as wholes impractical.
Social environments, in contrast, are at a second order of abstraction
from the multi-dimensional impact of the outside world. They can be
systematically classified by relatively few dimensions which define
sociality itself.

In modern western thought, the dimensions of sociality have been
most passionately discussed in the work of Hobbes, Locke, Rousseau
and other enlightenment philosophers. For these thinkers, the very
existence of social order was a problem to be explained. Individual
human beings were products of nature - of observable physical
processes. The aggregation of individuals into groups, and the subordination of individual wills to a group will, was not a natural
process, and (they argued) had to arise out of some mutual interest,
be it profit or survival. Despite their many differences, the
enlightenment philosophers agreed in underscoring the idea that
sociality involves the subordination of individuals to a supra-
individual pattern of interaction and therefore limits freedom of
individual action.

The two most general spheres of action limited by social order

are (1) whom one interacts with, and (2) how one interacts with them.
In order to classify social environments, we may treat these spheres
of action as two dimensions which vary according to the degree to
which individual freedom is restricted. Mary Douglas (1978) refers
to these dimensions as 'group' and 'grid' respectively.

The grid/group classification is intended to have the sort of
general applicability necessary for analyzing the relationship of
the social and symbolic orders. A few points should be made concerning
the limitations on this applicability.

1 It is a relative rather than an absolute tool, constructed of
   continuous rather than dichotomous variables. The four cells are
   primarily of heuristic value; actual distinctions among social
   environments may be less extreme depending on the scope of the
   comparison.
2 As it classifies social environments, it is technically incapable
   of distinguishing (as it stands) whole social systems or pan-system
   institutions; thus, capitalism, while ideally in square A (low/low),
   is operationally composed of at least A and B, and probably C and
   D as well.
3 The grid/group classification is not a causal model; it does not
   explain, or seek to explain, why a social environment changes, or
   an individual changes environments. The sources of such changes
   are the exigencies of the real world to which society and individuals
   must continually adjust. They are external to the dimensions of
   sociality and not generated from within.
4 It is not the only classification possible, or extant, which links
   social structure to symbolic structure; in fact, almost all
   social classifications make this linkage, if only implicitly. The
   link here is explicit.

Taking up this final point, we shall turn our attention to a
selection of established social classifications in order to show how
existing schemes share with grid/group an underlying concern to
account for the distribution of beliefs according to variation in
social experience. Such a systematic comparison may also help to
clarify the kinds of things which we interpret as indices of grid
and group, respectively, by relating them to classificatory dimensions
with which the reader may be more familiar.

For the purpose of this paper, social classifications may be
grouped into one- and two-dimensional schemes. The one-dimensional
schemes (being far more numerous) may be further divided into grand
dichotomies, special typologies, and evolutionary states.

Grand dichotomies

By grand dichotomies I mean those schemes which divide the entire
social universe into two mutually exclusive parts. Durkheim's
distinction between two types of social solidarity is an appropriate
first example. Durkheim argued that society integrates its members
by exploiting either their commonalities (mechanical solidarity) or
their differences (organic solidarity). Mechanical solidarity
demands a high degree of conformity, in behavior and belief, to the
strictures of the common conscience. Deviance from these norms is
regarded as a crime against society, and is met with repressive legal

sanctions. Organic solidarity, in contrast, encourages individuality.
Integration depends on individuals carving out their own social niches.
When deviance reaches a point regarded as criminal, it is usually
viewed as an interpersonal action and is met with restitutive legal
sanctions.

Durkheim presented this distinction in evolutionary terms, suggestin
that mechanical solidarity was characteristic of small, homogeneous,
primitive societies and gave way gradually to organic solidarity as
size and internal differentiation (the division of labor) increased.
A broader view of ethnography than was available to Durkheim makes the
evolutionary nature of his scheme untenable. Highland New Guinea for
example offers hundreds of examples of primitive societies predicated
on the individuality, competition and economic exchange characteristic
of organic solidarity.

Stripped of its evolutionary trappings, the mechanical/organic
distinction falls into a larger class of dichotomies which, while
employing various criteria and terminologies, are frequently reduced
to a distinction between conformism and individualism as principles
of social life. Sir Henry Maine (1861), primarily through an analysis
of ancient Roman law, argued that:

> from a condition of society in which all the relations of Persons
> are summed up in the relations of Family, we seem to have steadily
> moved towards a phase of social order in which all these relations
> arise out of the free agreement of Individuals.

Maine defined this process as a shift from status to contract. For
Maine, the transition from status-governed to contract-governed
behavior was a logical, irreversible, and definitely progressive
movement.

Tönnies's (1887) categories of Gemeinschaft and Gesellschaft, by
his own reckoning, have some congruence with Maine's status and
contract, respectively. Gemeinschaft represents a mode of society
governed by ties of kinship, friendship, and local tradition;
Gesellschaft describes a mode of society governed by individualism,
competition, and contract. Tönnies also noted the evolutionary
trend from the former to the latter, but for him this was a change
for the worse. Gemeinschaft was deemed the natural condition of man;
the trend toward Gesellschaft ultimately led to the total dehumaniza-
tion of society.

Weber's (1930) heuristic typology of traditionalism and rationalism
follows the same pattern. Traditionalism holds sway when an
individual's decisions are determined by social convention.
Rationalism gains ground to the degree that individuals become
unfettered by social relationships and are able to make decisions
in their own interest. Weber contended that a trend toward
rationalism was characteristic of human history.

Linton's (1936) distinction between ascribed and achieved status,
while of less global scope, follows the same line of demarcation set
down by his predecessors. Ascribed status is a social position
conferred upon individuals at birth (or other introduction to society,
such as adoption, capture, or purchase). It defines a permanent set
of relations, obligations, and expectations vis-à-vis other members
of society. An achieved status is just the contrary: a social
position obtained through individual effort and possibly at the
expense of other individuals.

From different perspectives and biases all of these dichotomies
cleave the social universe along approximately the same plane. To
the extent that a society is dominated by ascribed status positions,
it is clearly of the mechanical/status/Gemeinschaft/traditionalist
variety. As the scope for achieved status positions broadens, society
moves toward the organic/contract/Gesellschaft/rationalist pole. As
seen above, this was regarded as a natural, unidirectional evolutionary progression in the eyes of nineteenth-century Europeans, with
worldwide capitalism the glorious (or despicable) end. But the
existence of primitive capitalists and modern totalitarian states
calls the inevitability of this progression into severe doubt. What
remains is a bi-polar classification of societies according to their
mode of integration: conformism or individualism.
   Grid/group classification is indebted to the polarization of
sociological thought between individualism and conformism which is
represented by these grand dichotomies. However, in grid/group
analysis, the conformist-to-individualist movement is subdivided into
two separate dimensions, 'group' defining the choice of interpersonal
contacts, 'grid' defining the behavioral options within personal
interactions.
   The basic conformist/individualist dimension runs along the
diagonal through squares A and C where grid and group scores are
either both high (C-conformism) or both low (A-individualism). For
future reference, this will be labelled the stable diagonal. The
B/D diagonal, on the other hand, represents a set of alternative
social environments not envisioned in the old conformist/individual-
ist dichotomy: the co-existence of equally strong conformist and
individualist pressures in complementary aspects of social action.
I shall refer to this as the unstable diagonal.

Special typologies

Special typologies restrict themselves to a particular substantive
subset of the social universe. The individual types are always
clearly defined, but they may be somewhat unsystematic in their
relationship to one another. Durkheim (1951) again provides a good
first example in his study of suicide. Durkheim argues that suicide
is a social phenomenon triggered by the extreme conditions of
various social environments. Egoistic suicide is the hazard of
individualism carried to the extreme of isolation from normal social
ties. Altruistic suicide lies at the opposite extreme where
identification with the social body supersedes the sense of personal
preservation. Anomic suicide occurs in response either to severe
perturbations in the individual's social equilibrium, or to a general
lack of stability and regulation in the individual's social environment. Fatalistic suicide, in contrast, is a response to excessive
and unchanging regulations of the individual without social recompense
or reward.
   A clear congruence of this classification of suicide with the
four cells of the grid/group matrix may be established. The
egoistic/altruistic contrast falls along the stable diagonal, egoistic
suicide occurring at the extreme corner of individualistic square A,
altruistic suicide occurring at the diametrically opposite corner

of conformist square C. The anomic/fatalistic contrast falls along
the unstable diagonal, anomic suicide in the extreme corner of
socially unstable square D, fatalistic suicide in the opposite
corner of oppressed and alienated square B.

Other special typologies are less conveniently structured. Ruth
Benedict's (1934) delineation of three patterns of culture is
intentionally unstructured, yet the 'Dionysian' Kwakiutl, 'Apollonian'
Zuñi, and paranoid Dobuans would appear to be easily differentiated
by grid and group. The Dionysian conflict, personal ecstacy and
aggrandizement conform to our expectations of individualist square A.
The Apollonian ideals of structure and social harmony would seem to
be characteristic of conformist square C. The treacherous conflict
and witchcraft beliefs of the Dobuans would seem to place them
firmly with the simple groups in square D.

If we treat Sahlins's (1963) comparison of two types of political
leadership in Oceania as a typology, it falls neatly into the stable
diagonal of the grid/group matrix. In competitive square A the
Melanesian 'Big Man' leads by virtue of his personal charisma and
ability to outdo rivals in feasting while providing for his followers
In conformist square C, the Polynesian Chief leads by virtue of his
ancestry and according to formula.

Evolutionary stages

Multi-stage evolutionary typologies do not correspond neatly with the
grid/group classification, and for good reason. They deal with whole
social systems of progressivly increasing complexity, whereas the
grid/group categories are social environments within whole social
systems and do not necessarily vary or disappear as a function of
complexity. A certain grid/group category, reflecting the position
of the elite, may predominate at a certain evolutionary stage, but
even in this limited sense of correspondence, the progression of
categories is not unique. Rather, at each successive evolutionary
level there appears to be a spectrum of alternative methods for
organizing complexity, ranging from highly individualistic to highly
conformist. This is perhaps best demonstrated by fleshing out a
well-known evolutionary typology with some contrastive ethnographic
examples.

Morton Fried (1967) delineates four stages of human social
evolution based upon changing principles of political organization:
egalitarianism, ranking, stratification and the state. For our
purposes, the last two stages may be combined, since Fried argues
that stratification, without the apparatus of state controls, is
unstable and either degenerates back to ranking or emerges to
statedom.

In an egalitarian society there are as many high-status positions
as there are people to fill them. Although all are of equal social
standing, certain individuals may through their special abilities
and achievements gain differential respect and prestige among their
fellows. But none of this respect translates into differential
access to material goods or control over others' behavior. In the
real world, this simplest of political types is best approximated in
populations based upon nomadic hunting, gathering, and, sometimes,

horticulture. In these economies the individual family unit is close
to productive self-sufficiency, thus fostering a low-grid, individualistic environment. But the bulk of social interactions are limited to
the local co-resident group of families. This local group is important for defense and subsistence security (through food-sharing and
co-operative ventures). Thus, Fried's egalitarian societies fall
into the class of formalist groups in square D. But notice that,
even in this least complex stage, the grid/group category fails to
characterize the entire social system. Egalitarianism, in this case,
exists among males in the system, but females are almost universally
held in lower esteem. Their access to material goods and behavioral
options is almost always under the (at least nominal) control of
fathers, uncles, brothers, husbands and sons. They exist in a
higher-grid world than their male relations, somewhere towards
square C.

Ranking occurs when there are fewer positions of high status than
there are individuals to fill them. There is a clearly recognized
status differential, above and beyond the male/female split noted
above. Differential access to resources is a privilege of high rank,
but it is accompanied by an obligation to redistribute resources to
subordinates. The social value of rank is its stimulation of
production and specialization through mobilization demands from
above, and consumption demands from below. There are two basic
directions an evolving egalitarian system may follow to establish
a ranking system: rank, and the lines of mobilization and redist-
ribution, can be predetermined by kinship or they can be achieved
and maintained by competing entrepreneurs. The first direction
sends the system up-grid to square C, ascribed hierarchy. This was
the path of the classic Polynesian chiefdoms organized along the
lines of conical clans. The second direction sends the system
down-group, towards square A. This was the direction taken in the
New Guinea Highlands with Big-Man systems and in Afghanistan with
the warring Khans. Of course, the difference between entrepreneurial
and ascribed ranking systems is never absolute in reality. In the
most rigid of Polynesian chiefdoms there were always avenues for
individual achievement (mainly in war) as well as considerable
manipulation of genealogies. Among the Khans of Afghanistan
inheritance and family tradition played a large part in establishing
one's position. None the less, the difference in emphasis is
strikingly clear.

Stratification involves a qualitative separation in terms of
prestige, wealth, and power between those holding the high and low
status positions in society. Whereas in a ranked system high
status is dependent upon one's relationship to, and support from,
subordinates, in a stratified system high status is a function of
control over the resources which subordinates require to survive.
The personal and mutual ties of kinship and patronage are junked in
favor of class and caste hierarchies maintained by the military
apparatus of the state. As in the case of ranking, high status
positions may be rigidly determined by social convention, or they
may be achieved through entrepreneurial competition. The former
results in autocracies of various sorts, the latter in capitalist
republics. In the case of capitalism, the competitive upper-class
environment (square A) creates an oppressed (square B) lower-class

environment. In autocracies, the upper and lower classes both appear
in square C, but exist at different ends of a power differential.

Two-dimensional classifications

These are less common and (aside from the grid/group scheme itself)
I will examine only three two-dimensional classifications.
     Guy Swanson (1969) has developed a classification designed to
discriminate types of political organization. One dimension describes
whether participation in the organization is a function of one's
status outside the organization, or a function of status gained by
virtue of membership in the organization. In the first case, an
individual is an 'element', in the second a 'part'. Sex, age,
strength and achievements would be criteria for being an element;
kinship, caste, class, would establish one as a part.
     The second dimension distinguishes between organizations whose
participants work primarily for their self-interest, as opposed to
those where group interests come first. He labels these as
'associations' and 'social systems' respectively. Combining the two
dimensions yields a four-cell classification (see Figure 1.1).

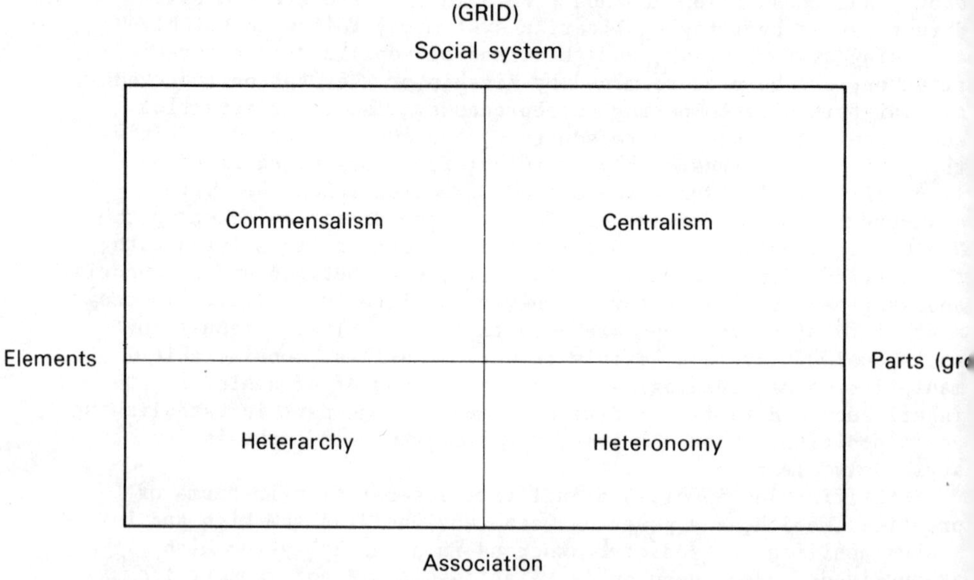

(GRID)

Social system

Commensalism	Centralism
Heterarchy	Heteronomy

Elements   Parts (gr

Association

FIGURE 1.1

     Valid parallels between the grid/group dimensions and Swanson's
organizational dimensions may be discerned. The elements/parts
dimension is congruent with the group dimension: to the extent
one acts as a part one is limited to the group which defines that
part (high group); to the extent one acts as an element one is free
to cross group boundaries and establish individual networks (low
group). The system/association dimension converges with the grid

dimension. An association provides a low-grid environment where self-interest reigns. A social system constrains individuals in a high-grid fashion to act in the group interest.

The resulting categories are similarly parallel to those of the grid/group classification. 'Heterarchy', an association of elements, is a collection of independent constituents meeting and discussing together with their own interests of primary importance; clearly a low-grid low-group environment. 'Heteronomy', an association of parts, is a group of independent constituents, who are none the less dependent upon membership in the group to maintain that independence; low grid, high group. 'Centralism', the social systems of parts, may be the analogue of 'Ascribed hierarchy'; high grid, high group.

The last category, 'Commensalism', a social system of elements, presents a problem at first glance. It would seem to correspond to the high-grid, low-group category, 'atomized subordination'. This cell tends to be an oppressed and exploited region of social space, usually under the domination of the entrepreneurs from square A. How then can it support its own type of political organization? Swanson (1969: 15) notes that, 'A commensal policy differs from heterarchy in that men participate in making ultimate decisions in their capacity as members-at-large of the society, not as participants in, or as representatives of, special subgroups in the population'. With a similar scheme, Swanson reads a different set of values for each square, and provides a more benign view of their restrictions. I would emphasize, on the contrary, that democracy for all its liberal ideals is indeed the home of the capitalist and proletarian: the former can afford to wage political campaigns, the latter sometimes can scarcely afford to vote.

In a study of Indian ideology and social structure, McKim Marriott (1976) has distinguished four types of inter-caste transactional strategies. There are asymmetrical strategies, ranging from 'optimal' to 'pessimal'. An 'optimal' strategy maximizes giving and minimizes receiving: 'pessimal' strategies reverse this priority. There are also symmetrical strategies which balance giving and receiving. These range from 'maximal', where the number of transactions is maximized, to 'minimal', where the opposite strategy prevails. Marriott associates these transactional strategies with the four Varna: Brahmin (optimal), Ksatriya (maximal), Vaisya (minimal), and Sudra (pessimal) in descending order of rank (see Figure 1.2).

The correspondence of these types to the grid/group categories is less immediate than in the case of Swanson's classification, but none the less may be discerned. Within a system as complex as Hindu caste relations there will of course be a variety of social environments, some tending towards the extreme values of square C, others tending toward A, B and D. Granting this, the correspondence between the two schemes remains illusory because the dimensions used are not congruent, even though the resulting types are. Symmetry and asymmetry are dimensions of exchange; they do not translate directly into dimensions of social space.

However, the possibilities of social interaction are not unlimited in this variety. Marriott's types of strategies have organizational effects which enable us to find congruence by a direct comparison of the derived categories. The 'optimal' strategists, Brahmins, are the

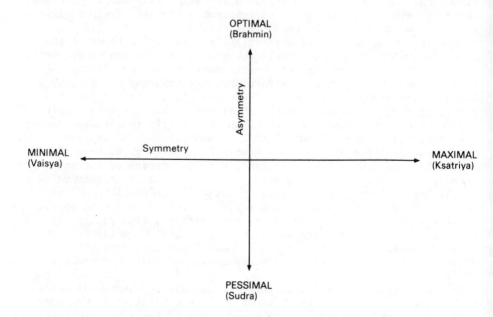

FIGURE 1.2

elite of the caste system and as such can be expected to operate under the strongest constraints of grid and group. The high-grid condition is indicated by the asymmetry of their intercaste exchanges: asymmetry establishes a hierarchical relationship of dependence and obligation. The high-group condition is demonstrated by minimization of receipts: refusing to take gifts from outside groups clearly establishes a group boundary and avoids domination from without.

Following this train of argument, the 'maximizers' (Ksatriya) should tend in the direction of square A (low grid/low group). Symmetry of exchange creates a lower-grid situation by equalizing exchange relationships, while maximization of receipts lowers group constraints by crossing a plethora of group boundaries. The Ksatriya, as it happens, are dominated by warring princes and large-scale landholders. They are easily the most entrepreneurial and competitive of the Varna caste groups.

These two examples seem to have provided us with dimensions with which we can reorder Marriott's types into a format isomorphic with the grid/group classification. The extent of grid constraints on individual behavior is indicated by the degree of asymmetry present in exchange relationships. Total asymmetry equals high grid, total symmetry equals low grid. The group constraints are indicated by the willingness to accept gifts from members of other groups. Minimization of receipts indicates high group constraints, maximization of receipts indicates low group.

Continuing with the last two types, the 'minimal' Vaisya strategy with symmetrical exchanges, minimizing receipts tends toward square

D (low grid/high group).   The Vaisyas are mostly merchants and skilled artisans.   They are small in population and relatively poor in assets, their primary asset being their specific occupational abilities.   They avoid inter-caste obligations that would hinder their (low grid) mobility as contractual skilled workers or traders, and yet depend heavily upon their (high group) caste membership for livelihood.   Marriott notes that other minorities, notably various religious sects, also follow the minimal strategy.   Behavior in these groups conforms well with the expectations of square D.

The pessimal Sudra strategy, with asymmetry and maximization of receipts, tends toward square B, the zone of the oppressed.   This is appropriate as the Sudra form the bottom of the Varna ladder.   They are without rank, wealth, or power, and must depend upon patronage from above.   The revised classification of Marriott's strategies, therefore, looks as shown in Figure 1.3.

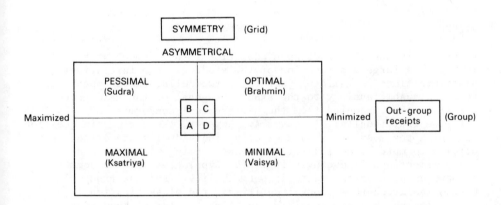

FIGURE 1.3

Whether the changed focus will provide new insights into the caste behaviour and religious cultic practices will depend on new research in this direction.

I now turn to Basil Bernstein's (1971) studies of socialization which use a two-dimensional scheme describing educational environments (Figure 1.4).   The 'classification' dimension measures to what degree the pool of information potentially available to the student is divided into unambiguously bounded categories.   The 'framing' dimension measures the degree of control over what information will be given and how it will be presented.   A school with strong classification and framing represents a highly structured and hierarchical educational environment.   Weak classification and weak framing provide

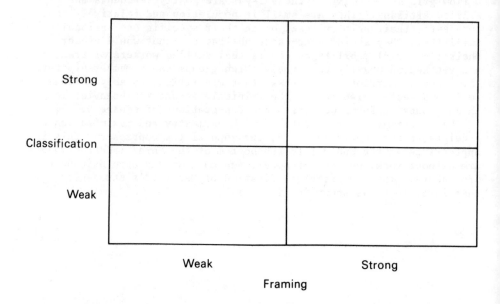

FIGURE 1.4

an extremely unstructured, open educational environment where
learning is largely a function of the students' own initiatives and
discriminations. Examining just these two cells, there appears to
be a reasonable analogy to the stable diagonal of the grid/group
classification, ranging from the hierarchical conformism of square
C to the individualism of square A. However, the options in question
deal with the mode and substance of an individual's education. Any
attempt to match the classification and framing with grid and
group dimensions is unconvincing. The typologies have in common
a focus on boundaries and their permeability. But the group
boundaries are between social entities; the classification
boundaries are between cognitive entities, fields of knowledge.
Thus, while Douglas is using two social dimensions in order to
derive social environments with predictable cosmological correlates,
Bernstein is placing a social dimension against a cosmological
dimension in order to derive socialization environments. Both
procedures are appropriate because they are operating within
different time scales. Douglas's analysis assumes that, given
enough time, cosmology must be flexible enough to adjust to the
social environment. Bernstein, on the other hand, is dealing with
the relatively short time-period of the socialization process in
which the prevailing cosmological system is itself a prominent and
relatively unyielding part of the child's environment.

THE COSMOLOGICAL DERIVATIVES OF GRID AND GROUP CATEGORIES

To this point, social classifications have been examined without much

reference to their implications for symbolic variation. Rather, I
have attempted to demonstrate that many social classifications,
whatever their particular substantive focus, share certain underlying
concerns which may be characterized by Mary Douglas's concepts of
grid and group. Not all classifications mesh easily with the grid/
group format, but the exceptions may prove to be a function of scale.
Evolutionary typologies differentiate entities of greater social
complexity and longer time span than the social environments of
Douglas's scheme; Bernstein's socialization environments deal more
subtly with a more limited time scale. Grid/group analysis, along
with most other social classifications, operates in the middle ground
between socialization and social evolution: the range of social
niches to which individuals must adapt.

If we accept the premise, which seems to be shared by the
typologies we have been looking at, that the symbolic framework
within which an individual views the world is a cardinal aspect of
his adaptation to social constraints, what predictions can be made
for the grid/group quadrants? For the purposes of this paper it will
be sufficient to examine a few basic cosmological elements in order
to trace how they may be logically inferred from grid/group
categories and used to construct distinct cosmological types. There
are three levels of analysis involved in this procedure: dimensional,
interactional, and emergent. The dimensional level indicates what
aspects of a symbol system vary according to each dimension
independently. The interactional level examines those symbolic
elements which vary along a secondary dimension created by the
covariance of the primary dimensions (i.e., the stable vs. unstable
diagonals). The emergent level analyzes the cosmological configurations which arise from the combination of dimensional and interactional symbolic elements in each quadrant of grid/group space.

Dimensional level

Operating under a Durkheimian hypothesis that the structure of
symbolism parallels the structure of social life, we would expect
symbolic systems to vary along grid and group in much the same way
that social environments do. Thus, as the group dimension measures
the individual's degree of identity with a specific group, it should
also measure the degree to which he views himself and his society
as part of the natural universe. Under high-group constraints
society and nature are seen as one integrated system. Low-group
conditions, since they treat the individual as a separate entity
from society, would tend to foster the symbolic separation of
society and nature.

The group dimension also distinguishes the goals of symbolic
action. The focus of symbolic action in high-group environments is
on the preservation and continuity of the group. In low-group
environments, the object of symbolic action is likely to be ego-
oriented (e.g., personal salvation).

	LOW GROUP	HIGH GROUP
1	Society separate from nature	Society part of nature
2	Ego-oriented goals for symbolic action	Group-oriented goals for symbolic action

Just as the grid dimension monitors the degree of restriction on
how individuals may behave in general, it also applies specifically
to symbolic action. In high-grid situations, where behavioral option
are relatively few, symbolic action is likely to be extremely
routinized in terms of how, where, when, and why it may take place.
Low-grid conditions loosen the restrictions on symbolic action. It
is able to become more spontaneous, flexible, and personalized.

LOW GRID	HIGH GRID
Personalized means of symbolic action	Routinized means of symbolic action

Interactional level

The interaction of the grid and group dimensions produces a contrast
between those areas of social space where the dimensional strengths
are equal (high grid/high group; low grid/low group) and those
where they are unequal (high grid/low group, low grid/high group).
There is some justification in labelling these the stable and
unstable diagonals, respectively, in that environments dominated by
either square A or square C have formed, or can form, an enduring
stable social structure. Such a structure is presumed by the
high-grid/high-group constraints of square C; it is inherent in the
weight of individual assets and abilities brought to bear in
square A. The cells of the unstable diagonal are not capable of
generating an enduring social structure - in square D because of the
inherent trend to fragmentation, in square B because of the
constraints on interaction between individuals.
    The effect of this stable/unstable contrast on symbolic variation
is twofold. First, since the stable diagonal is the home of
successful elites, they place a positive value on their cosmological
order. In square C, the synthesis of society and nature is viewed
as harmonious and necessary to everyone's well-being. In square A,
the separation of society from nature is regarded as an improvement
upon nature. Man conquers nature through his own ingenuity and for
his own benefit. For inhabitants of the unstable diagonal, however,
the social order itself is seen as a constant source of danger, and
their view of cosmological order relating nature and society will be
correspondingly complex and more negative.
    The second effect of the stable/unstable contrast is on the degree
of elaboration in the symbolic system. Along the stable diagonal we
may expect a high degree of elaboration. Long traditions of
doctrine, interpretation, and complex codes of symbolic action are
likely to develop along with a specialized organization of practi-

tioners. The elaboration will tend to be greater than any individual, and certainly any non-specialist, can master. Along the unstable diagonal there may be folk traditions, but none so complex that they cannot be fully inculcated by individuals; there may be specialists, but usually on a part-time and unorganized basis. In general there will be a low degree of elaboration. In the case of square B, individuals are subject to the elaborated symbol system of those who regulate them, but they are unlikely to accept it in this form. They will partake in it in a passive, desultory fashion.

UNSTABLE DIAGONAL   STABLE DIAGONAL

Negative value on   ──────────→ Positive value on
  cosmological order   cosmological order

Unelaborated   ←──────────   Elaborated symbolic
  symbolic system   system

Emergent level

Combining the previous levels of analysis, we are given five state-ments concerning the symbolic order for each quadrant: two on the cosmological order (its structure and value), two on symbolic action (its means and goals) and one on the degree of elaboration (see Figure 1.5).

These statements, as they stand, form rather abstract and disconnected lists of attributes. Each list may be integrated, however, to form a distinct cosmological configuration.

Square A, with its positively valued separation of society and nature, encourages a view of Man as master of nature. To subdue and have dominion over nature means that its fruits must be actively seized, or the individual perishes. Similarly, the individual, through personalized symbolic action, must take an active role in assuring his own place in the cosmos. The ultimate goal is the salvation of his particular soul; the primary means are personal, supplicatory communication with cosmic forces (e.g. prayer), and worthy, worldly accomplishments (e.g. good works). This emphasis on personal performance also pervades the ranks of symbolic specialists and accounts for the direction taken by elaboration of the symbol system. Along with traditions of organization, myth, and ritual, there develops a tradition of critical review and reinter-pretation. Christian practitioners, for example, provide weekly reinterpretations of doctrine in light of contemporary events, and have a lengthy tradition of religious scholarship to fall back upon. Confidence in an internal critical review is a fundamental charac-teristic of western science and politics, as well as religion.

Moving up-grid to square B, the elaboration of the symbol system declines, because both the system and most of its practitioners are imposed from some other quadrant. The inhabitants of B do not have a real stake in the intellectual substance of the system and know mainly its form. Symbolic action is limited largely to participation in ritual. As to belief, personal salvation may still be the goal, but lacking coherent formulae for earning it, the individual is likely to develop a fatalistic reliance on ritual forms.

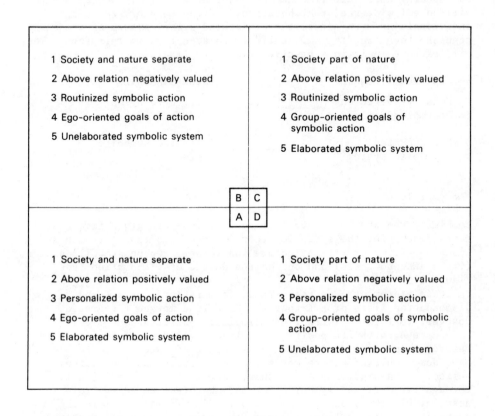

FIGURE 1.5

The society which corresponds to square C exults in the harmony of
society and nature. Man does not subdue nature, but maintains a
delicate balance. A disruption of the social equilibrium will be
answered by a disruption of the natural equilibrium, and a distur-
bance in nature is a portent that something is rotten in the social
fabric. Symbolic action is therefore oriented to the preservation
of this balance. Ritualization of symbolic action is paramount,
because to deviate from form is in itself a disruption of the social
status quo. Ritual form is one thing that can be perfectly regulated,
and thus used to symbolically regulate nature. The emphasis on form
and structure outweighs the significance of content. Thus, Hindu
mantras differ from Protestant prayers in that they rely on the
pattern of sounds rather than their meaning. Elaboration of the
symbolic system in square C also takes the form of considerable
scholarship and research, but without powerful critical review.
Traditional doctrine may be refined, embellished, and expanded, but

not fundamentally challenged from within. Challenges that do occur tend to create new traditions which co-exist with the old one. Much internal elaboration takes the form of refined systems for predicting nature (astrology, numerology, etc.).

Descending along the grid dimension to square D, we find people's views of society and of nature linked in disequilibrium. They are both fragmented into mutually antagonistic groups and both suffer constant danger from predators, human, natural and supernatural. Existence depends upon membership in a group, and therefore the goal of symbolic action is the protection of the group from outside threats. Sometimes these threats are physical assaults; more often they are the result of witchcraft or magic of some kind, and reveal their presence by sickness, death, a bad harvest or other misfortune. Personalized symbolic action in this square takes the form of divining the malefactor, expelling him, should he be a member of the group, cancelling his spell, and responding with one's own magic. The square D symbolic practitioner has a private pipeline to the supernatural with which he outwits his enemies and protects his friends, kin, and clients. Elaboration is at a low level because specialists are not organized and no enduring social structure exists which would support such organization.

The cosmological configurations above are the product of a logical exercise. It remains to be seen how valid or useful they may prove to be in the analysis of real social and cultural systems. Two points concerning their applicability should be reiterated. Firstly, while they have been heuristically characterized into four types, they actually represent four directions in which symbolic systems may be expected to vary in response to a corresponding shift in the constraints of the social environment. The important part of this analysis is not the types but the dimensional contrasts from which they are built. Secondly, although the above cosmological types have been described largely in terms of religious and magical systems, we would expect analogous configurations to occur in any symbolic field, such as science and the arts.

BIBLIOGRAPHY

BENEDICT, RUTH (1934), 'Patterns of Culture', Boston, Houghton Mifflin.
BERSTEIN, BASIL (1971), On the classification and framing of educational knowledge, in B. Bernstein (ed.), 'Class, Codes and Controls', vol.1, London, Routledge & Kegan Paul: 202-30.
DOUGLAS, MARY (1973), 'Natural Symbols', London, Penguin.
DOUGLAS, MARY (1978), 'Cultural Bias', London, Royal Anthropological Institute, occasional paper no.35.
DURKHEIM, EMILE (1933), 'The Division of Labor', trans. G. Simpson, Chicago, Free Press.
DURKHEIM, EMILE (1951), 'Suicide', trans. J. Spaulding and G. Simpson, Chicago, Free Press.
FRIED, MORTON (1967), 'The Evolution of Political Society', New York, Random House.
THE HOLY BIBLE (King James version).
LINTON, RALPH (1936), 'The Study of Man', New York, Appleton-Century.

MAINE, HENRY (1861), 'Ancient Law'. Quote in text from 1917 edition, New York, Dutton: 99.

MARRIOTT, McKIM (1976), Hindu transactions: diversity without dualism, in B. Kapferer (ed.), 'Transaction and Meaning': 109-42, Philadelphia, Institute for the Study of Human Issues.

MARX, KARL and F. ENGELS (1948), 'The Communist Manifesto', New York, International Publishers.

SAHLINS, MARSHALL D. (1963), Poor Man, Rich Man, Bigman, Chief: political types in Melanesia and Polynesia, 'Comparative Studies in History and Society', 5:285-303.

SWANSON, GUY (1969), 'Rules of Descent: Studies in the Sociology of Parentage', Ann Arbor, University of Michigan Press.

TÖNNIES, FERDINAND (1887), 'Gemeinschaft und Gesellschaft', trans. C.P. Loomis as 'Fundamental Concepts of Sociology, New York, American Book Company.

WEBER, MAX (1930), 'The Protestant Ethic and the Spirit of Capitalism', trans. T. Parsons, London, Unwin.

Chapter 2

A THREE-DIMENSIONAL MODEL
Michael Thompson

INTRODUCTION

It is often difficult to explain behaviour related to environmental
problems, and this is a pity because, if only we could explain such
behaviour, we could save ourselves a lot of trouble and a lot of
money. Nowhere is this intellectual difficulty, and the waste
consequent upon our failure to overcome it, more apparent than in
the peaceful use of nuclear energy. In no other field have the
policy reversals been so spectacular, so unexpected and so alarming
in their consequences.

In Sweden, ex-Prime Minister Olaf Palme has claimed that it was
the opponents of his plan to expand nuclear energy who tipped the
scales against him and turned out his Socialist Party for the first
time in forty-four years. In Germany, sometimes violent anti-
nuclear demonstrations have led to court rulings that have halted
construction on two reactors and have brought to a virtual standstill
the most extensive nuclear energy programme in Europe. Similar
questionings of nuclear projects reverberate through France, Britain,
Italy and Spain.

Of course, the simplest and most attractive explanation for these
reversals is that new evidence has come to light since the initial
policy decisions were taken: either that risks hitherto unsuspected
have been discovered, or that the knowledge of these risks, hitherto
concealed, has become public. The evidence, alas, is against this
explanation.

In 1945 the 'Bulletin of the Atomic Scientists' was established
to deal publicly with nuclear controversies of all kinds, in England
the Campaign for Nuclear Disarmament was created in the 1950s, and
in the United States the Committee for Nuclear Information began its
activities in 1958. In other words, concern about the negative
consequences of unlimited nuclear proliferation has been expressed
from the beginning. Most of this concern has been directed at the
unpeaceful uses of nuclear energy and only in the 1970s, when the
policies have long been established and the technologies well proven,
has concern been so suddenly directed at the peaceful uses. Nor
would it be any use arguing that this is because we can now afford
to be sensitive to risks that previously we had to accept. There

has been no marked diminution of the risks involved in the unpeaceful uses of nuclear energy, nor have we suddenly stumbled across other less dangerous energy sources. Quite the reverse. The protests have reached a crescendo at the very moment that our societies have come to recognise their dependence upon energy to maintain our way of life, and we are faced with the paradox that we are rejecting this source of almost unlimited power only as we come to realise our tremendous need for it. How can we find a rational explanation for such behaviour: behaviour that would seem to be based on rationality-in-reverse?

   In cases such as this the answer to the question, if there is one, is not likely to be found near at hand in those disciplines – economics, management or political science, for instance – that have long had their hands on the policy tiller. The answer, an adequate explanatory framework for what is going on here, does not at present exist but can be provided by bringing together insights from two remote and seemingly unlikely places: topology and anthropology. More specifically, an explanation can be provided by marrying catastrophe theory to Professor Mary Douglas's ideas about the connections between different kinds of social context and different kinds of cosmology. (2)

SOCIAL CONTEXT AND COSMOLOGY

Douglas believes that anthropologists, having for so long immersed themselves in the study of comparatively simple but spectacularly diverse peoples, should now bring this esoteric knowledge to bear on their own societies. She argues that, though people see things differently, there are not that many different ways of seeing things differently. At the same time, though people may find themselves in very different social situations, there are not that many different kinds of social situation to find oneself in. If she is correct, the way is opened for the transcending of two great traditions that have always been assumed to be mutually contradictory: cultural relativity and cultural universality.

   Douglas holds that just two dimensions are enough to describe the important variations of social context: one, the extent to which a person's social life depends on his membership of social groups (group), and two, the extent to which his social life is restricted by rules which preordain his social relationships (grid). Further, she holds that simple qualitative distinctions between strong and weak group and between strong and weak grid are sufficient to describe the correlation between social context and cosmology (by cosmology is meant the theories about the nature of the universe that sustain moral judgments). The result is a simple, but bold, typology in which four sorts of social context are associated with four sorts of cosmology. The full description of these four contexts and their associated cosmologies, and of the manner in which the various kinds of moral judgments tend to stabilise these associations, is a lengthy and complicated business and need not concern us here. For present purposes a brief illustration of the theory, in terms of varying responses to pollution, should suffice.

   We should expect that individuals with high-group contexts, because

of the emphasis on boundaries, will be pollution-conscious. With
weak grid (where there is little internal differentiation of the
group) pollution can arise only at the boundary of the group and the
culture will be biased in the direction of scapegoating and of
witchcraft. As we move up grid, from weak to strong, so the level of
differentiation within the group increases. In such contexts,
concepts of pollution will relate, not just to inside/outside, but
to more complex separations based upon hierarchy. The culture where
such strong-group/strong-grid contexts are prevalent will be biased
towards ritual and sacrifice.

In weak-group contexts there is much more opportunity for
individualistic manipulation. Those with weak grid, the successful
manipulators, will tend to subscribe to a pragmatic view of the world
in which no distinctions are absolute and everything is negotiable.
Concepts of purity and defilement, if present, would impede these
entrepreneurial processes. The result is that in weak-group contexts
generally there is little concern about pollution. The manipulated
occupy the last quadrant, weak group/strong grid. They share the
entrepreneur's lack of concern for pollution but, since their lives
are everywhere constrained by preordained rules, they have no scope
for negotiation and do not share his pragmatism. These are the
people whose lives Mrs Gaskell described as being like a lottery.
They find it difficult to construct a very coherent world picture but
are attracted by the prizes that millennial movements promise.

'World view' or 'culture' are other concepts that are commonly
used in attempts to describe the different ways in which people
relate to their social and physical environment. Douglas chooses
the word cosmology because she wishes to emphasise the coercive
element in world view or culture: the way in which people justify,
to themselves and to others, the decisions and actions that they
take. She is concerned to stress that a world view does not emerge
simply by a logical process of seeing and understanding. Its
persistence, its common currency and its credibility are, she holds,
only made possible by a constant effort of will: by a positive
and shared commitment to that world view in preference to other
possible ones. This effort, this commitment, that is constantly
needed to maintain the stability of a world view is the locus of
morality. A particular way of seeing recommends itself to us not
just because it furnishes us with a way of understanding, a means of
maximising the level of meaning that we can extract from our
situation, but also because it is right.

The very boldness and simplicity of Douglas's typology tends to
obscure the significance of what she is saying, which is that the
stable relationship between culture and social arrangement - that
most anthropologists tend to take for granted - is really quite
extraordinary and demands some sort of explanation. Douglas's
explanation runs something like this.

A particular world view or culture is not, in itself, stable. It
is stabilisable only in association with a particular kind of social
context and in association with a shared moral commitment among the
occupants of that social context. Such stabilisable situations are
really quite limited and Douglas maintains that there are only four
of them and that they can be described by this simple picture shown
in Figure 2.1

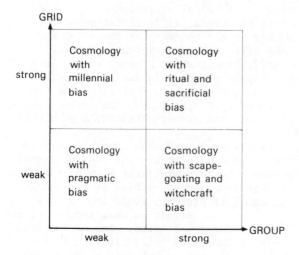

FIGURE 2.1

This typology is explicitly static. It simply says that, for each of these four kinds of social context, a shared moral commitment to a particular kind of cosmology will give stability. Implicit in the argument is the idea that this stability is only maintained by a constant turmoil in which each individual's actions are sorted out for reward or punishment in terms of the moral judgments that the particular type of cosmology appropriate to that particular social context makes possible.

It is as if Douglas, looking at the English countryside, has noticed that populations of foxes and rabbits are always present within it. A typology, a list of the common English mammals, would include the information that rabbits and foxes are present in some sort of equilibrium. At the same time, she is well aware that this stability is the outcome of a constant turmoil in which the foxes eat the rabbits and the rabbits try to avoid being eaten by the foxes. Equilibrium (the continued presence of both foxes and rabbits) and disequilibrium (resulting in the extinction of either rabbits or foxes or both) can both result from this turmoil and the problem is to understand how equilibrium and disequilibrium states are possible and why it is that we sometimes get one and sometimes get the other. In other words, rabbits and foxes are not just there: they constitute a dynamical system. The same, Douglas insists, is true of social contexts and cosmologies.

My aim is simply to take Douglas at her word and to ask what sort of dynamical system could generate the four stable equilibria that are depicted in her typology. She has provided a model of the stabilisable outcomes of the turmoil: my aim is to model the turmoil itself.

THE DYNAMICAL SYSTEM

Introduction

Some clues as to how to set about modelling the dynamics of context,
cosmology and morality can be obtained by taking Douglas's typology
and trying to set it in motion. At any moment an individual's social
context in terms of grid and group must lie in one of her four
quadrants and, if we know his quadrant, we know his cosmology. But
if, as a result of his involvement in social life, his context is
changing, then what happens if he moves out of one quadrant into
another? Should we regard the boundary lines between the quadrants
as conventions for what are, in fact, gradual transitions from one
cosmology to another or should we assume that they represent sudden
discontinuous changes in cosmology of the kind that Saul experienced
on the road to Damascus? If this latter is the case, why should
these lines in grid/group space be specially privileged in that
sudden discontinuous changes occur along them and not along other
lines that can be drawn in the space? In particular, how on earth
do we understand what is happening in the case of an individual whose
changing context happens to pass through the point where her four
quadrants meet? Since context and cosmology are stabilised by
shared moral commitment, the transition from one stable arrangement
to another is problematical. Such a transition requires the relaxing
and relinquishing of one sort of moral commitment followed by the
acceptance and embracing of a different one. How can this happen?
    These, I hasten to add, are problems for me, not for Douglas.
Such changes occur as a result of process and her typology is
concerned not with process but simply with the stable equilibria
that can emerge as a result of process. But the advantage of posing
these problems in this way is that they suggest four clues to their
solution. The first is that it looks as if I will need more than
two dimensions. The second is that I will need to ask what sort of
processes could generate her three determinants of stability: grid,
group and morality. The third is that, as it stands, the point
where the four quadrants meet is going to present difficulties.
The fourth is that I will have to allow for the growth and decay
of commitment.
    In fact, I need three dimensions: one concerned with the sort of
process that gives rise to the group component of social context
which I identify as group dynamics, one concerned with the sort of
process that gives rise to the grid component which I identify as
network-building, and one concerned with the exercise of the
coercive possibilities that the cosmologies present which I identify
as manipulation. In this last process, involving manipulation, there
is no need to assume that, if coercive possibilities are present,
they are automatically taken up. For Douglas's equilibria to emerge
they have to be taken up: stability requires commitment. But,
since transition is a sequence of unstable situations, it seems
likely that during it these coercive possibilities are not taken up
and that, indeed, transition is possible precisely because of this
temporary loss of commitment. I therefore need, in the first
instance, to speak of world view. Cosmology is the special case:
world view plus commitment.

A rather surprising consequence of looking at the processes
behind these determinants is that it turns out that Douglas's typology
is not exhaustive. There are, in fact, not four but five stabilisable
situations, and the one Douglas has missed lies somewhere near the
middle of her picture and so resolves the problems presented by the
point where her four quadrants meet (see Figure 2.2).

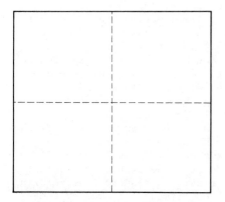
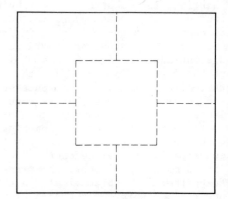

BEFORE: four equilibria
         meeting at a
         problem point.

AFTER: five equilibria.
        Problem point
        removed.

FIGURE 2.2

The autonomous individual

To get at the dynamics we need to look at the processes behind
Douglas's grid and group dimensions. The group dimension appears
to be quite simple. If a person obtains his entire life support
from within the group, we can say that his social context has strong
group. If he obtains none of his life support from within the
group, we can say that his social context has weak group. But this
separation of strong- and weak-group contexts says nothing about
how he comes to be included or excluded. As Douglas points out,
groups are concerned with the preservation of their boundaries:
emphasising the differences between those inside and those outside,
carefully monitoring the admission of outsiders, ruthlessly expelling
those inside who are perceived as threats. These actions, in
aggregate, result in group dynamics: formation, fusion, fission,
collapse. At some stage along a series of expulsions a group will
become unstable. To start with, offending crew members are being
forced to walk the plank. Towards the end, transmogrified, they
are rats deserting a sinking ship. (3) Douglas is able to lump them
all together as having weak-group contexts but, if I want the group
dimension to reflect the process of group dynamics, I will have to
keep them apart.

Similar problems arise with the grid dimension. If a person sits
at the centre of a vast network in which he is connected, not just to
a lot of people, but to a lot of important people, he will at the
same time be unconnected to a lot of unimportant people. For the
wheeler-dealer, his personal network is all. For those selected
against by the wheeler-dealer, other people's networks are all. The
wheeler-dealer is very much a free agent. The little man finds his
life largely prescribed by the ramifications of the networks of
others. How does this continuous network-building process relate to
Douglas's grid dimension?

The little man finds that his options are closed by the proliferation of networks which do not include him or, at best, include him
only at their peripheries. This closure of options receives
expression in the form of prescriptive rules which provide two
justificatory bases: the self-help ethic of those whose actions
give rise to exclusion, and the fatalistic acceptance of preordained
social relationships by those who are excluded. In Douglas's terms,
the little man's context has strong grid. The successful wheeler-
dealer is 'gridded' only to the extent that others are even more
successful than he. Douglas would say his context has weak grid.
But weak and strong grid do not adequately describe all the contexts
that can result from this kind of social process. There is another
possibility.

A person may choose to stand aside, or aloof, from all this
network-building. Dismayed by the excesses of the rat-race he tries
to remain autonomous avoiding where possible involvements that would
enable him to call on the support of others and, at the same time,
enable others to make calls upon him. Of course, it is very unlikely
that he will be able to avoid all connections. Even the celebrated
Tibetan hermit Milarepa, living in a Himalayan cave and eating boiled
nettles, had some vestigial relationship with the person who had
provided him with the pot in which to cook his nettles. When he rid
himself of this last undesirable contact, by deliberately breaking
his nettle pot, he also destroyed his already tenuous life-support
system. Full autonomy, it seems, can only be sustained for limited
periods - forty days and forty nights is the traditional estimate -
but at least the autonomous individual keeps his network to a
minimum, engages wherever possible in self-liquidating transactions
and avoids placing heavy demands on such networks as he has.

Douglas is aware of the autonomous individual and of the
distinctive world view that he is drawn towards. However, since
full autonomy seems to imply the elimination of community, it is
difficult to visualise just how the shared moral commitment so
necessary for stability can be achieved. The evidently temporary
nature of complete autonomy reinforces one's suspicions that the
autonomous individual has only a world view and not a cosmology. It
is for these reasons that Douglas takes the autonomous individual
'off the social map'. Yet he is obviously a key figure as far as
social processes are concerned and, since my aim is to depict both
world views and cosmologies (and the processes by which each is
transformed into the other), I cannot disregard him.

In fact, I find it helpful to take this autonomous individual,
who by definition is outside the processes of group dynamics and of
network-building, as my starting-point and to fill out my picture by

considering the various ways in which he can become involved. A
surprising feature of the picture which emerges is that the autonomous
world view turns out to be a cosmology as well. That is, the context
and world view of the autonomous individual can be stabilised. This
leads to some awkward questions. How can a commitment to the ideal of
autonomy be shared? And how can the moral imperative to avoid any
coercive involvement with others give rise to judgments that coerce
others? I will leave the resolution of these delightful paradoxes
to my second essay in this volume (chapter 13).

The grid dimension

I need to draw this context variable in such a way that it reflects
the processes that give rise to it. I cannot, therefore, fit the
context of the autonomous individual in somewhere between weak and
strong grid. Weak-grid and strong-grid contexts are the direct
results of network-building whilst the context of the autonomous
individual is attained by avoiding network-building. Thus the
context of the autonomous individual is not so much half way between
weak grid and strong grid, but in contrast to them both. This means
that I will have to redraw the grid dimension.

   In contrast to this autonomous individual, look at the various
individuals caught up in well-developed networks. One of the
classic anthropological examples of this sort of thing is the Big
Man in New Guinea Highlands society. The Big Man is a forceful,
competitive entrepreneur who builds up a massive personal network
through his many wives, his relatives, his followers and his
students or henchmen. His exuberant egalitarian bonhomie conceals
a shrewd screening process in which only important followers enjoy
easy access whilst the less important must usually remain content
with indirect contact. Most screened of all are the least important
individuals known in pidgin as 'rubbish men'.

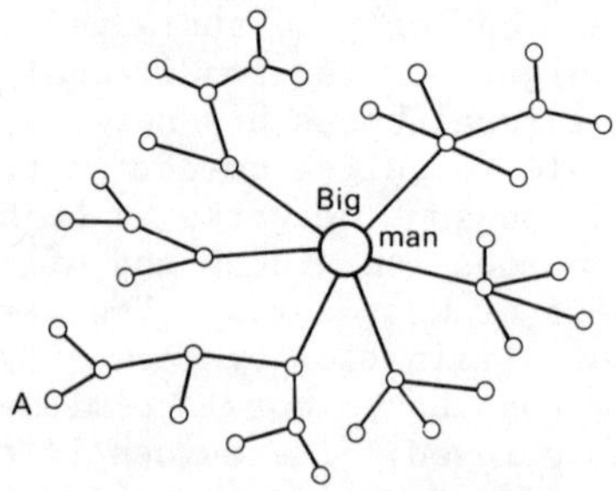

FIGURE 2.3

   So far as social context is concerned, the crucial property here
is centrality. The social context of the Big Man is obviously very
different from that of one of his less important followers, A, for
instance. All roads lead to the Big Man; only one road leads to
A (see Figure 2.3). The Big Man is central; A is peripheral.
Exactly how one would set about quantifying centrality/peripherality
need not overconcern us here. All we need to note is that emphatic
centrality corresponds to Douglas's low grid and emphatic peripherality corresponds to her high grid. Autonomy corresponds to the

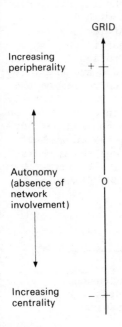

FIGURE 2.4

absence of both centrality and peripherality. The grid dimension
can be redrawn as shown in Figure 2.4. (It might seem that an
individual much involved in network-building could be central to
some networks and peripheral to others. If this were the case he
would fit in the scale somewhere near the zero which, of course,
is supposed to represent autonomy - the absence of network-building.
I suspect that, in practice, no such individuals will be found.
The reason lies in the fact that social relationships are, to some
variable extent, transitive. That is, in general if A is related
to B and B is related to C then A is related to C. Transitivity
in network relationships has, it would seem, the effect of
eradicating such bold contrasts in an individual's network involvement.)

The group dimension

The autonomous individual in his search for self-sufficiency is
hardly likely, once he has extricated himself from the rat-race, to
immerse himself in one of those tight little communities which
appear so attractive to some. Such groups may well be self-sufficient
but they insist on the subordination of individuality to the well-
being and survival of the whole. The autonomy-seeker must shun group
membership as assiduously as he shuns network involvement. How do
we describe the context dimension that runs from that of the autonomous individual, who is indifferent to group membership, towards, on
the one hand, the person happily immersed in and sustained by his
group and, on the other hand, towards the person miserably excluded,

perhaps even expelled, from the group to which he looks in vain for
his support. Again, without overconcerning ourselves with just how
it can be quantified, all we need to take into account for the description of that part of social context deriving from group is the
intensity of inclusion or exclusion. The autonomous person is indifferent; his life support unthreatened. The included and the
excluded are far from indifferent. The included person relies on the
group for his life support; the excluded person is only too painfully
aware that this security is denied him. Inclusion within or exclusion
from a group whose members provide little support for one another, or
a group that has fuzzy and ill-defined boundaries, is obviously less
intense than acceptance within or rejection from a group the members
of which never look elsewhere for support and which has clearly
defined and energetically policed boundaries. The group dimension
can be redrawn as in Figure 2.5.

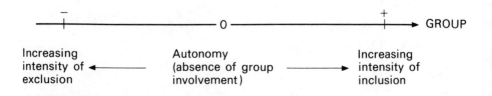

FIGURE 2.5

The manipulation dimension

In deriving the social context dimensions of grid and group we have
recognised that a person finds himself in this or that situation
as a result of process - of network-building and of group dynamics -
but the dimensions have been constructed in such a way that they
simply describe a person's context and say nothing, explicitly or
implicitly, about how he gets there. He gets there, and moves on
from there, as a result of the hurly-burly of social life: as a
result both of his own actions and of the actions of his fellow
men. Of course, the sort of actions he and others take are not
uninfluenced by the sort of contexts in which they find themselves.
With so much going on we can hardly expect that stability will
always prevail. He will, in general, either alter his context as
a result of his own actions or have it altered for him by the
actions of others, or both. Only when these actions both have zero
effect, or when they happen to cancel one another out, will we
obtain the stable special case. So what we are talking about is
manipulation: doing things, wittingly or unwittingly, to yourself
and having things done, wittingly or unwittingly, to you by others.
    The autonomous individual is at pains not to manipulate anyone
and to avoid being manipulated himself. In effect, he chooses not
to manipulate and the unstated assumption is that, if he so chose,
he could enter the fray and manipulate along with the best of them.
The very fact that he is able to exercise this choice suggests that
the other possibility - that, if he entered the fray, he would

himself be manipulated - is not very likely. Turning to the fray,
we find it composed of two sorts of position vis-à-vis manipulation,
and two sorts of manipulation, resulting therefore in two times two,
that is four, sorts of social context. There are those individuals
who, energetically manipulating, stay in the fray because that is
where they want to be, and there are those who have no choice. They
stay in the fray, and are manipulated, because they lack the where-
withal to manipulate others or to withdraw into autonomy.

   The third dimension, manipulation, can be represented by a zero
corresponding to autonomy: the ability to manipulate is present but
not acted upon: and a positive and a negative direction depicting
the ability acted upon (manipulating) and the absence of that ability
(being manipulated) respectively (see Figure 2.6).

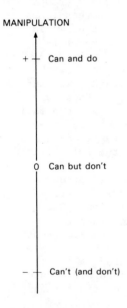

FIGURE 2.6

Contradiction

Manipulation is power made manifest. This manifestation can emerge
within the process of network-building or within the process of
group dynamics. In network-building it exhibits an individualistic
quality: forceful individuals gathering all unto themselves. In
group dynamics it exhibits a collectivistic quality: individuals
effacing themselves through the impersonal insistence upon, and
imposition of, the rules that serve to guarantee the group's
external separation and internal cohesion. In saying this I am
aware that I am not saying anything new, but it is in taking the
next step, the description of what happens when both network-building
and group dynamics are present - that is, the description of what
happens in real society - that I believe myself to be saying something

that has not been said before. It has not been said before for the
simple reason that, in the absence of catastrophe theory, it is
unsayable.

In the situation where group predominates but there is some
network-building the individualistic quality, which in a pure
network-building situation would make power manifest, becomes counter-
productive. In the group-dominated situation, where power is manifested collectively through the imposition of generalised rules,
manipulation increases as prescription increases. The energetic
network-builder is increasing his own freedom of action and thus
decreasing prescription. As he decreases his prescription, a course
of action which, if network-building were predominant, would be the
sensible thing to do, he will find to his dismay that his manipulation
has decreased. He is, in effect, biting the hands that feed him and
inviting the owners of those hands to expel him from their group.
To increase his manipulation he should increase, not decrease, his
prescription, that is, he should do the opposite of what he would
do in a predominantly network-building situation where power is
manifested individually.

Turning now to this reciprocal state of affairs where network-
building is predominant but there are some groups present, we find
that the obverse applies. Here manipulation accrues to those who
reduce their prescription by both increasing their network centrality
and spurning group membership. Here to maintain or increase group
membership becomes counter-productive since it inevitably increases
prescription. There is little point in sticking to the rules if the
way to get on is to break the rules.

In these clear-cut situations, that in which group is predominant
and that in which network is predominant, the appropriate strategy
for the individual is obvious: there is no contradiction. One
course of action will increase his manipulation, the other will
decrease it. As we go, via autonomy, from the predominantly group
situation to the predominantly network situation so these sensible
courses of action become reversed, but at no point along this
sequence is there any confusion as to which is the sensible counsel.
Sometimes one is tenable, sometimes the other, and sometimes (near
autonomy) neither, but never both. But there are some sorts of
situation, those in which both network-building and group dynamics
are well developed, where these collectivist and individualist
counsels are both tenable, that is, they are contradictory, and the
individual will search in vain for the criteria that elsewhere would
enable him unequivocally to decide which counsel he should heed.
Again, all this is, perhaps, not new but what is new is the
possibility of handling both non-contradiction and contradiction
within the same formulation. Specifically, I shall show that
catastrophe theory allows us, as social context varies, to describe
and predict the appearance and disappearance of contradiction. It
will allow us to give a sensible pictorial description of something
which, if expressed in words, must always remain nonsensical.

From all this it is evident that the relationship between social
context and social process is complex and that a crucial element in
it is the individual striving at all times to make as much sense as
possible out of the ever-changing situations in which he finds
himself. This idea of man as a 'meaning-maker' is a commonplace in

anthropology, and the way in which he homes in onto a whole framework of meaning - a world view - has always been the subject of
lively debate.

I intend to transcend this debate by suggesting that the sometimes
contradictory views that are expressed within it are best understood
not as attempts to explain how world views are possible (though this
is how they are presented), but as committed arguments in favour of
this or that world view. (That is, each rival theory aims to
convert the world view that it embodies into a cosmology. A theory
may be an intellectual resting-place but it is also a moral rallying-
point.)

This idea that social inquiry is ideological enjoys wide
currency, and is usually followed by the conclusion that objectivity
is unattainable. By contrast, a transcendent theory, far from
entering into the debate, will furnish an account of it. As such
it will represent a sizeable step in the direction of objectivity.
Such a transcendent theory will have to provide answers to the
following questions: how does an individual home-in onto his world
view?; why does he home-in onto one particular world view?; how
does he change from one world view to another, especially when they
are contradictory?; are these processes deterministic or do chance
and choice also play their part?; and why should there be five, and
only five, stabilisable sorts of world view (i.e. cosmologies)?

Transaction theory

The classic model of the homing-in process is provided by transaction
theory. The idea is that an individual has, initially, a ragbag of
disparate values and that, on the basis of these values, he engages
in transactions with other individuals over various valued objects.
This ragbag of evaluations constitutes his world view and provides
him with some sort of basis for deciding what courses of action are
open to him and for predicting their likely outcomes. Being an
intelligent and thinking man, he follows the course of action that
his world view suggests is likely to be most advantageous to him.
In transacting over a valued object he will probably find that his
ragbag of values is differently constituted from that of the
individual he is transacting with. In other words, it is very
likely that there will be a mismatch between the expected and the
actual results of his actions. In the light of this mismatch, he
rearranges his values in the hope of doing rather better next time.
The end result of this sort of behaviour in myriad and often
overlapping transactions is that his ragbag of values gradually
becomes more systematised, more internally consistent and more like
those of the individuals with whom he has been transacting. In
this way, world views become more orderly, more accurate in their
prediction and more shared.

The trouble with this transaction theory model of the homing-in
process is that it is too good. It results in all the transactors
ending up with the same world view, and different world views can
exist only between populations that don't transact with each other.
In other words, it is too deterministic.

This overdetermination results from the invalid assumption that

everyone's ragbag has got the same contents and that just the values
attached to them are different. But the fact is that the universe
of objects is so vast as to be unhandleable and, if we wish to
handle it, we must first whittle it down to manageable proportions.
Our world view must, willy-nilly, be constructed only from those
objects that we happen to have in our ragbag in the first place.
Inevitably we suffer a cognitive bias: the contents of our ragbag
furnish us with a way of seeing, and a way of seeing is also a way
of not seeing.

When this requirement for cognitive bias is incorporated into
the transaction model it results in one small but crucial change. A
transacting individual now modifies his values, not on the basis of
the results of his actions, but on the basis of the perceived
results of his actions. If two transacting individuals happen to
have rather different cognitive biases it is now, with this
modification, quite possible that in the process their world views,
whilst each becoming more systematised and more internally consistent,
will at the same time become less shared. In other words, they will
both still be homing-in but onto different objectives.

This is a sketchy but adequate outline hypothesis for the
homing-in process but, to complete my transcendent theory, I will
have to offer some convincing reasons for there being only a limited
number of possible objectives. The redrawn grid and group axes
provide the clue since they now describe, in a nicely symmetrical
way, five extremes of social context: one, autonomy, associated
with withdrawal from the fray, and four others that result from
the two kinds of position vis-à-vis manipulation, and the two kinds
of manipulation that develop once the fray is entered.

THE FIVE STRATEGIES

Bias, morality and the separation of objectives

Transaction theory is curiously amoral. If, as it insists, there
is only one sort of world view for people to home-in on then common
sense alone will lead them to it. But, if there is more than one
sort of world view available, common sense will not be enough to
attract and retain adherents. Common sense will lead a person to
a world view, morality will lead him to the right one. The problem
now is to model this selective homing-in process by relating
cognitive bias to social context and social context, via manipulation, to shareable world views.

This can be done by looking at people in all sorts of different
social contexts and plotting their positions in terms of the three
variables: group, grid and manipulation. The results of this sort
of investigation can be summarised in terms of inhabited and
uninhabited regions within this three-dimensional space.

Starting with (1) zero group and zero grid, this context is
where one would expect to find the autonomous individual: the
classic example is the hermit, secure in his harmless and austere
self-sufficiency. So the inhabited region for zero group and zero
grid is near the middle - zero manipulation - and it is difficult
to see how positive or negative manipulation (which require group

and/or network involvement) could also be inhabited.

Taking next what are likely to be the more familiar contexts, those associated with a society that emphasises individuality, consider (2) negative group and positive grid. An individual in this context, spurning or being rejected by such groups as there are and peripheral to networks, is going to find himself manipulated. No matter how he reduces his needs and tightens his belt he is unlikely to achieve autonomy and only through ceaseless work and shrewd attention to his network involvement can he hope to achieve network centrality and become a manipulator. Many of the people who inhabit this region of negative manipulation experience an unwelcome stability: they are the non-coping families near the bottom of the slippery slope, they are trapped in the cycle of deprivation. And, in some measure, they are trapped there as a consequence of the unlooked-for aggregate effect of those individuals lucky enough not to be there. Furthermore, you remain just as manipulated whether you are expelled from group (negative group) or simply ungrouped (zero group: either indifferent to existing groups or unable to join groups because there aren't any). However, if the grid component of your context decreases it means that by network-building you have managed to reduce the extent to which you are manipulated, and if it decreases enough you will have built up a network sufficient for you to manipulate others. In other words, you will be moving towards the sort of social context (3) where there is zero or negative group and negative grid (network centrality). You are well on your way to becoming one of 'the savage beasts of capitalism'.

Look now to less familiar situations such as are found in some primitive societies (those with a strong emphasis on group) and in India and Nepal (caste): (4) positive group and positive grid. This is the context, unfamiliar in the West, where group is dominant and therefore manipulation (group mediated) is increased by individuals impersonally insisting that the rules be observed: increasing their prescription. Individual members of the higher castes have little personal freedom of action, for their position within the hierarchy demands all kinds of avoidances and observances. The insistence on prescriptions, such as ensuring that the shadow of a lower-caste member does not fall upon your cooked food, may be restrictive of individual freedom but collectively it imposes and maintains the caste order. The lower-caste member is free of such prescriptions: it does not matter whose shadow falls on his boiled rice. He therefore inhabits the other corner of the square, (5) positive group and negative grid, and has negative manipulation.

But such social contexts are not entirely absent from western society. For many in the armed services, the civil service and in trade unions, the way to collective dignity, if not salvation, is by the book: sticking to the rules. It follows that manipulation will collectively accrue to those who have the most prescriptive book of rules and, conversely, that those groups that do not enjoy such a high level of prescription will find themselves manipulated. You cannot work to rule if you have no rules to work to.

A moment's reflection will confirm that often it is precisely those whose group membership is most hazy or uncertain who are the most insistent imposers of prescription and that, conversely, those

who do not (or cannot) impose prescriptions often find themselves less
and less bounded by group membership and more and more manipulated.
In India it is the relatively ungrouped merchants and craftsmen who –
doing as the brahmins say, rather than as the brahmins do, and
pedantically insisting on the correct avoidances and observances –
are the real imposers of the caste order. (4) In other words,
manipulation can remain strongly positive when grid is high even if
group becomes zero and, conversely, manipulation can remain strongly
negative when grid is low even if group becomes zero.

The hypothesis

Clearly, the delineation of all these inhabited and uninhabited zones
within this three-dimensional space is probably the task of a life-
time. All I can do here is beg your indulgence as, on the basis of
this sketchiest of outlines, I fill out my hypothesis. These five

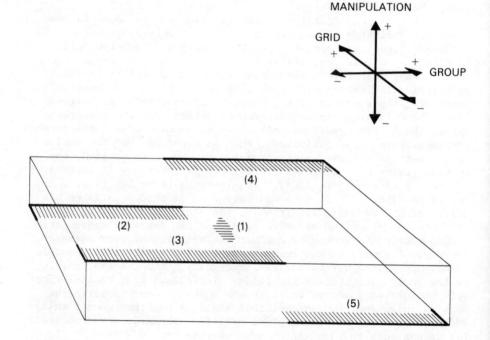

FIGURE 2.7

inhabited regions may be shaded in on the three-dimensional space
as shown in Figure 2.7.

The next step, on looking at these fragments, is prompted by the
intuitive hunch that it looks as though the inhabited regions all
have a sort of sheeted quality and that, taking the simplest
possibility first, perhaps they all lie on just one single curvy
sheet. I am encouraged to act on this hunch by catastrophe theory
which explains how, if certain conditions are satisfied, this can
be so and specifies the nature of the possible curvy sheets.   In
fact, this simplest possible way of joining these five fragments
together (as shown in Figure 2.8) to form a single surface completes
the outline of my hypothesis.

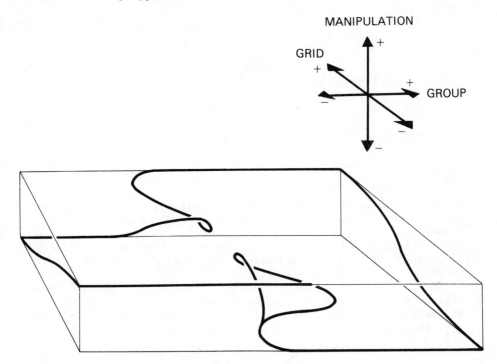

FIGURE 2.8

Bimodality and discontinuity

The two curious overhanging sections of this surface are spread out
in the vertical dimension and there is nothing comparable in the
two horizontal directions. This points to a difference between
manipulation on the one hand and group and grid on the other. In
general, for any point on the horizontal base there is one corresponding value for manipulation, but under the overhanging section there
are suddenly three values: one on the top surface, one on the
bottom surface, and one on the inverted surface in between. The
inversion of this middle surface means that this value is unstable.
So, in this region of triple values, one is unstable and two are

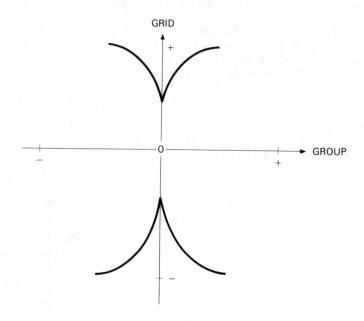

FIGURE 2.9

stable. This is the pictorial representation of contradiction and this region of triple values has some interesting and surprising properties.

If the surface is projected down onto the horizontal base then each region of triple values becomes outlined by a pair of lines meeting at a cusp point (Figure 2.9)

If an individual's social context, initially well outside these regions of triple values, gradually changes so that it enters one of these regions, moves across it, and then passes out at the other side (Figure 2.10), what will be happening to his manipulation?

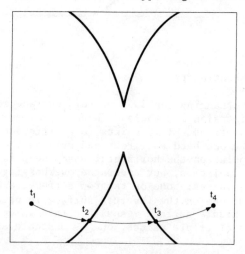

FIGURE 2.10

Initially at t_1 (with negative group and negative grid) there is one
appropriate value of manipulation: strongly positive. He is a
forceful wheeling-and-dealing network-builder. At t_2 he enters the
region of triple values and there are now two stable possible values
for manipulation. Which does he take? The answer is given by the
homing-in process. This process results in an individual's world
view homing in onto some objective, and the requirement for cognitive
bias ensures that there is more than one such objective. Thanks to
his cognitive bias and to the homing-in process, an individual will
be pretty firmly locked on to one particular sort of world view and,
acting on the basis of this world view, he will find himself enjoying
a high level of manipulation. In other words, he is held stably in
his world view by the homing-in process and, until he enters the
cusp, no other stabilisable possibilities exist for him. Once in
the cusp, however, another stabilisable possibility emerges and, if
he could unlock himself from his current world view, it would be
possible for him to home-in onto a very different one: the
difference being that, acting on the basis of this new world view,
he would enjoy a stable but very low level of manipulation.

But it would take a very large effort on his part, or a very
large jolt from outside, to unlock him from his current world view.
Another way of putting this is to say that his cultural bias
militates against this possible transition. He has put a lot of
effort into seeing things the way he does and he has put a lot of
effort into not seeing things the way the newly possible world view
would require. In other words, he won't change from the one to the
other until he has to. And he has to change at t_3 because, at this
moment, the objective he has for so long been stably locked onto
disappears. Inevitably, he locks onto the new stable objective
and so finds himself undergoing a sudden and dramatic change from
manipulating to being manipulated (see Figure 2.11). (Were he
travelling in the opposite direction the change would be from being
manipulated to manipulating and would occur as he moved out of the
cusp towards negative group.)

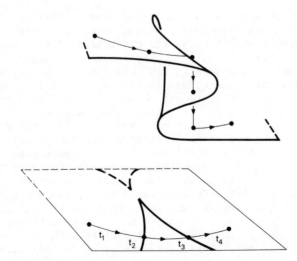

FIGURE 2.11

Such a transition is likely to involve him in an intense and
perhaps alarming personal experience. It seems to him that, in a
blinding flash (blinding because, for a moment, he has no way of
seeing) the whole world is altered, but of course the world is still
the same: it is his view of it that has altered. So this hypothesis
provides a pictorial description of dramatic conversion: of sudden
discontinuous changes in world view. But elsewhere it provides a
description of a smooth and gradual transition from one world view
to another, for instance, along the sequence of changes shown in
Figure 2.12.

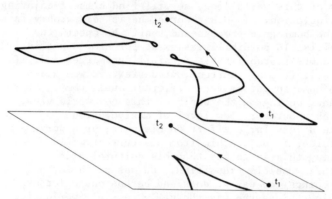

FIGURE 2.12

As if this were not enough, the existence of the three-dimensional
surface explains why, in certain instances, one particular line in
the group/grid horizontal plane (the fold line depicting the exit
from the region of triple values) is privileged and does depict a
sudden discontinuous change from one world view to another.

Topology's contribution

Clearly, the way the surface is folded to give this region of
triple values gives rise to a powerful concept: it is called the
cusp catastrophe; cusp because its projection of the two fold lines
is a pair of lines meeting at a cusp point, and catastrophe because
(in conjunction with a dynamic, in this case the homing-in process)
it entails discontinuous change in the value of the vertical
dimension in response to gradual changes in the horizontal dimensions.
Catastrophe, in this sense, is value free. Whether a discontinuous
change in world view is a good or a bad thing is a value judgment
much influenced by the social context of the individual who makes
it ('he who hesitates is lost' versus 'look before you leap').
   Topology allows us to describe pictorially something that is
not easily described in words. The translation from pictures to
words has little difficulty with the dynamic, the homing-in process.
This is often given verbal expression in terms of rational learning
behaviour: an individual operating in his best interest and, at
the same time, modifying his mode of operation in the light of his
experience. His best interest is defined by the objective of his

homing-in process and it is here, in understanding not the goal-
seeking (the homing-in process) but the goal-setting (what it is that
the process homes-in on), that the translation difficulties are
located. The picture tells us that it would be wrong to say there
was only one objective (cultural universalism) and that it would
also be wrong to say that the objective could be anything at all
(cultural relativism). The picture says: 'Economic rationality is
not enough. But do not despair. To follow a rational course of
action an individual has to be able to grasp a cultural setting
within which the idea of that course of action can emerge and be
comprehended, and such graspable cultural settings are really quite
limited'.   The rather unlovely title of this approach is cognitive
economics. It permits us to make due allowance for the notion of
man as a meaning-maker without insisting on it to such an extent
that all else is excluded.
     Now it might seem that the maximisation of meaning (which is one
way of describing what the dynamic is doing) is a pretty odd sort
of maximising when in two areas (strongly negative group with
strongly positive grid, and strongly positive group with strongly
negative grid) it results in the individual homing-in onto strongly
negative manipulation. But these areas of the surface depict
rockbottom. The maximum meaning that can be extracted from these
sorts of social context comes from the realistic acceptance that,
come what may, the dice are pretty heavily loaded against you.
In other words, survival is the name of this game, and in these
areas we can expect the sort of world views and general cultural
settings within which the sensible courses of action that can
emerge are consonant with a survival strategy.

Strategy and cosmology

But the cusp catastrophe is not the only powerful concept contained
in this three-dimensional picture. It turns out that the two areas
of the surface that represent rockbottom, the survival strategy,
are asymptotic to the horizontal plane corresponding to strongly
negative manipulation. There are two other horizontal planes, and
two only, to which the surface is asymptotic: the plane through
zero manipulation (one area) (5) and the plane through strongly
positive manipulation (two areas). Thus there are just five areas
of the surface that are asymptotic to the horizontal. Could this
be the reason why there should be just five stabilisable conjunctions
of social context and cosmology? What is more, just three horizontal
planes - the top, the bottom and the middle - are involved. Could
there be some special significance to these planes?
     Though I have made a verbal distinction between cultural settings
in general and graspable cultural settings in particular, I have
not yet translated this distinction into pictorial form. The
special significance of the asymptotic, or flattish, areas of the
surface is that they define these graspable settings. This is
because these flattish regions are, in a sense, doubly stable.
First of all, the whole surface is stable in that it depicts all
the objectives that the homing-in process can home-in onto, but the
flattish areas are also stable in the sense that an individual

located in one of them will find that quite large changes in his
social context produce only small changes in his level of manipulation. Outside these flattish areas, on the steeply sloping parts
of the surface, a small change in an individual's social context
causes quite a large change in his level of manipulation. So, in
the flattish areas, his world view suggests courses of action that,
when acted upon, give roughly the same sorts of results and leave
his level of manipulation pretty well unaltered. This 'repeatability' disappears as he moves onto the steeper slopes of the
surface. There, quite a small change in social context will result
in consecutive actions producing quite different results. This
means that, thanks to the homing-in process, he will make quite
extensive modifications to his world view. The result of this sort
of response over a whole sequence of transactions is something
that looks like a dialectical relationship between world view and
social action. He will, on the steep slopes, tend to be on the
move whilst, on the flatter regions, he will tend to stay put.

   Another way of explaining how the flattish areas correlate with
graspability is in terms of the extent to which world views can be
shared. If, for the sake of argument, we assume that people are
evenly distributed over the surface then an individual on a flattish
area will find that those people in his vicinity have the same sort
of world view (in the sense that, when they act on their world views
they result in pretty much the same level of manipulation). What
is more, they go on having the same sort of world views. By
contrast, on a steeply sloping surface even those very near to him
will have quite different world views and, to make matters worse,
both theirs and his are likely to be changing all the time. So,
only in the flattish areas, are you likely to find world views that
are both lasting and shared. It seems unlikely that, on the steep
slopes with little repeatability and little prospect of sharing
world views, individuals will be able to formulate much in the way
of strategies for action.

   In catastrophe theory the whole surface (except for the inverted
bits) is called an attractor since, in conjunction with an effective
dynamic, phenomena seem to be captured by it. The inverted middle
sheet of a cusp catastrophe is called a repeller, since its effect
is to drive phenomena away towards the upper or the lower sheet of
the attractor.

   In general the horizontal planes to which the attractor happens
to be asymptotic are not singled out and accorded any special
significance but in this case, because of these qualities of
graspability and shareability that they confer upon world views,
they are in some way privileged. Translated into social terms
such planes correspond to ideals. At least, to translate them as
such opens up some suggestive and exciting prospects.

   Concepts are static, real situations are in general not static.
The surface represents the real possibilities, the nearest
asymptotic plane represents the cultural concepts that will make
that reality most meaningful. The divergence of plane and surface
accounts for the discrepancy between what people say they do and
what they actually do, whilst this asymptotic relationship accounts
for the perceived quality of the ideal as something to be striven

for. Further, attainable and unattainable ideals correspond to
attractors and repellers respectively. I would suggest that a person
inside one or other of the cusps but close enough to zero grid to
still espouse autonomy is, in his pursuit of this unattainable ideal
(it is attainable only outside the cusps and near to zero group and
zero grid), acting in such a way as to drive himself (and others)
towards either the upper or the lower sheet of the attractor. The
hypothesis therefore gives a qualitative prediction of the conditions
that will have to be met if the pursuit of a (perhaps passionately)
desired ideal is not to be distressingly counter-productive. It also
gives a qualitative indication of the sorts of changes in social
context that will have to occur before people find themselves
sufficiently close to some attainable ideal for it to commend itself
to them as an image of a reasonable and desirable state of affairs.

The policy connection

Some naive critics of catastrophe theory have suggested that it is
politically dangerous and that social scientists should have nothing
to do with it for fear that they will put a powerful weapon into the
hands of unscrupulous politicians. Quite apart from the fact that,
since most politicians (be they scrupulous or unscrupulous) are
able to read, such a panic response is unlikely to avert this
supposed disaster, it is surely desirable to improve the likelihood
that a state of affairs advocated by some politician and endorsed
by a majority of the electorate will be brought nearer by the
policies that, once elected, he implements.

The complete hypothesis

So, if asymptotic horizontal planes are ideals, and if, as seems
likely, the bottom plane is the survival strategy ideal, then the
middle one should be the autonomous strategy ideal and the top one
the manipulative strategy ideal (see Figure 2.13). Furthermore,
as we go from negative to positive group the quality of meaningful
social action changes from individualistic to collectivistic.
Obviously, a collectivist manipulative strategy will emerge within
a very different kind of cultural setting from that in which an
individualist manipulative strategy will emerge. The same goes
for the collectivist and individualist forms of survival strategy.
So, if my hypothesis has any substance, we should expect to find,
not five kinds of social context (for social context varies smoothly
and continuously over the group/grid plane), but five kinds of
strategy emerging from five kinds of cultural setting. In certain
specifiable circumstances we can expect smooth gradual transitions
between strategies and in certain other specifiable circumstances
we can expect the transitions to be sudden and discontinuous.
    These five kinds of cultural setting (Figure 2.14) roughly
correspond to Douglas's cosmologies. (6) Each has a distinctive
bias associated with a distinctive strategy. The bias defines a
particular set of goals and the strategy enables an individual to
maximise these goals. Provided the strategy remains effective, bias

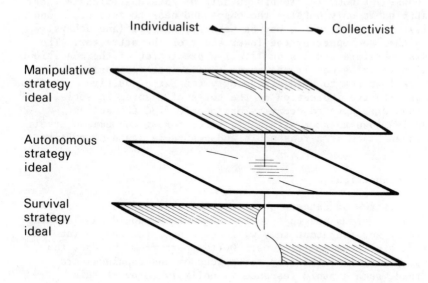

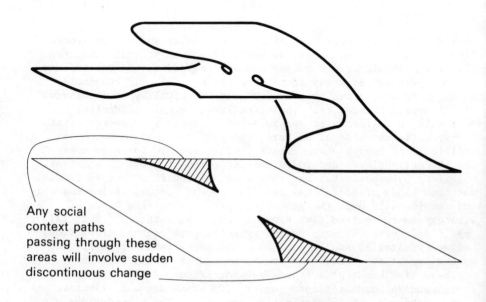

Any social
context paths
passing through these
areas will involve sudden
discontinuous change

FIGURE 2.13

SURVIVAL INDIVIDUALIST
Little developed but eclectic.
Passivity.
Wild views on abroad.
Little developed time
     perspective.
Erratic child-rearing
     (alternating between
     indulgence and violence).
Millennialism.
Anomic suicide.

MANIPULATIVE COLLECTIVIST
Transcendental metaphysics (society
     and nature isomorphous).
Ritualist (ensures proper harmony
     between society and nature).
Natural law.
Cautious about abroad.
Sacrifice. Strong on tradition.
Tough discipline/child training.
Altruistic suicide

AUTONOMOUS
Nature mysticism (nature and
     society as one).
Simplicity and naturalness valued.
Approves of abroad. Live in
     present.
Natural goodness of children
     (progressive theory of
     education).
As yet unidentified type of suicide?

MANIPULATIVE INDIVIDUALIST
Nature and society separate ('every
     prospect pleases and only
     man is vile').
Intellectual rigour. High
     standards. High culture.
Looks to autonomy in unthreatened
     moments (so progressive theory
     of education but with hidden
     controls).
Frantically in favour of abroad.
Strong (manipulative) sense of
     history.
Egotistic suicide.

SURVIVAL COLLECTIVIST
Homespun philosophy ('small is
     beautiful').
Us (vulnerable) v. Them (predatory).
Scapegoating (denatured humans).
Poison. Contamination. Purge.
Witchcraft accusations.
Tough discipline/child training.
Xenophobic.
Strong on tradition.
Fatalistic suicide.

FIGURE 2.14

and strategy can constitute a stable system in which individuals
will find that the more they strive to maximise their goals the more
shareable those goals become. In other words, only within these five
conjunctions of social context and cosmology is shared moral commitment possible.

Douglas's four cosmologies remain unaltered in their contents but
they are joined by a fifth (which Douglas has described but taken
'off the social map'). The redrawing of the group and grid axes,
and the addition of the manipulation axis, reveal that social context
alone is not enough to completely separate the cosmologies and that
in two regions of social context there are two cosmologies that can
give stability.

Static and dynamic: special and general

I should now pause to explain how this dynamical system relates to
Douglas's typology. Her four stable arrangements are very separate
from one another. Each context and its associated cosmology forms
a self-sustaining system: its rigidity, its permanence and its
separation being maintained by a shared commitment among the occupants
of that context to that cosmology. As they transact with one another,
their shared commitment to their cosmology, to the rules concerning
the nature of the universe, everywhere and always provides them with
a basis for moral judgments. What is more, not only do they have
this common basis, they act upon it: continually justifying the
world to themselves and to others, continually rewarding those who
by their words and actions confirm that world and continually
penalising those who threaten it.

Stability therefore requires of an individual:
1 Rational transacting behaviour in his social context resulting
   in him homing-in onto an appropriate world view. (In terms of
   the picture: moving onto the surface.)
2 A feedback process between his world view and his context in
   which each modifies the other in such a way that his world view
   becomes more shareable. (The tendency to move from the sloping
   parts of the surface towards the nearest flattish bit.)
3 An effective strategy. His shareable world view will indicate
   to him certain courses of action as preferable to others. For
   this strategy to be effective the results of his following the
   preferable courses of action must, on balance, be to his
   advantage and the results of his following the less preferred
   courses of action must, on balance, be to his disadvantage.
   (The equilibrium that holds him on the flattish part of the
   surface must be stable.)
These conditions obtain only in the special case and it is this
special case that is depicted by Douglas's typology. The first
condition ensures that an individual homes in onto the world view
appropriate to his social context. The second condition ensures
that he changes his context and his world view until they become
shareable. The third ensures that he becomes committed to his
shareable world view. That is, it ensures that his world view is
transformed into a cosmology.

My picture contains Douglas's typology as a special case (and,

incidentally, reveals the existence of a fifth context, zero group/
zero grid, where these conditions can be satisfied) but it does not
start off by assuming that any of these three conditions obtain.   It
does not assume that an individual has an appropriate world view.
If he has an appropriate world view, it does not assume that it is
shareable.   If he has a world view and it is a shareable world view,
it does not assume that he is committed to it.

1   Whilst I believe that rationality is what makes the social world
    go round, I do not assume that all behaviour is rational.   I do
    not assume that everyone is always on the surface and that the
    rest of the cube is uninhabitable.   I am saying simply that most
    of the time most people are on or near the surface and most of
    the time most people behave rationally.   That is, they strive
    quite successfully to make as much sense as they can of where
    they find themselves.   (If this were not so there would not be
    any society there for us to study.)   A person who, voluntarily
    or involuntarily, does not do this will tend to move away from
    the surface and may find himself in a position to construct all
    kinds of alternative realities.   He may find himself respected
    as a magician or reviled as a madman, for his pains.
       A necessary condition for a rational and intelligent individual
    to be on or near the surface is that the dynamic, the homing-in
    process that moves him towards the surface, should have a faster
    time-scale than the feedback mechanism that moves him across the
    surface.   We should not assume that this is always so.   If the
    time scales change until they are of the same order, then even
    the rational and intelligent individual will no longer remain
    on or near the surface.
       For instance the rapid social change fostered by technological
    progress represents a potential speeding-up of the feedback
    process, whilst the increase in both the amount of communication
    and the rapidity and range of its transmission represents a
    potential speeding-up of the dynamic.   These rates of change are
    not uniformly distributed between different social contexts.
    In those contexts where there is speeded-up communication but
    little technology-induced social change, individuals will tend
    to be strongly attracted towards the surface and the cost of
    deliberately maintaining oneself some distance away from the
    surface (moral disapprobation) will be large.   In those contexts
    where communication remains slow and little developed but
    technology-induced change is rapid, individuals may well just
    drift away from the surface as the cost of deliberately
    maintaining oneself away from it shrinks to zero.   Under such
    conditions even Douglas's stable states will cease to be stable.
    That is, the picture tells us how and when society can become
    impossible.

2   Douglas sees the feedback process as the mechanism that maintains
    the separation of her stable states.   She stresses that the
    individual responds to his context and that his response can, in
    turn, modify his context.   In other words, there is personal
    scope for changing context.   She sees this personal scope being
    exercised in such a way as to move the individual towards one
    or other of her stable states and, indeed, this is often the
    case.   But not always.   Such endogenous change can sometimes

result in a movement away from a stable condition. This is
because a stable equilibrium is really a huge confidence trick:
the individual supports the whole and the whole supports the
individual.

An individual who exercises his scope for changing his
context will inevitably change the whole as well, but usually
that change will not be very great. This local behaviour, based
on the assumption that the global situation will remain largely
unaffected, is summed up for instance in the justification:
'If I don't do it, somebody else will.' This local/global
disjunction involves the logical error of combination - the
assumption that what is true for the parts is true for the
whole - and this false but inevitable assumption on the part of
an individual can result in the erosion of the stable equilibrium he is trying to uphold. Look, for instance, at the sort
of endogenous change that can result in a transfer from negative
to positive group.

I would suggest that the difficulties in maintaining economic
growth indefinitely, and the insecurities generated by the oil
crisis in particular, constitute restrictions that are more
keenly felt in network than in group relationships. As the
rewards of entrepreneurial activity decrease, a rational
individual is likely to slightly reduce his more energetic
network-building and to channel that effort into his more
reassuring relationships: those of long standing, perhaps with
kin, or those with whom he can at least invoke ties based on
shared interest, experience or locality. That is, the
individual's response to such restriction is to cool things
a little bit: to try to move himself a short distance up grid.
But the aggregate effect of everyone pulling in their horns
like this is to shift them all, at right angles, quite a long
way towards positive group.

In expansive times the burgeoning networks of relationships
cut across and obscure any latent groupings within the overall
pattern. In restrictive times these cross-cutting relationships
are the first to atrophy and, regardless of individual intent,
groups begin to emerge and reassert their influence.

3 When he first feels the restriction, the entrepreneur is still
firmly committed to his manipulative individualist strategy and
to the world view that justifies it. Pulling in his horns a
little is a tactic suggested to him by this strategy. If he
alone resorted to it, it would be an effective tactic and would
end up confirming him more strongly in his strategy. Because
everyone resorts to it, it ends up undermining his strategy
and lessening his commitment to its associated world view. With
his strategy undermined and adrift from his cosmology, he is
now free to reinterpret his relationships.

Of course exogenous change, as well, can dislodge people from
their stable equilibria but the interesting feature of the three-
dimensional hypothesis is that it shows how this can happen simply
as a consequence of the local/global disjunction. It should now be
put to the test for one should not assume that even so beautiful
an hypothesis as this cannot be wrong.

RISK AND RESTRICTION

I began by posing the paradox that, at the very moment of becoming aware of our tremendous need for energy, so many of us are, for the first time, rejecting the almost unlimited supply that nuclear reactors promise. My hypothesis provides a possible resolution of this paradox by showing that our realisation of energy need imposes restrictions upon us: we realise that we simply cannot go on doing as we did before. In other words, to the extent that these restrictions are imposed, our various social contexts are changed and, if our social contexts change, so may our cosmologies change. These changes in cosmology would entail changes in associated strategy and these changes in strategy might, in aggregate, entail significant changes in the socially acceptable level of risk. So, I am suggesting that changed perception of risk results from changed social context.

Since those most involved in the opposition to nuclear reactors are organised into groups (like the Friends of the Earth (7) in Britain and the multiplicity of groups involved in the Bürger-initiativen in West Germany) - groups that until recently were not there - we should investigate the possibility that these changes in risk perception result from changes in the social contexts of their component individuals towards positive group. (8) Since these changes in risk perception have occurred suddenly, taking those not involved largely unawares, we should expect that some at least of these changes towards positive group have been via one or other of the cusps. Two questions now arise. First, why should these hypothetical changes occur? Second, why should they involve dramatic shifts in risk perception?

The general setting within which restriction worms its way into every home and every purse is perhaps not easily described, least of all by those who are the inhabitants of the homes and the owners of the purses. It is for this reason that a Dutch journalist provides the clearest diagnosis of West Germany's current malaise. (9)

Like a man in the highest income bracket who planned his finances on the assumption of perpetually increasing prosperity, West Germany is now being forced to limit luxuries for the first time since the country became rich.

The rest of the world would agree with the Chancellor, Herr Schmidt, when he rightly points out that the West Germans have precious little to complain about.

But if, as is the case with the average voter, your yardstick is not how badly the neighbours are doing but how much better you were doing yourself four years ago, all becomes clear.

The oil crisis ended the economic miracle, but many of the expectations it engendered were buried only this year with the mortal remains of its creator, Professor Ludwig Erhard, and some of them are still alive.

This air of stagnation and disillusion constitutes a creeping crisis which is no less real for being hard to define. The symptoms of the malaise, which amounts to a crisis of self-confidence, are so diffuse that they often appear unrelated to one another. (10)

Is it too optimistic to suggest that my picture allows me to define this creeping crisis, the symptoms of which appear diffuse and unrelated? For it should be possible to go out and plot where people are, and where people were, on the surface, and so obtain a precise understanding of the malaise.

But, if restriction is the cause of the malaise, what is the cause of the restriction? Is our realisation that things cannot go on as they have been doing externally imposed (by the oil crisis) or is the restriction generated internally (in the sense that people simply cannot keep up an atmosphere of continuing expansiveness indefinitely)? But even the oil crisis was not external. It was not precipitated by some cosmic event, or by the sudden evaporation of the earth's fossil fuel, but by people: Arab people. Whether the restriction was internal or external depends on which sort of people you are talking about. So the indications are that the external (or natural) restrictions are always there but that the realisation that they are there is likely to be internally generated. I am not saying that there are no external (or natural) restrictions, but simply that our awareness of them is what we act on, and that there is often little correlation between the two. For man, unlike other animals, has culture interposed between himself and his environment. Unlike both environmental determinism and cultural determinism, my aim is to try to say (and subsequently do) something about this lack of correlation between external and internal restriction.

Before looking to see whether the West German malaise involves significant shifts in social contexts in the direction of positive group, I should ask why such changes should involve changes in risk perception. The answer lies in the differences between individualist and collectivist strategies. The great personal risk undergone for great personal reward - be it fame, fortune or both - makes perfect sense in the general cultural setting of individualism. It is often paraded as the definitive and justificatory characteristic of rampant capitalism: the idea that it is only right that those individuals who risk their capital, or their talents, should reap suitably large rewards. For those operating the survival strategy risk-taking is often just one of the facts of life, and the one really big risk (usually criminal) the romantic means of escape. To such individualists the idea of shared risk-taking is abhorrent (for example, their view of the likely outcome of the shared risking of talent - a camel is a horse designed by a committee).

But in the general cultural setting of collectivism, great personal risk should only be courted if it is for the benefit, not of the individual, but of the group. Here selfless heroism, patriotism and team spirit are the valid forms of risk-taking. Captain Oates walking into the Antarctic night and the little Dutch boy with his finger in the dyke share positive group contexts. Evel Kneivel, jumping the Grand Canyon on his solo motorcycle, has no group at all.

So the collectivist strategies encourage risk-spreading: you may never become rich and famous (unless dead) but at least you enjoy the warmth and security of your group. The individualist strategies encourage risk-narrowing: Dick Whittington went to

London, not because the streets were paved with gold, but because he
had to get away from his group so as to be in a social context where
he could take the big personal risks that would make his fortune.
If the creeping crisis that currently afflicts West Germany (and
other industrialised nations) is an aggregate creep towards positive
group, then we should expect a significant shift from risk-narrowing
to risk-spreading: from optimism to pessimism. The current widespread concern about socially acceptable risk suggests that many are
now uneasy about risks which until recently they found acceptable.
It is the people, not the risks, that have changed.

Yet there is a sense in which the risks change as well as the
people. The person moving from ungrouped individualism into strong
communality will find that new risks swim into his ken. These are
long-term risks which he is now able to apprehend thanks to his
increased time-perspective. And, of course, it is these long-term
risks about what we may be inflicting upon unborn generations that,
above all others, accompany nuclear energy. When Keynes made his
famous retort, 'In the long run we are all dead', he was (despite
his marginal involvement in the ill-defined Bloomsbury Group)
speaking from a negative group (and negative grid) social context.
In the positive group context we cannot ignore the long term, for
our commitment to our group requires us to believe that, though
in the long run we ourselves may all be dead, our group will live
on.

The autonomous strategy is neither to narrow nor spread risks
but to avoid them. One of the best ways of reducing one's
perception of risks is to be ignorant of their existence. The
autonomous individual lives in the present and his time perspective
is suitably truncated. Thus the only risks he needs to avoid are
the very short-term ones: as far as all the others are concerned,
ignorance (deliberately cultivated, rather than imposed) is bliss.
The biblical text for the autonomous individual, communing with
Nature and preferring her works to those of man, is:

> Consider the lilies of the field, how they grow; they toil
> not, neither do they spin: and yet I say unto you, that even
> Solomon in all his glory was not arrayed like one of these.
>
> Take therefore no thought for the morrow: for the morrow
> shall take thought for the things of itself. Sufficient unto
> the day is the evil thereof. (11)

The motto of the optimistic individualist is more likely to be 'He
who dares, wins', whilst the pessimistic collectivist will console
himself by reflecting that a trouble shared is a trouble halved.

CONCLUSION

So much for the broad sweep of the argument for the resolution of
this nuclear paradox. Can I finish by trying to pinpoint how it is
that this argument is able to succeed where others fail?

The fundamental reason why we have difficulty in explaining
behaviour related to environmental problems is that we do not know
what an environmental problem is: we think that an environmental
problem is something that arises in the environment. Both
Douglas's typology and my attempt to model the dynamics that give

rise to it suggest that the environment is often little more than a medium for the expression of social concerns. Once we see environmental problems as social rather than environmental phenomena, many of the obstacles to our understanding of them disappear.

Grid/group theory shows that an individual's perception of environmental risks can change. So can the level of risk he is prepared to accept. These changes, which can be large, sudden and widely spread within a population, can result in the appearance and disappearance of environmental problems. This means that, in all probability, our environment is most threatened when there isn't an environmental problem in sight.

The real problem is not the environmental problem: it is the mismatch between it and the actual condition of the environment.

NOTES

1 The ideas expressed in this paper have not appeared overnight nor have I produced them unaided. I would like to thank Massachusetts Institute of Technology, The International Institute for Environment and Society, Berlin, and the Russell Sage Foundation, New York, for their support. Also, I am indebted to Rob Coppock, Professor Mary Douglas, Professor Geoff Harrison, Jim Q. Smith and Professor Christopher Zeeman for help and constructive criticism.

2 Mary Douglas, 'Cultural bias', London, Royal Anthropological Institute, occasional paper no. 35.
   E.C. Zeeman, 'Catastrophe Theory: selected papers 1972 - 1977', Reading, Mass., Addison-Wesley, 1977 (particularly relevant is ch.3, differential equations for the heartbeat and nerve impulse).
   R. Thom, 'Structural Stability and Morphogenesis' (French edn 1972) trans. D.H. Fowler, New York, Benjamin, 1975.

3 The late Professor John Mackintosh MP believed that the Labour Party was about to become unstable in this way. See his article in 'The Times', 26 September 1977.

4 For a full description of these unfamiliar contexts see McKim Marriott, Hindu transactions: diversity without dualism, in 'Transaction and Meaning', ed. B. Kapferer, pp. 109 - 42, Philadelphia, Institute for the Study of Human Issues, 1976.

5 Strictly speaking, three areas: two of them being on the inverted middle sheets of the cusp catastrophes. The meaning of these other two areas is explained on pages 52 and 53.

6 I should stress that the aim of grid/group theory is to describe what Benedict called patterns of culture, not culture itself: Ruth Benedict, 'Patterns of Culture', London, Routledge & Kegan Paul, 1935 (paperback edition 1961).

7 And the Network for Nuclear Concern which is not a network in our sense of the word but a grouping of groups.

8 They may be (and indeed very likely are) changing in the grid dimension as well, probably towards positive group.

9 Again malaise, like catastrophe, should really be value free. Politicians, economists and journalists tend to see it as a bad thing: a malaise. Others in different social contexts may see

it as a recovery from a protracted mental illness: West Germany
at last coming to its senses.

10   Dan Van der Vat, West Germany: a special report, in The Times,
22 June 1977.
11   Matthew vi.28 - 9, 34.

Chapter 3

GIVING THE GRID/GROUP DIMENSIONS AN OPERATIONAL DEFINITION

James Hampton

Some may consider any attempt to measure the dimensions of grid and group in quantitative terms to be ill-considered. It is easy for the finer insights and subtler elements of a theory such as this one to be lost or blunted in the process of pressing them into the mould of empirical methodology. All too often, claims to have disproved a theory are based on empirical predictions derived on the basis of naive and literal interpretations. This state of affairs is particularly likely to occur where the original statement of the theory employs figurative and abstract language, and has been largely developed as an interpretative tool for making sense of otherwise meaningless collections of data. In this light, a parallel can be drawn between grid/group analysis and the psycho-dynamic theories of Freud and the post-Freudians. In both cases new concepts are defined which can bring sense to a bewildering variety of observations (on the one hand cultural and social diversity, and on the other the great variety of normal and pathological mental states involving symbolic meanings). In both cases the richness of the theory can make it difficult to derive critical empirical predictions without making simplifying assumptions. In spite of such objections, the development of an empirical test of the theory of grid/group analysis can be defended on a number of grounds. First, there is the need to satisfy the world of empirical science that the theory is in fact a scientific theory, saying something about the external world, and with testable consequences. If conducted with a proper regard for the inadequacies of existing measuring techniques in the social sciences, and with a sympathetic understanding of the dangers of not doing justice to the theory and its insights, an empirical test can be of value, and its results enable the theory to be developed or modified further. The second reason for pursuing this endeavour is that regardless of whether or not the results of the test may be believed, or may be subject to serious methodological criticism, the very process of expressing the theory in empirical terms can force the researcher to sharpen the theoretical concepts involved and to make them more explicit. In particular, attention becomes focused on various parts of the theory which are as yet unspecified, but for which answers must be found. It is to such problems as

these that the final section of this paper will turn. First,
however, the method used and the results obtained will be presented.
    The project was conducted by Mary Douglas and the author at
University College London. We set out to use a very simple questionnaire technique to examine the grid and group dimensions, and to test
a possible relation between a person's social context (as defined
by the two dimensions) and the cosmological beliefs and values which
he or she espoused. We made two separate surveys, in which the
same set of social context questions (with a few minor modifications)
were put (a) to a heterogeneous sample of 80 men and women of many
different occupations in Britain, and (b) to a sample of 100
professional and managerial men and women in three different urban
areas of Britain.
    The aim of the project was first to analyse the concepts of grid
and group into two sets of basic elements, such that each element
would be logically related to the others. These elements then
formed the core definition of the two social dimensions (see Douglas
1978 for details). From these definitions we then devised a number
of questionnaire items which were intended to measure a person's
position on the social dimensions of grid and group. These questions
then constituted our measure of the social context of the individual.
    It is clearly not feasible to have one questionnaire that can be
used for everyone in a complex society. Compromise must be made
between relevance to the individual and generalisability. For
several reasons we chose to concentrate our questions on the social
context of the work-place. For the group dimension, questions
about both work-group and home-group strength were included. The
second aim was then to demonstrate that these various measures of
the two dimensions would be intercorrelated to give some construct
validity to the concepts of grid and group. Finally we hoped to be
able to show that measures of the individuals' values and beliefs
would be correlated with the social context positions on grid and
group, in the ways predicted by the theory. We used the term
'cosmology' to refer to this second part of the questionnaire
dealing with values and beliefs. In presenting our findings, I
shall first deal with the construct validity of the grid and group
scales for our two samples, and then describe the results of our
attempt to predict cosmological views on the basis of the social
context dimensions.

GRID AND GROUP SOCIAL CONTEXT

From the social context questions, 28 grid and 12 group measures were
constructed by scoring the answers appropriately (see Table 3.1).
(In the second sample, the number of group measures was increased
to 14.) If the grid and group dimensions are to form a useful way
of summarising the differences between people's answers to the
questions, then one may expect measures of the same dimension to
be positively correlated with one another, and not to correlate
with measures of the other dimension. One way of testing this
internal consistency of the dimensions is to correlate each measure
with the total scale obtained by summing all the measures. For
this test Kendall's nonparametric coefficient of correlation, tau,

TABLE 3.1   Indices of grid and group dimensions used in questionnaires

GRID		Index	Value for high grid
A Competition	1	Short of time at work	Never
	2	Useful in work to have a speciality	No
	3	Job future	No change
	4	Work involves outside contacts	No
	5	Job is a competitive one	No
B Insulation	6	Can choose hours of day to work	No
	7	Promotion given by explicit criteria (e.g. seniority)	Yes
	8	See people from work in free time	No
	9	Rules and regulations at work	Yes, and important
	10	Make decisions and get informal feedback	No
	11	Responsibility limited to well-defined areas	Yes
	12	Work in a hierarchical organisation (more than three levels)	Yes
	13	Segregated facilities at work	Yes
	14	First names used at work	No
	15	Would you invite your boss home?	No
	16	Stop thinking about work when get home	Yes
C Autonomy	17	Can choose use of time at work	No
	18	Can take time off when you want	No
	19	Can decide to waive rules	No
	20	Can choose those who work with you	No
	21	Have a boss	Yes
	22	Work involves originality	No
D Control	23	Supervise others' work	No
	24	Make decisions affecting others	No
	25	Work involves responsibility	No
	26	In charge of distributing resources to co-workers	No
	27	Make rules for others to follow	No
	28	Could find another job of same type easily	No

Note: In the second survey, indices 13 and 25 were poorly correlated with the other measures, and were excluded from the scale

TABLE continued

TABLE 3.1   (continued)

GROUP		Index	Value for high group
A At work	1	Work as part of a close team	Yes
	2	Reluctant to leave job because of friends	Yes
	3	Don't take time off for sake of others	Don't
	4	Unwritten rules at work involving co-operation	Yes
	5	Have drinks with colleagues regularly	Yes
	6	Have lunch with work group	Yes
	7	Help out others at work if have some misfortune	Yes
	8	Have collections and parties when people leave	Yes
B At home	9	Family in same business and help out	Yes
	10	Close-knit family	Yes
	11	Work colleagues in home social network	Yes
	12	Family and friends know each other	Yes
	13	Friends know and see each other	Yes
	14	Belong to clubs with regular meetings	Yes

Note: (a) In the first survey indices 3 and 4, and 7 and 8, were scored together.
(b) In the second survey, indices 5 and 10 were poorly correlated with the others and were excluded in creating the scales for home and work group.
(c) In addition, indices 8 and 9 were excluded from the overall scale of group for the same reason.

was used (Siegel 1956). For the first sample of people, all the part-whole correlations were positive both for grid and for group, and all but four were significantly greater than zero beyond the 0.05 level. For the second sample, only one measure failed to have a significant positive correlation with the scale total. Furthermore, there was no significant correlation between the scales of grid and group (Kendall's tau = -0.039 for the first sample, and -0.11 for the second). The correlational structure of the measures therefore gives good support for the independence and internal construct validity of the two scales.

A more exacting test of the correlational structure was undertaken using the technique of factor analysis. The level of structure in both samples was relatively low. For the first sample three main factors emerged. These were a strong grid dimension and two weaker group dimensions, one involving work-group questions,

and one the home-group.   In the second sample, there were again
three interpretable factors: a strong grid factor, and then a
weak group factor with some grid measures loading on it, and finally
a factor concerned with stability. This third factor was strongly
reflected by questions concerning how long people had been in a job,
how long they intended to remain, and whether they were reluctant to
leave and not seeking career advancement. The measures of group at
home showed little consistent structure in this second sample. It
is likely that the whole sample was weakly organised as to group
and also that the questionnaire technique is less adapted to
eliciting strong-group behaviour. It appears that grid is a much
easier dimension to measure using a questionnaire technique than is
group. Grid comes out as a strong consistent factor, differentiating
between people, both in a sample of mixed occupations, and in one
restricted to professional and managerial people. Comparison of the
factor analyses of the two samples reveals that it is the same set
of questions which load most strongly on the grid factor for both
samples. One can conclude that the grid dimension is largely
independent of class differences, since the same pattern is found
in a sample of heterogeneous occupations, as in one of high-status
ones. The group dimension produced less clear results, and ideally
one might want to use observational and sociometric techniques to
achieve a better measure of a person's position on the group
dimension.

COSMOLOGY

We can now turn to the problem of predicting cosmological views
from the social context measures. In the first survey a traditional
type of attitude scale was constructed. Forty statements were
presented to the subjects who had to indicate their agreement/
disagreement on a 5-point Likert scale (Likert 1932). The statements were such that people in different quadrants of the social
context grid/group map might be expected to agree with and disagree
with different sets of statements. The results were disappointing.
When each item of the cosmology was considered separately, only 9
of the 40 items came out as significantly correlated with the
social context scales in the predicted direction. Another 7 had
one of the scales correct, and either a zero correlation on the
other predicted scale, or else a significant correlation on the
other where none was predicted. The lack of independence among
the highly intercorrelated cosmology statements makes the interpretation of this number as a significantly positive result rather
dubious. The only result which appeared to be illuminating was
that people in the high-grid half of the sample made fewer 'No
opinion' responses than those in the lower half (chi square = 3.94,
significant at 0.05). There was also an insignificant trend for
people in the low-group half to make fewer 'No opinion' responses.
This result is in accord with our expectations that the high-grid/
low-group corner has an unquestioning, passive cosmology. It would
appear that the remaining corners were likely to question the
assumptions behind the attitude statements and not feel able to
agree or disagree with them.

The failure of the social context dimensions to predict the
cosmology responses could be due to several factors. In particular
it was felt that indicating agreement or disagreement with an
abstract, general statement is not a very meaningful task. Fishbein
(1966) has pointed out that the more specific a particular attitude
statement can be made, then the more reliably will measured attitudes
reflect behavioural intentions. For the second sample therefore an
attempt was made to find questions which were more personally
relevant and direct.

Twenty-six questions were devised for the second cosmology
questionnaire. Once again they were chosen with the aim of
differentiating the four cosmological patterns predicted by the
grid/group theory for the four quadrants of the social context map.
However, because the first sample had cast some doubt on the
correctness of the previous predictions, and because the actual
connection between social context and cosmology is not central to
the theory of grid and group, no firm predictions were made as to
the way different cosmological areas would respond. At an early
stage in the development of a theory it is often wiser to allow
the patterns to emerge, if they will, so that they can form the
basis of further predictions and so that the theory can be modified
in their light if they prove to be reliably replicable. Thus while
we expected certain responses to be associated with certain grid/
group positions (and this motivated our choice of the questions),
our prediction was merely that there would be some significant
mapping of social context on to cosmology.

The method adopted for testing the association between social
context and cosmology was to draw up a table for each cosmology
question, showing the distribution of answers of each type across
the four quadrants of the social context map. In order to do this,
cut-off points had to be placed on the social context grid and group
dimensions in order to divide the sample into high and low scorers.
Before this was done, the two social context scales were made more
internally consistent by excluding those social context measures
which had more negative correlations with the other measures in
their scale than positive ones. The result of this manipulation
was to remove two of the 28 grid measures and 4 of the 14 group
measures. This 'cleaning up' of the scales had a marked positive
effect on the number of cosmological questions which were associated
with the social context scales.

Obviously the more manipulations and tests that are performed,
the greater is the chance of finding associations, and hence the
less significance attaches to all the results found. It was felt
at this stage of the project to be more useful to bring out the
trends in the data than to know the exact probability of the trends
being entirely due to chance factors. Because the survey was of an
investigative, piloting kind, two other manipulations were examined
to see how they might bring out further associations. First the
group variable was divided into questions about home group, and
questions about work group. (Earlier analyses had suggested that
the connection between the two sets of questions was not strong.)
These two new group dimensions, labelled home and work, were also
'cleaned up' by excluding measures with more negative than positive
correlations with other items. They were then used in place of the

group dimension proper so that altogether three maps of social context
were produced - grid x group, grid x home, and grid x work. The
second manipulation was to adopt three levels for the cut-off point
on each dimension - a high, a central and a low criterion, dividing
the sample approximately in the ratios of 1:2, 1:1, and 2:1 respectively along each scale. In this way it is possible to pick out
effects where a cosmological response is typical only of people at
the extreme end of one of the social context dimensions.

RESULTS

Two kinds of test were made, one for main effects of the social
context dimensions on the cosmology results, and one for other
possible deviations from randomness that involve the interaction of
the two dimensions. For example, in a cosmology question with a
simple Yes/No response, the pattern of answers for a main effect of
one dimension might look like one of those in Figure 3.1. Inter-

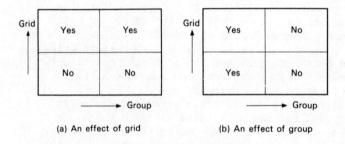

FIGURE 3.1 Examples of main effects

actions would have one of the forms shown in Figure 3.2. In Figure
3.2(a) and (b), opposite corners respond alike, thus removing any
overall main effect of either dimension. In Figure 3.2(c) a main
effect of (say) grid is only found at high group and vice versa.

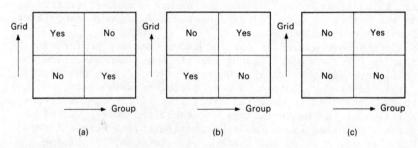

FIGURE 3.2 Examples of interactions

Chi-square tests were used. For the main effects tests, a 2 x 2
chi-square test corrected for continuity was applied to the cross-
tabulation of the social context dimension (e.g. grid, high v. low)
with the cosmology question (e.g. yes v. no to a particular question).

TABLE 3.2   Cosmological responses associated with the grid x group
social context map

High grid low group		High grid high group	
Question	Response	Question	Response
Are you in favour of children being given corporal punishment in schools?	YES	How far back does your oldest surviving friendship go (not counting family)?	(LONGER THAN AVERAGE)
Should the state care for the chronically sick or elderly, regardless of whether they have families that could look after them?	NO	Should the state care for the chronically sick or elderly, regardless of whether they have families that could look after them?	YES
Do you think it is an advantage or a dis-advantage to be unusual in appearance?	DISAD-VANTAGE	Do you think it is an advantage or a dis-advantage to be unusual in appearance?	ADVANTAGE
Has good or bad luck played a large part in your life?	YES	Has good or bad luck played a large part in your life?	NO
Which things are really important in the up-bringing of a child? - Developing person-ality as an individual?	UNIM-PORTANT	Which things are really important in the up-bring of a child? - Developing person-ality as an individual? - Acquiring skills and qualifications for a job?	UNIMPOR-TANT UNIMPOR-TANT

TABLE continued

TABLE 3.2 Continued

Low grid low group		Low grid high group	
Question	Response	Question	Response
Are you in favour of children being given corporal punishment in schools?	YES	How far back does your oldest surviving friendship go (not counting family)?	(LONGER THAN AVERAGE)
Should the state care for the chronically sick or elderly, regardless of whether they have families that could look after them?	YES	Should the state care for the chronically sick or elderly, regardless of whether they have families that could look after them?	NO
Do you think it is an advantage or a dis-advantage to be unusual in appearance?	DISAD-VANTAGE	Do you think it is an advantage or a dis-advantage to be unusual in appearance?	ADVANTAGE
Has good or bad luck played a large part in your life?	NO	Has good or bad luck played a large part in your life?	YES
Which things are really important in the upbringing of a child?		Which things are really important in the upbringing of a child?	
- Developing person-ality as an individual?	IMPOR-TANT	- Developing person-ality as an individual?	IMPOR-TANT
		- Acquiring skills and qualifications for a job?	UNIMPOR-TANT
In your favourite kind of meal, do you prefer traditional or exotic food?	TRADI-TIONAL	In your favourite kind of meal, do you prefer traditional or exotic food?	EXOTIC

TABLE 3.3 Cosmological responses associated with the grid x home social context map

High grid low home		High grid high home	
Question	Response	Question	Response
How far back does your oldest surviving friendship go (not counting family)?	(SHORTER THAN AVERAGE)	How far back does your oldest surviving friendship go (not counting family)?	(LONGER THAN AVERAGE)
Are you in favour of the censorship of adult films?	YES	Are you in favour of the censorship of adult films?	NO
Are you in favour of the fluoridisation of public water to give people healthier teeth?	NO	Which things are really important in the upbringing of a child? - Developing personality as an individual?	UNIMPORTANT
Should people suffering from incurable diseases have the choice of a painless death?	NO	How many days a year do you reckon you have to miss work due to illness?	(MORE THAN AVERAGE)
		Do you celebrate your birthday with a party?	YES
		Should people in middle age aim to look younger than they are?	NO

Low grid low home		Low grid high home	
Question	Response	Question	Response
How far back does your oldest surviving friendship go (not counting family)?	(SHORTER THAN AVERAGE)	How far back does your oldest surviving friendship go (not counting family)?	(LONGER THAN AVERAGE)
Are you in favour of the censorship of adult films?	NO	Are you in favour of the censorship of adult films?	YES
Should people suffering from incurable diseases have the choice of a painless death?	NO	Should people in middle age aim to look younger than they are?	YES
Do you celebrate your birthday with a cake with candles?	YES	Do you celebrate your birthday with a cake with candles?	NO
		Which things are really important in the upbringing of a child? - Developing personality as an individual?	IMPORTANT

TABLE 3.4   Cosmological responses associated with the grid x work social context map

High grid low work		High grid high work	
Question	Response	Question	Response
Which would you rather do given a choice for a 2-week holiday?		Which would you rather do given a choice for a 2-week holiday?	
(Prefer:) GO AWAY TO A FAVOUR-ITE HOLIDAY PLACE THAT YOU KNOW AND LIKE, HAVING BEEN OFTEN BEFORE.		(Prefer:) TRAVEL TO NEW PLACES AND MEET NEW PEOPLE	
Would you like to see the death penalty brought back for terrorist crimes?	YES	Would you like to see the death penalty brought back for terrorist crimes?	NO
Has good or bad luck played a large part in your life?	YES	Has good or bad luck played a large part in your life?	NO
Do you think it is an advantage or a disadvantage to be unusual in appearance?	DISAD-VANTAGE	Which things are really important in the upbringing of a child? - Developing personality as an individual?	UNIM-PORTANT
Which things are really important in the upbringing of a child? - Developing personality as an individual?	UNIM-PORTANT		

Low grid low work		Low grid high work	
Question	Response	Question	Response
Do you have many friends of other generations?	NO	Do you have many friends of other generations?	YES
Would you like to see the death penalty brought back for terrorist crimes?	YES	Would you like to see the death penalty brought back for terrorist crimes?	NO
Which things are really important in the up-bringing of a child? - Developing person-ality as an individual?	IMPOR-TANT	Which things are really important in the up-bringing of a child? - Developing person-ality as an individual?	IMPOR-TANT

For interactions a goodness-of-fit chi-square test was applied to
the distribution of each response type across the social context
quadrants, using the overall sample distribution as the basis for
the expected cell frequencies. By application of these tests, the
cosmology responses significantly associated with social context
dimensions at the 5 per cent significance level were selected.
Tables 3.2 - 3.4 summarise the results for the three maps of social
context. The responses typically associated with each quadrant are
displayed in that quadrant. (2)
    To summarise the results, there were only 8 of the 26 cosmology
questions that showed no significant associations with any of the
social context dimensions. This failure rate is encouragingly low.
Of the significant results, some (for instance on child-rearing and
luck) fit well with the cosmologies anticipated by Mary Douglas
(1978). Others (for example capital punishment) are less obvious.
By using a sample taken from a single socio-economic status bracket,
the confounding effects of class can be discounted although one may
not generalise the results to other classes. However, there are
other possible variables which may be confounded with our social
context dimensions, and hence might be responsible for the observed
associations. For example, the number of years of education a
person has had has been found to be a good predictor of those who
are in favour of violent punishments. Future surveys of the kind
presented here would have to collect more biographical details of
the respondents in order to control for such confounding effects.(3)
It must also be remembered that many tests were performed on the
data, and so one should not expect all of the results presented here
to be reliable. However, considering that the construction of new
scales usually involves a long process of perhaps half a dozen or
more stages of modifying some questions, and adding or deleting
others before reliable results can be produced, the social context
scales of grid and group are extremely promising. It was interesting
that group at home and at work were differentiated to some extent.
This differentiation was borne out in the cosmological themes that
were associated with the two group dimensions. They are summarised
below:

    HOME GROUP

    Censorship of films   Education
    Fluoridisation of water   Days off work
    Voluntary euthanasia   Aim to look younger
    Length of friendships
    Birthday parties and cakes

    WORK GROUP

    Holidays
    Death penalty
    Unusual appearance
    Luck
    Friends of other generations

Finally, an analysis of the 'don't know' responses showed that there
were far fewer than in the first sample. There was an insignificant

trend for people in low grid, low group to make more, and people in high grid, high group to make fewer 'don't know' responses.

PROBLEMS AND OTHER ISSUES

The final section will discuss some of the issues and problems which have been raised by undertaking this project. These issues are probably of equal value in the development of grid/group analysis as the results themselves. Five areas will be dealt with.

(a) Objectivity

Perhaps the most obvious problem with using people's own assessment of their social context position is the problem of the subjectivity of their judgment. Interestingly this question appears to interact with the problem of levels discussed below, in that reasonably objective measures (such as the physical environment, regularity of group occasions, codified systems of rules) apply more readily to defining the grid/group position of groups (such as tribes or institutions) than to defining individual positions within a group. Thus it is unclear at present to what extent we define an indivi- dual's position in terms of the actual grid/group constraints acting upon him as seen from some perspicacious observer's vantage point, and to what extent it is crucial that the individual is actually aware of the constraints. Measures based on interview or questionnaire techniques can only hope to reflect the social context as it appears to the person in it. This being so, there is also the vexatious possibility that the reported view of the social context is biased by the distorting lens of the person's cosmology. Grid/group position will then have a double effect on the subjective report of that position – first through the actual constraints acting on an individual, and second through the interpretation imposed on them by the cosmological bias. It may be the case, therefore, that the distinction between sociological and psycho- logical explanations of cosmology becomes untenable, since the two form a single interacting system of influences on beliefs and attitudes.
  However, there is one kind of psychological explanation of the correlation between social context and cosmology which can be tested. This explanation would run as follows. Individuals differ in their personalities (for purely psychological reasons if such things exist). They therefore will be led to prefer and to choose different kinds of social environment and also different systems of belief which are sympathetic to their personality. Hence if we measure their social environments and cosmologies, we may discover a correlation, but it would be invalid to infer that the social environment generated the cosmology. (I am indebted to David Bloor for pointing out this argument to me.) The argument as it stands may contain serious flaws. What for example is it about a social environment that makes it conducive or sympathetic to the individual? Even so, a longitudinal study of people who have sudden changes in social environment thrust upon them (as, for example, in leaving

university or being conscripted into an army) might be able to show
that social environments can be instrumental in altering a person's
cosmological viewpoint. The social psychological literature on
attitude change may also be relevant here (e.g. Bem, 1967). I
return to this question in discussing the position of the individual
below.

An interesting piece of evidence on the question of objectivity
emerged from the results of the second survey. When the grid
measures were divided informally into two sets, one selected to
reflect more objective kinds of question, and the other the questions
more prone to subjective effects, then it turned out that the more
objective questions were better correlated overall with the grid
dimension. This evidence however is clearly not sufficient to
answer the problems raised.

(b) Cosmology

The measurement of cosmology has raised various questions. One is
the extent to which cosmology must be measured in a context-
specific fashion. Thus the issues used in order to test the systems
of values and cosmological beliefs must be of relevance to the
particular context in which the individual lives. If this is not
the case then people will respond according to a stereotyped
cosmology that does not reflect their own condition - i.e. that is
never used for the justification and legitimation of their own
actions.

A teasing example of the pitfalls to be avoided here was
suggested by Gert Hofstede (personal communication) who has conducted
the analysis of a huge multinational survey of attitudes and
perceptions about work (Hofstede, 1975-78). He pointed out how the
same people would be happy to agree that they preferred their boss
to act in an authoritative manner, while at the same time agreeing
with the statement, 'Lower levels of management should have more
say in the running of the organisation'. It is therefore necessary
to distinguish the desired - being the personally relevant judgments
of value - from the desirable - the general principles that are seen
to apply at a less personal level. The theory of grid/group
cosmologies must therefore make explicit just what kinds of value
would be predicated as derivable from social context position -
leaving open the possibility that there may be other kinds of value,
and other media of transmission. A look at typologies of belief
and value systems (e.g. Rokeach 1960, Fishbein and Ajzen 1975)
could provide some clarification of this issue.

(c) The position of the individual

I have already mentioned a serious problem that concerns the
relation between grid/group analysis as applied to groups or
societies and the analysis of an individual's position within a
society. At present the same conceptual framework is used to deal
with both these levels. How far this will be possible is an
empirical question that urgently needs attention. To use another

example from Hofstede's work, he found that two dimensions could be positively correlated at one level and negatively correlated at another. Thus for example the dimensions of stress and job satisfaction were negatively correlated within each occupational group - the lower the stress the greater the satisfaction. However, between the occupations the relation was a positive one - the more stressful the occupation, the more job satisfaction went with it.

A second question about the position of individuals concerns the notion of a mismatch between social context and cosmology. Individuals may find themselves launched into a new area of the social map, for one of two reasons. They may have precipitated the move themselves, or they may be the victims of some external changes. In the first case the theory of grid/group analysis ought to consider what are the tensions that will make an individual more or less content with his present position.   Is it purely a question of his past history in the grid/group map, or should one also bring in personality variables? This seems to me to be a fruitful possibility for a link with work in psychology. For the other case, where change is forced on a person, the theory should make predictions about how the justifications can be made for a change of cosmology; personality could also play its part here in (i) the degree of inconsistency between old and new cosmologies that can be tolerated, and (ii) the lability of a person's held cosmology, the ease with which it will accommodate itself to the new surroundings. Examples from the psychological literature of these kinds of personality traits are abundant (e.g. Adorno et al. 1950, Fromm 1941, Rokeach 1960). Similarly it would be a fruitful field to link up grid/group analysis with psychological studies of obedience (Milgram 1974) and conformity (Asch 1956) which appear to be concerned with very similar issues.

A final issue concerns the problem of individuals who ostensibly have two quite distinct social contexts - for instance one at home and one at work - with quite different grid/group positions in each. At present the theory assumes that their cosmology will reflect some average position between the two areas of their life, perhaps weighted according to the personal relevance attached to the different activities. Empirical research is needed here to find out how common situations like this are, and how stable they can be. Informal evidence suggests it may be very possible to have, say, a high-group home background, with a relatively low group at work. Should we then expect to see inconsistent and self-contradictory cosmologies emerging for these individuals, or might the resolution of two cosmologies result in a hybrid, eccentric form of cosmology? The ability to maintain two social context positions simultaneously may yet again reflect an individual personality variable.

(d)   The problem of the centre

This problem concerns the generality of the grid/group scheme for industrialised societies. The theory is presented as a general scheme for all societies, but for exposition purposes it has been largely described in terms of the four extreme positions, corresponding to the four corners of the diagram as shown on p.4 (Figure 1)

(plus the fifth withdrawn low-grid, low-group cosmology). As such
we must ask how many people in a modern society can meaningfully be
placed towards one of these extremes, and how many are distributed
somewhere around the centre? As this is a question about distributions
one might look to a quantitative empirical answer. However, this
answer is difficult to give for the following reason. When constructing a measuring scale based on a number of different measures combined
in a polythetic manner, the criterion used to identify a meaningful
dimension is the strong intercorrelation of the various measures that
are intended to reflect that dimension. Thus for instance in our
survey research we showed that grid was a valid way of summarising
differences in social context because the various grid measures
were all intercorrelated. If we then construct our scale by adding
these measures, however, this means that the distribution will be
determined by the pattern of correlations and will emerge as bimodal,
with more people ending up towards the extremes of the scale than in
the centre. In other words there is no independent way of motivating
the definition of the scale so as to give a meaning to the actual
size of intervals along it (an interval scale) as opposed to giving
meaning to the rank ordering of items along it (an ordinal scale).
With only an ordinal scale for defining social context (and it may
be argued there are very few real interval scales in the social
sciences), we should then perhaps look to the consistency of
cosmologies to tell us what happens in the centre. The question
then becomes one of whether the four (or five) cosmologies described
by Mary Douglas are the only self-sustaining cosmological positions,
such that people will tend to migrate towards one or another, but
cannot maintain a stable position in between them. Until we have a
good technique for assessing cosmologies this remains a question
that is open to speculation but not to direct test. It would
indeed be disappointing if it turned out that the majority of the
population of a heterogeneous society fell into some central grey
area of eclectic, loosely integrated cosmologies, and that the
clear-cut areas in each corner were limited to a relatively small
proportion of people.

(e) The withdrawn cosmology

As a conclusion, I shall turn to a problem that has been evident
for some time - namely the placing of the hermit recluse on the
grid/group map. A person who withdraws totally from society cannot
be subject to the constraints of grid or group. Hence in her
writings Mary Douglas has hesitated between taking him right off
the diagram, or putting him in the low-grid/low-group corner.
Unfortunately, this corner is then occupied by two very different
cosmologies - the one of the successful entrepreneur, the 'big
man', who is manipulating the others around him and is in a position
of power, and the other for the withdrawn individual who has no
interest in meeting others at all.
    Alternative solutions to this question have been suggested.
Rayner (personal communication) suggests a band of extreme low grid
where this withdrawn cosmology will be found, thus placing the
entrepreneur slightly higher up the grid dimension. In a previous

paper (Hampton 1976), I suggested taking the hermit off the map altogether, while Thompson (personal communication) would like to see him at the centre of a three-dimensional cube, with grid and group as two of the axes, and power as the third. Indeed the connection of power with the grid/group map is also discussed by Ostrander (chapter 1 of this volume) where he refers to the stable and unstable diagonals. The addition of a third dimension seems to be a good way of dealing with the withdrawn cosmology, but as Thompson's map is a plane drawn within a three-dimensional space, it will not differentiate positions on the grid/group diagram (except in the 'catastrophe regions' where the plane is folded over itself).

A different solution would be to have a third dimension for the grid/group map which, like grid and group, is a measure of social interactions and which would also be independent of them (unlike the power dimension). One would then have a cube in which any position may theoretically be occupied. Thus the hermit and entrepreneur would both be at low grid and low group, but they would occupy positions at different ends of the third dimension. Taking these two examples, it seems that what differentiates them most is the quantity of social interaction in which they are engaged. The entrepreneur represents a high extreme, and the hermit a low extreme. This third dimension (which I shall refer to as activity) may also be fruitfully used to differentiate the other three quadrants of the grid/group diagram. For instance in high grid, low group, a person with much social interaction would be a struggling entrepreneur who was losing the battle to remain at the centre of his networks, while a person with a low level of activity would be the alienated factory worker. In the low-grid, high-group corner, high levels of activity would describe the tightly-knit revolutionary sects (see Rayner, chapter 11 of this volume), while low levels would be exemplified by a monastic order with very little status differentiation and very little interpersonal communication. Finally for high grid, high group, a high level of activity might describe a large organisation such as an army regiment, or a hospital, whereas low levels might correspond to life in a geriatric ward or in certain kinds of prison, where interaction was very rare, and always with the same few people.

This third dimension is only one possible variable which could prove useful for elaborating the theory of grid/group analysis in different directions. Clearly, caution must be taken in building new parts into a theory which is already rather 'top-heavy' in the relation of theoretical power to empirical evidence. However, the proposed new dimension should not prove difficult to define and measure empirically, and it does appear to follow the logic of the derivation of the grid and group social context dimensions. Thus, to follow Ostrander's characterisation (in chapter 1), grid is how one interacts, group is with whom, and activity is how much.

CONCLUSION

The understanding of how different societies are able to generate widely differing cultural viewpoints is crucial for placing a proper perspective on all our knowledge and beliefs. This paper has been addressed to those with a proper scepticism about conceptual schemes that interpret the world without stating how the concepts may be operationalised, or making predictions about the outcomes of experiments. It is hoped that the project described here will have gone some way towards demonstrating the feasibility of grid/group analysis, so that fieldworkers may feel encouraged to draw on its insights for the development of their own research, and so contribute further to the development of the theory.

NOTES

1   This research was made possible by a grant from the Social Science Research Council of Great Britain.
2   Whether or not both directions of an association are shown, depends on the level of the criterion dividing high from low which produced the significant result. If it was a central criterion, then both (say) yes-with-high, and no-with-low are shown as typical responses. If it was a high criterion, then only the response associated with the high portion of the sample is considered significant. Similarly for a low criterion, only the no-with-low association would be shown.
3   One might of course argue that grid/group analysis could explain why the previous association had been observed. People might be in favour of violent punishments because an early end to their education led them into a particular grid/group social context. Thus the theory may be able to offer links that will explain previously observed connections between attitudes and social variables.

BIBLIOGRAPHY

ADORNO, T.W., Else FRENKEL-BRUNSWICK, D.J. LEVINSON and R.N. SANDFORD (1950), 'The Authoritarian Personality', New York, Harper.
ASCH, S.E. (1956), Studies of independence and conformity: a minority of one against a unanimous majority, 'Psychological Monographs' 70, whole no.416.
BEM, D.J. (1967), Self-perception: an alternative interpretation of cognitive dissonance phenomena, 'Psychological Review', 74:183-200.
DOUGLAS, M. (1978), 'Cultural Bias', London, Royal Anthropological Institute, occasional paper no.35.
FISHBEIN, M. (1966), The relationships between beliefs, attitudes and behaviour, in S. Feldman (ed.) 'Cognitive Consistency', New York, Academic Press.
FISHBEIN, M. and I. AJZEN (1975), 'Belief, Attitude, Intention and Behaviour', New York and London, Addison-Wesley.
FROMM, E. (1941), 'Escape from Freedom', New York, Farrar & Rhinehart.
HAMPTON, J.A. (1976), Grid-Group Analysis: a tool for cultural comparison, unpublished paper presented at a conference on 'American and European Values' in Jekyll Island, Georgia.
HOFSTEDE, G. (1975-78), Series of fourteen papers published as part of the Working Papers of the European Institute for Advanced Studies in Management, Brussels.

LIKERT, R.A. (1932), A technique for the measurement of attitudes, 'Archives of Psychology', no.140.

MILGRAM, S. (1974), 'Obedience to Authority: An experimental view', New York, Harper & Row.

ROKEACH, M. (1960), 'The Open and Closed Mind: Investigations into the nature of belief systems, and personality systems', New York, Basic Books.

SIEGEL, S. (1956), 'Nonparametric Statistics for the Behavioural Sciences', New York, McGraw-Hill.

Chapter 4

TWENTY INDUSTRIAL SCIENTISTS: A PRELIMINARY EXERCISE

Celia Bloor and David Bloor

This essay (1) is based on an analysis of a mass of interview data provided by a sample of industrial scientists. The aim was to see whether the material could be interpreted in the light of grid/group theory. The word 'interpreted' here refers to two distinct processes. First, could the industrial scientists be located along the grid and group dimensions? This meant trying to construct the dimensions in a way that made them applicable to the various industrial organisa- tions in which the scientists found themselves. The analysis must be able to discriminate between these organisations, for the typology must be construed as being about sub-groups in our society rather than about societies as a whole. The second, and more exciting question, is whether knowing the position of a scientist on the grid/group diagram allows us to predict the picture of science and nature that scientists will discern in their experimental work. For example, do scientists evince 'cosmological bias' which bears analogy to the cases described by anthropologists? Here we have focused on certain salient features of cosmologies predicted in 'Cultural Bias' (Douglas 1978). We have paid special attention to the attitude to the scientist's task, the attitude to the natural world, and the attitude to other scientists, expecting to find them combined in contrasted patterns. Along these lines we found four different cosmological schemes. According to one, the work of the scientist is to discover and measure regularities, inventing the right key, as it were, to turn the lock and reveal nature's secrets, deemed in themselves to be essentially unmysterious and knowable. This scientist would value exactitude and correct performance of testing procedures; good scientists would be like good instruments, standardised, ranked commodities, complementary to one another and substitutable. Another cosmological scheme presents a complete contrast on all these points: nature is endlessly mysterious and unknowable; the task of the scientist is to make a clever gadget that works, the grand theory of how it works is not a high priority; the scientist needs flair, imagination and skills in transacting with diverse colleagues. In this scheme the good scientist is a unique, creative individual. In a third cosmological scheme these contrasted theories about nature and scientific inquiry hardly receive any attention: such concerns are submerged beneath a welter

of confusing social problems. In the fourth case the scientist
lives too segregated a life either to entertain theories about
science and nature, or to experience intensely absorbing social
relations.

Though the materials in this essay are suggestive, the exercise
has an entirely exploratory character. It is like a pilot experiment
which tests the apparatus, discerns snags and indicates the scope of
the effects being studied. Unlike the official findings of subsequent
work such exploratory exercises do not usually surface in the
literature. Nevertheless, knowing about them can be useful. They
yield the hints and warnings usually conveyed through informal networks of communication. What follows is offered in that spirit.

THE DATA

In 1973 forty industrial scientists were interviewed for a period of
about two to four hours each. The interviews - which were tape-
recorded - were semi-structured, but all covered the same ground.
They were designed to find out what sort of problems the scientists
experienced in moving to their industrial jobs from the academic
environment in which they had worked for their doctorates. All the
scientists had been at work for about one year after their leaving
university physics and chemistry departments.

These interviews were part of a larger study designed to test
the claim that an industrial environment would clash with the so-
called 'scientific values' of freedom to publish, open criticism and
free choice of research topics. This claim, stemming from the work
of Robert Merton, had already encountered criticism in the literature,
but no one had looked at a pure sample of PhDs before. (2)

In the course of the interviews the scientists were encouraged to
describe the way in which their work was organised; with whom they
worked; what their daily routine was like; what problems they
encountered; what they liked about the work; how they imagined
their career progressing; the assessment procedures to which they
were subject and the structure of the firm. As well as this the
scientists were asked about their attitudes to science; what
techniques they used; what approaches fascinated them; what sort
of scientific problems engaged them and what sort of results they
liked. So as well as bearing on their social situations, these
interviews contained data that might reveal their attitudes towards
the natural world.

The verbatim transcripts of the interviews amounted to some one
and a half thousand pages. In order to reduce the task of giving
them a detailed scrutiny to manageable proportions the sample was
randomly divided into two halves. What follows will therefore be
data derived from twenty of the scientists. By way of illustration
let us first look at some interviews which were typical of those
that we encountered. We have chosen cases which seem to us to
represent the four extreme positions on the grid/group diagram.

ILLUSTRATIVE CASES

(i) High grid/high group

Dr Ravelston works on developing a microwave device for defence use,
though he is employed by a commercial electronics firm. The group
aspect of his working relations came over very clearly in his description of the general atmosphere of the firm:
  They've got a good atmosphere there. I mean, most of the people
  there are my friends outside work as well. Really it is just one
  big, happy club.
    We usually go out drinking on a Friday afternoon if there's an
  odd moment and the boss usually sends us out with a £1 note every
  so often. We organise Christmas dinners together, darts matches
  against other teams. Some days it's more like a social club than
  a work place. You know, you do know what other people are doing -
  what problems they've got. Every so often you'll see them having
  to work a bit harder, and you don't really feel you're shut away
  in a corner. [. . .] There's always a darts match going on at
  lunchtime, always a group at the pub, there's always another
  group going shopping.
As well as this account of the overlapping of social relationships, there is a further piece of evidence pointing towards high
group. This is the fact that the project on which Dr Ravelston is
working is fairly long term. A feasibility study had already lasted
for one year and the work was due to last five years more. Over
this long period Dr Ravelston would be in charge of about five
people and the firm did not have a high turnover. Indeed Dr Ravelston
himself had been employed there for about three years between his
first degree and the beginning of his PhD study. He had then
returned to his old company, who had paid him a retainer during his
research.
  The question of measuring grid is slightly more difficult. There
is a general reason for assuming that grid must be high. Nothing
about Dr Ravelston's work involves much by way of transacting with
people. He is not doing people good turns in order to reap the
advantage; he is not selling himself or his ideas, nor is he
engaged in contractual bargaining. Rather, he is greatly preoccupied
with organising things, with sequencing and ordering them. Because
the work is for a government contract the year's project feasibility
study dealt in detail with costing and planning of resources.
  These days you don't only have the technical specifications, but
  there are development documentation systems, quality assurance
  plans and reliability plans and component evaluations and all the
  formal reporting procedures to do with financial reporting and
  accounting and whether it's going to be run on the computer or
  not.
Work of this kind involves drawing up an enormously detailed plan
of the order in which components have to be invented and produced and
problems about them solved. The time and money that can be allowed
for each phase of the research, development and production of the
piece of electronics must be accurately scheduled.
  In order to make this plan work, Dr Ravelston is very much
concerned to keep an eye on the people who work under him and in

association with him. He must make sure that everyone is keeping to
schedule and has a clear sense of what he ought to be doing - something
which he is keenly aware applies to him too.

Although the work involves travelling up and down the country to
meet ministry representatives and to get together with the other
contractors, these meetings are described as 'rather formal'. Not
much detail was provided, although the relations with other firms and
the ministry were described, more than once, as 'like chess'.

Another feature which suggested a high-grid rating was the rather
orderly hierarchy of the firm itself. This was signalled by the fact
that salaries were usually related to age, though Dr Ravelston hoped
for an exception to be made for himself. Asked whether salary was
merit-related, he replied:

> No, well - barely so. People, as far as I know, have definitely
> been slotted in according to age and no one has really ascended
> out of his age group ... if anyone does do, it'll be me of course.
> I'll do it this Christmas or April.

Hierarchy in the firm was symbolised by the usual grading of furniture.
Dr Ravelston did not seem to perceive any existence of power struggles
at the top of the hierarchy. When asked about such struggles, he
just described the symbols of status and seemed to contemplate his
progression upwards:

> I haven't come round to carpets yet. It is only the divisional
> manager who has got a carpet, but one day I shall have a carpet,
> and a red telephone, but that's a bit higher up the tree, that is.
> Higher up than that, you get a picture on the wall as well, but
> that's a long time into the future.

What sort of cosmology would grid/group theory lead us to expect
from someone in Dr Ravelston's position at high grid/high group? We
need to know how to identify the equivalent, in science, of a belief
in the magical efficacy of ritual. Plausibly this would take the
form of a pious belief that the right methods and formulas, properly
followed, will automatically produce the desired results. Nature
would be expected to be orderly, and woe betide those who do not
follow the right procedures.

Significantly we find that for Dr Ravelston the sophisticated
electronics research and development that he is organising is just
the next step up from schoolboy tinkering with alarm clocks.

> I don't know any theoretical physicists. I suppose there are
> theoretical physicists. There are daydreamers and philosophers
> and things, but most people like either tinkering with cars or
> start taking batteries and radios and alarm clocks apart. Of
> course, when you're young, they don't go back together again,
> but a bit later you learn to take things apart and put them back
> together again. I've got to the stage where I am designing
> things which have never been put together at all - definite
> progression there.

In his own words, electronics is just an extension of meccano:

> It's much better than a meccano set - masses of people milling
> around - it's immensely technically complicated, a tremendous
> challenge.

Dr Ravelston is describing a view of science that might be called a
'key-in-lock' view. The unknown in nature is seen as a technical
challenge, that is, a puzzle, something complicated but with an

assured answer, given enough perseverance, enough man-hours and trained
competence.
    Even more telling is Dr Ravelston's concern over the process of
measurement. His research in electronics is very closely bound up
with the necessity of having accurately calibrated instruments. All
of the instruments in his laboratory are periodically checked and
all of them bear a little label indicating when they were last
calibrated - 'down to the last knife and fork', as Dr Ravelston
rather neatly put it. Everything would go awry unless this procedure
were carried out reliably. One of Dr Ravelston's most vividly
described memories concerns his experience of academic research in
physics. What he recalls finding there, after his initial experience
in industry, is that his fellow researchers were very sloppy over
this matter. They would construct apparatus beset by a whole range
of sources of unreliability, thus rendering their results useless.
Dr Ravelston is deeply contemptuous of this: it is very repugnant,
'a crazy way to go on'.
    You've got to make sure it's accurate and calibrated and doesn't
    drift and doesn't fail - all these dynamic ranges and noise
    levels and linearities and all sorts of things, different measuring
    techniques. Most people at colleges, they've got something to
    measure and if they can see it on a scope, fine. If they can't
    see it on a scope, they try and amplify it and put it on a scope,
    and there's very little thought put in. Most results from PhDs
    are totally meaningless in fact - very, very few are actually
    accurate. Few of them attempt to assess their own accuracy with
    the results. It's bad; it's criminal in fact.
It does not see too fanciful to suggest that Dr Ravelston's concern
with calibration is at least analogous to a form of ritual purity -
where ritual is not, of course, empty or mechanical, but is seen as
necessary for establishing proper relations with nature.
    On a more personal level, we would expect Dr Ravelston not to
show much interest in the subjective side of men so much as in their
outsides - the role rather than the role player. Consistently he
says
    you can only work ... do so much, depending on how many people
    are working on the job. It's quite amazing how much the average
    applies. You know, you've got a certain job to do and you must
    have a certain amount of space or a certain amount of people to
    within the 10 per cent or so. You can't take one or two
    brilliant people, if it takes four people to do it, two brilliant
    people can't do it. Three brilliant people might do it, but
    four average people can do it. It's strange really.
And again:
    I mean, when you think about engineers, really you can just buy
    engineers. They are just like units, they are pretty much inter-
    changeable, and if you want someone for a particular job ... you
    can put an advert in the paper at the right salary.
So far this fits very nicely.
    The sort of event that is likely to lend excitement to life in
an orderly universe of measurable facts is the unfrocking and
exclusion of error. The highlight of Dr Ravelston's own academic
research was the very accurate measurement of a physical constant.
There had been trouble over his result, some authorities not agreeing

with it. It had not been accepted and only now was his PhD going
through, for recently a new theory had been developed which predicted
a value to which his result was an incredibly close approximation.
His opponents, he now felt, would have to go back to their apparatus
and find out where the errors had crept into their work - the
inaccuracy of which had now been exposed.

So here is the cosmology much as predicted for members of a
hierarchical group. We have found a key-in-lock view of nature, a
stress on its routine aspects, its regularity. The need for care
and precision takes on moral overtones and corresponding to this is
the need to identify and reject inadequate performance.

Let us now look at another case, this time a man whose environment
would seem to be in the diametrically opposite corner of the diagram.
This will help highlight just how different can be the attitudes and
experiences of the sample. If the views of Dr Ravelston seemed in
some way obvious or unproblematic, the contrast with Dr Grange which
follows should alter that appearance.

(ii)   Low grid/low group

Dr Grange is employed in the central research laboratory of a large
electrical concern. He is also engaged on accurate measurement, as
he is a consultant on instrumentation. If his fellow scientists and
engineers require some special measuring process that they cannot
develop for themselves, they turn to the department in which Dr
Grange is employed. He will research into the problem and develop
some appropriate transducer for turning the behaviour of the process
to be measured into useful and detectable signals.

The first reason for assigning Dr Grange to a low position on
the group axis is that he essentially works on his own. The client
either approaches him directly or, if the work reaches him through
his superior, he is left to work out the answer himself. He sees
his boss about once a month. The working relationships with his
clients are described by Dr Grange like this:

> I don't have to work with them all the time. I'm working with
> them quite intensively say for a couple of months and then I
> drop out of their lives completely and let them carry on and do
> the experiment .... I find this a nice level to keep industrial
> friendships at - not living in each other's pockets, but at the
> same time if you see each other in the labs, you say 'hello'.

This contrasts with Dr Ravelston who drops into the pub with his
long-term colleagues rather than dropping out of their lives.
Dr Grange then goes on to provide a very clear characterisation of
the style of the relationship between himself and the people to
whom he addresses his cheery 'hello'. He refers to the importance
of knowing:

> each other's good points and bad points - for example, on the
> simple social level, I know who's good at welding, who's good at
> cars, who's good at television ... and at the same time, I also
> know who's got such-and-such an instrument. If I go and talk to
> him nicely, he might lend it to me for a week, so that I can try
> out this new idea of mine.

What is called 'the simple social level', then, is a level of useful barter and this style extends upwards into the work relationships. 'It's useful in that it helps me get my work done': this theme is expanded by Dr Grange when he says:

well through my work with various clients, I've come to know which PhDs in the lab or which physicists are good for talking to about certain subjects. So-and-so is good at optics and so-and-so is good at electronics and so-and-so at solid state. If I do a study on perhaps an instrumentation system for stress waves in solids, I can go straight to the acoustics bloke and say, 'look, is this right?'.

So here we have Dr Grange finding out what use people are to him, building up his contacts and swapping pieces of knowledge. He is transacting with them. He thinks of his clients as forming a sort of following and the greater the following, the more his credit. Thus:

If clients get given a piece of work which they consider to be good and is a good piece of physics, they say, or I hope they say, 'Roger Grange, he's a good bloke, remember that'.... In fact I'm getting people coming to see me who've been directed to come and see me by people I've done work for.

The picture which emerges strongly from the whole interview is of a person actively benefiting from each exchange, increasing his stock of goodwill, prestige and success in the eyes of his clients and supervisors. He stresses the importance in his job of selling his ideas to people and in his description of the encounters at which this selling takes place, he insists on the hard bargaining that is necessary - he is not dealing with men who are easily satisfied, so his suggestions and ideas have to be good ones. His many victories have not been easily won: 'the clients are, well, very highly qualified people. There's no point or chance of pulling the wool over their eyes.'

As would be expected for low grid/low group, the social forms which are valued are the rules of fairness, not ascription. Thus, Dr Grange expresses his dislike of salary scales which go up by age rather than by pure merit. He is rather annoyed by the fact that some people older then himself earn more, even though in his 'considered opinion' they are doing less than he is. On the other hand, the hierarchy of positions in his firm - that is, 'research officer', 'group leader', 'section leader' etc. - 'is not as rigid as it sounds'. This is a good thing in Dr Grange's view and he is relieved by the fact that mere status in the hierarchy does not always correspond with salary. The mechanism of salary assessment used in his organisation, called the 'technical assessment panel', is deemed satisfactory by Dr Grange because 'it goes a little way in reducing the effects of nepotism and other nasty things that occur'.

Attitudes towards nature predicted for low grid/low group present it not as strictly ordered, but emphasising its irregularities. It will be seen as responsive to the special skills of the uniquely endowed individuals who study it. Since there will be differences from person to person, the world will be seen as a mysterious thing, not a key-in-lock matter.

For someone who is busy with may clients - and Dr Grange was

running two or three projects at once - time is at a premium, routine
work is time-consuming, and it is novelty that is potentially
marketable.

Dr Grange has clear views on scientific theory and its approach to
nature:

> I've never been one for taking a monotonous series of results and
> processing series of results - the systematic study of an effect.
> Whilst it might further the pure physics or the knowledge of the
> subject-matter, it doesn't really appeal to me.

He goes on:

> Compared to getting reams and reams of experimental results,
> spending three months working them out on a computer or a hand
> calculator and drawing graphs and then spending another month or
> more writing a couple of paragraphs and discussions of these
> results, and then having them argued about by people who might
> put a different theoretical interpretation on the results that
> you've obtained ... they are not cut-and-dried; it's not as
> cut-and-dried as having a black box which works up to a
> specification and that's it. And as I've said, once the black
> box is there and working, I quite like to see the back of it.

There are two important points here. First, things which are cut-
and-dried, like a black box which satisfies a customer's specification, allow a bargain or a contract to be deemed concluded. The
goods have been delivered and the cash or the reward is now due.
Endless haggling over theoretical interpretations, rather than
pragmatic criteria of workability, is as frustrating for Dr Grange
as a chaotic and idiosyncratic accounting system must be to someone
who wants to know whether a deal is or is not profitable.

Second, Dr Grange said that once the black box is working he
likes to see the back of it. He does not want to be bogged down
in the routine development of his ideas - he wants to move on to
the next interesting problem. What is more, he has organised
things so that this is indeed what happens. He strategically
detaches himself from this side of the problem. To begin with, the
client and his boss generally work through the problem to remove
those aspects of it which are just 'stringing pieces of meccano
together'. Only when they hit on a fundamental problem in physics
do they, according to Dr Grange, pass it on to him. What happens
then is that Dr Grange studies the problem and hands on his ideas
in the form of a drawing to an engineer:

> And then they'll make something up for me and they'll plonk it
> on my desk - 'here you are, go and play with it' - an interesting
> black box. So I then have to go out into the lab., play about
> with it and find out its properties, difficulties and short-
> comings and advantages if it's got any and think of amendments
> and get the amendments done.... When that's been done it's almost
> out of my hands, because all I do is to take it along to the
> workshop and say 'copy it'.

He hands it over to others and rushes on to the next interesting
problem. The long-term flow chart which orders and sequences
activity is not to be found here. Dr Grange copes with the problem
of his multitude of clients and the need to focus on but one part
of the problem by the deft use of a screen of technicians. This all
accords with his general preference for the singular, the elegant

and the unique - 'it's repetitions which go against my grain, as it were'. Later in the discussion he expressed his distaste for highly empirical and complex subjects, like fluid dynamics, and stated his attraction for striking paradoxes like the fact that the sky at night is dark, a fact which points to the need for a dramatic theory like that of the expanding universe. He calls scientific work like this 'after-dinner physics' - the point of the designation would seem to be that these ideas enhance the social prestige of those who can delight their audiences with them. They are attention-getters: vivid, concrete, the achievement of appropriately brilliant men who hurry on to the next trick as the distinguished after-dinner speaker hurries on to the next joke. And surely nothing could represent the irregular in nature more than the citing of that most singular event of all: the original big bang.

So, if Dr Ravelston is a pious worshipper of truth, Dr Grange is a scientific version of a New Guinea Big Man. Their contrasting attitudes towards mistakes is interesting. We have seen that Dr Ravelston in his high-grid/high-group position finds error morally offensive, something criminal that demands expiation. Dr Grange is really not at all worried about mistakes: he often makes them. He is quite happy to go up to the acoustics expert with an idea that is laughed at as scientific nonsense. He is not abashed, nor deterred from trying again in the same or another specialty. He learns from his mistakes, he trades knowledge with so many people that mistakes will get filtered out sooner or later and the customer's instrument will get built and delivered. Again the predicted bias in attitude has been found. Instead of the key-in-lock view of science, we have a view which is optimistic and morally neutral, except for the requirement of success. The symbol of science as meccano is replaced by that of a mysterious black box: the scientist is no longer the standard replaceable unit of conscientious endeavour, but the dynamic individual endowed with the special touch.

Two more positions on the grid/group diagram remain to be illustrated. First, a case of witchcraft in the laboratory.

(iii) Low grid/high group

Dr Merchiston is a chemist who specialises in the chemistry of a specific element and is working on a long-term project associated with nuclear reactors. His project concerns impurities in the chemicals. He is a member of a group of seven scientists under a section leader who all specialise in the same chemical - although concerned with different aspects of it. The reason for rating him fairly high on the group axis is that there is evidence of a degree of interdependence between the members of the group - they help one another - but, more important, they seem rather conscious of a group identity and boundary. He was asked, 'Do you have any team feeling about the way you work or do you work mainly independently?'

Yeh; certainly, yeh there is, because expertise for work on sodium is within that group, and we get this sort of feeling that in fact we are working as a team although we are working on independent projects, and the link is the sodium if you like - the actual expertise in handling sodium. It's quite dodgy stuff.

[Interviewer]: Is that actually much help to you in fact, the working contacts?

Yes it is. There's a lot of discussion goes on between the members of the group. I mean we're not working in complete isolation and ... yes it's a tremendous help - the different talents of the group and talking to each other and different opinions on projects.

The sense of boundary around the group which contains the expertise in handling this dangerous chemical arises because other research groups, such as engineers and metallurgists connected with the design of the nuclear reactor, need help with sodium. Dr Merchiston says there is some resentment generated in this interaction:

I'm not entirely happy, and this is a general feeling in the group, with the recognition we get for helping out other people within the laboratories. What tends to happen is: you help somebody out, you give somebody advice and they go and get on with something and churn the results out and it comes out as if they did the whole work and this sort of thing. So I am not entirely happy in that respect.

So the experience of exchanging information across the small group boundary has proved less than profitable: such inequities may help to create a sense of a good inside and a bad outside.

On the other hand, inside the small group there are problems - there is a lack of direction and a sense of confusion is conveyed. All of this points to low grid, an absence of rules controlling behaviour. For example, when asked how he got started on his project, how his work was allocated when he arrived, Dr Merchiston said:

I was given a brief to look at a certain area and this was essentially sort of ... how can I put it? ... this was more or less just looking at impurities in sodium, OK? So I was given a brief and I wasn't told anything particular to do, I was ... the only thing I was told was to look at what was going on in that area, and find something to do basically.

Dr Merchiston rounded off this somewhat desperate statement with the incongruous words 'it's pretty good actually'. This incongruity is heightened later when he launches into a statement of his frustrations with management.

There doesn't seem to be any direction. We're supposed to be getting data and so on and so forth for the commercial reactor, but they don't seem to be directing ... I don't think they're directing the effort in the right direction. There's not ... although there's a lot of interaction between research officers in different groups and in different divisions, there's not really a lot of interaction between division heads and section leaders, and what tends to happen is that you get duplication of effort and for example you get people doing work on sodium who should never be doing work on sodium. We're also in a pretty situation now when we're ... we're working - sodium - in a building that's devoted to sodium work and there are three sections in that sodium building. There's a sodium chemistry section, a sodium technology section, and a sodium safety section and reactor safety.

Dr Merchiston then goes on to describe the consequences of this
'pretty' situation which we shall look at for ourselves in a moment.
What has emerged so far is that his small team is huddled together
in frustrating and rather undirected relations with other similar
teams, interacting rather jealously within the confines of the same
building.

According to our theory, the inhabitants of small, unstructured
groups will be mutually dependent and yet they will learn to their
cost that they cannot trust one another. They will be subject to
contradictory goals and conflicting duties, such as loyalty and
competition. Whilst the outsider represents the unknown, there will
also be reason to fear the malicious intentions of one's neighbours.
Experience will thrust upon them the dichotomy between the inside
and the outside, good and evil, the proper and the perverted or
inverted. They will respond by finding representatives of the
outside in their midst to explain their misfortunes. This is why
the members of such groups accuse one aother of lacking loyalty and
mysteriously causing evil. Purges will be organised to sweep away
evil and restore the purity of the group.

Within Dr Merchiston's general outlook there is very strong
evidence of contradictory goals and tendencies pulling him hither
and thither. In fact, the remarkable thing about reading this
interview transcript is that it is riddled with hesitation, equivocation and contradiction. Here are some examples. He states that the
reactor has to be ready in seven years, then says it is three years.
He calls the body he works for a non-profit-making body and then
says it does make profits. He says he has three projects and then
hesitates over whether it is three. On a variety of occasions he
says he has considerable freedom and then chafes over his lack of
freedom. He will leave the firm, then he won't leave the firm;
he will get out of work on sodium, then says it would be foolish
even to think of not working on sodium, and so on. The point is not
whether in their precise statement these claims are logical
contradictions, or whether, by due qualification, they could be
rendered compatible - the point is that they are behavioural
evidence for unresolved tensions in Dr Merchiston's reactions and
intentions.

Dr Merchiston wants more freedom for research, although he has a
brief which is made out to be directionless. He feels somewhat
abashed about this desire and more than once calls it merely a
'selfish' desire on his part - mere self-interest. Yet at the same
time this sort of guilty desire for freedom is linked to a vision of
wonderful scientific consequences. Wasn't Einstein unconstrained?
he asks, presenting a picture of Einstein sitting in his patent
office creating relativity theory. It may be carping to question
whether a patent office is many men's idea of unbounded freedom, but
one can note the tension between this pragmatic justification of
freedom and its previous characterisation as selfish.

Significantly the main source of constraint on Dr Merchiston's
present situation is located in the person of his immediate manager.
This is where he spells out the consequences of the 'pretty' state
of confusion mentioned above.

We are in a position now where we've got a section leader from
another division who's got a lot of problems understanding what

we do, who ultimately decides whether we get apparatus built or
not ... and it's very frustrating to think that not only another
section leader, but someone, a section leader in a completely
different division, can influence the way you work. The thing
is, he's been made responsible for sodium safety and he knows
less about sodium safety than anybody else in the building
probably.

Then there follows another equivocation over the consequences of the
situation. Dr Merchiston concluded:

these are petty things that are peculiar to ... I don't know if
you want this sort of thing ... you get these little petty
frustrations, you know.

[Interviewer]: Are they things that have a petty effect or is
the effect quite serious?

Oh it's quite serious, it's not a petty effect ... it can
certainly put the work back.... We're in the process of trying
to alter it. We're working on a united front to try to get a
few things changed.

Dr Merchiston then supplies a vivid picture of the inverted and
abnormal world occupied by the evil forces he is trying to sweep
away.

You've got this situation, for example - I've just been up to
[names one of his firm's major experimental sites], and you've
got this inverted pyramid sort of structure where you've got a
couple of blokes down there working at the bench, turning out
the results and the management sort of goes like that [holds up
both arms to form a V]. And you've got about ... for example,
in the chemical services place where I was, in the offices
upstairs there were about five or six management people who were
scientists - but they were sort of management. You've got two
blokes down at the bottom who were turning out the results and
those six blokes were getting a living out of those two blokes.
Whereas it was totally different at university. You know,
you've got maybe the prof, then you've got lecturers and then
maybe a whole host of researchers; it's not the same.

So the prof, by contrast, is at the top of the pyramid world
the right way up.

We seem to have here an equivalent of the frustrating world of
witchcraft accusations. Unfortunately the interview does not reveal
how this orientation might filter its way even more deeply into
thought about the dangerous material, sodium, with which the men
worked. It is not difficult to guess how blame would be allocated
in the event of an accident. But enough has been said to suggest
the predicted bias in attitudes.

The final representative case, in the remaining quarter of the
diagram, is a scientist who is found in a high-grid and low-group
social environment.

(iv) High grid/low group

Dr Lindoch, who is female, is employed as a data analyst studying
the output of a nuclear power station, monitoring and predicting

its performance. The work is long term - her project is due to
last one to two years, at least. The aim is also long term: to
build better nuclear power stations by knowing more about the
performance of existing ones.

The reason for putting her very low on the group axis is that she
works mostly on her own and generally complains of feelings of
isolation. Thus when asked if she worked in a team, she said:

> It is as a member of a small team really, but I work mostly on
> my own. I talk to the people who're involved in the experiments
> and the analysis in slightly different ways, but I actually work
> on my own.

Describing her office accommodation, she said:

> There's myself and another research officer and ... well it varies,
> sometimes ... there aren't any others at the moment. So you
> aren't completely alone, but you tend to be just sat there at
> your desk working all the time, which is something I haven't done
> before.
>
> [Interviewer]: You're very much more isolated than you were at
> university?
>
> I should say so, yes. I mean, when you were at university you
> sit alone and do a lot of work in your own room, but you go and
> do practicals and meet people during practicals and go to lectures
> and things. It's more like having a tutorial now when all I can
> do is go and talk to my group leader at work.

An idea of how little contact this desk-bound job of data analysis
entailed is conveyed strongly in the following contrast:

> It gets a bit monotonous sometimes going into work every day,
> doing your work in an office, coming home and ... you don't get
> very much contact. This last week we've actually been doing an
> experiment as a trial run for the experiments we're going to be
> doing ultimately. It made such a change, actually doing something
> and having people around.

But if the isolation suggests low group, the degree of insulation
between her and other people defined by the pattern of authority,
status, age and academic discipline also seems considerable. In
other words, grid is high. For example, she has little or no choice
in what work she does. Thus:

> My group leader has been there four or five years now, so he
> knows most of what goes on and it's through him that I get most
> of my knowledge of what to do. He says just what to do and 'that
> wants doing; so do it', so you can go away and think how to do
> this, that and the other, and then you do it.

This lack of freedom of choice is further described later in the
interview:

> I mean, I was never really asked if I wanted to do this work.
> I was told, 'right, you're doing this', but it's difficult to
> chop and change between jobs. I mean, now I'm set up in this
> it's going to take a couple of years I think ... before the
> system ... I may have some say then in what I do next.

Even the rather one-way transactions between the boss and Dr Lindoch
are somewhat attenuated by disciplinary boundaries. Describing her
boss, she said:

> For a start, he's a mathematician. It's a bit strange at times,

and sometimes we don't communicate very well ... we tend to have different approaches to problems ... it's a bit difficult conversing sometimes.

So sitting at her desk with data coming in from a power station, a computer waiting to receive it, a limited number of programmes available to use, hardly anybody else around but a mathematician with whom to hold stilted, slightly frustrating conversations, we have a scientist trapped in high grid/low group.

Grid/group theory does not say much about the unfortunates in this position although they might be very numerous. The context might encourage a bias towards mere conformity - it is an impoverished location, devoid of significant experience out of which to build a cosmology. Indeed, conformity is Dr Lindoch's key-note. For example, consider the question of the degree of freedom a scientist ought to have to publish his or her results. This is precisely the freedom which is sometimes said to cause a value clash in university-trained scientists. But when asked whether freedom to publish was something that a scientist ought to have, Dr Lindoch replied in complete conformity with the industrial role she occupied:

No I think that's definitely wrong. I mean, if you're working for someone and they don't want this knowledge imparted to other rivals ... then that's fair enough and you should not publish. If you wanted to publish, then you should watch the sort of job you're going in for, and what sort of work it is. I think it's fair enough that they should restrict publishing.

Over and above this conformity, it appears that Dr Lindoch does in fact feel rather empty, helpless and powerless. She took the job as a compromise because she failed to get an academic job. She obviously feels controlled by the company, rather resents it, but feels powerless to change it. At the very end of the interview Dr Lindoch, who was one of the least enthusiastic and forthcoming of the sample, was asked if there was anything else to add. She came out with a clear expression of the feeling of being controlled.

I think the main thing is having done a PhD but being marked as a data analyst. They look at your PhD, see what you've done, see if it's any use to them, say 'Ah yes, you're a data analyst' - in future you can no longer be a physicist.

So she felt marked, categorised, confined and used. As far as views of nature or science were concerned, there was very little to say. Her present work was not viewed as real science, it was just sophisticated data analysis. Real science was the particle physics Dr Lindoch had done for her PhD. There the results are unpredictable, what you find depends partly on how you look at the results - what you are looking for. But these themes are not elaborated nor is the distant ideal boldly drawn.

COMMENTS ON THESE EXAMPLES

These illustrative cases all came up in the first half-dozen or so interviews that were selected for scrutiny. They convey something of the flavour of the material and the kinds of comment that were attended to and used as cues for arriving at grid/group ratings. They also illustrate the type of attitude or belief that we fastened

upon as the counterpart of the cosmologies studied by anthropologists.
Clearly, of the four illustrations the last two revealed very little
by way of views about nature. The first two cases, however, those
of Dr Ravelston and Dr Grange, represented quite definite opinions
about nature and the optimum ways of relating to it. These were
dubbed the key-in-lock and black-box views respectively. Different
features of nature were highlighted and assumed significance: the
key-in-lock view stressed its regularities; the black-box view its
irregularities. They embodied quite different attitudes towards
'mistakes' and their role in good scientific practice. These patterns
recurred in the subsequent interviews.

Grid/group theory expects these biases to arise out of the
different social uses of knowledge. They are not passive 'reflections'
of social circumstances but the result of active contrivance for
social purposes. It will be interesting to see how this expectation
is fulfilled in the case of our first two examples. Again, what
follows is intended to be illustrative of how empirical material may
be read in the light of the theory.

Recall the different working arrangements in the two cases: the
first was dominated by long-term obligations to a cost-conscious
government; the other was a busy market-place of short-term contracts.
The different sorts of pressure that can be put on people in these
two situations - and the different strategies available for people
to get cover against criticism - explain the different emphases in
the two views of the natural world. The failure to fulfil a long-
term government contract would send men scurrying for protection.
It would be necessary to insist that all reasonable precautions had
been taken; due caution had been exercised; all the routine
procedures had been scrupulously observed. Mistakes and irregularities
of procedure would matter because they might represent weak points
in the face of future criticism. Risk-taking assumes a different
character for the scientist coping with many short-term contracts.
It is beneficial to take risks; it is a waste of time to cover
oneself too fully against the possibility of failure, for some
failures are inevitable. The distribution of effort needed for
optimum rewards is different. Because it is better not to be too
cautious, the features of nature which are morally and socially
exploitable are now different.

The distribution of rewards for the expenditure of time and
effort, and the pay-off matrix for risk taking, are all socially
determined. They are properties of social structures - and they are
exactly the factors that provided the foci of the different accounts
given by Dr Ravelston and Dr Grange. Our claim, then, is that the
preferred styles of work; the sense of optimum orientations to
nature; the ideas of the morally permissible in science, do not
come from the technical constraints of the work or from an earlier
experience in university but from the social constraints current in
the organisation of work.

SYSTEMATIC EXAMINATION OF THE SAMPLE

The procedure was to read each interview and extract from it every
statement that seemed to bear upon the grid or group positions of

the scientist. (Our sense of relevance was of course guided here by our intuitive understanding of these terms.) The result was a long list of all the pieces of evidence that might be used to allocate an interview to a position. The next step was to reduce this list to a much smaller number of cues. These were meant to collect together repeated references to the same event or phenomenon and remove the effects of redundancy.

It seemed to us that ten different cues could be discerned for the group dimension. For example, (i) was there evidence of sharing social activities with workmates or colleagues? (ii) was there evidence of group action to right wrongs? The grid dimension was a little more complicated. We judged that twenty different types of cue had emerged. Of these nine seemed to be indicators of high group and eleven of low group. For example, if a scientist said that people in his firm were set in traditional ways of doing things, that it was difficult to get changes made, then this was a cue for high grid. If on the other hand he gave evidence, like Dr Grange, of scope for entrepreneurial activity and building up a clientele, then this was counted as a cue for low grid. The list of cues that emerged is given in Table 4.1.

TABLE 4.1 Grid and group cues used for rating industrial scientists

---

GROUP CUES

---

1   Group working together, i.e. on same project, in close physical proximity, etc.
2   Working with same people on long-term project.
3   Evidence of sharing social activities with workmates - immediate colleagues, more distant colleagues, management.
4   Feeling of group identity, ethos, boundary - identification with group's (working group's or firm's) interests.
5   'Everybody knows everybody else' and 'knows what everybody else is up to' - immediate colleagues, more distant colleagues, management.
6   Any evidence of intermarrying or nepotism.
7   Lots of fringe benefits in the company and incentives to company loyalty, e.g. sports facilities, help with mortgages, bonus schemes, etc.
8   Evidence of any group action to right wrongs.
9   Evidence of conflicts with other groups defined in relation to the group.
10 Evidence of rumours, bitching about other people - conflict within the group.

(table continues)

TABLE 4.1   (contd.)

GRID CUES

(Plus)

1   Very bureaucratic structure with definite responsibilities and
    tasks associated with each level, defined channels of communication
    and a hierarchy of command.
2   Little room for manoeuvre in the way the work is done.
3   Formal explicit monitoring - lots of formal report writing, memos
    and formal meetings.
4   Formal salary assessment scheme, salary related to seniority
    rather than merit, etc.
5   Knows exactly how the job will progress over the next few years -
    career progression is open and there are definite routes.
6   People are set in traditional ways of doing things - difficult to
    get them to change. Much inertia in the system. Buck-passing as
    a defence.
7   Have to keep to regular hours.
8   Symbols associated with status, e.g. different-sized carpets.
9   Facilities, e.g. canteens etc., segregated into a hierarchy.

(Minus)
1   Flexible organisation with little structure, few restrictions,
    few specified rules and interactions determined idiosyncratically
    according to immediate needs and people's personal qualities and
    talents, rather than because of hierarchy.
2   Has a free hand in how he works, organising his own time, deciding
    on his own priorities, etc.
3   Monitoring is informal or invisible, e.g. casual discussions
    with boss.
4   Salary assessment is individualistic or mysterious.
5   Career progression is not laid out or open.
6   Much scope for entrepreneurial activity - generating work for
    himself, building up clients and people dependent on his knowledge
    (patron-client type relationships), getting to know people who can
    be useful, selling himself and his own abilities all the time -
    much transacting and negotiating.
7   Work involves wide spread of approaches, picking up new techniques
    very rapidly, talking himself out of tricky situations, being
    thrown in at the deep end - sink or swim.
8   Follows his own ideas through from beginning to end.
9   Bosses come and go, higher-up back-stabbing. Low-down people
    trying to curry favour with superiors.
10 Is responsible for his own mistakes, has to carry the can, etc.
11 Strong time-pressure - tims is of the essence.

It was decided to give a score of one point for each of these cues
and then add them up in an entirely mechanical way to produce an
approximate grid/group rating for each scientist. The existence of
separate cues for high and low grid meant that some people may score
on both. Our response to this was to adopt the arithmetically brutal

convention of giving a positive value to each high-grid cue and a negative value to each low-grid cue and then add them to get the final grid rating. Obviously this whole procedure will not recommend itself to delicate methodological stomachs. The outcome of this piece of crude expediency is given in Fig. 4.1.

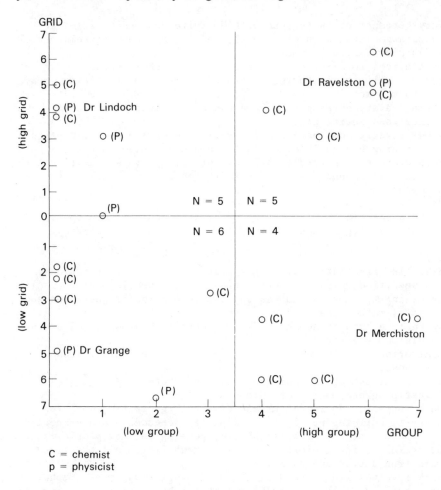

C = chemist
p = physicist

FIGURE 4.1   Twenty industrial scientists

Obviously the precise distribution of the twenty scientists across the diagram is only significant in as far as it suggests that the rating method is capable of making discriminations.

We are interested to see if the attitudes evinced by the scientists correspond in the predicted way to their grid/group ratings. Unlike the grid and group assignments, our procedure for recognising and categorising their cosmologies was not broken down into cues - though our impression was that this could have been done without too much difficulty. For simplicity we judged the cosmologies informally by matching them with the examples given in the illustrative cases. The

number of instances in which the cosmology corresponded to the grid/
group position in the manner described in the illustrations amounted
to fifteen out of the twenty. Let us take the diagram quadrant by
quadrant to see how this total is made up. Of the five scientists
in the high-grid/high-group quadrant we judge all of them to be
recognisable as 'ritualists' with key-in-lock views of science.
Moving down to the low-grid/high-group quadrant we found three out
of the four felt persecuted by their managers and betrayed traces of
what might be called a witchcraft cosmology. The six scientists in
the competitive low-grid/low-group corner of the diagram yielded
three go-getting Big Men characteristically pressed for time and
subscribing to a black-box view of science and nature. Finally four
out of the five high-grid/low-group scientists were typically
passive and conformist. If this accounts for the fifteen out of the
twenty who appear to conform to the prediction, what of the remaining
five? Of these, one seemed too mixed to classify clearly, and four
did not give enough information on questions of attitude to be grouped
with any of the types.

METHODOLOGICAL PROBLEMS

A number of insurmountable problems beset the procedure adopted in
this experiment and prevent its conclusions being anything other than
suggestive. We shall briefly list the main difficulties - no doubt
there are others. These mainly derive from the fact that other
theories can be produced to account for the findings and that the
procedures used are informal and subjective.
1 The reader has no means of knowing the extent to which the
authors have interpreted or selected the data. This problem is
particularly acute in the assessment of the cosmologies, though it
is a consideration that applies to the interpretive link between the
grid and group cues and the sentences on the interview transcript.
Only the most rigorous coding procedures checked for consistency of
outcome across different coders could overcome this difficulty, by
which time the exercise would have ceased to be a pilot experiment.
2 Because the interview data represents the scientist's own
perception of his social situation (rather than one independently
arrived at by the investigator) any connection between it and
attitude or 'cosmology' could be an artefact. It could derive from
the scientist's personality. According to this psychological
coloration theory aggressive and ambitious personality 'types'
might always recount their interactions - whatever they are
objectively - in ways that make them appear low grid/low group,
and similarly with their preferred modes of scientific operation.
Add to this type the authoritarian personality, say, and the paranoic
and the passive types and the results follow.
3 Then there is what may be called the 'psychological selection
theory'. It is possible that because of self-selection, or because
of screening by the firms themselves, only certain sorts of
personalities come to occupy the various quadrants of the grid/group
figure. In as far as this happened it becomes possible that these
personality types simply imported beliefs which were not generated
or sustained by the various patterns of interactions. If certain

personality types were prone to adopt certain attitudes to either nature or science then this would create a spurious correlation - spurious, that is, from the point of view of the theory we are experimenting with. But it is important to stress that by themselves neither self-selection nor institutional screening are incompatible with the theory. What is incompatible is the psychologistic claim that certain beliefs may be present irrespective of their role in patterns of interaction - that they are located in the grid/group figure like the paper crowns on Wittgenstein's chessmen, i.e. as adornments that have no genuine role in the game.

The present data contains no means of answering these objections or ruling out these alternatives. The only response that would meet them would be to conduct another study using objective measures of patterns of interaction and using two stages. The scientists would have to be followed into different grid and group positions (derived, say, from their changing jobs) to see its effect on their 'cosmology'. The outcome of the pilot experiment is to suggest that further inquiry along these lines would be a worthwhile exercise.

CONCLUSION

When we began this work it was not even clear to us that any sense at all could be made of data about industrial scientists by using the grid/group approach. But once the theory was applied to empirical material it became apparent that in a largely unselfconscious way, people do describe their social experience in a fashion that can be related to the grid and group axes. Things that the scientists said which were just so much background material, given the aims of the original research, sprang into prominence. The figure/ground characteristics of the data changed dramatically. Even if this pilot experiment has in no way constituted a test of the theory against alternatives, still a severe test of another sort has been imposed on it. This is the discipline of being applied to detailed factual findings. Although the task of operationalising the central concepts of grid and group has only just begun, it proved impossible to resist the conclusion that here was a tool of analysis that genuinely allows progress to be made.

NOTES

1 This paper was first read in the Anthropology Department, University College, London, 23 November 1976.
2 See Celia Merrick (now Celia Bloor), 'Young Scientists and their Work', PhD thesis, 1975, University of Kent at Canterbury.

BIBLIOGRAPHY

DOUGLAS, MARY (1978), 'Cultural Bias', London, Royal Anthropological Society, occasional paper no.34.

Chapter 5

A NOTE ON STYLES IN ACCOUNTING
George Gaskell and James Hampton

Financial accounting is a necessary and ubiquitous aspect of any
organisation. It involves the recording of financial transactions
that have already occurred but also entails the significant functions
of forecasting and budgeting, functions which impinge on almost
every aspect of the enterprise. That accounting is not neutral with
respect to people is not a novel concept. Hopwood (1974) is one of
a number who have written on the impact of accounting on human
behaviour.

Accountants, as Hopwood says, have never operated in a behavioural
vacuum. They make working assumptions about the way people are
motivated, how reports are used and interpreted, and how particular
systems fit into the realities of power and influence within an
enterprise. In Hopwood's view the effectiveness of any accounting
procedure, be it in the context of planning, co-ordinating or
controlling various complex and interrelated activities, ultimately
depends upon how it influences the behaviour of the people in the
enterprise. The choice and operation of a particular accounting
system is therefore an important aspect of the management style in
that any system is based upon, and is justified by, a set of
generalised beliefs and values about the right and wrong ways of
organising people's activities.

The problem then is to relate the structure or social context of
an organisation to the operation of its accounting system. Grid/
group theory predicts that the generalised ideals about right and
wrong ways of accounting will be found in particular organisational
contexts. Thus, if organisations can be categorised in terms of
grid and group, then the accounting system, the operationalising of
the management's cosmology, should correspond to the grid/group
categorisation of the particular organisation.

In 'Managers and Magic', Cleverly (1973) describes accountants
as the priesthood of the organisation. As a priesthood they are
organised in a hierarchy, possess arcane knowledge, operate a
jealously guarded membership into which entry is accompanied by
rituals of initiation. They are disciplined and act as guardians
enforcing strict codes of behaviour and morality, both within and
outside the profession. Their most important role is that of
'mediation' which only they can perform in the organisation because

they alone 'know they are right'. The worshipping managers rely
on the accountant priests for advice, protection and prediction to
help them through the insecure and chaotic world of business.

Accounting was selected as the focus of the present inquiry
because its procedures imply decisions based on cosmological elements,
generalised beliefs and values. As already noted, the selection of a
method of accounting within an organisation implies certain generalised
ideals about the control and influence of people and the right way to
achieve objectives within a particular context. The grid/group theory
predicts that personal theories about ideal accounting procedures
arise out of the context of organisations. These personal theories
will be imposed upon a particular organisation and the ultimate
generalised ideals held by an individual will be generated within
that social structure. Couched in more concrete terms, certain
relevant differences should be observed in the theory of accounting,
in its procedures and in the uses made of accounting in organisations
with different grid and group characteristics. In order to achieve
this we need the conceptual analysis and associated methodological
tools to differentiate between first-order social contexts (attitu-
dinal indices comprising the organisational dimension) and second-
order moral or cosmological attitudes.

Thus we assess the social context dimensions using objective
methods of inquiry. First-order attitudes and practices can then
be assessed by self-report of the person in that social context.
Finally, the second-order moral value system can be elicited by
questioning the person about his views of the justifying principles
by which he feels one should ideally operate. The test of our
predictions then lies in the match or lack of match between these
different levels of analysis for a particular organisation.

SOCIAL CONTEXT

The assessment of social context must be based on objective aspects
of the particular organisation in order to avoid the informant's
values colouring his account of his perceived situation. We can
differentiate two levels of objective inquiry which would allow for
an assessment of the grid and group position of an organisation.
1 The materials constituting the framework and traffic elements
   of the organisation.
2 The regulative legal and lesser principles governing and
   controlling the employees.
Any organisation leaves some material traces of its processes. The
more obvious are the arrangements of the building, the provision of
facilities for different employees, including parking spaces, offices,
secretaries, sanitation, carpets and canteen facilities. Such things
as writing paper, transport services, the type of food served are
material traffic elements.

The regulative aspects are apparent in the macro-legal documents
setting out the duties and liabilities of persons within the
organisation, towards one another and to the outside world; contracts,
the charter of incorporation, audits and minor regulations concerning
security, preventing fraud, time-tabling, and union and staff association rights. Aspects of the wages and incomes policy of the
organisation would also be important.

   Given a description of those objective aspects of the organisation
which are relevant to the working environment of the accountants it
would be possible to classify their social context. All material and
regulative aspects systematically reflecting differences in status
hierarchy in terms of the provision and quality of facilities, the
extent and definition of responsibility and accountability would
indicate grid strength. Group strength would be reflected in the
interdependence of units within the organisation, the frequency of
departmental and interdepartmental communication and meetings, shared
morning coffee, staff lunches, the importance of staff associations
and coffee clubs.

FIRST-ORDER COSMOLOGY: THE ORGANISATIONAL DIMENSION

Ten aspects of accounting procedures have been selected to indicate
how the grid/group theory might be applied in the investigation of
first-order cosmology (see Table 5.1). The grid and group dimensions
are distinguished and the use of each aspect of accounting seen in

TABLE 5.1 Characteristics of accounting procedures associated with
the grid and group dimensions

Grid dimension	High strength	Low strength
1 Origin of capital expenditure proposals.	Only by few people at the top.	By people at many levels.
2 Centrality of control of resources.	Central control, compulsory use, no accountability.	Decentralised, optional use, accountable for efficient usage.
3 Assessment of budget performance.	Budget-constrained.	Profit-conscious.
4 Treatment of uncertainty in accounts.	Concealed.	Revealed.
5 Agreement on success criteria.	Poor agreement.	Good agreement.

Group dimension	High strength	Low strength
1 Shuttling of blame.	Doesn't occur.	Common.
2 Disbelief in accounts.	Doesn't occur.	Common.
3 Use of budget information.	Form of group ritual.	Scoring system of assessment.
4 Status of accountants in firm.	Low level.	Higher levels.
5 Penalties for exceeding budget.	None.	Serious.

the context of high and low strength on the two dimensions. In the
following paragraphs we outline these accounting procedures and their
implications for grid and group.

THE GRID DIMENSION

1 Origins of capital expenditure proposals

Accountants are normally asked to predict the flow of such proposals
and to assess them. One would expect that in a low-grid context
such proposals could be produced at all levels of the organisation,
whereas in a high-grid context only the highest authorities would
have the freedom to produce them. The explicit systems of control
(low autonomy) and strongly defined limits to job definitions
(insulations) of high grid greatly reduce the scope for original
ideas to emerge from the lower levels of the hierarchy.

2 Centrality of control of resources

There are three areas in which a contrast could be made between
central control of resources and divisional autonomy.
  (a) Use of capital
       In high grid, all capital resources would be allocated by
       a central authority which also provides accounting
       information about returns on capital etc. By contrast in
       low grid, individual managers would be responsible for the
       return on capital employed within their own section, and
       would thus have more control and autonomy over the use of
       capital.
  (b) Research and development
       In a similar way, the provision of research and development
       facilities within an organisation could either be done
       through a central laboratory (high grid) or through each
       division having its own resources for which it is indepen-
       dently accountable (low grid).
  (c) Consultancy and data processing services
       Again, these services could be provided free of charge,
       but with a mandatory use, by a central authority, or
       alternatively, the individual divisions could choose to use
       them as need arose, and be accountable for the use made of
       them.
          The issue of central control is also associated with grid
       for the following reason. When each department is individu-
       ally accountable for the use it makes of capital, research
       and development, and other services, there is then an open
       competition possible between different departments, and
       every activity undertaken becomes a factor in the assessment
       of cost effectiveness. Thus competitiveness as well as
       autonomy contributes to the low-grid value of a decentralised
       organisation.

3   Assessment of budget performance

When managers come to be assessed for their performance with respect
to meeting their budgets, Hopwood (1973) has distinguished two main
ways in which the assessment can be made. The first is a budget-
constrained method, where the constraints on spending are fixed in
advance and assessment is purely concerned with whether these
constraints have been broken. The alternative method is a profit-
conscious assessment, in which extra profits generated are offset
against overspending. The second method allows managers more scope
for initiative in the same kind of way as described in 2 above. The
profit-conscious method is, therefore, an indicator of a low-grid
context, as compared with the high-grid budget-constrained method.
Interestingly, another aspect of grid - the increased uncertainty
experienced in low-grid contexts - is also apparent here. The
profit-conscious method of assessment might be found to be necessary
when there is turbulence and uncertainty in either production or
marketing of a product. Where such uncertainty exists, there is a
far greater need for risk-taking and opportunist flexibility in
spending, and hence in those circumstances a profit-conscious method
of assessment probably should be preferred to the inflexible budget-
constrained method, which allows little autonomy to individual
managers.

4   Treatment of uncertainty in accounts

As mentioned above, one aspect of low grid is the way in which
uncertainty is dealt with. One can, therefore, expect that budgeting
information in a low-grid context will display this uncertainty, and
try to take some account of the probabilities involved in different
situations. For example, when submitting a proposal, a manager
would be required to give estimates of the best, worst and most
likely possible outcomes of the scheme. In high grid, however,
uncertainty tends not to be revealed in the budgeting information.
The methods are fixed rather than flexible, and no attempt is made to
estimate the range of accuracy of forecasts.

5   Agreement on success criteria

Dew and Gee (1973) have worked on the amount of agreement or disagreement that exists between superordinate and subordinate managers
on the most important criteria by which the successful performance
of the subordinate's job should be judged. They found a surprisingly
large discrepancy existed in many cases between the criteria selected
by the superordinate and those selected by the subordinate. One can
expect that grid will be having an effect in this area as well. In
high grid, where different levels are strongly insulated, with
differential status and relatively formal channels of communication
between them, one would expect a far greater disagreement concerning
success criteria (and other aspects of the job description) between
different levels, than would be found for a low-grid firm. At low
grid, there are few barriers between different levels, and hierarchical

organisation is tempered by many cross-cutting areas of interaction. One would, therefore, expect people to have a much better idea of each other's goals, and to share a similar order of priorities.

THE GROUP DIMENSION

1 Shuttling of blame

In a low-group firm, one might expect that each section would feel no compunction about blaming its failures of budget performance on a lack of proper support from other sections. Where group is high, however, this shuttling of blame should be absent. In particular, when grid is also high, there should be well-defined responsibilities so that blame-passing is simply not possible. With low grid and high group, the absence of blame-passing would be due to group pressures of loyalty; while it could not take place overtly, however, some underground system of covert suspicion may well be found, similar to the witchcraft-ridden societies described by Douglas (1970) as belonging to this corner of the diagram.

2 Disbelief in accounts

It is sometimes found that different sections of a firm keep their own records of accounting information, and express doubt and criticism about the accuracy of information put out by other sections. This form of scepticism should occur particularly in firms with a low-group structure between departments, since two independent information systems could not co-exist within a tightly-knit group. It should be noted that group strength within each department, however, may be quite high, encouraging an 'us/them' attitude to other departments. This proviso applies equally to the shuttling of blame described above.

3 Use of budget information

In a low-group firm, budget information is taken seriously. People hold their jobs by right of their efficiency and a contribution which is strictly accountable. The budget is a competitive scoring system for assessing individuals. With a high-group firm, however, a person has his job by virtue of belonging to the group. Failure is, therefore, an embarrassment for all, and would be treated as an illness. In these high-group firms, therefore, the budget becomes a form of ritual, in which all the effort and discussion goes into the preparation, and very little attention is paid to assessing performance against forecasts. As a prediction, very little use would be made of budget information in high-group firms.

4 Status of accountants in firm

Given that high-group firms do not find it easy to justify assessing

people by their performance, one can expect that the role of the
accountant in such firms will be kept to a low level in the power
structure. An approach that is continually concerned with competitive
assessment of individuals is not tolerated in high-group firms, where
the inefficiency of particular individuals is an embarrassment that
must not be brought out into the open. The low-group firm, however,
could well have accountants in senior positions.

5 Penalties for exceeding budgets

It follows from the two previous points that a very different
attitude to penalties for exceeding budgets would be found in high-
and low-group firms. In low group, dismissal, transfer or a reduction
in autonomy may well follow a serious failure in budget performance.
Overspending is a crime which carries penalties. For high-group
firms, however, little attention is paid to budget, and there are no
penalties imposed for failure to keep to a budget. Overspending is
a form of illness which can be cured by increased group support,
leading to an increased commitment to the group by the individual.

SECOND-ORDER COSMOLOGICAL ATTITUDES

Selected from the list of more general structural hypotheses there
appear to be at least two particular fields in which the judgment
of right behaviour can count as cosmological in the sense of
reflecting opinions concerning the basic principles of social or
professional life. These fields are attitudes to truth and
credibility on the one hand and attitudes to rewards and punishments
on the other. Here some tentative but specific predictions with
respect to the relations of social context to second-order cosmology
are proposed.

Truth and credibility

(a) If the management and accountants know that the budget
     figures are subject to a great deal of uncertainty, should
     this be acknowledged? Would it be right in an ideal firm
     for everyone to be told the full extent of the uncertainty?
     Or would it be best for this to be known only to the
     specialised and responsible offocials?
Prediction: Individuals in companies with high grid strength
would tend to believe in concealing uncertainty.
(b) It may be difficult to arrive at an accurate allocation of
     responsibility for costs. Is it inevitable that any given
     assessment of cost between units be disputed? Does it
     matter if blame tends to be shifted from one unit to another?
Prediction: Individuals in companies with high group strength
would disapprove of blame-shuttling.
(c) When dealing with information from the accountant, do the
     units in the organisation accept it as a true statement, or
     is there a tendency to find such information incomprehensible
     or inaccurate?

Prediction: Individuals in companies with high group strength would tend to accept the validity of accounting information, as a matter of principle.

Penalties

The use of penalties reflects a very basic part of the cosmology of an organisation. In line with the first-order behavioural predictions, the following cosmological values may be predicted.

(a)   Penalties may be simple monetary ones, or involve a complex system of promotion deferment, allocation of status rewards etc.

Prediction: High-grid companies use status and long-term penalties. Low-grid ones use financial ones. Beliefs in the efficacy of different penalties will be found justifying these systems.

(b)   Penalties may be imposed for failure to comply with rules (such as budgetary limits) or for poor overall performance (such as profit figures).

Prediction: High-grid companies penalise failure to conform to rules, low-grid ones penalise failure to produce profits. Beliefs concerning managerial success will be in line with this system.

(c)   The use of penalties at all is a possible source of weakening group commitment.

Prediction: High-group companies will be less likely to have any explicit penalty system, and will express the belief that such systems do not work.

This conceptual analysis is presented as a challenge both to organisational and grid/group theory. The challenge to organisational theory is that grid and group offers a convenient taxonomic system and provides in addition a systematic approach relating the important aspects of organisations - structure, climate and performance. In its conception of the links between the individual and the social context grid/group theory integrates the psychological and sociological levels of analysis and incorporates the cultural dimension.

The challenge to grid/group theory is that an empirical evaluation will require detailed predictions to be made for a specific situation including the operationalising of the concepts of social context and cosmology in a new setting. In this paper the basics are laid with respect to accounting, but one aspect of an organisation. Seen in the context of accounting the complexities introduced by organisational size, technology and market stability must be worked through.

This is an interdisciplinary undertaking and one involving many problematic theoretical and empirical issues. However, the current state of organisation and grid/group theory suggests that a marriage might be convenient, the former characterised by a body of empirical data in need of theory and the latter a theory in search of empirical validation.

ACKNOWLEDGMENT

We are greatly indebted to Dr K. Gee of Lancaster University for
assistance in the analysis of the technical aspects of accounting in
relation to grid and group.

BIBLIOGRAPHY

CLEVERLY, G. (1973), 'Managers and Magic', Harmondsworth, Penguin.
DEW, R. and K.P. GEE (1973), 'Management Control and Information',
London, Macmillan.
DOUGLAS, M. (1973), 'Natural Symbols - Explorations in Cosmology',
Harmondsworth, Penguin.
HOPWOOD, A. (1974), 'Accounting and Human Behaviour', London,
Accountancy Age Books.

Part Two

COMPARATIVE STUDIES IN HISTORY AND
THE HISTORY OF IDEAS

INTRODUCTION
Mary Douglas

George Kelly's essay deals critically with methodological problems.
He uses grid/group analysis to interpret the role of the philosophers Voltaire, Montesquieu and Diderot in eighteenth-century
France. He specially considers the traps and ambiguities that lie
in the approach as formulated now for the historian who tries to
use it. His essay might well belong in the first section on method.
We have placed him at the head of the section on comparative studies
in history since he uses his deep familiarity with enlightenment
thought and with the biographies of the thinkers to test just how
far this historical material supports the claims made for grid/group
analysis. He ends with questions that seem to be answerable with
the same caveats which have been applied to the same problems raised
by all the writers on method. What counts as a group, for example?
It is difficult to say how much more of a distinctive group the
philosophers were than the aristocrats or other categories.
Disarmingly, George Kelly says that perhaps eighty years is too big
a spread of time and that the allegiances would crystallize more
clearly in a micro-study. But I do not think so. He is working
over a time span similar to that of Martin Rudwick's essay. The
latter is able to discern geological styles through the nineteenth
century. The difference is that George Kelly in tracing the growth
and maturity of a particular movement is inevitably aware of rough
edges and curious adhesions to his definition of the subject.
Martin Rudwick has a field already defined by the subject of geology
and within it he identifies particular cognitive styles.
   So George Kelly's problem is not to be solved by scale reductions.
He also asks interesting questions about stability and instability
in any given historical arrangement of ideas and about the relations
between one group and the rest of society. He takes away the
reproach of a static delineation of grid/group mapping by suggesting
how the cosmological components interlock uncomfortably within the
mutual horizons of a group and cause disquiet, 'harbinger of
intellectual revision and social movement'. Thus he gives full
credit to the internal coherence of ideas for power to sustain a
society and to incoherence for power to provoke challenge and
collapse. Two of the most interesting points he raises, in tracing
the shift of ideas from those appropriate to an aristocratic and

monarchical society in C of the diagram to the individualism of A,
concern attitudes to nature and to history. In 'Cultural Bias' I
had surmised that the traditionalist stratified society would tend
to bring nature into its internal arguments always on the side of
society as such, so that nature and society would tend to be treated
as one. By contrast, I expected a sense of alienation between
nature and society in the atomized individualistic culture. Again,
in the case of historical judgment, I had predicted that the praise
of past heroes and their exemplary lives would be put to full use in
sustaining the former type of society while critical historiography
would replace it in the latter - on both scores George Kelly's essay
shows me how wrong I could be. It suggests plenty of scope for
reconsideration and development.

Katrina McLeod is engaged in interpreting new archeological
writings of the long period of the Warring States in classical China
between the fifth century BC and the second century AD. She suggests
that the jurists' more baffling statements yield sense if seen as a
long-drawn-out epistemological argument between top right and bottom
left parts of our diagram. Between the eighth and the fifth century
BC, when the story starts, the control of kings had waned until the
fully ritualized kingship replaced active political exercise of
power. Among the ritualists, words became attached indissolubly
to things, not only words but also rites and the people performing
them. In their central palaces and temples the knowledge system
would have had to be completely static and sacred. But ritualism
was politically weak. By the beginning of the fifth century BC
fragmented power allowed local rulers to compete with each other.
As unconstrained, freely negotiating individuals they started by
seeking the supporting strength of religious sanctions, but ended
by employing professional administrators.

[The high grid proprieties of hierarchy] sanctified by ritual
division of labour were not, after all, conducive to the
formulation of the sort of propositions, whether of a moral or
mechanical nature, which were likely to bring about the development and deployment of new weapons (such as the trebuchet and
the cross-bow) capable of defeating a neighbouring city state.

Expert in the new technologies of weaponry, strategy,
metallurgy and fortifications as well as in the techniques of
creating law and centralized administration, the peripatetic
generals and managers of the states negotiated ... on their own
terms with the rulers [and] were usually able to withdraw their
services.

This (McLeod, this volume, p.141) is the model description of the
entrepreneurial low-grid situation. These administrative mercenaries
exemplify in their many writings exactly the philosophies of public
expediency and private self-cultivation to be expected in low-grid
individualism. During the disturbed period those who deplored
political fragmentation and disorder perceived it to be linked with
epistemological incoherence. If only labels could be correctly
matched to things, the proper demarcations would be drawn and moral
rectitude restored.

Katrina McLeod boldly uses grid/group analysis to interpret what
Arthur Waley called the 'language crisis' of this period. She sees
the discussion of morals and politics transferred to the epistemo-

logical problem of the relations between labels and things labelled. If this archeologist can demonstrate that the philosophical writings of a long period of ancient Chinese civilization yields richly to grid/group analysis, one is tempted to try the same work upon the epistemological views of one's philosopher friends. On the other hand the professional administrators, low-grid individualist entrepreneurial career men, seem to have been introspective, pessimistic, not seeing any direct connection between the way things fall apart and their own role in the dissolution. They reflect on the relation between man and society but have no clear ideas of what it could or ought to be. Their self-analysis sounds so like our own contemporary questionings it seems appropriate to follow this essay with Don Handelman's on the restricted scope for self-knowledge which different quadrants of our diagram afford the possibilities of self-reflexion through play and public ceremony through the works of Richard Sennett (1974) and Victor Turner (1974: chapter 6).

Don Handelman here considers the grid/group setting of the social environment and argues that different kinds of public events afford different degrees of reflexive scope. The individual can reflect upon the self in relation with other individuals, or upon the boundary of the group, or upon all the compartments of the whole society. He argues persuasively that only certain kinds of social arrangements can produce certain kinds of play performances, so that the scope for reflexivity is affected by the grid/group structure. This is a very thought-provoking assessment of the structuring of individual consciousness which lies within the power of culture. Many would argue that the clear, fair view of society is only to be had by standing aside from it but Handelman gives reasons for doubting the possibilities of self-knowledge for those who choose to inhabit the margins of society.

In the history of ideas the usefulness of the grid/group method seems to be most interestingly developed. In the next chapter, David Bloor takes the attitude to anomalies and to boundaries as diagnostic. A theory that encounters an anomaly can be protected either by refusing to take account of the exception to its rules or by adjusting the definition by making more and more subdivisions, either approach refusing to allow the main boundaries of the theory to be altered. Either of these approaches shows a bias in favour of the literal strength of the original theory. Words and ideas are being used as labels for things as if by labelling the things correctly the status of the discipline would be preserved and as if this was the one overriding concern. It is as if the labels protect the ancient citadels of learning from dissolution. But the freelance theory-brokers who constitute the intellectual vanguard are intrigued by anomaly, their careers thrive on discovering reasons why the labels on things ought to be changed: for them, classificatory schemes are mere expedients. Concept-stretching and reclassification are the daily occupations of this kind of theorist. Words are not expected to reflect any ultimately real demarcations between things - there are not boundaries which words must respect.

David Bloor's review of Lakatos's posthumous 'Proofs and Refutations' starts by delineating a taxonomy of mathematicians' attitudes to a theoretical puzzle. It ends by connecting types of theoretical responses to the social experiences of the community of mathematicians,

specially to changes in German universities. In the mid nineteenth
century the controllers of these institutions made an explicit
decision about their organization. It resulted in mathematicians
being taken out of a context of static, local, group loyalties to an
international competitive environment. A new dialectical discourse
inevitably developed. This essay is admittedly tentative, but it
is extremely suggestive for directions in which this kind of analysis
can be tried. Along the stable diagonal we start to expect a deep
epistemological shift. Various forms of nominalism are passionately
adhered to in the top right, where traditionalists wield their arch-
priestly authority and distribute the gradings.   They would much
prefer never to have to confront the very unscholastic thinking
practised in the bottom left. Pragmatic stretching of words to mean
whatever the new conceptual challenge requires is another epistemological style. Whereas on the top right of the diagram anomaly is
either unperceived or roundly rejected, on the bottom left there is
a sturdy eclecticism and tolerance.

   The essay by Martin Rudwick was directly inspired by David Bloor's
on polyhedra. We should be prepared by now to find among low-grid
geologists equivalents of the anomaly embracing mathematicians on
the frontiers of theory, and equivalents of the professional Chinese
administrators who innovated so successfully. We also expect
geological ritualists parallel to the early hierarchical Chinese
kingdoms and the anomaly rejecting mathematicians in small isolated
German universities. Following David Bloor, Martin Rudwick pays
attention to the styles of problem-solving and particularly a way
of dealing with anomaly as indicators of different ultimate
principles sustaining the respective arguments for different grid/
group conditions. He identifies four. The abstract synthesizing
analytic style matches Lakatos's modern mathematician, dialectical
in argument, open to all disciplines, welcoming to apparent anomalies,
powerful in analogical imagination, a style which also matches the
ancient Chinese professional administrators who competitively
promoted such brilliant technological development. Second is the
pragmatic, classificatory style, conscious of one defined method
and of bounded problems, using a more concrete language and
expecting things to correspond to correct labels: 'Facts are plain
and unambiguous for any right-minded and unprejudiced observer.'
This style has order for its primary goal. The third style he calls
agnostic, sceptical of the possibility of synthesis, open but
unsystematic. The last is a 'binary style' which divides geologically
significant events into a simple before-and-after a great dividing
moment, a division between distant and close. Like Bloor's
mathematics departments, the geologists are sorted out according to
the closed or open professional boundaries they maintain around
their discipline. These boundaries are the social dimensions to
which correspond the coherence of the classifications they develop
in their subject matter, their sensitivity for theoretical boundaries,
their response to theoretical anomalies. Martin Rudwick has sifted
biographies for signs of group loyalties and respect for rank, seeking
to trace the distinctive theoretical styles accurately to positions
on the grid/group diagram in respect of the professional situations
of their exponents. The famous innovators who are exponents of his
abstract style have essentially been a small minority of geologists

in any generation - few, but very significant in their contribution
to the subject, and self-evidently modern. The concrete style is
represented by the majority of the geologists, many very distinguished,
'but the real locus ... lies in the ordinary books, memoirs and
articles on geology by lesser known figures ...'. These are the two
styles of the stable diagonal. An agnostic style in geology is
practised by 'the many local amateur collectors of rocks and fossils
in the nineteenth century, the subordinate "officers" of geological
surveys, and in the present century, the subordinate members of
geological research and exploration teams of mining and oil companies'.
Lastly, he identifies fundamentalist, binary style, the literalists,
scriptural geologists of the early nineteenth century who were creating
a sectarian form of geology to support a religiously sectarian
viewpoint.

BIBLIOGRAPHY

DOUGLAS, MARY (1978) 'Cultural Bias', London, Royal Anthropological
Society, occasional paper no.35.
SENNETT, RICHARD (1974), 'The Fall of Public Man', Cambridge
University Press.
TURNER, V.W. (1974), 'Dramas, Fields and Metaphors', New York,
Cornell University Press.

Chapter 6

'LES GENS DE LETTRES':
AN INTERPRETATION
George A. Kelly

Grid/group theory provides certain opportunities and places certain traps for the historian. Some of these explicitly affect what writing history means, what the boundaries of the discipline are, how the undertaking should be performed, and how various other disciplinary tools of conceptualization should be brought to the aid of the historian. I can only touch on such broad matters in passing.

In a more restricted focus, it is plausible that grid/group theory can be used by certain kinds of historians or by historians who dwell on particular topical or chronological materials. Most of this essay will be concerned with the possibilities of the theory at this level, from the point of view of a student of eighteenth-century France (Old Regime, Enlightenment, and Revolution). My approach is a mixture of social and intellectual history, though with greater emphasis on the latter.

After some opening remarks about the nature of the theory and its wider resonances I shall use it to interpret the role of the eighteenth-century 'gens de lettres'. This complex issue surely cannot be settled in a brief essay that will perforce neglect disputes and omit matters of great importance. But I hope to be able to acquaint the reader with the type of interpretive fit I see between the theory and the problem, while at the same time exposing the ambiguities of that fit.

I regard grid/group both as a theory (in its internal explanatory coherence and particularly in its aspiration to polycultural applications) and as a grand hypothesis whose cosmology and resulting typology appear to have been in part inductively obtained from anthropological observation and interpretation, in part concluded deductively or intuitively by procedures of rule-derivation. Most general social theories seem to be of this amphibian kind (unless they are expressly metaphysical): what seems crucial, however, is that the theorist should have a formal system in which to fit the cases, which is distinguishable from the status of the cases themselves, i.e. synthetic. Thus grid/group is to be tested with an eye to the satisfactory ordering of situations and in no sense to be imposed on the situations by fiat; it is also to be tested against the explanatory power of theories of a comparable scope, e.g. Comte, Marx, Parsons, Foucault, etc.

Pictorially speaking, Douglas's theory can be represented as a four-box matrix. Within these ideal-typical territories the social context of groups is expressed in 'cosmologies' (culture-constructs that order the justification and conduct of existence). In 'Cultural Bias' Douglas suggests the shape of A, B, C, and D cosmologies in terms of views on nature, time, human nature, and social behaviour, further divisible into sub-categories. Where the cosmological fits are out of sorts with expectations of the ideal-typical model of any of the quadrants (assuming that the observer's cosmological data is correct), a number of interpretive possibilities arise: (1) the observer might conclude that his own criteria for establishing the composition of a 'group' had been faulty; (2) the observer might conclude that the world-picture of a group was suffering incoherence and draw the appropriate implications; (3) the observer might find valid reasons for reconciling the countervailing cosmological elements in order to situate the group studied in the most appropriate area of the quadrant or perhaps across quadrant boundaries; or (4) the observer might regard cosmological discord in a group as a causal element in a theory of social change and thereby extend the ostensibly taxonomic properties of grid/group theory to encompass social dynamics as well as a mere sighting of longitude and latitude. Finally, but only after rigorous experiment with specific groups and cultures, (5) the observer might decide that the theory was inadequate, either in its designation of ideal-types (it might be insufficiently exclusive), or in the rule-derivations for the quadrants, or in the cosmological descriptions associated with them. Indeed, he might conclude that there was a problem of circularity between the derivation of rules and the descriptive features of the social mentalities.

For our purposes we can exclude (5), because a theory deserves its day in court before conceivable abstract objections to its potency are granted any decisiveness. The other possibilities, however, are all of interest to the historian trying to work with grid/group.

The first of these (1) involves the definition of a 'group' (presumably a contiguous, researchable social unit) itself. In Douglas's theory not just anything can be a group, although the innate properties of A, B, C, and D will, according to the case, make a group boundary more or less spacious, e.g. 'C ... can be bigger than groups at D since it can devolve, federate, become tributary to another.... [It] can expect to persist longer without fission' ('Cultural Bias': 20). Yet a group cannot be an entire complex society: the theory seems expressly posited to explore the features of the internal relations of diffuse societies, rather than to define their conglomerate thrust.(1) Much less can a group be a 'civilization'. In the manner stated by Douglas it is illicit (or banal) to extend the analytic properties of grid/group theory to entities such as the British Navy or the Roman Catholic Church. This somewhat dampens the historian's propensity (especially true in the history of ideas) to fix his focus on populations widely extended in time and space. It also calls for the rigorous monographic examination of rather small and well-defined segments of society. It is not of course precluded that analytically separable groups might exist side by side and even competitively

within a single quadrant. Nor is there any doubt that a plethora of
qualifying groups (to the extent that historical research can inform
us) existed in eighteenth-century France, e.g. the Parlement of
Rennes, the Maréchalat of France, the General Assembly of the Clergy,
the Princes of the Blood, the Académie des Sciences, the Section of
Gravilliers, etc. I further believe that, with proper precautions,
certain larger categories can be additively constructed, e.g.
Jansenism, Freemasonry, the Jacobin clubs, etc. But the problem of
scope and parameters is something that the prudent historian must
bear in mind. That problem is not made easier by Douglas's alternating
use of 'group' to signify a dimension on her map as well as a
collection of persons to be placed on the map by two-dimensional
logic.

Possibilities (2), (3), and (4) are all loosely connected. With
respect to the most fruitful uses of grid/group theory it is surely
important to make precise placements within each quadrant according
to the specificity of valid cosmological criteria. Certain features
of corporative structure may drag a group upward and rightward from
the individualistic imbeddedness of A; a whiff of anomie may push
a group toward B; an egalitarian posture that continues to
emphasize solidary interaction may dislocate a group from C into
high D, and so forth. In such regards, the double axes of grid/group
theory overcome the simplistic linear models of most social theory
(e.g. status and contract, Gemeinschaft and Gesellschaft, traditional
and rational/legal, etc.). The complexity that the added dimension
gives to the social map makes eighteenth-century France decipherable
to me in a way that it could not be according to any bipolar scheme.

At the same time, it is permissible and indeed necessary for the
historian to discover stability or instability in any empirical
cosmological arrangement. It may be that the variables which appear
to situate a group, say, in the lower left portion of C-quadrant
tend to stabilize that group, either because of its specific internal
functions or because of its relations to other groups in the context
of the total society. But it is equally possible that a given
cosmological conjuncture will betoken instability, even impending
chaos. It may be that the cosmological components cannot easily
dwell with one another within the mental horizons of members of the
group, and that this disquiet is a harbinger of intellectual revision
and social movement. Indeed, grid/group theory considerably
complicates and enriches our notion of social change because we can
draw from its resources not only the portrait of clashing cosmologies
identified with well-defined social groups and actors but also the
image of motions inspired by internal incoherence, encompassing both
challenge from without and collapse of certitude within. Both these
motives are appropriate to any adequate description of what went on
during the last century of the Old Regime.

Another specification that seems to me to conform to the
historical truth is what I call Douglas's voluntaristic principle
('Cultural Bias': 13). Grid/group theory

> treats the experiencing subject as a subject choosing. It does
> not suppose that the choices are pre-determined, though costs may
> be high and some of the parameters may be fixed. The method
> allows for the cumulative effect of individual choices on the
> social situation itself.

This seems far more compatible with events observable in the Age of
Reason than theories that preach either economic or geographical
determinisms or providentialist teleologies.

Let me summarize up to this point. Grid/group theory constrains
us to select as our primary matter for concentration a well-defined
'group' or at least to justify with great care the social units to
whose mentalities and behaviour we are making reference. It invites
us to attempt their taxonomic placement in a quadripartite scheme
that is presumably exhaustive of the major social variables. But it
also allows us to assess cosmological incoherencies productive of
social disruption and the group's destiny on the map. A sufficient
emplotment of the inertia and motion, stability or deviancy of groups
would be one way of giving us a portrait of the performance of a
large social ensemble, incorporating both descriptive and explanatory
elements at a rather high degree of abstraction. To be sure, the
theory, or parts of it, might be wrong, or at least wrong for
specific cases. The theory might bear too much of a burden. Or
its taxonomic presentation might not easily permit the leap to the
dynamic explanations interesting to historians. But such issues
are at stake in any theory. I personally have the intuitive sense
that grid/group is neither too ideological nor too culture-bound,
neither too simplistic nor too cumbersome to reach results.

The fascinating thing about eighteenth-century French society is
that, globally speaking, its momentum and incoherencies distributed
persons in all four sectors of Douglas's matrix. However, the
cosmologies of its most powerful and articulate elements tended
toward C (high grid/high group). The rules of C, while they
functioned relatively well, described most of the conditions of the
Grand Siècle; the history of the eighteenth century, from the time
of the Regency (1715-23) on, consisted of the progressive malfunc-
tioning of these rules until, by the time of the Revolution, their
shell was robbed of a good deal of its living substance. Although
Douglas's theory does not claim to be an interpretation of modern
western civilization, it is tempting to say that the main march of
that civilization has been on the diagonal C-A (labelled by David
Ostrander as the stable diagonal), akin to what Maine described as
the movement from status to contract. These anticipations were
already showing in France, even in aristocratic or privileged groups
such as the parlementaires or the military officers, in the latter
half of the eighteenth century.

We live today (and so, to a lesser degree, do the French) in
social clusters characterized by weak-group rules and commitments
at low-grid A, among the more advantaged parts of the population.
But, amid the breakdown of the functioning rule-set of C, the French
did not enter A without much disorder or without trailing large
residues of C into the New Jerusalem of modern individualism.
Indeed, conversely, the French already possessed ideologies of
individualism (largely inherited from Roman law, pagan learning,
and moralists like Montaigne) that affected their mentalities far
more than their social dispositions and were, as such, not incompatible with C. Still more important to note (this both brings out
the particularity of the French experience and commends the
resources of grid/group theory for dealing with it), the secular
glide from C to A was not accomplished without a serious side-trip

into D (Jacobinism). This episode need not be regarded as merely
freakish or illusionary (as Marx and virtually all historians of
'modernization' tend to see it). At any rate, what appears clear on
the evidence is that, prior to and during the Revolution, there was a
variety of motions down-grid, whether toward A or toward D, and
considerable assimilation of previously insulated B elements of
society to the intense group relations and sectarianism of D.
(Whether their expectations were realistic or utopian is not at
issue here; the point is to account for their social strength, which,
as Douglas predicts, was not very durable.) The motion from B to D
was not unaffected by the counter-motion of some old and many new
elites from C to A; indeed the development of Jacobinism is
unquestionably linked to some of this confusion.

Like all cosmic generalizations, the preceding sketch lacks both
nuance and unexceptionability. Yet I believe that a deep plunge into
the historical facts would corroborate it. I mention it here only
for two purposes: (1) to provide a basic context for the specific
remarks to follow; and (2) to give a preliminary indication of how
and why I think the two-dimensional capacity of grid/group theory
provides an access to an understanding of social and mental change
in eighteenth-century France that would be unavailable if we worked
with a bipolar scheme.

Now I would like to turn to the specific question of the gens de
lettres and their role as historical agents. Much of my own work
has been concerned with the issue of death in eighteenth-century
France; inevitably this theme - one of Douglas's major elements of
cosmology - will obtrude somewhat in the wider discussion. In
treating the gens de lettres - no easy task, for, if they regarded
themselves as a party of humanity, they were also hardy intellectual
individualists - I shall try to illustrate their hesitations between
C-cosmologies and A-cosmologies under the rubrics of 'nature' and
'history' with the valuation of life and death as a kind of unifying
link. Although I believe that what I shall have to say has further
bearing on such touchy matters as the relationship between Enlightenment and Revolution, I cannot, in the present essay, extend my
remarks in that direction. I shall merely try to connect the
philosophy of the century with grid/group phenomena.

It is often implied or stated that the gens de lettres - Voltaire,
Montesquieu, Diderot, Helvétius, etc. - either created or expounded
a philosophy of the rising bourgeoisie, emphasizing worldliness,
sociability and social reform, and the despiritualization of the
Christian cosmos. In other words, they are seen as being in the
vanguard of the march from C-values (represented by Catholic
Christianity and the Old Regime) to A-values (represented by science
and modern competitive individualism). But the question seems to me
much more complicated. For one thing, it does not seem entirely
clear that a coherent bourgeois philosophy was pre-formed in the
pre-Revolution by a bourgeois class, to use Marxian language, in
and for itself. Neither can one be totally persuaded that, radical
as they often were in their opinions and commitments, the philosophes
and savants regarded themselves as spokesmen for such a position.
The gens de lettres were a complex mixture of social strata. They
were frequently patronized by the privileged; the aristocratic
biases of much of the 'Republic of Letters' must give pause to any

simple notion that its members were propounding an ideology on behalf
of the bourgeoisie. Above all, the intellectual (homme de lettres,
académicien, philosophe) felt solidarity with his own kind, quarrelsome
as he often was intramurally. (2) 'We must take care,' writes Paul
Bénichou, 'to see that those whose role is to produce thoughts and
give voice to values, philosophers and writers, have every reason to
consider themselves a group apart from all the others and to think
according to their common condition' ('Le sacre de l'écrivain', Paris,
1973: 17).   This solidarity gives us reason to consider the gens de
lettres as a group, regardless of the diversity of their intellectual
production. And Voltaire, for one, insisted that authors have a kind
of nobility.
     If the preceding is correct, we have now to make some kind of
assessment of the relations between the gens de lettres and the grid/
group patterns of society. My contention will be that the savants
(allowing for all their differences) did not unambiguously open the
floodgates in anticipation of a social movement from C to A, but that
they hesitated in their choice of these values (if, retrospectively,
it can be called a choice). Though 'engagés' and at their highest
pitch raising 'a war cry ... [for] reason, tolerance, humanity'
(Marquis de Condorcet, 'Escuisse d'un tableau historique', Paris,
1933: 161), they also attempted to achieve certain social and cosmological conciliations, even while conspicuously attacking 'féodalité'
and both the doctrinal and positive forms of post-Tridentine Catholic
Christianity, especially the fear of eternal punishment in an afterlife ('Take away the fear of hell from a Christian,' Diderot wrote,
'and you will take away his belief' - Addition aux 'Pensées
philosophiques', XVII).
     We will have trouble attaching the precociousness of philosophy
to grid/group behaviour. In part, this is because of some of the
anomalies I have mentioned and will discuss: especially the conflict
between, as the anthropologists say, 'culture' and 'nature' (see
Douglas, 'Cultural Bias': 24). For the moment, suffice it to say
that if the philosophes practised some of the rules of A and
promulgated cosmologies representing A's 'critical spirit', they
merely helped to enable but did not complacently sponsor the vision
of a world in which A-relations would be triumphant. But there is
a deeper problem: the role of philosophy itself, despite the
'committed' bent it took in the age of Louis XV. In the last
analysis it is best to see Englightenment philosophy with its
literary and scientific appurtenances as an agent of grid/group
displacement, not as a series of mapped positions in its own right.
It is, after all, society with its thoughts and actions that inhabits
the map. In this view, the primary role of philosophy is that of
mediating and overcoming the discordancies of experienced social
cosmology with abridgments and alterations that render it more
'group-worthy', more credible and easier to live by.
     There are of course multiple examples that we can draw both from
the 'philosophy of the century' and from certain of Douglas's
cosmological precisions that give a dominant A-flavour to Enlightenment thought: it is, in some sense, in the measured words of
Georges Gusdorf, the movement that 'invented the ideas of values
constituting our mental structure (ordre mental) up to the middle
of the twentieth century' ('Les principes de la pensée au siècle des

lumières', Paris, 1971: 32). The rampant individualism and
utilitarianism of Helvétius point unambiguously toward A. So does
the humanitarian commitedness of Voltaire or Condorcet. So do the
practical and educative aspects of the century's epistemological
project. Also, the 'philosophes' evidently had much to do with
rationalizing time as a personal resource rather than a community
resource (as is held characteristic of C: see 'Cultural Bias': 28).
The preoccupation of at least some of the gens de lettres with
critical historiography (as opposed, say, to the providentialism of
Bishop Bossuet) is likewise a perceptible indicator ('Cultural Bias':
30). And one could go on.

But in terms of the specific cosmological criteria derived by
Douglas from the mental horizons and social behaviour of persons
inhabiting a quadrant there is a stopping-place. Curiously enough,
in the case of the gens de lettres the principal barrier to their
A-commitedness would seem to be their metaphysic of nature, with
implications extending into other facets of their world view,
including their valuation of life and death, their notion of history,
and their outlook on punishment, to name but three. I say that this
is curious not because it is obscure, but because the concept of
nature in the eighteenth century, ambiguous as it often is, undercuts
the Christian cosmos of revelation, miracles, and afterlife and yet
remains, antagonistically but substantially, a co-participant in
the C quadrant or, at very least, is unable to fly free of it. As
Jean Ehrard writes, I think correctly: 'The leading idea of the
Enlightenment is not the idea of progress but that of nature....
The unfolding of human affairs is not generally conceived as an
inexorable decay or as a progressive improvement but as a series of
oscillations around an eternal nature' (L'idée de nature en France
à l'aube des lumières', Paris, 1970: 389). And as Douglas specifies
of C: 'Nature, especially in its symmetries and regularities, is
conceived to be on the side of the good society' ('Cultural Bias':
23).

To be sure, two secondary citations scarcely make a proof. It
was the philosophes who wrote of 'perfectibility', who radically
denied the shrouded Providence of the Augustinian tradition and
shattered the union of Aquinas's grace and nature. The Christian
forms of understanding were not extinguished, yet the Christian
correspondences between the personal life and species-life and
between intelligence and morality were upset, not always without
regret but almost always in the conviction that the Christian view
of man, in the debased hands of a privileged orthodoxy, had shackled
his most human and rational capacities. Most of the Enlighteners
believed in a distant, hypothetical creation, followed by a vastly
more significant human self-creation in which the notion of grace
was absent and the designs of the world were left essentially to
'nature' or to the decisions of the most intelligent worldlings.
Moreover, the sceptical, experimental, utilitarian side of Enlightenment thought certainly prefigured an exit from C.

Yet, when all is said and done, when we go to the vital core of
the writings of Voltaire, Diderot, or Rousseau, reason remained in
nature. A nature, in many respects still 'naturata', remained
normative for human understanding and conduct. Nature of course
meant many things, everything from the peasant's daily routines

with his crops and animals to the laws of Newton and their extension
into morals and politics. But we are far from a Darwinian nature;
and the vocabulary of the century bespeaks an aspect of C: 'état de
nature', 'homme naturel', 'droit naturel', 'ordre naturel'. Although
the eighteenth century ventured the notion of a man-made history,
history had none of the metaphysical primacy that the next century
would assign it. Although we speak familiarly and without apology
of the 'historical consciousness' of the eighteenth century and know
that a longer view of the past and of the future had been obtained,
the reason of man that penetrated and appropriated the secrets of
nature was not historical reason. The great challenge was to
preserve institutions believed consonant with nature or to diminish
the ones that nature, as interpreted by reason, abhorred. The
debate over the 1755 Lisbon earthquake had been waged within the
context of a C-variety explanation: 'one should expect an intellectual
effort to elaborate a transcendental metaphysics which seeks to make
an explicit match between civilization and the purposes of God and
nature' ('Cultural Bias': 23). And almost forty years later, the
inauguration of the Revolutionary calendar, with its Year I and its
months celebrating the climates of nature, had the intent of
'restoring nature' and denying history an independent power.
    Since many moves were going on at the same time in the intellectual
life of France during our period - some of whose confusions I have
commented on - it would be disingenuous either to argue that the
concept of nature used by the intellectuals adequately defines their
cosmological position or to deny that the society was moving down-
grid. Neither assertion would be true. No doubt among the gens de
lettres there was not only a tendentious movement into A-category
thought but some inflection toward D as well (this substantiated
in some of the rules of the 'Republic of Letters' as well as by some
notable instances of sectarian quarrel: e.g. Malesherbes, by 'group'
definition a parlementaire but on the fringes of the literati,
once accused Voltaire, though not Montesquieu, of being a 'chef de
parti' - letter to d'Alembert of 1779, cited in Pierre Grosclaude,
'Malesherbes: témoin et interprète de son temps', Paris, 1961: 161).
But by almost all of Douglas's cosmological criteria, the gens de
lettres were not in D; most especially they did not prefigure, to
use Goethe's phrase, 'literary sansculottism'. I think it correct
to say that a fair part of the Enlightenment was still in C, partly
because of the social habits of its votaries (some ascriptiveness,
a sense of hierarchies, royal and aristocratic patronage, especially
through the academies), partly because of a potent, though gradually
waning, conviction that philosophy could repair or rebalance
cosmology without sacrifice of too much of the culture of C. The
most obvious exception here was Christian orthodoxy. Instead, a
Newtonian metaphysic of nature would become man's artificial limb.
Was it so artificial? I was at first a bit stunned when I read in
Douglas, as an example of C, the couplet of Alexander Pope: 'Nor
think in Nature's state they blindly trod;/The state of Nature was
the reign of God' ('Cultural Bias': 23). Bossuet and deism had
seemed to become marriageable partners. Of course there were no
such nuptials in the Age of Reason. And of course Pope's well-
chiselled expression of nature in C, with its apparatus of the
'great chain of being', was progressively dismantled as the century

wore on, especially in the resolute attack on theodicy after the
Lisbon earthquake. Yet if one took Newton very seriously, one still
had to accept a bit of Pope. As I rethink many aspects of this
bewildering century, including the mix between Jeffersonian deism
and the residues of the Great Awakening in the foundation of the
American republic, I can only respect the complexity of the
problem. (3)

    There are other clues to be found under the rubric of history.
Here the argument moves from the question of the character of
history, to the judgment of what is historically admirable or useful,
to the notion of history as biography, as an account of man's life
and death. Once again elements of A and C are ambiguously mingled.
And once again - within present boundaries - we may assert that the
confusions of C are the major cosmological events of the century.

    Concerning the nature of eighteenth-century French historiography,
it is now, following the pathbreaking work of Cassirer, Meinecke,
and others, widely acknowledged that the greatest writers - Voltaire
and Montesquieu - undertook new forms, both critical and synthetic
in intent, to restore the philosophical status of historical
knowledge. D'Alembert praised this effort in his 'Preliminary
Discourse to the Encyclopedia' of 1751: 'Excellent authors have
written history; precise and enlightened minds have probed its
meaning' (trans. R.N. Schwab, New York, 1963: 100). Critical
historiography is, according to Douglas, a salient A-characteristic.
Let us see how d'Alembert viewed the issue. He drew a distinction
between 'civil' and 'literary' history. The first of these concerned
nations, kings, and conquerors; the second, geniuses, men of
letters, and philosophers. There was an explicit, though nuanced,
antagonism between the two kinds: evidently the gens de lettres
and scientists were benefactors of humanity, while the others
rarely were. It is important to grasp this moral intent behind the
new methodology of social history. It is also important to note
that although histories of science and philosophy were beginning to
be written in the Age of Reason, the heavy emphasis of literary
history is on the person: 'the new hero', as Condorcet once called
him. This is also highly moralistic; it is what Bolingbroke
called 'philosophy teaching by examples'. It is, in fact, a
Plutarchianism of the intellectuals, and it must be seen as a
significant complement to the epistemological contributions of
their 'critical historiography'.

    All of this sounds very much like an extension of the individual-
istic world view of A. In a certain sense it is. In the eighteenth
century, especially in the hands of Fontenelle, Condorcet, and
d'Alembert himself, its major vehicle became the academic eulogy,
prepared by the first two for the Académie des Sciences and by the
third for the Académie Française. The intention in the hands of
these scrupulous practitioners was to tell the truth about the
worldly and public achievements of the deceased, although, wherever
possible, highlighting his meritorious acts and downplaying moral
deficiencies or scandal. In brief, it was a reunion of the classical
forms of 'laudatio' and 'historia'. But it is no less true that
the celebratory and hierarchical tendencies of the eulogy, despite
concentration on the person, made it also a kind of surrogate for
the Christian 'exemplum' and 'imitatio' and, in the context of the

royally sponsored academies with their co-opted membership, an aspect of corporate ritual. Not only were the savants being given due reverence but they were being advanced, wherever possible, as models for the living and as part of a continuous and critically screened hierarchy of intelligence and virtue. There are, then, imbedded in the tradition of the eulogies aspects of high-grid/high-group behaviour, although the manipulations of the meaning of the continuum of life and death are scarcely Christian.

By the mid-eighteenth century a very substantial part of the scientific and literary estate had surrendered or at least 'bracketed out' any orthodox belief in immortality or the rewards and punishments preached by a partly discredited Church. At the same time most of them had difficulty in conceding to the neo-Epicurean notion of a meaningless natural world where philosophy could counsel only resignation and the banishment of fear. Above all, they themselves wanted to live on by being remembered as monuments. They rationalized this in the earthly but lightly spiritualized notion of posterity (whose most fervent advocacy can be found in Diderot's 'Lettres à Falconet' and whose most scathing enlightened opponent was Jean-Jacques). They in part created the Encyclopedia and certainly the collections of eulogies not only so that knowledge might live on but that they might live on, remembered by a grateful humanity. One of the difficulties with this project, as the Church reminded them, was that it was highly elitist, not a valid moral motive for the mass of men. But the Church was ill-placed to offer lessons in human valuation. In many respects the aspiration for and consolation of 'posterity' carried the day. However, it later became much attenuated in the 'absurdity' and anomie of A-group cultures. In the eighteenth century it still resonated with positive vibrations. A challenge to Christian doctrine, it was still a plausible move to restore the equilibrium of life and death in a society that was still, to a very large degree, corporate and hierarchical. Thus it serves as another example of what I said earlier about philosophy's mission of cosmological adjustment, while further delineating the nature of the special group I have been examining.

The employment of the gens de lettres as a group points to certain ambiguities regarding the conditions of being a group. Douglas freely concedes that groups can vary considerably in magnitude. The gens de lettres of the Enlightenment were not, at the one extreme, men of wit, 'beaux esprits', nor, at the other, were they mere erudites like the antiquarians. They could 'move in many fields of knowledge' (Voltaire, article Gens de Lettres, 'Diction-naire philosophique', III, in 'Oeuvres complètes', ed. Garnier, 52 vols, Paris, 1877-82, XIX: 252). Their number was several score; their immediate audience reached perhaps as high as ten thousand; their 'posterity' has of course been enormous.

I feel quite confident in designating the gens de lettres as a group by function and by general intellectual solidarity (despite cosmological conflict). But they are also, in a sense (like the nobles), an 'internationale', ranging from Philadelphia to St Petersburg, as well as an explicit agent in French society. And they do not especially cultivate a homogeneity of living conditions. Unlike a primitive tribe, they are not a social ensemble having

foreign relations, but a part of a social ensemble. They are not
physically contiguous, although most of them correspond with
frequency. If a group is to be defined by function and professional
solidarity, it will be likely to appear as a blotch covering a tidy
enough area of the grid/group map. If it is to be predetermined by
identity of cosmological attitudes, its area will retract greatly,
but it may lose in functional specificity. In either case there will
be different implications for grid/group mobility and social change.
Here, although I may have taken unwarranted liberties, I think that
Douglas owes us some further theoretical refinement.

But the resources of grid/group theory for clarifying numerous
problems of the time and place I study are, I think, considerable.
I hope to have shown why in my analysis. I have tried to discuss
briefly (and, let us grant, partially) a very complex case so as to
guard against the imputation of triviality and to suggest how much
further these points can and ought to be taken. It may be that
grid/group theory does not have and ought not to be thought to have
the flexibility that I have introduced. For I have treated the
gens de lettres both as a group possessing cosmological attitudes
and as a catalyst for the influencing of other (unmentioned) grid/
group positions in eighteenth-century France. Douglas might
consider such a move illicit. Historians might think my ideas
biased in their own right or deliberately set askew by the theory
that has served as my major vehicle of interpretation. If this
were so, I would respond to Douglas that the historian must juggle
somewhat with her theory where a result beyond mere theory-testing
is sought. But if she asked me to work on a smaller canvas I would
be sympathetic. I would allow to the historians that I have made
little enough discrimination between kinds of savants or the
individual philosophes themselves; that I have neglected to say much
about social history; that I have resoundingly collapsed a time-
dimension of some eighty years. Of course more than grid/group
theory or any competing theory is needed if one is to do the job of
history well. But I would avow that I have asserted nothing here that
I would be reluctant to assert in some other argot and that I have
found grid/group theory a highly useful, though not miraculous,
vehicle for conceiving and working through some undeniably serious
issues.

NOTES

1 It is evidently otherwise in some of the relatively rudimentary
   societies traditionally studied by anthropologists.
2 I use the term 'gens de lettres' to indicate those persons engaged
   principally in the production or exposition of 'high culture'.
   Not all 'gens de lettres' were 'académiciens' and few were genuine
   'philosophes', but the overlap was considerable. Ideally, an
   'académie' was composed of 'persons of distinguished capacity, who
   exchange knowledge and reveal their discoveries for mutual benefit'
   (Article 'Académie', Encyclopédie, I: 52a).
3 To get off on the American track would take us too far afield. I
   should, however, add that I of course do not believe that the
   Enlightenment and Protestant evangelical strains in the New World

bear the same relationship as Enlightenment and orthodoxy in
Catholic France. On America, see Sidney E. Mead, 'The Old Religion
in the Brave New World', Berkeley and Los Angeles, 1977: 69-72, and
references. My point is to stress the shared complexity, not the
similarity, of these instances.

BIBLIOGRAPHY

DOUGLAS, MARY (1978), 'Cultural Bias', London, Royal Anthropological
Society, occasional paper no. 34.

Chapter 7

THE POLITICAL CULTURE OF WARRING STATES CHINA
Katrina C. D. McLeod

INTRODUCTION

Foucault tells us in the preface to 'Les Mots et les Choses' (1966) that his book came into being with the disorienting laughter provoked by Borges's citation of the animal taxonomy in 'a certain Chinese encyclopaedia'. In this embroidered sliver of Chinoiserie

it is written that 'animals are divided into: (a) belonging to the Emperor, (b) embalmed, (c) tame, (d) sucking pigs, (e) sirens, (f) fabulous, (g) stray dogs, (h) included in the present classification, (i) frenzied, (j) innumerable, (k) drawn with a very fine camelhair brush, (l) et cetera, (m) having just broken the water pitcher, (n) that from a long way off look like flies'.

The effect of juxtaposing these objects and qualities in an alphabetic sequence is monstrous and absurd but it is also carefully designed at several levels: as a text from a radically 'other' but bookish culture; as a play upon our notions of randomness and relatedness; as possibility in the ordering of perception. Foucault's analysis of Borges's quotation from the Chinese leads to his study of the arrangement and historical disposition of the human sciences in the Enlightenment. Although 'Les Mots et les Choses' is a work of European cultural exegesis, Foucault, having raised the spectre of an alien taxonomy, continues to reverse a familiar philosophical problem. He applies to European - or rather French - historical sources the perception of strangeness and difficulty in translating or 'knowing that' which anthropologists and historians of other cultures have thought to be peculiarly their domain.

The ontological problems involved in translating polysemic terms from one language to a radically different one have been much discussed following the 'twins are birds' controversy (Evans-Pritchard, 1956). More recently ethnolinguists have explored the systematic covariation of taxonomic and social structures. But in looking at Chinese materials we are confronted not only with an implicit symbolic order but with explicit rules for the construction and transmission of knowledge. In this context, Borges's encyclopaedia with its fabricated uncertainty about the rules for sameness, relatedness, subordination, containment, exclusion and contradiction,

is an uncomfortable reminder of the difficulties inherent in
representing real Chinese classifications.

Apart from the divinatory and bronze inscriptions of the Shang
(second millennium BC) and the Western Chou (?1122–771 BC) the earliest
continuous prose and poetry written in Chinese dates from the
beginning of the first millennium BC. No revealed texts appeared in
the Yellow River basin but by the fifth and fourth centuries BC,
texts of a ritual, philosophical and historiographical nature were
being written, circulated and associated with the reputed founders
of particular schools of thought: Confucius's 'Analects', for
example, the 'Chuang Tzu' and Lao Tzu's 'Tao te Ching'. With the
imposition of a single political and legal structure on the several
Chinese states and the founding of empire in the third century BC,
an effort to produce systematic representations of knowledge grew
in strength among the professional literati. One of the spectacular
results of this was the 'Shih Chi' of Ssu-ma Ch'ien who unabashedly
wrote the history of the world and then gathered together in the form
of treatises all that was known about those topics the control of
which was considered essential to legitimate authority: Ritual,
Music, Pitchpipes, Heavenly Bodies, Feng and Shan sacrifices,
Watercourses, Weights and Measurement. Related to this systematising
tendency was the designation of certain texts as classics. In
particular those works associated with Confucian philosophy,
historiography, poetry or ritual became the subjects of recension
and exegesis and were eventually transformed into fundamental
articles of traditional Chinese culture.

The metamorphosis of a text into a classic ensures that its
contents assume an importance scarcely present in the original
author's intention. The headings of thought or argument in such a
work become very similar to encyclopaedic classifications, frozen in
classical time and, by means of arrangement and tabulation, in
visual and epistemological space. Texts treated in this manner
become not only the repositories of knowledge but also of morality,
of what may be rightly thought and written down. For example, the
arrangements of Confucian historiography in the Han dynasty ordered
the perception of political behaviour within a context of ritual
rules, sexual metaphors and cosmology which in their turn determined
the semantic groupings of early Chinese dictionaries, thereby
coalescing the study of language and the study of ethics.

Problems of translation appear therefore not only in transferring
implicit meaning between anisomorphic semantic and syntactic
structures, but also in representing explicit epistemological
arrangements as they are both produced by and constrain their
particular social contexts. It will become clear from subsequent
sections of this essay that in the Warring States period (c. 475–222
BC) radically different ways of perceiving the natural world and
human society were argued and formulated within the contexts of
philosophical and political discourse. The problem of translation
of these Warring States texts is further compounded because, from
the Han dynasty, many of them were treated not merely as records of
what was said or thought, but were taken to be, in the manner of
sacred texts but without the corollary of divine intervention,
conscious representations of cultural knowledge and the manner in
which the natural world as well as human society ought to be perceived.

Under subsequent dynasties of Chinese history, notably the T'ang, Sung and Ming, the encyclopaedic tradition of preserving and classifying both classical and contemporary knowledge was elaborated. Huge compendia were written for the use of the emperor and his high ministers. It is true that other encyclopaedias, of more modest proportions, were produced as examination aids for civil service candidates, but it seems to have been a matter of considerable significance that the Son of Heaven should have had in his possession and therefore under his control, written, systematic and comprehensive knowledge of the Chinese world.

These encyclopaedias aroused the wrath of Lévy-Bruhl (1910: 448-9) who declared that 'Chinese science offers a notable example of ... arrested development'. (He has been discussing some of the instances of illogicality to be found in primitive thought.)   Continuing with all the moral and intellectual certainty of a European of the Belle Epoque, he says,

> Chinese science has produced enormous encyclopaedias which contain astronomy, physics, chemistry, physiology, pathology and therapeutics, etc. All this is, in our eyes, abominable nonsense. How could so much application and ingenuity be spent throughout many centuries for [such] a negligible result .... Each of these so-called sciences rests upon crystallised concepts which have never really been submitted to the test of experience.

In so far as Lévy-Bruhl believed the Chinese to have produced no empirically tested science or technology, Joseph Needham and his collaborators have shown Lévy-Bruhl to be magnificently wrong. The investigations of 'Science and Civilisation in China' (Needham 1954) have made the old question of China's scientific backwardness in comparison with the West obsolete. The new question which arises from the discussion about how the Chinese analysed the natural world and manipulated its objects is 'why, between the first century BC and fifteenth century AD Chinese civilisation was much more efficient than the Occidental in applying human natural knowledge to practical human needs' (Graham 1973:47, quoting Needham 1964a).

In trying to understand the Chinese classifications of natural knowledge and the Chinese disposition of natural objects, processes or human observations, it is not clear, however, that Needham's volumes have brought us to an understanding of the alien, other systems of Chinese knowing, beyond, that is, the evocative laughter of Borges or the derision of Lévy-Bruhl. Like all great scholar-explorers, Needham has changed the cognitive map, especially with regard to what Foucault calls the 'atopia' (the non-existence in real Western understanding) of China and Chinese science. But a glance at the format of 'Science and Civilisation in China' shows that Needham's method of representing scientific knowledge in its context of civilisation has more to do with Lévy-Bruhl's list of subjects or encyclopaedic classifications than the way in which the Chinese represented the natural world to themselves. After all, whether the thinker or experimenter was Buddhist, Taoist or Confucian, or something of an eclectic, he rarely considered knowledge of the natural world to be abstracted from politics and ritual. Needham's oeuvre is presented in a series of completed or projected subjects, for example chemistry and chemical technology, physics and physical technology, biology and biological technology, including medicine and

pharmaceutics. There is little discussion about whether or not the
epistemological and empirical objectives of these units of enquiry
were identical in Chinese thought with those in the West. What is
suggested by Needham, however, is that the Chinese sometimes did
much better in these fields than contemporary Westerners and certainly
much better than they have been given credit for by Western historians
and philosophers of science. But this approach in itself implies
that the Chinese intended to disclose the same information,
procedures and natural regularities as those summarised by the
headings of the Western scientific encyclopaedia.

Since this paper is concerned with the social contexts of knowledge
and perception in Warring States China, I offer an early historical
example of this sort of difficulty in an excerpt from Needham's study
of iron and steel technology (1964b). In an early Han dynasty source,
the smith Kan Chiang is unable to make the iron melt and flow. When
his teacher encountered the same difficulty, he 'and his wife threw
themselves into the furnace, and afterwards the work was complete'.
Kan Chiang fortunately also has a wife, Mo Yeh, who asserts that
'"your teacher knew when to give his body to the flames in order to
accomplish the work; I would not hesitate to do the same". So
cutting off her hair and paring her nails, she threw them into the
furnace.' The swords are made successfully. As Needham notes, the
use of human sacrifice in primitive furnaces to make metal flow is
a common motif, but 'most interesting of all is the statement that
Mo Yeh threw something into the furnace (or the crucibles) to make
the metal flow more easily'. Later on in the same work, Needham
brings up the question of small quantities of phosphorus which may
have been added by early smelters to 'promote full fusion of the
metal and its perfect running in thin moulds'. Thus an early form
of flux, Needham suggests, 'might be the reality behind the symbol
of the black hair which Mo Yeh threw in Kan Chiang's furnace'.
Is Needham correct to assume that this is merely an instance of
proto-scientific empirical discovery or is it necessary to understand
the full symbolic meaning and context of the action, and the
connection between the uses of the human body and its manipulation
in technological procedures? To what extent is it relevant that
the making of weapons and the smelting of iron were analogues of
the sacrifice in that the spirits were assembled to oversee the
process and the techniques involved? There is nothing particularly
unusual in the use of hair and nails to represent the entire human
body: the motif appears in a legend about the culture here T'ang
who after five years of unremitting drought assumes the guilt of
others in an act of devotion which became a model for later rulers.
Before Shang Ti and the Spirits 'he cut his hair, pared his nails
and used his body as a sacrificial victim' (Lü-shih ch'un-ch'iu
1975: 9.3b).   Further investigation of texts contemporary with
Needham's story from the Wu-yüeh ch'un-ch'iu shows the importance
of human hair and nails in mortuary rituals, rites of expiation,
and the devotion of a general to the spirits in the ancestral
temple before military campaigns. The binding, folding, plaiting
and dressing of hair in elaborate arrangements as well as its use
to display caps and strings among both men and women at this period
denoted important social facts: mourning or age-status, social
or military rank, ritual role at the sacrifice, etc. Treatment and

symbolism of hair was perceived to be a major distinguishing feature
of Chinese ethnicity, separating Han Chinese from barbarians and
melevolent kuei spirits who presented a scandalous appearance with
hair either loose and undressed or standing on end. During imperial
times, the work schedules of the scholar-officials, whose ritual
purity was known to be vital to the moral and political order of the
state, were divided by regular days for lustration and hair-washing.
Amongst the many other symbolic manipulations of bodily effluvia are
the frequent appearance of roasted hair and nails in traditional
Chinese medicine. With other products of the human body such as
teeth, blood, bone and milk, hair and nails were considered medically
efficacious in a wide range of diseases and remained in the official
Chinese pharmacopoeia at least until 1964 (Cooper and Sivin 1973:
217 ff.). It would therefore seem that the significance of throwing
hair and nails into the furnace in Needham's quotation must not only
be elucidated in scientific terms by the practical value of adding
a phosphorus-bearing substance to iron as a flux but also in the
cultural context of the perceived efficaciousness and potential of
the human body and its products in social and religious representations as well as in the curing of disease.

NEW INFORMATION ABOUT EARLY CHINA AND GRID/GROUP THEORY

In recent years the study of classical China, broadly defined for
present purposes as the period between the fifth century BC and the
second century AD, has been presented with a remarkable challenge.
Chinese archaeologists have uncovered a large number of ancient
building sites and tombs. Some of the tombs were found to contain
not only caches of grave goods in the form of artifacts but also
texts and documents written on both bamboo and silk. There are the
earliest recensions of texts such as the Book of Poetry (Shih Ching)
and the Lao Tzu but also entirely new materials on varied topics:
medicine, astronomy, divination, philosophy, administration, the
military and law (Loewe 1977). In the last section of this paper
I shall be referring to a set of documents discovered at Shui-hu-ti,
Yün-meng, in Hupei province in 1975. In the coffin with a corpse
which had been buried in the late third century BC were over a
thousand bamboo strips: legal enactments, pro forma documents and
information on administrative practices in the state of Ch'in, one
of several autonomous political units into which China was then
divided. By the time these particular records were buried in the
tomb of an administrator the Ch'in state, under the leadership of
the First Emperor (Ch'in Shih Huang Ti), had succeeded in conquering
the rest of China and in founding an Empire. These new documents,
as well as others which have been found, provide information about
topics such as early law and the internal regulatory mechanisms of
the early Chinese state on which only fragmentary evidence had
previously been available. In general, the finds require a re-
evaluation of many traditional notions about the nature of classical
Chinese culture.
    However, it is not only texts which have to be read, but also
the structure and contents of the buildings and tombs uncovered by
archaeologists. The economics of death and the procedures of burial

and mourning occupy a prominent place in Warring States texts.   But despite the frequent protests made in contemporary literature both against the burial of enormous wealth and also against the sacrifice of human beings in the tombs of rulers, we know very little in terms of explicit information about the Chinese view of death and the relation of the dead body (sometimes embalmed or encased in jade because ideally the corpse should not rot) to the existence of the dead as ancestors or spirits. We do know that by this time a long life of normal span was no longer the prime religious concern of some members of the elite but, rather, this prayer had been replaced by the quest for bodily immortality, to be obtained by the ingestion of drugs and the practice of yogic techniques of 'no death' (wu-ssu) (Yü 1964-65). But the aspect of completeness, the thoroughgoing extravagance both in terms of symbols and economic resources as well as the organisational application needed to mobilise the labour necessary for some of the burials at this period demand analysis and exploration.

In 1978 the ruler of the minor state of Tseng was discovered to have been buried with an entire orchestra of bronze bells, string and wind instruments, chiming stones and drums dating from the late fifth century BC and accompanied by the bodies of twenty-one young women who possibly served as court musicians (Wen Wu 1979: 7). The tumulus of the First Emperor (d. 209 BC) remains as yet unexcavated but pits sunk in the vicinity have revealed a complete army of several thousand lifesize, painted clay figures. In full armour, accompanied by horses and chariots, there are crossbowmen, halberdiers, swordsmen and cavalry standing in formation in brick-lined chambers (Wen Wu 1975: 11, 1978: 5). How do we interpret this army? No text is of assistance. Was this monumental representation of the conquering Ch'in army a sacrifice to a chthonic deity, analogous to the burial of jade, metal or silk? Did it serve to protect the dead emperor? What views of death, the Ch'in army and statuary were responsible for the burial of such a curious combination of symbolic might and ultra-realism, the details of each soldier complete down to the last hair-fold and plait and even, it would seem from photographs, showing individual facial expression?

With the new textual material as well as the objects unearthed new theoretical approaches, apart from the purely philological, are needed. Disciplines and methodologies will have to be used to interpret the new evidence and re-evaluate the old other than those which have been traditionally used by sinologists.

The rest of this paper is concerned with a beginning attempt to apply an anthropological theory of some considerable explanatory power to a limited range of textual material on early China.

In several recent publications Mary Douglas has elaborated the dimensions of grid and group (Douglas, 1970, 1975, 1978). A preliminary caveat is that the grid/group dimensions do not present an explanation of knowledge or perception in terms of social class, nor do they offer causal or teleological explanations. For present purposes I am not, therefore, so much concerned with why a particular philosophy or school of thought developed in classical China, but with how universes of meaning were constructed and used within that society. One of the values of grid and group is that they have been projected not only to contain the field of phenomenological constraints

within a given culture but also the possibilities for the individual
to remove himself or his system of thought from such structures.

Unlike the dichotomies of theorists such as Weber and Durkheim
which show evolutionary development from one type of society to
another, whether from mechanical to organic solidarity or from
traditional to legal-rational society, grid/group is a polythetic
classification designed to show the pattern and relative strength of
groupings and constraints within a given society at a particular
point in time.

In this analysis of some early Chinese material I am not trying,
therefore, to typologise Chou, Ch'in or Han society as a whole in
relationship to each other, nor am I documenting the reasons for
change from one type of society to another. This is, rather, an
exercise in textual sociology designed to elicit and elucidate
implicit structures and implicit meaning within the constraints
imposed by both limited and problematic literary and philosophical
materials.

The dimension of grid is one of increasing classification moving
from zero, or the point of greatest individuation, to the north-west
corner of the diagram. Grid reveals not so much what is classified
but the relationship between contents and the nature of their
differentiation. Thus the movement from zero to high grid would
represent the increasing strength of insulated categories and the
increasingly impermeable nature of the boundaries which define the
classifications of knowledge, language and action. At high grid an
implicit cosmology of penalty-carrying rules isolates the individual
in a well-demarcated hierarchy and structures both the interactions
between individuals and the nature of morality and deviance. Moving
down grid, the boundaries become increasingly weak and subject to
arbitration among increasingly competitive individuals. Towards
zero, law, religion and social relations as well as warfare and
cosmology are governed by the abstract rules and ethics of the
market. Those who philosophise tend to become concerned with self-
evident propositions about the nature of meaning, language and the
natural world.

Moving from zero to high group indicates the extent to which the
individual's social being and his perception of the external world
is bounded by others and controlled by those with whom, often on a
basis of quality, he must work, eat, marry and fight. Social
experience and the generation of knowledge at high group is
constrained by the crucial external boundary maintained by the group
against outsiders. Under these conditions deviance and dissidence
are considered to be breaches in the group boundary and are
controlled by the threat or practice of expulsion, usually in the
form of death or exile.

KINGSHIP, POLITICAL CULTURE AND GRID/GROUP IN CHOU CHINA

It is often assumed by Western historians that Chou China was a
feudal society, but recent research has shown that the late Shang
and Western Chou can only be seen as minimal states (Keightley,
1978). Chou China was a ranked society in which the King formed
military alliances with his relatives or sub-chiefs. The administra-

tion of royal power lacked the internal regulatory capacity usually
associated with a state and only a few permanent channels and
procedures of government apart from ad hoc commands can be recognised.
Division of labour, apart from certain forms of skilled artisanry,
was also minimal: agricultural work, construction of tombs, walls
and buildings as well as soldiering often being carried out by the
same personnel (Keightley 1969: 344-5). The poetry, historical
writing and bronze inscriptions of the period provide much information
about the Chou kings and how their kingship was perceived by other
members of the elite.

The Chou kings can, perhaps, best be seen not as the monarchs of
traditional states but instead as redistributive chieftains; lower
on the scale of grid than their unfree workers and lower on the
scale of group than the lineages with whom the King was allied. As
in Polynesia, so in Chou China 'the chief is the centre of the tribal
economy, concentrating goods made available by the various households
and re-allocating them for community activities' (Sahlins 1958: 3).
The goods for re-allocation by the Chou kings came, to some extent,
from the allied lineages in the form of tribute, but mostly from the
King's management and deployment of artisans and herders as well
as general workers (either native bond-servants or war captives)
in the King's fields, industries (metallurgy and pottery) or crafts.
These high-grid workers are always mentioned in the sources
collectively. They never appear as individuals or actors but only
as producing, fighting or being sacrificed (surely the most high-
grid experience of all). Challenge to the Chou King came either
from the surrounding tribes or from those further along the axis
of group, the royal relatives or allied chieftains who had been
given the lands of the defeated Shang to cultivate. The lineages
were themselves constrained by rules governing their duties to the
royal chief as well as those relating to the worship of ancestral
spirits and, connected to this, the exchange of women and exogamy.

Not only was the Chou King responsible for the production of
goods, materials and people to put on an impressive show of military
might and religious ceremony, he also had to provide luxury items,
gifts, food and entertainment on a lavish scale. At the most basic
level, the Chou King was responsible for the seasonal allocation of
food, clothing and tools to his workers. He also participated in
two sets of reciprocal relations. Firstly there was the relationship
of mutual guarantee and protection with the ancestral Spirits. In
return for fu (blessings) such as rain, crops, grandsons and a long
life, the King entertained the Spirits with meat either cooked (from
hunting expeditions and the domestic flocks) or raw (the sacrifice
of the defeated in war or at least the cutting off of their ears),
the various types of grain and other foodstuffs served in splendid
bronze vessels sometimes inscribed with the name of a particular
ancestor.

> He makes libation with clear wine,
> Then follows with the Russet Male,
> Offering it to the forefathers, to the ancients.
> He holds the bell-knife
> To lay open the hair;
> He takes the blood and fat.
> So he offers the fruits, offers the flesh

So strong-smelling, so fragrant.
Very hallowed was this service of offering,
Very mighty his forefathers.

(Waley 1960: 212)

The ancestral Spirits were not only fed; they were invited to get
drunk on the King's wine and to listen to and enjoy the music and
dancing with which the King entertained them. Given the repertoire
of attentions which the Chou King could offer the Spirits, it is no
wonder that if the crops failed or if the rain was insufficient, this
was perceived to be the King's fault and the remedy his responsibility.

On the other hand, if the King could succeed in war and the hunt,
maximize agricultural production and accumulate the necessary luxury
materials or manufactured goods, he could bestow these upon his
allies to gain prestige and overawe them. (Contemporary sources
always portray the ideal King as one who is worked to skin and bone.)

The Chou kings gave fields and workers as well as families of
artisans to the royal relatives and sub-chiefs. They also gave jade,
bronze (for bells and ritual vessels), flags and emblems, chariots,
horses and trappings as well as other things of value in the Chou
world. Perhaps the most celebrated act of prestige in the Book of
Poetry is the providing of entertainment by the King. The music,
dancing, drinking and eating of the ancestral sacrifice as well as
games and archery contests were offered to the Chou kinsmen.

Sauces and pickles are brought
For the roast meat, for the broiled,
And blessed viands, tripe and cheek;
There is singing and beating of drums.
(Waley 1960: 207)

Here, too, is soup well seasoned,
Well prepared, well mixed.
Because we come in silence,
Setting all quarrels aside.
(Waley 1960: 217)

It is the descendant of the ancestors who presides;
His wine and spirits are potent.
He deals them out with a big ladle,
That he may live till age withers him.
(Waley 1960: 208)

In return for the grants of agricultural land and people, the
gifts and feasts, the Chou King received intermittent tribute and
the military support of the sub-chiefs and their kinsmen. Military
service was not, however, routinised and, when heavy, occasioned
some poetic grumbling.

The year is running out.
But the king's business never ends....
What great carriage is that?
It is our lord's chariot,
His war-chariot ready yoked,
With its four steeds so eager.
How should we dare stop or tarry?
In one month we have had three alarms.
(Waley 1960: 122-3)

From the eighth to the seventh centuries BC the Chou kings were
pushed out from their position as redistributive chiefs. Following
upon the defeat of the Chou by the Western barbarians the local
sub-chiefs gained in power and administrative capacity. Military
conflict and the appearance of more complex forms of political and
military organisation created the possibility for social mobility
so that by the time of the Warring States (fifth to third centuries
BC) some jobs and political functions were filled by men chosen for
their ability. The exact period of the emergence of a true state
is unclear, but conditions of political and social innovation
allowed negotiating individuals at low grid low group to manipulate
unstable political conditions in order to obtain political power.
As the states achieved varying degrees of centralised administration
(task-specific officials, delegation of control to local areas as
well as regular legal and fiscal procedures) the nature of political
leadership also changed. From being a redistributive chief,
personally involved in all the aspects of the exercise of power and
controlled by the expectation of the sub-chiefs and allies, the
ruler in the Warring States became an employer of personnel, a
decision-making administrator, a gatherer of information and,
moreover, he delegated military authority by sending out generals
to lead the army on his behalf.

Relations between the competitive states were regulated by means
of covenants whose terms were negotiated and upheld by ritual rules
and sanctions. In the absence of an overriding political authority,
the Spirits were invoked in the covenanting ritual as guarantors.
Procedure was strictly followed: the agreement took place in the
'wilds' (that is in neutral space outside the political and
religious area of the city-state); after the text of the covenant
was drawn up, the blood of a sacrificed animal was smeared on the
lips of the contracting parties and the agreement as well as the
animal were consigned to the guarantors by burial in the ground
(Dobson 1968). Vital to the working of such formal covenanted
relationships between states were abstract concepts such as 'good
faith', without which it was said 'covenants are useless'.

During the Spring and Autumn period and the Warring States,
both the formation of military and political alliances and their
breakdown were extremely frequent, resulting in the emergence of
a few large states and numbers of skilled, literate, younger members
of the competing lineages who were, through reasons of unemployment
or military defeat, without territorial allegiances (Hsü Cho-yun
1965). Some of these shih began to formulate new techniques of
philosophical speculation, administration and legal and fiscal
structures. Because of political dislocation, the shih were withdrawn from high group, but their careers and writings also exhibit
an effort to remove themselves from the constraints of grid:
kinship hierarchies, sanctified by ritual division of labour, were
not, after all, conducive to the formulation of the sort of
propositions, whether of a moral or a mechanical nature, which were
likely to bring about the development and deployment of new
weapons (such as the trebuchet and the crossbow) capable of defeating
a neighbouring city-state.

Expert in the new technologies of weaponry, strategy, metallurgy
and fortifications, as well as in the techniques of creating law and

centralised administration, the peripatetic generals and managers
of the states negotiated for the adoption of their methods and
policies on their own terms with the rulers. They were usually able
to withdraw their services and leave the court of a ruler who
displeased them and their writings display parrhesiastic verbal
exchanges with their employers who almost always lose the argument.
Competed for between the states and competing among themselves for
dominance within a particular state, the managers dealt in the only
form of currency which seems to have mattered to their patrons:
varieties of effective statecraft and military organisation. Little
is known of the biographical details of these low-grid/low-group
administrators (apart from a little information about the most
famous such as Confucius) but a number of them left behind manifestos
or expositions of their philosophies and policies. Sometimes, as
in the case of Confucius, the managers founded schools and disciples
recorded their conversations.

   Many of the political arguments in these texts deal with the
nature of good government; they are usually (with the exception of
Legalist writing) supported by reference to moral values which were
recognised to be open to conflicting interpretation, contradiction
and the exercise of individual judgment. It is, perhaps, this
emphasis on ethics and introspection, found in low-grid/low-group
philosophers such as Mencius, Hsün Tzu and the early Mo Tzu, which
makes the philosophers of the Warring States seem so modern in
temperament.

   One of the consequences of the entrepreneurial attitude to
politics, the generation of new knowledge and technology in the
Warring States, was the perception that certainty had disappeared.
Remedies for political disorder and conflict abound. A dilemma was
posed for those officials who were removed from most of the
constraints of hierarchy but who still wished to maintain the
rules of filial piety, sacrifice and distance in social relations.
At the same time thinkers such as Mencius and Confucius were
greatly concerned with developing an ethic of service to the state
among the shih. There is considerable discussion about what the
individual official should do were his own values to be in conflict
with those of the ruler whom he served. The literate shih of the
Warring States often perceived a conflict between self-cultivation
(the maintenance of absolute moral purity) and the obligation of
political engagement.

   Tzu-lu commented, 'Not to enter public life is to ignore one's
   duty. Even the proper regulation of old and young cannot be
   set aside. How, then, can the duty between ruler and subject
   be set aside? This is to cause confusion in the most important
   of human relationships simply because one desires to keep
   unsullied one's character. The gentleman takes office in order
   to do his duty. As for putting the Way into practice, he knows
   all along that it is hopeless.' ('Analects' ch. 18; trans.
   Lau 1979: 151).

In the political rhetoric of the Warring States texts, dualities
of types of defilement and purity made analogous the condition of
the human body, distance in kinship and political relations, the
natural world (in particular the aquatic environment) and political
administration. Defilement or pollution is described in a complex

vocabulary of specialised terms when it was perceived by Warring
States thinkers that the contents of categories which should be kept
well-defined and insulated from one another spilled over inappropriately and mixed.   Cognitive and moral dissonance was linked
metaphorically to uncontrolled rivers, anomalous natural events such
as eclipses, the overflowing, seeping and mixing of liquids, the
blocking of conduits, the mutilated human body, illicit forms of
sexual relations, rotting and bodily effluvia.   To restore purity or
maintain it, on the other hand, rituals are advocated or used which
are based on exorcism with a vocabulary of symbolic terms related to
wholeness, separation of ritual categories, correctly organised
clothes, food and music, lustration, fasting, clear-flowing, well-
bounded water-ways.

The perception of cognitive dissonance in the philosophical texts
was underlined by what Arthur Waley has called the 'language crisis'
of the period (1964: 21-2).   'Names' it was thought 'are the means
by which the sages regulate the ten thousand things' (Kuan Tzu,
13.5a) so that 'when there are names, then there is government;
when there are no names, then there is disorder' (Kuan Tzu, 4.9a).
Warring States philosophers wrote about their perception that words
(literally 'names') and objects (literally the 'solid' or 'really
existing') no longer matched or corresponded.   'Now the sage kings
are dead', Hsün Tzu said,

> terms are carelessly preserved, strange nomenclature arises,
> terms and realities are confused and the form of right or wrong
> is not intelligible so that even an official who guards the laws
> or a scholar who chants the classics are all confused.   Should
> a King arise, he would certainly follow the ancient terms and
> reform the new terms.   Then he could not but investigate the
> reason for having terms and reform the new terms, together with
> the means through which similarities and differences are found,
> and the fundamental principles in applying terms to things
> (Hsün Tzu 16.2b, trans. Dubs 1966: 283).

This perception of the loss of epistemological coherence was
linked to the political fragmentation and disorder of the times by
contemporary thinkers.   Both in organising the historical record
and in recommending policy, the ascription of moral fault or guilt
becomes increasingly important in explaining this loss of certainty.
While it was not believed that crime, guilt or moral fault could
cause cosmic disturbances, it was, however, thought that human
fault and, in particular, the impurity or immoral administration of
the ruler, could be signified by anomalies in the natural world.
Landslides, floods and eclipses indicated disorder within the
state;   the court of the righteous ruler was visited, on the other
hand, by manifestations of the sacred: dragons, phoenixes and the
growth of unknown plants.   The moral condition of man and his
environment was linked, but one of the qualities of a ruler with
'virtus(te)' was his assumption of responsibility for disaster and
its avowal.

With the fragmentation of the political order and the absorption
of small states by the more powerful, there was a shift of the
procedures of warfare.   In the Spring and Autumn period, the rules
of battle were not clearly demarcated from those of the hunt;
elaborate gaming, verbal challenges and ritual dominated the

procedure of warfare. But the low-grid, low-group generals of the
Warring States were more interested in winner-takes-all battles
than in the maintenance of the constraining rules of up-grid ritual
conflict. Professional generals trained their soldiers to kill
rather than joust. The emphasis on new technologies, on the mass
production of weapons and the planning of strategies using surprise
and deception to overcome the enemy was another characteristic of
the competitive, individualistic managers of military and political
affairs in the late Warring States.

CONJUNCTIONS OF WARRING STATES PHILOSOPHY AND POLITICAL-SOCIAL GROUPS

Confucians

State managers associated with the political views of Confucius
range, on the diagram, from low group/low grid to very high grid.
This indicates the range of response to political service on the
part of the shih; from those who were willing to work for any ruler
in the hope of being able to influence him to their views, to those
state managers who took up a much higher grid position because of
holding aloof from the ruler or from administration - which were
perceived to be so morally suspect that the serving official would
encounter unavoidable ritual or moral defilement. Both attitudes
to the conflict between ritualist and ruler are discussed in the
Mencius:

> Po Yi would serve only the right prince and befriend only the
> right man. He would not take his place at the court of an evil
> man nor would he converse with him. For him to do so would be
> like sitting in mud and pitch wearing a court cap and gown....
> Liu Hsia Hui, on the other hand, was not ashamed of a prince
> with a tarnished reputation, neither did he disdain a modest
> post.... That is why he said, 'You are you and I am I. Even if
> you were to be stark naked by my side, how could you defile me?'
> Mencius added, 'Po Yi was too straight-laced; Liu Hsia Hui
> was not dignified enough. A gentleman would follow neither
> extreme.' (Mencius, 'Kung-sun Ch'ou' 2A; trans. Lau 1970: 84)

Although Mencius, Confucius and their followers were low-grid/
low-group shih, their ethical concerns were based upon the right
ordering of, or possible pollution accruing to, essentially religious
relationships. That of father and son was, of course, the most
fundamental because it became, with the passage of time, the source
of opposition and structure in the ancestral cult. The other major
relations of man/wife, ruler/minister (an analogue of the sexual
relationship), spirit/people were organised according to rules and
rituals of distance and separation. The categories of same and
other were demarcated by lustration, washing and exorcism so that
the dangers of contact were controlled.

Because of the fundamental nature of ancestral religion, the
rituals taken most seriously in the Confucian texts are those
related to funerals and mourning, in particular the mourning of son
for father. Lengthy and debilitating mourning affected the body and
the social interaction of the descendants. The most extreme form,

commented upon by those such as Mo Tzu who opposed complex rituals
of death, caused the son to withdraw from his official position in
the state and, indeed, from all work, for twenty-seven months, to
live in a hut outside the walls of his home and to refrain from
sacrifice, listening to music and from sexual relations.   The body
of the mourner was supposed to become emaciated from fasting or the
eating of only small amounts of unseasoned food;   bodily postures
indicative of grief were necessary;   the mourner stripped the top
half of his body for the funeral and in mourning would change the
binding of his hair and might wear unhemmed clothes made of plain,
coarse-fibred cloth.

The phenomena of ritual such as food, textiles, music and animal
and grain offerings at the sacrifice as well as the everyday
treatment of the intact human body were divided according to
epistemological schemes and regulated for purity by the strength
of insulations, space or intervals that existed between one correct
(cheng) form and another.   The Confucians who advocated this high-
grid system of ritual argued that just as human relations, the
relations between men and the Spirits, or the waters of rivers
could spill over inappropriately and not in season, so the
prescribed sounds, colours, tastes and bodily movements which
encoded meaning in sacrifices and in rituals of passage could
overcome the appropriate boundaries of form and quality which
separated them from their related others in the same conceptual
scheme.

> The energies become the five tastes, are emitted in the five
> colours, are manifested in the five sounds.   If they overspill,
> then there is confusion and disorder and the people lose their
> natures. (Tso Chuan, Duke Chao XXV; cf. Legge 1971: 708)

Because of the emphasis of the ritualists on highly insulated –
and therefore high grid – classifications of human relations,
sacrifice, food, manipulations of the body, they were relatively
uninterested in the generation of new knowledge.   The exposition
of a tradition, even if it involved innovation sub rosa, was more
important to the ritualists and led them to focus on the attainment
of a state of knowing rather than a course of action designed to
lay out the rules for future knowledge.   In this regard, as with
rituals and mourning, the Mohists were epistemological adversaries
of the Confucians.   The state to which a ritualist aspired was
that of being a chün tzu, 'superior man', usually translated with
unfortunate Edwardian overtones as 'gentleman' but conveying some
of the same sense of being both a moral and a ritual adept.   A
lower-grid epistemology would have laid out the exact requirements
and necessary stages of knowledge for the transformation of an
individual to the state of being a chün tzu.   The aspiring followers
of Confucius, however, had to make do with example, inference,
implicit instruction and cryptic allusion.   This rhetorical
indirection is apparent in the Analects.   Confucius does not
formulate his arguments on the basis of propositions but on the
logic of ritual perceptions: his analogies and lapidary remarks
are related to the form of high-grid knowing in which words are
perceived to be only a small part of the legible text of the
phenomenal and social world.   Sound, including speech and the music
of bronze, string, stone and wind could be deciphered as an

expression both of the phases of the natural environment and of the condition of human society. The shape of sacrificial vessels, posture and movement in the rites, facial expression, the combination of colour in textiles and flavours in sacrificial food as well as the physical condition of rivers, mountains and heavenly bodies were all thought to bear semiotic value analogous to that of the written word. The text, in the sense of a written exposition of a philo- sopical position, was therefore conflated with a perception of the world and subject to the same procedures of gloss, interpretation and moral inference. Speculation on the basis of abstract rules of knowledge was not as important for the high-grid ritualists as the evaluation of the correspondences between a man's political actions and the colour and ornamentation of the textiles in which he chose to present himself and the sounds which he chose to hear.

In the Warring States, the proponents of high-grid/low-group ritual were, despite their willingness to serve a righteous master, often unemployed. After the debacle of the Ch'in Empire and the establishment of the Han in 206 BC, the Confucians met with some considerable success after the ritually purist view of political engagement had undergone modification. The rules of the rites in all their detail and complexity were retained and even expanded, but a higher group element was grafted on to form the successful, political type of Confucianism of the Han Dynasty. Access to power and the family based nature of the obligations of power introduced the need to justify and persuade. The Han Confucians elaborated already existing dualities of ritual purity and the avoidance of pollution. Justifying metaphysical arguments, commentaries on received texts, accusations of heterodoxy as well as claims to irrefutable, primitive orthodoxy competed for adherents and for access to political authority. Moving across the diagram to high grid, high group, the Confucians remained scattered depending upon their ability to act with political effectiveness.

Mohists

The Mohists are placed on the diagram from low grid/low group to high group, slightly higher grid. The ideas and ways of life of the Mohists are known to us from a corpus of diffuse materials which give very little indication of the social origins either of Mo Tzu, after whom the movement was named, or of his followers. Their interest in the technological aspects of military engineering, however, and the plain, unadorned nature of most Mohist prose make it likely that their movement 'was rooted in the trades and crafts of the towns, among people otherwise inarticulate in ancient China' (Graham 1978: 6).

Mohist leaders offered their services and those of their organised followers to Warring States rulers on a temporary basis for the defence of their city-states. The style of warfare advocated by the Mohists was innovative in several respects. Firstly, it was primarily defensive; secondly, they extended existing technologies such as metallurgy, wood and earth constructions to create specialised forms of military engineering; thirdly, their soldier- engineers were not temporary conscripts but professional fighting

men organised into tightly disciplined military units (Yates 1980).
     The early Mohists of the Warring States outlined an ethical
position in opposition to what they perceived to be the contemporary
norms of competitiveness and aggressive warfare. They endeavoured
to work for only those rulers who agreed to abide by the Mohist
views. Unlike the high-grid ritualists, however, whose relations of
exchange and service were based on ranking and ritual hierarchies,
the early Mohists advocated equality and universal love (chien ai);
the later military groups were organised by rules which, in so far
as function permitted, treated all members equally in terms of
military law. Universal love, it was stated quite clearly, precluded
both the loves of personal interest and the extreme forms of devotion
to family hierarchy prescribed by traditional kinship and ancestral
religion.
     But what is the way of universal love and mutual aid? Motse said:
     It is to regard the state of others as one's own, the house of
     others as one's own, the persons of others as one's self....
     When all the people in the world love one another, then the strong
     will not overpower the weak, the many will not oppress the few,
     the wealthy will not mock the poor, the honored will not disdain
     the humble, and the cunning will not deceive the simple. (Mo Tzu
     p'ien 14; trans. Mei 1973: 82)
The later Mohists became well known for their successful military
organisation, technology and strategies; the writings show a shift
up-grid and up-group as the paramount concern became not the
formulation of an ethical position perceived to be diametrically
opposed to Confucianism, but the defence of the city-community
against the superior numbers of external enemies. The military
leaders of the Mohists advocated a type of permanent martial law
based on notions of group liability and mutual surveillance very
similar to those of the Legalists. The constant fear of attack
(real enough in the political environment of the Warring States)
as well as the Mohist view of the world as a literally threatening
pressure upon physical and moral boundaries, are evident from the
way in which the Mohists advocated the mobilisation of entire city
populations into armies. Women and children, as well as the men,
were organised to fight and were subject to the same rules of
military law as the men; mutual liability was developed to the
point that those who held administrative posts in the Mohist cities
were required to place their relatives as hostages in surety houses
as a guarantee of loyal and competent military behaviour. If
deviance from the group norm or immorality at any level of society
was not caught within the web of military law, punishment could
come from the irruption of spirits who, sometimes acting on the
behalf of the ouranic deities Heaven and Ti, took revenge or
punished the guilty as in the case of the wicked King Hsüan who,
it was well known, had been shot through the heart by the spirit
of an innocent man whom he had put to death.
     Extant writings of the Mohists show little interest in meta-
physical speculation or in the symbolic use of language and ritual.
Instead they show a sophisticated interest in grammar and the rules
for constructing logical and self-evident propositions. The
Mohists explored their observations of the natural world by discussing
optics, mechanics and measurement. They also analysed forms of

knowing and types of change as well as the logical structure and
fallacies of the statements put forward by the sophists and
rhetoricians of the Warring States. Mohist cosmology and religion,
on the other hand, take a comparatively simple form. Spirits are
considered to exist and to be present at the sacrifice because they
have been observed by reliable witnesses. But even if the spirits
could not be induced to attend the eating and drinking ceremonies,
Mo Tzu suggests that it does not really matter: the food and drink
are not wasted because the families and villagers who participate
in the sacrifice are gathered together in celebration. Victor
Turner's description of the generalised social bond of 'communitas'
(1969: 96) seems to have been more relevant to Mohist perceptions of
sacrifice than the symbolism and categories of sharply demarcated
objects, movements and words which the Confucians considered
essential to the ritual process.

Also in distinction to the Confucian view of religion, Mo Tzu
contains two treatises against elaborate funerals and against music.
The denunciation of the latter may seem rather odd until we remember
Tseng Hou I's grave with its complete orchestra and especially the
concentration of immensely valuable quantities of metal and labour
in the sixty-five bronze bells, some of them of great size and
weight. The music of the ruler could be costly and so could the
funerals of his subjects if carried out according to the traditional
rules. Mo Tzu speaks cavalierly of the 'rotting flesh' which is
buried with so much wealth and mourned with so much loss of time
to the economy and administration of the state.

> When the government is run like this (that is with the consequences
> of complex and wealthy burials) God and the spirits would deliberate
> from on high, saying: 'Which is better, to have these people exist
> or not to have them exist? It really makes no difference whether
> they exist or not.' Therefore God and the spirits will send
> judgment upon them and visit them with calamities and punish and
> desert them. (Mo Tzu p'ien 23; trans. Mei 1973: 129)

Chuang Tzu and the followers of the Tao

Critical of all systems of classification, especially those of ritual
as well as of all social and political constraint, Chuang Tzu rejected
the Confucian concern with the Rectification of Names or the purity
of nominal categories. He argued, instead, for a view of language
which contrasted the faulty precision of meaning derived from social
or worldly knowledge with the ambiguity and arbitrariness of language
perceived by the followers of the Tao. Through paradoxes and gaming
with antonyms and contraries, Chuang Tzu showed that words could be
used in such a way as even to contradict the common sense of
observation; it could be argued, for example, that Mount T'ai was
no larger than the tip of a hair.

Although the categories and language of common sense and contemporary social representations are vociferously rejected in the
Chuang Tzu, it is also apparent that their symbolic value is not
being ignored. The ritual vocabulary, metaphors and symbols
employed by other Warring States philosophers are basic to both the
Chuang Tzu and the Lao Tzu. But in order to serve the rhetorical

purposes of the author the symbols are played with, used facetiously,
manipulated humourously, juxtaposed as incongruously as Borges could
wish, and, sometimes, as we shall see below, quite systematically
inverted.

Chuang Tzu argued for the cultivation of the body and spirit to
the point that both harmonised completely with the natural world
and became a passive part of the cosmos or Tao. The purity and
spontaneity of this naturalness could only be achieved by withdrawing
from the world, from ritual and ancestral religion and from the
constraints of action or service in the administration of the state.

> So it is said, with the sage, his life is in the working of
> Heaven, his death the transformation of things. In stillness he
> and the yin share a single virtue; in motion he and the yang
> share a single flow.... He discards knowledge and purpose and
> follows along with the reasonableness of Heaven. Therefore he
> incurs no disaster from Heaven, no entanglement from things, no
> opposition from man, no blame from the spirits.... His spirit is
> pure and clean, his soul never wearied. In emptiness, nonbeing
> and limpidity, he joins with the Virtue of Heaven. (Chuang Tzu
> p'ien 15; trans. Watson 1968: 168-9)

The extreme low-grid/low-group position of the Taoists did not,
however, mean that they were outside the constraints imposed by the
need to communicate their philosophical ideas and to persuade
others of their validity. Even thinkers of such minimal engagement
in political society as Chuang Tzu had advice for those with
political power. Action, particularly that of regulating a state,
provoked damage to both the body and spirit: true knowledge, that
of the natural world and the Tao, could only be achieved through
minimalised action (wu wei) and contemplation.

> To be pure, clean, mixed with nothing; still, unified and
> unchanging; limpid and inactive; moving with the workings of
> Heaven - this is the way to care for the spirit. (Chuang Tzu
> p'ien 15; trans. Watson 1968: 169)

An interesting effect is created on the grid/group diagram
because the Legalists also took up the concept of minimalised
action (wu wei): they argued that the ideal ruler could, by
instituting a complex enough hierarchy of rewards and punishments
as well as intensifying the constraints of mutual liability, reach
the point where, merely by the ruler assuming his position, the
state could be ordered in perfect equilibrium (a mechanical metaphor
of balance and fulcrum was used). The thinkers of the Warring
States apparently perceived the paradox of creative inactivity as
a dialectic of minimal and maximal control both of the body and the
state at the extremes of high grid/high group (Legalism) or low
grid/low group (Taoists).

Some seekers of the Tao were said to have managed to withdraw
so completely from the human world that they must be placed off
the grid/group map. They did not have disciples, write philosophical
works or even criticise the society from which they had withdrawn.
Known as sages or Transcendants, it was thought that they had so
purified their physical and spiritual being that their bodies were
permeated by the Tao (the orifices of the sages' bodies were
unblocked because they had removed themselves from systems of
classification) and that they were able to travel through the

dimensions of the cosmos on the clouds or wind. Since they had
withdrawn from all usual sensory experience, it was only to be
expected that the sages were said to live on the tops of mountains -
the Chinese equivalent of a Desert Father's hermitage - and that
they were silent. The sages' more philosophical colleagues could
not, however, refrain from mentioning them nor from exhibiting their
radical disdain of contemporary society: the Transcendants
cultivated spontaneity instead of the measurement of ritual and
communed with the impersonal Tao by eating and drinking cosmic
substances; they practiced yogic techniques and were exceptionally
long-lived because they avoided the corruption and impurity of human
society and, of course, spurned the eating of cereals, known
collectively as the 'Five Grains', which were a condensed symbol of
Chinese agricultural society and of its structured sacrificial
relationship with the Spirits.

He said that there is a Holy Man living on faraway Ku-she
Mountain, with skin like ice or snow, and gentle and shy like a
young girl. He doesn't eat the Five Grains, but sucks the
wind, drinks the dew, climbs up on the clouds and mist, rides
a flying dragon, and wanders beyond the four seas. (Chuang Tzu
p'ien 1; trans. Watson 1968: 33)

Perhaps nothing would have appeared more shocking to contemporaries than Chuang Tzu's rejection of mourning and the rites of
burial. When his wife died and a friend came to condole, 'he
found Chuang Tzu sitting with his legs sprawled out, pounding on
a tub and singing'. The friend remonstrates with him but Chuang
Tzu replies that he has been looking back to

Not only the time before she had a body, but the time before
she had a spirit. In the midst of the jumble of wonder and
mystery a change took place and she had a spirit. Another
change and she had a body. Another change and she was born.
Now there's been another change and she's dead. It's just
like the progression of the four seasons, spring, summer,
fall, winter. (Chuang Tzu p'ien 18; trans. Watson 1968: 192)

Chuang Tzu is, of course, not merely citing the endless tour of
natural process. He is attacking a ritual considered fundamental
to ancestral religion. The lengthy period of mourning for a close
relative was a period of liminality before the bereaved was re-
integrated into the pattern of kinship. The Taoists themselves
are, however, permanently liminal; not yet Sages and completely
able to dispense with the forms of society and yet not accepting
its structures either.

Concomitant with the Taoist position approaching zero on the
grid/group diagram is the inversion in the texts of the culturally
significant. Neither the Lao Tzu nor the Chuang Tzu see anything
to be avoided or controlled in death or decay. Both texts exalt
the feminine in contrast to the masculine emphasis of the ancestral
cult. The ritual categorisation of the senses in terms of colour,
taste and sound was perceived as destroying the natural faculties.
One of the attributes of the Sage was to be su, plain or undyed,
and p'u, unornamented or uncarved. Su, not to be confused with
white, was a withdrawal from colour: it is mentioned in Warring
States texts as the non-colour of mourning clothes, of the ruler's
clothes and chariot after military defeat or when quitting the

boundaries of the state. Su therefore denoted an obligatory
withdrawal from the coloured or dyed structures of normal society;
it referred to the potent and yet humiliating process of being
recast in a new social role. Similarly, what was cultured and
Chinese as well as ritually significant was also patterned and
ornamented.

The Taoist ideals of being su and p'u, therefore, emphasised the
Taoist withdrawal and threw the many ritual contexts of these
symbols into high relief by applying them not to textiles, wood
and ritual goods but to the Taoist Pure Man. That is the individual
whom the Taoists believed to be endowed with spiritual possibility
because he had not only departed from structure but had also negated
it, and turned it upside down, like the pot which Chuang Tzu used
as a drum to accompany his song instead of mourning his wife.

Legalists

Most successful of those who competed to put their policies into
action by gaining the support of state rulers, the Legalists were
able in the state of Ch'in to build a military and administrative
structure which could be used to integrate the other states into
an Empire. Although the Ch'in Empire itself was shortlived
(221-209 BC) the succeeding Han rulers used all the basic features
of the Ch'in legal and administrative system.

Legalists writings from the fifth century onwards advocated two
major strategies for the construction of a unified polity. On the
dimension of social incorporation, the group (of affines, neighbours
or co-worker) was treated as the basic unit of legal responsibility.
On the other hand, up-grid policies were implemented which were
designed to introduce distinctions of status and function and to
make clear the boundaries of administrative task and delict.

One of the familiar methods of Legalist control of the population
was to intensify the constraints of family and village ties by
treating the five-man or five-family group as the guarantors of
each other's behaviour and performance in duties to the state
(military service, corvée labour etc.). While the origins and exact
meaning of the five-man group are unclear, Warring States materials
stress the military aspect of this institution. Military administration divided the population, at least roughly, into five
household groups, each producing a five-man squad for battle. In
the new Ch'in legal materials (McLeod and Yates 1981) the members
of the five-man group are clearly to be held legally responsible
for the crimes of their fellow group members. They were also
responsible for the protection of group members against violence or
theft from the outside, and although being in mourning seems to
have temporarily removed the onus of liability for the group from
the individual, it may be inferred from the statement that officials
working in government offices 'should not be held liable for their
five-man group' that those officials who were not resident away
from home were so liable for the actions or non-performance of
their fellow group members. Knowledge of fault in another obliged
the individual to investigate carefully and make an official
accusation so that, as it was said, the hearts of the group were

bound or linked within a structure of surveillance and compliance rather similar to the way the Mohist hostages distrained upon the loyal activities of the relatives whose behaviour they guaranteed.

The effectiveness of the five-man residential and work group for the control of behaviour depended upon the fostering of particular notions of the relations between individuals. Institutionalised and centralised group control demanded a very different framework of rules from the political culture of the early Warring States which had provided an ideal environment for the activities of the freely-negotiating individual who could transact with his equals under the rubric of abstract values such as good faith, sincerity and human-heartedness. Instead of assessing the ethical behaviour of the individual, group management was based on notions of reciprocity, positive and negative guarantee and mutual liability.

The technical term tso, meaning in ordinary parlance to sit or, in the army, to take up a position, appears with great frequency both in the Ch'in documents and in Han sources to describe the individual's linkage to the actions of others and, if an official, to administrative accounting procedures. The new documents state that 'the household is liable for (the actions of) its bondservants; the bondservants are not liable for (the actions of) the household'. Apart from this single limitation, it would seem that the entire Ch'in population incurred liability for the actions of fellow group members when co-resident with them. Indeed the legal definition of a household was that its members 'completely match liability for the guilty individual'.

Ch'in officials were considered liable for the debts incurred or the discrepancies discovered in procedures of verification carried out after they had left a particular job or been dismissed. A general rubric in the Ch'in laws states that 'those who share an office; each has his own job; each is liable for that of which he is in charge. If a government bailiff is dismissed, the county prefect orders someone to verify his office.' The official, and in some cases, his fellow workers, is responsible for the results of this accounting procedure, and, in general, officials are liable for the actions of their immediate superiors and inferiors in the administration. Group was, therefore, under the Ch'in a means of control whereby the family, five-man group as well as co-workers were linked in a network of clearly defined rules.

Apart from the responsibility for the crimes of others which fell upon both men and women as a result of inclusion within one group or another, the Ch'in documents provide examples of several types of guarantee which reinforced the control exercised upon the individual by those with whom he was resident or with whom he worked. The pao form of positive guarantee which was a warranty of certain achievement was used to indicate the responsibility of family members to ensure that an exiled relative reached his destination without dying or absconding. The cognate form of pao or negative guarantee, 'standing surety lest...', placed relatives who stood as guarantors in a legal position similar to that of the internal hostages of the Mohist texts where, in protected towns, the relatives of key officials are said to be lodged in special surety houses (Yang 1961).

Not only was the individual in Ch'in law bound to his group by liability and to those whom he guaranteed in the manner of a hostage, but the documents also insist that group members are obliged to be cognisant of the behaviour of their fellow group members. If a crime or administrative delict occurred, the people who were considered to be in a position to see and know would also be prosecuted. If a wife, for example, can be shown to have known that her husband committed a robbery because instead of denouncing her husband she hides him, she is then, herself, classified as a robber. If ignorance can be assumed, then the wife would be treated merely as an arrestable person involving the lesser liability of being a family member rather than joint liability for the crime. The category of sharing guilt is applied to those who know about a crime and subsequently eat meat (possibly that of the sacrifice) with the criminal. It is, surely, what would be expected from high group control: sharing food and the knowledge of the diurnal affairs of others binds the individual to his kin or work group both symbolically and legally.

The Ch'in documents contain pro forma transcripts of legal processes and instructions on procedural matters. Ch'in prosecution manifests its high-grid/high-group character as an inquisitorial and confessional process. At least in the present documents of the late Ch'in state and early Empire, most of the agonistic elements which may be observed in the establishing of covenants or agreements between individuals or states in the Spring and Autumn period are missing. Instead, the Ch'in process emphasises, through an elaborate and bureaucratic series of documentary comparisons, the establishment of reality. It has already been noted that shih - the really existing - was of great importance to the philosophers of the Warring States who gave thought to their perceived language crisis. Under Ch'in law, the liable or guilty individual has to submit or confess before the legal process can be completed.

If the epistemological relevance of the submission by the individual to collective reality seems far-fetched, the Ch'in procedure may be compared with that of other societies. In Common Law, the verdict is a result of contest, probability or proof by means of the assessment of admissible evidence; notions such as 'admissible', 'evidence', or 'probable', being the subject of previously formulated rules. In the legal procedures of small-scale societies in which the irruption of the sacred is sought to determine guilt or innocence, ordeals may be used to provide satisfactory answers to the problem of deviance (Brown 1975). The Ch'in process, however, concentrates upon the establishment of what really happened - predicated upon group liability - and the need for the individual to submit to the truth as it has been discovered.

All the Ch'in cases begin with a report or denunciation which was itself a serious matter because one of the purposes of the legal process was to determine the validity of an accusation as well as the guilt of the person accused. If it was shown that someone had made a denunciation without proper investigation or had made one in the knowledge that it was untrue, then that individual was, himself, guilty of a crime. After the denunciation, the instructions for procedure read,

In general, in questioning parties to a case, you must first hear their statements in their entirety and record them, with each

party developing his replies.... When you have interrogated him
to the greatest extent possible and he has lied repeatedly, has
changed his statements but not submitted ... then investigate
by beating.

The accused must, therefore, submit to the official view of the case
or be tortured. The documents give information about the channels
and types of documentation which passed between local and county
officials before a final determination was reached. Reports are
frequently returned with demands from superior officials for
further information on the accused: Ch'in law seems to have been
nothing if not bureaucratic. Finally, after admitting the charge,
the guilty individual declares any other liabilities which he might
have incurred before the sentence is decided by the administrative
official.

I have already argued that several schools of thought in the
Warring States perceived the contemporary environment both literally
and in the figurative political sense to be at risk. Apart from the
reinforcement of high-group strategies of control, the Legalists
also adopted policies and legal definitions which led to the high-
grid structuring of function in the state and the restructuring of
the individual family or lineage's relation with the state. An
important dichotomy in texts such as the Han Fei Tzu is private
versus public or state interests. Public laws were held to be
incompatible with the obligations of kinship (prominent in a
chieftaincy or proto-state) which intervened between the individual
and the government in a true state. But even the Ch'in state had
to take ancestral religion into account so that filial impiety is
treated as a capital offence.

In general, the up-grid policies of Ch'in administration
emphasised the intervention of the state in what seem to have been
previously regarded as private disputes. The ability of the
individual to act outside the procedures of the state was further
demarcated by the prosecution of acts done on one's own responsibility or by arrogating authority. These terms were used to
describe those actions which were not intrinsically illegal, but
which, if carried out by people who were not authorised by the
appropriate function, could incur punishment. From the numerous
instances in the Ch'in documents of references to the rule that
fathers should not punish errant sons 'on their own responsibility',
we may infer that such punishments of intra-family delicts were
common but that the Ch'in state tried to accrue as many of these
actions to the public procedures as was possible. Acting on one's
own responsibility was to permeate the boundaries of definition
because one thereby encroached improperly upon an action which
properly belonged to the ruler or to a particular official.

After the establishment of the Ch'in dynasty, it is recorded
in the Shih Chi that there were set up in honour of the First
Emperor stelae at points in his progress around the newly unified
Empire. The inscriptions salute the new age and credit Ch'in Shih
Huang Ti with the separating of the sexes, the measuring, the
defining and separating necessary to the establishment of pure
officials. It is interesting that some of the same descriptive
vocabulary is used in the Confucian texts to refer to inappropriate
ritual forms and the inaccurate deployment of condensed symbols

such as colours and sounds. But whereas the Confucian writers use
the metaphors of water and sex to emphasize ritual pollution, the
Legalists used them for the evaluation of political and administrative
behaviour. That this was not merely the style of public rhetoric
but part of the administrative vocabulary of the Ch'in state can be
seen by the appearance of the same terms in a letter of instruction
and 'The Way of being an Official', circulars to local officials
which were excavated from the same tomb as the Ch'in legal materials.

After they acquired political power in the state of Ch'in the
Legalists had been able to apply a significantly up-grid policy,
the 'Rectification of Names', to administrative and legal practices.
Legalist obsession with the lack of structure or corruption
engendered by the lack of fit or, as it is put in both the Legalist
texts and the Ch'in documents, the 'not matching' of language and
reality led to the recommendation of severe punishments for those
officials who jumped out (yü, yüeh) of category, status or function.
This jumping out or, as it is sometimes described, traversing of
borders or walls, could destroy the carefully constructed high-grid
boundaries of function or at least make them undesirably permeable;
in turn this threatened the certainty and purity of knowledge which
Legalist writings and policies were designed to create.

when an intelligent ruler keeps ministers in service, the
officials cannot jump out of functions and obtain merits thereby
nor utter words not adequate to deeds. Whenever they go beyond
their functions they are put to death, and whenever their words
are not adequate to deeds they are held guilty. (Han Fei Tzu
P'ien 7 'Erh ping', 2.7a)

This is surely an extreme form of job specification. But it is
not just an indication of divisions of administrative labour. The
Legalist philosopher, Han Fei Tzu, points out that the matching of
name and reality or form ensured that punishment extended not only,
as might at first be supposed, to the official 'whose word is big
but whose result is small', but also to the official 'whose word is
small but whose result is big'.

This is not because no pleasure is taken in the larger accomplishment but because it is not in accordance with the name given to
it. The injury done is greater than if the larger accomplishment
had not been performed and therefore they are punished. (ibid.)

In political, legal and administrative activities the Legalists
conceived of a relationship of debt between verbal statements,
intentions and ultimate performance. As in the imaginary law of
Venice and the pound of flesh, it was vital that the action not
overspill the boundaries of its definition.

We may see from this that rational bureaucracy, in the Weberian
sense of the term, was not the primary concern of the Legalist
policy-makers, but, rather, the creation of rules of administrative
practice constrained by high-grid epistemology. The formation of
Empire and the extension of the structures of the true state were
perceived to require the reorganisation of the boundaries of
knowledge. The most important knowledge for the legalists and
other ambitious administrators of the late Warring States was that
which removed the possibility of discrepancies between officials
and their work; knowledge, that is, in the form of insulated
classifications of administration which were established by the
borders and boundaries of law, task and function.

CONCLUSION

It would seem that the directions and tendencies represented by the axes of grid and group provide insights into the conjunctions and disparities of language, religion and political structure which it is sometimes difficult for the historian interested in 'mentalité' to relate. The elaborations of minimal and maximal constraint along the dimensions of grid and group allow not only for the location of collective representations but also for the location of the individual voice in a traditional culture (see Figures 7.1 and 7.2). This possibility of showing multiple contingencies and the strategies for avoiding them is often absent from orthodox structuralism and from the sort of phenomenological attention to dominant ways of knowing advocated by Foucault. The grid/group dimensions allow us to see a complex range of possible semiotic contexts within one particular culture and how the individual in his political role as persuader may manipulate and recreate that context. The documents and texts of an ancient culture can be seen, perhaps, not just as isolated remnants of philosophy or historiography but as inter-connected and participating in common concerns and levels of discourse to which their authors provided very different answers (see Figure 7.3).

Let us take, for example, the attitude to death in the Warring States which has been discussed at some length and which was evidently a matter of concern and - for some - great concentrations of wealth. The Mohists, as we have seen, advocated minimal death ritual, the Confucians an elaborate control of corpse pollution and the Taoists no ritual at all. These attitudes are not the result of one set of economic or social causes. They have, surely, to be understood not in isolation but within their universe of related meanings and cultural constraints: social grouping, relation to others, uses of language and attitudes to knowledge, perceptions of the sacred and political structures.

David Ostrander (ch.1 of this volume) has suggested that the interaction of the grid and group dimensions produces a contrast between those areas of social space where the dimensional strengths are equal (high grid/high group, low grid/low group) and those where they are unequal (high grid/low group, low grid/high group). He has labelled these directions across the diagram as the stable and the unstable diagonals. This is a tempting point at which to leave the discussion of early China. The Han Dynasty (206 BC - 220 AD) managed to combine the high-group policies of the Legalists with the up-grid philosophies of the Confucians, thereby removing many of the conditions of low-grid and low-group competitive society which had existed in the Warring States. The movement up the stable diagonal does, indeed, coincide with the construction of a large and stable Chinese Empire. However, destabilising factors of that Empire were manifested in the existence of militant sects characteristic of the high-group/low-grid part of the diagram. Sects such as the Yellow Turbans controlled the irruption of the sacred and contained it within their large groups of adherents. Taoist in philosophical inclination (they should be distinguished from Chuang Tzu and his followers by their emphasis on the super-natural), the Yellow Turbans were uninterested in the elaboration of

systematic texts or theologies but like the later Mohists they
organised military societies to counter external threats and the
impurity of contemporary society. The other manifestation of
destabilising high group at the end of Han was the lineage: powerful
local landlords who became disaffected with central Han government
and withdrew from its administration to their own clan-based local
societies. At many points in Chinese history the millenarian group,
driven by a mixture of high-group organisation and low-grid eschatology
has been a political factor of some consequence. As the Yellow Turbans,
so the high-group/low-grid T'aip'ings and the Boxers. I would
therefore suggest that should the type of analysis elaborated in this
paper for Warring States China be extended to later periods of
history, it might well yield further insights into the social contexts
of traditional Chinese knowledge and perception.

GRID GROUP, MAJOR ACTORS AND PHILOSOPHIES

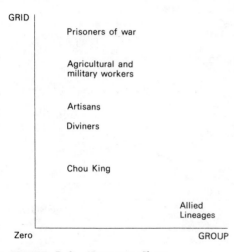

FIGURE 7.1   Western Chou

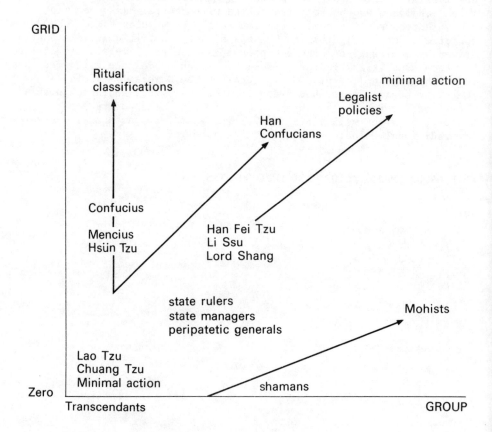

FIGURE 7.2 Warring States

GRID

Insulated classifications of knowledge. Ritual categories rigorously maintained: music, colour, taste, rites de passage. 'Distancing' of the spirits; separation of sacred and profane. War as sacrifice of raw meat. Emphasis on 'states' of knowledge.	Minimal action (wu wei). Hierarchy. Metaphysical systems of Han philosophers. Commentaries on classics, exegeses and forgeries. Ascriptive ranking. Doctrines of Just War. Multilated bodies of punished criminals symbolise deviance.

COSMOS AS THE SIGNIFIER OF
POLLUTION IN HUMAN SOCIETY

	Inquisitorial/confessional legal procedure based upon discovery of 'reality'. Submission of the individual to the group's definition of 'the facts'. Five-man mutual liability groups.
Achieved ranking; rank as negotiable commodity. Minimal symbolism. Self-evident philosophical statements. Rule-based covenants and agreements. Winner takes all warfare; strategy and deception in battle. Ethical philosophies. 'Natural'/spontaneous identification between body and cosmos. Minimal action (wu wei).	Military law and internal hostages applied to threatened civilian groups. Defensive and guerrilla warfare. Irruption of spirits into the group; sometimes controlled by shamans. Sects and secret societies. Expulsion from group by ostracism or death (sometimes modified by military law). Punishment of individuals by the spirits.

Zero

GROUP

Withdrawal
of self: rejection of
condensed symbols: food,
colour, mourning

FIGURE 7.3   Cosmologies

ACKNOWLEDGMENT

I wish to thank the Russell Sage Foundation for a grant which
supported the writing of this paper, and Mary Douglas, David
Keightley, and Robin Yates who commented on an earlier draft.

BIBLIOGRAPHY

BROWN, PETER (1975), Society and the supernatural: a medieval change
'Daedalus' 104.2:133-51.
COOPER, WILLIAM C., and NATHAN SIVIN (1973), Man as a medicine:
pharmacological and ritual aspects of traditional therapy using
drugs derived from the human body, in 'Chinese Science: Explorations
of an Ancient Tradition: 203-72, ed. Shigeru Nakayama and Nathan
Sivin, Cambridge, Mass., MIT Press.
DOBSON, W.A.C.H. (1968), Some legal instruments of ancient China:
the Ming and the Meng, in 'Wen-lin: Studies in the Chinese
Humanities': 269-82, ed. Chow Tse-tung, Madison, Milwaukee and
London, University of Wisconsin Press.
DOUGLAS, MARY (1970),'Natural Symbols: Explorations in Cosmology',
New York, Random House, Pantheon Books.
DOUGLAS, MARY (1975),'Implicit Meanings: Essays in Anthropology',
London and Boston, Routledge & Kegan Paul.
DOUGLAS, MARY (1978), 'Cultural Bias', London, Royal Anthropological
Institute, occasional paper no.35.
DUBS, HOMER H., (1966 (1928)), 'The Works of Hsün tze', Taipei:
Ch'eng-wen.
EVANS-PRITCHARD, E.E. (1956), 'Nuer Religion', Oxford University
Press.
FOUCAULT, MICHEL (1973 (1966)), 'The Order of Things: An Archaeology
of the Human Sciences', New York, Random House, Vintage Books.
GRAHAM, A.C. (1973), China, Europe, and the origins of modern
science: Needham's 'The Grand Titration, in Shigeru Nakayama and
Nathan Sivin (eds), 'Chinese Science: Explorations of an Ancient
Tradition': Cambridge, Mass. MIT Press, 45-69.
GRAHAM, A.C. (1978), 'Later Mohist Logic, Ethics and Science', Hong
Kong, Chinese University Press.
'Han Fei-tzu' (1970), 'Ssu-pu pei-yao' ed. Taipei, Chung-hua shu-chü.
HSÜ CHO-YUN (1965), 'Ancient China in Transition: An Analysis of
Social Mobility 722-222 B.C.', Stanford, Stanford University Press.
'Hsün-tzu' (1970), 'Ssu-pu pei-yao' ed. Taipei, Chung-hua shu-chü.
KEIGHTLEY, DAVID N. (1969), Public work in Ancient China: a study
of forced labor in the Shang and Chou (PhD Dissertation, Columbia
University), Ann Arbor, University Microfilms International.
KEIGHTLEY, DAVID N. (1978), The late Shang State: its weaknesses
and strengths, paper presented at the Conference on the Origins of
Chinese Civilization, University of California, Berkeley.
'Kuan-tzu' (1973), 'Ssu-pu pei-yao' ed. Taipei, Chung-hua shu-chü.
LAU, D.C. (1970), 'Mencius', Harmondsworth, Penguin.
LAU, D.C. (1979), 'Confucius: The Analects (Lun Yü)', Harmondsworth,
Penguin.
LEGGE, JAMES (1971 (1872)), 'The Chinese Classics vol.5, The Ch'un
Ts'ew with the Tso Chuen', Taipei: Wen-shih-che ch'u-pan-she.

LEVY-BRUHL, L. (1910), Les Fonctions mentales dans les sociétés inférieures, Paris, F. Alcan.
LOEWE, MICHAEL (1977), Manuscripts found recently in China: a preliminary survey, 'T'oung Pao' 63.2-3: 99-136.
'Lü-shih ch'un-ch'iu' (1975), 'Ssu-pu pei-yao' ed. Taipei, Chung-hua shu-chü.
McLEOD, KATRINA C.D. and ROBIN D.S. YATES (1981), Forms of Ch'in law: an annotated translation of the'Feng-chen Shih' in 'Harvard Journal of Asiatic Studies', June 1981.
MEI YI-PAO, (1973 (1929)), 'The Ethical and Political Works of Motse', Westport, Hyperion.
NEEDHAM, JOSEPH (1954 -) 'Science and Civilisation in China', Cambridge University Press.
NEEDHAM, JOSEPH (1964a), Science and society in East and West, 'Centaurus', 10.3: 174-97.
NEEDHAM, JOSEPH (1964b), 'The Development of Iron and Steel Technology in China', Cambridge, The Newcomen Society.
SAHLINS, MARSHALL D. (1958), 'Social Stratification in Polynesia', Seattle, University of Washington Press.
TURNER, VICTOR (1969), 'The Ritual Process: Structure and Anti-structure', Chicago, Aldine.
WALEY, ARTHUR (1960 (1937)), 'The Book of Songs', New York, Grove.
WALEY, ARTHUR (1964 (1938)), 'The Analects of Confucius', London, George Allen & Unwin.
WATSON, Burton (1968), 'The Complete Works of Chuang Tzu', New York and London, Columbia University Press.
'WEN WU' (1975), Lin-t'ung-hsien Ch'in-yung-k'eng shih-chüeh ti-i-hao chien-pao, in 'Wen Wu' 11: 1-18.
'WEN WU'(1978), Ch'in Shih-huang ling tung-ts'e ti-erh-hao ping-ma-yung-k'eng tsuan-t'an shih-chüeh chien-pao, in 'Wen Wu' 5: 1-19.
'WEN WU'(1979), Hu-pei Sui-hsien Tseng Hou I mu fa-chüeh chien-pao, in 'Wen Wu' 7: 1-24.
YANG LIEN-SHENG (1961 (1952)), Hostages in Chinese history, in 'Studies in Chinese Institutional History', pp.43-57, Harvard-Yenching Monograph Series no.20, Cambridge: Harvard University Press.
YATES, ROBIN D.S. (1980), The Mohists on warfare: technology, technique and justification, in 'Journal of the American Academy of Religion', supplement vol.47.3: Studies in Chinese Classical Thought.
YÜ YING-SHIH (1964-65), Life and immortality in the mind of Han China, 'Harvard Journal of Asiatic Studies' 25: 80-122.

Chapter 8

REFLEXIVITY IN FESTIVAL AND OTHER CULTURAL EVENTS
Don Handelman

This is a preliminary attempt to connect, schematically, certain
cultural events, in which often are embedded messages of play, to
different contexts of grid/group analysis (Douglas 1970, 1978). I
will suggest that play is a medium of self-reflexivity within these
events: but that the measure of reflexivity which is brought to the
fore is related itself to the grid/group contexts with which these
events may be associated. Thus, each kind of cultural event may
carry different reflexive messages of play to the contexts with
which it tends to be associated - and therefore also to the persons
who live in these contexts, and who participate in these events.
In general, through media like that of play, society is enabled to
comment to itself about its own routine conditions of existence,
their values and their contradictions. (2)
    The cultural events to be discussed, through ethnographic
examples, are those of the festival, modes of symbolic reversal,
joking relationships, and the spectacle. These categories of event
were chosen, first, because the medium of play and its messages
often are embedded within them; and second, because I think that
these categories of events tend to be associated with different
grid/group contexts. (3)

PLAY AND CONTEXT

Before turning to the discussion of cultural events and their
reflexive messages for related grid/group contexts, let me outline
briefly how the idea of play is used in this essay. The logic of
play - its perception and activity - is organized differently from
that of ordinary, or other, reality. This permits the juxtaposition
of novel combinations of experience (Miller 1973). Given the radical
differences in their respective logic of perception, the co-existence
of ordinary reality and that of play is paradoxical: because the
world of play is based on an idea of make-believe, it raises
questions and doubts about the validity of ordinary experience
(Bateson 1972b; Handelman 1977a).
    The world of play is brought into being through the cognitive
meta-message, 'this is play' (Bateson 1972b): this message bridges

the logical incongruities between ordinary reality and that of play. (4)
In turn, this cognitive bridge permits messages, which arise within
the world of play, to comment on the ordering of ordinary life, on
its arbitrariness, and on the subjectivity of its experience (cf.
Huizinga 1970: 85; Douglas 1968; Csikzentmihalyi and Bennett
1971).(5)

It is those meta-messages which arise within the world of play,
and which in turn comment on ordinary life (or on another reality of
reference), that make the reality of play a medium of self-reflexivity. Given the nature of play, its premises of make-believe and
pretense, it is a medium particularly suited to doubt and to
question the routine postulates of other realities. Thus it is
this negation of the taken-for-granted exigencies of routine life,
and this dissolution of necessity in the means-ends relationships
of causal epistemologies, which make those messages that arise in
play such acute commentaries on the realities of reference within
which the world of play arises. Unlike, for example, ritual and
ceremony which 'discourage untrammeled inquiry' (Moore and Myerhoff
1978: 14) into the phenomenal coherence of cosmic and social order,
the messages of play do exactly the converse. They take apart the
clock-works of reality, and question their organization, and indeed
their very validity as human and as cultural constructs.

Whether through inversion, reversal, parody, satire, or other
plays-upon-form, play-messages necessarily call forth reflection
and re-evaluation of those accepted principles which compose the
templates of cosmic and social order. (6) The idea of reflexivity,
awakened by the medium of play, probably is that of contrastful
experience itself. (7) I would stress the experiencing of such
principles, because play, like other aesthetic media (e.g. dance,
drama, art), often is organized perceptually in terms of presenta-
tional symbols (Langer 1953), which are evoked by the kinds of
cultural events to be discussed here. Thus, expressive media,
which arouse emotions about how taken-for-granted categories of
persons or relationships become unlike or alike one another, and
therefore question the bases of such distinctions, must be considered
reflexive in their effects on the self.

Here I am suggesting that, through play, the self is freed
temporarily from the ideal and real strictures of cosmic and social
order. In this state, the self becomes open to receive those
messages which are commentaries on its situations within everyday
life. Within play, the self-as-subject can regard itself and others
as object. This loss of, or distancing from, subjectivity, permits
one to gain unusual perspectives on oneself, on oneself in relation
to others, and on oneself in relation to principles of order.
Throughout the remainder of this essay I will suggest that different
cultural events encourage the freeing of the self in varying degrees,
and with different foci; and that these variations are related to
those grid/group contexts with which these events tend to be
associated.

The contexts to be discussed are created by the intersection of
the dimensions of grid and group, to generate a range of contexts
from that of high grid/group to that of low grid/group. Here I
mention briefly those attributes of the four major types of context
which are particularly relevant to the forthcoming analysis.

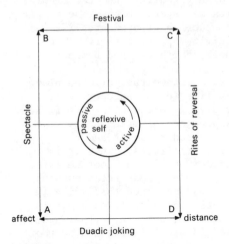

FIGURE 8.1   Grid/group contexts, cultural events and the self
(letters A, B, C, D denote grid/group contexts, as cited in Mary
Douglas 1970)

In the high-group/low-grid context (quadrant D; see Fig.8.1), the
external boundary of the group is maintained strongly, against all
outsiders. Accordingly, members are subject to controls in the
name of the group. But, within the group, there is a relative
absence of formal classification and specialization of role and
status. Therefore, relations between members tend to be ambiguous;
and a prime concern of the group will be to remove perceived
inequalities within it. Conflict tends to be masked, or to be
attributed to causes outside the group boundary. But the relative
weakness of internal lines of classification tends to engender
schism, fission, and expulsion. Cosmologically, in this context it
is assumed that both culture and nature have their rotten core – so
both have their vulnerable and predatory aspects. Put otherwise, a
prime concern of the group is the 'unmasking of wolves in sheeps'
clothing' (Douglas 1978: 22); and metaphors of scapegoating and
purgation are common.
In the high-group/grid context (quadrant C), the external
boundary of the group is also very resilient, and the individual is
subject to constraints in the name of the group. But internal lines
within the collectivity are clearcut: categories of persons are
divided into ranked compartments; there is a high degree of role-
specialization; with ranking there tends to follow an unequal
distribution of resources among members. Instead of being submerged,
internal conflict is dealt with more openly. In cosmological terms,
the group persists by validating its external boundary, and by
justifying the inequality, but overall integration, of its internal
lines and categories. Here the predicted conception of the relationship between society and nature is reciprocal, mutually supportive
and harmonious.
In the low-group/high-grid context (quadrant B), emphasis is on
the internal insulation of roles: personal autonomy is minimal, and

individual choice is highly limited by clearcut internal lines.
There are few rewards to which a person can aspire; while the power
which maintains all these insulating strictures is remote and
impersonal. Although the individual may belong to the largest
category of population, he is peripheral to all decision-making.
This context is the prototypic mass society: there is no group
boundary enclosing the person, for he is excluded from such groups
as may exist. In this context, his most adaptive stance is simply a
high measure of passivity.

   In the low-group/grid context (quadrant A), the individual is
largely on his own: life is highly competitive, is marked by personal
autonomy, and rewards the innovator. Persons are constrained neither
by external boundaries nor by internal lines of ascribed status: in
fact, all classifications tend to be provisional and negotiable.
Thus relationships tend to be ambiguous, but also threatening to the
extent that persons rely upon one another for support. Therefore
dyadic alliances may be of more significance than is group membership.

   The analysis which follows should be understood as exploratory.
The tenets of grid/group analysis are met best through a method of
'controlled comparison', that is, through an accounting of covariance
within a region of cultural and social-structural continuity, which
then can serve as a basis of common reference for the comparison of
alterations in the dimensions of grid and group. However, since
hardly any thorough regional study has been done on the questions
addressed in this essay, I have had to use disparate examples in
order to present my argument in a preliminary way. But the points
raised in this essay should be considered more systematically within
regional defined cultures when such materials are available.

MESSAGES OF PLAY IN FESTIVAL

The event of 'festival' tends to be associated with a context of
high group/high grid, and to a lesser extent with that of high grid/
low group, where it begins to tail off into 'spectacle'. The
etymology of the English word suggests that it derives from the
Latin noun festum, denoting 'festival time', and from festivus,
meaning 'gay, merry, light-hearted'. It is a time of celebration
marked by special observances, by joyous attitudes, and by a mood
of mirth, of cheer, and of rejoicing (OED: 172).
   Caillois (1959) suggested that the festival is marked by large
gatherings of boisterous participants, whose behavior may peak in
states of exaltation, and who are given to various kinds of excess
which connote the renewal and rejuvenation of social order (1959:
98-102). Pierssens refers to the festival as a 'total collective
performance', through which the social unit ' can totalise *the
consciousness it has of itself,* and symbolise its activities and
beliefs' (1972: 10). He correctly emphasizes the self-reflexivity
of the whole social unit, as it communicates to itself, about itself,
through festival.

   It becomes, entirely, the symbol of a retrieved homogeneity ...
   the staging of a total unity. The town *turns in on itself* and
   gives itself over to the exclusive law of mingling. It closes
   off, fences itself in; and the circle in which it shuts itself

off is found again and again in each of its festive activities in favour of the sign of rediscovering meaning' (1972: 12, my emphases).

Festival often is a celebration of the overall unity and integration of cosmic and social order. Within it, perhaps at its core, are revealed symbols or sacra of extreme significance to all participants. These may be re-enactments of common myths of origin, sacred relics of the basic indivisibility of group members and their relation to the cosmos, or symbols which venerate a communal sense of cultural and historical identity. When such information is placed within a medium of play (Handelman 1977a), participants are enabled to reflect upon the enduring verities it contains.

In the context of strong group/strong grid, festival brings together very diverse, often distant, categories of persons whose stations in life are clearly demarcated. In holy festivals, like that of Kataragama in Sri Lanka (Kapferer 1977), the inner core of sacred meanings may be juxtaposed with messages of play. Then metamessages of make-believe dissolve the rigid everyday strictures of this context, which are imposed on the self. Categories of persons, ordinarily separated by moral edicts and by social rules, are brought together within a medium which vividly encourages each to reflect upon the validity of his own position in relation to all others. In such holy festivals, through messages of play, there are dissolved both external boundaries and internal lines - distinctions between the sacred and the mundane, and between social roles.

Other festivals introduce messages of play, not only by altering the valencies of the everyday (as in many holy festivals), but also by erecting a mock model of society. This allows both for the erasure of social distinctions and for the active parodying of social order - through allegory, satire, irony, buffoonery, and so forth. Numerous examples of such events can be found in European civic festivals, of which the Schembartlauf of Nuremberg is one. Here commentary is focused on a wide spectrum of mundane existence. By destroying modes of the everyday, which threaten misunderstanding and conflict.among categories of persons, the solidarity of the social unit is reaffirmed. Civic virtues are here pointedly paid as much attention as are the cosmic bases of social order.

Late medieval Nuremberg, with its patricians, burghers, and guild and craft associations, would rank well within the strong-group/ strong-grid context. Its annual Shrovetide Schembart Carnival took place frequently between the years 1449 and 1539. Its legendary origin emphasized civil order and civic virtue. In 1348, when mutinous artisans revolted against the patrician council of the city, the butchers' craft remained loyal. As a reward, they were granted an annual dance which, over the years, evolved into the Schembart Carnival. An early commentator, writing in 1548, stated that the festival was a '"mirror of a bygone revolt, to remind the common people never to participate in such rebellious madness"' (Sumberg 1966: 30). Thus a real overturning of social order was replaced by its model, cast within a medium of play, fun, gaiety, and laughter. In turn, this opened the way for commentaries on that order.

The 'Laufer' (dancers), one of the main attractions of the

festival, were one of the few groups permitted to mask. Ideally, for a given carnival, half their membership was to come from the wealthy classes ('von den Erbarn'), and half from small-craft associations ('aus der gemain'). In practice, the Ehrbare tended to predominate among the dancers (Sumberg 1966: 60); but the privilege of being captain of the Laufer was shared equally between both classes (Sumberg 1966: 61-2).

Masked and anonymous, the egalitarian composition of the Laufer represented the dissolution of important lines of political power, wealth, and occupation. Frequently their songs were commentaries on the everyday: obscene, gossipy and scandalous (Sumberg 1966: 89). The themes of their critiques were urban and civic; and the Laufer danced both in brothels and in the homes of the Ehrbare, along their route.

The Laufer were accompanied by groups of 'grotesques' who amused, amazed, and terrified the onlookers with their costumes and antics. Some of their outfits were clearly satiric. Sumberg describes a costume which, 'presents a remarkable travesty on the sale of indulgences, in the form of a guiser arrayed in a white tunic made entirely of letters of indulgence; to each letter is appended a red seal on a ribbon, and on the largest of the seals the symbol of the keys of Heaven is discernable.... The character of [this guiser] ... is a very dramatic one, representing the great conflict that became the basis for the Reformation' (1966: 107-8). This and other burlesques and parodies attacked the boundary between society and order, and its everyday overlap, which was represented by the immorality of the mundane, and the veniality of those whose task it was to protect the sacred.

The highlight of every Schembartlauf was the Holle (literally hell), a pageant or float drawn on runners or wheels. The Holle was a condensation and summation of messages of the overturning of the world, which were only intermittent in the songs of the Laufer, or in the costumes of the 'grotesques'. In the Holle, complex metaphors of the infernal, of themes which plagued mankind, were brought into the city, within the medium of play, and made the centre of attention. The Holle became the world of the city, in miniature - a magnified model of life as it was, but should not be, lived.

The Holle often took the form of a castle, a motif of feudal power, or that of a ship of fools. Frequently it carried symbols of evil - dragons, basilisks, demons, children-eating ogres, and old women. A favorite allegorical theme was that of folly: fools were cleansed in wells, baked in ovens, polished on wheels, and planed down in mills (Sumberg 1966: 186).

In the climax to the festival the Laufer laid siege to the Holle, and a burlesque struggle ensued. The Laufer climbed siege-ladders, set off fireworks hidden within the float, did battle with its demons and fools, and eventually burned the whole structure (Sumberg 1966: 139), destroying this model of the world upside-down.

The Holle, like the whole festival, dissolved the boundary between the sacred and the secular, and between the citizenry and their evil or misguided selves. It also dissolved internal lines of status, wealth, and power, which divided the populace in everyday

life. It is significant that it is the masked Laufer, who themselves
bridge the secular and sacred realms through their obscene songs
and leaps of fertility, and who represent the temporary equality
of patricians and craftsmen, who storm and destroy the Holle. Their
act restores sacred virtue and civic solidarity: external boundaries
and internal lines. For Laufer, fools, demons, dragons, ogres,
and the Holle all belong to the same world of make-believe. In
destroying the Holle, the Laufer also eliminate themselves; and
daily existence is revalidated.

But during the festival celebrants took perspectives which
encouraged them to reflect on themselves, and on others, in a
holistic way: all order temporarily was put to question through
play, but in keeping with a medieval European world view. Thus
Gourevitch (1975: 75) argues that 'the Medieval sense of the
grotesque is not opposed to the sacred', for it may represent 'one
of the forms that disguises an approach to the sacred. It profanes
and affirms the sacred at the same time.' For example, in one
festival the motif of the Holle was a windmill, within which a
fool-miller fed fools into his mill to grind them into better men.
According to Sumberg, the grinding of the mill was also an erotic
symbol. But its grinding also represented 'the mill of holy
wafers', which symbolized 'the renewal of life through Christ'
(Sumberg 1966: 160-1). Thus the Schembartlauf never did away
completely with the natural order. Instead, the self-dissolution
of the world of play permitted other levels of meaning to re-emerge
from their embeddedness in symbols which only pretended to deny
their verity.

I now want to consider one example of a festival which uses play
to reorganize reality, less by dissolving boundaries than by
magnifying and by testing them, as an exaggerated model of everyday
life - the Palio of Siena. Modern-day Siena is divided into
seventeen contrade, or wards. Each, as was medieval Siena, is
essentially an independent city-state, with its own territory, seat
of government, church, museum, hymn, motto, and insignia. The
contrada is both a mutual-aid society and social club. According
to Dundes and Falassi (1975: 35) the contrada permeates the daily
existence of all Sienese. Every major rite de passage comes within
its jurisdiction. Moreover, within each contrada, 'a great point
is made of the solidarity of the contradaioli. Rich and poor,
left-wing and right-wing, nobleman and plebian, all are bound up in
the commonality of contrada spirit' (Dundes and Falassi 1975: 21).
Other social divisions are significant, but are modified by the
cohesive identity of the contrada. Furthermore, each contrada is
opposed to all others, as the city of Siena itself is opposed to
other social units beyond its boundaries. The city of Siena should
rank high on the dimension of group, as should each of its contrade.
(8)

The Palio is a horse race, run twice yearly in July and August
in honor of the Virgin Mary, a divine person of especial importance
to Sienese (Dundes and Falassi 1975: 8-9). Each contrada enters a
horse, which through ritual and social intensification becomes
'the' representation of its ward. (9) The race itself is preceded
by an elaborate parade which recapitulates the history of the
golden age of Siena - that period between 1260 and 1555 AD when it
was an independent republic.

The Palio, parade and race together, is a representation of
Sienese historical and cultural identity, and of the everyday
existence of its citizenry. It is an essential version of Sienese
themes, which are magnified, elaborated, and condensed within the
event. The Palio is discussed frequently throughout the year, and
is the subject of complicated alliances among contrade.

In the days preceding the race a careful diachronic and structural
balance is kept, between Siena as a solidary civic and religious
unit and the mutual oppositions of its constituent contrade. The
day before the race the Palio banner, symbolic of the whole event
and of the victory of one contrada, is brought in procession to a
city church, there to be blessed by the archbishop himself (Dundes
and Falassi 1975: 68-9). The day of the Palio itself horse and
jockey of the contrada are brought into its church, to be blessed
by the local priest. Although the bringing of the animal into a
church is a reversal of sacred reality, on this day it is required
behavior. Should the horse defecate within the church, this is
considered a sign of good luck in the coming contest (Dundes and
Falassi 1975: 96).

The blessing of the banner by the archbishop precedes that of
the horse by the local priest, as later the solemn and stately
recapitulation of the historic unity of Siena precedes the chaotic
opposition of the race. The blessing of the banner is also symbolic
of the unity of all Siena, as a religious and civic entity. Thus
it frames, through a more encompassing symbol activated by a higher
sacred functionary, the blessing of the horse by a lower functionary
within the confines of a local contrada church. In one domain the
overall identification of religious and civic solidarity is stressed.
In another, religious sentiment is identified with local territorial
lines. These domains become opposed to one another: but the
higher subsumes the lower, structurally and chronologically. And
it is in the lower local and territorial domain that the boundary
between the holy and play is confounded and intermingled. Thus
sacred messages of truth frame and subsume the make-believe ones
of play: the strength of oppositions, magnified in the race, become
pretense in the face of the enduring solidarity that is the city.

In everyday life each contrada is the city in miniature. But in
the Palio, two models of the city are counterposed to one another.
One is the pageant which precedes the race. For two hours, with
stately majestic fanfare, the golden age of Siena is reborn, and
stresses the continuity of Sienese life, up to the present (Dundes
and Falassi 1975: 102-3). In procession together, there parade
separate groups representing guilds, military societies, the
contrade, urbanites and their peasant vassals, and the patricians
who ruled Siena. This model of essential themes of common cultural
and historical identity and unity precedes the race, in much the
same way as the archbishop's blessing of the Palio banner preceded
the blessing of the horse by the local priest. This is a ceremonial
model of the eternal verities of the city, and their legendary
roots. In it there is harmony among its diverse components.

The second model is that of the horse. The horse becomes an
essential version of its contrada. But each horse also becomes the
embodiment of contradictory symbols and sentiments, which are usually
kept controlled or separated in Sienese life: the sacred versus the

profane, the exaggerated oppositions among contrade, the stark
conjunction of past glory and present reality, and the holistic
identification of universal sacred symbols with local territoriality.
But the horse is also a vehicle of play: and play encourages the
conjoining and counterposing of novel combinations of experience.
Therefore, within the representation of the horse, not only do
contradictory symbols (and the sentiments they evoke) co-exist, but
their boundaries also become confused and, in a sense, erased. (10)
On one level, pageant and horse reflect upon one another, as differing
versions of reality: these respectively adumbrate a civic order
which contains and balances its contrade, and contrade which
aggrandize or erase those distinctions upon which such order is
based. But again, the former is phrased as a serious ceremonial
frame which encompasses the latter. On a second level, those
contradictory symbols, which are brought into conjunction within
the figure of the horse, also reflect upon one another. On the
first level, in which pageant and horse reflect upon one another,
the distinctiveness of their differing versions of reality is drawn
with clarity. But, on the level of symbolic contradictions contained
within the horse, these differing realities are confounded and
intermingled.

Thus the Sienese models of pageant and horse, taken together,
simultaneously assert and challenge the validity of the moral and
social order of the city. Within the play-model of the horse,
contradictory symbols are conjoined and confuted, then brought into
counterpoint with the morally-correct delineation of boundaries
within the pageant.

The figure of the horse encourages reflexivity through anomaly –
the admixture of incompatible attributes – while through the
connection of pageant to horse, play evokes reflexivity through
contrast – the counterpoint of morality and its confutation. My
purpose in bringing out the complexities of these arrangements is
to emphasize that the reflexive characteristics of play operate on
all symbolic levels of the Palio – but that this becomes evident
only when these levels are seen to be in relation to one another.

In the race each horse does not resolve the confounded attributes
it carries, but any winning horse demonstrates that the underlying
unity of its contradictory attributes together can be carried
successfully to victory. Therefore this horse demonstrates,
implicitly, the potential power of the correct moral ordering of
boundaries and symbols, which is presented explicitly in the
pageant.

Through the Palio, the city is renewed in two ways. First, the
winning contrada is said to be reborn after its victory: its
members parade sucking pacifiers (dummies), or wearing giant rubber
nipples (Dundes and Falassi 1975: 138-9). But, since the contrada
is the city in miniature, it may be suggested by analogy that the
whole of Siena also is reborn symbolically. Second, after the
race, the respective statuses of the winning contrada, its allies,
and those of the losers are re-shuffled (Dundes and Falassi 1975:
187). Then the exaggeration of contrade divisions, and its upsetting
of moral proportions, are reduced to their proper scale. As the
contrade once again relate to one another in their usual mode of
opposition, so the city again becomes that entity which subsumes the

balance of its contrade. It is also in this sense that the routine
order of the whole city is renewed.

Let me conclude this discussion of festival with an event which,
under a common rubric, but on different occasions, takes the form
either of festival or of symbolic reversal. In this section I
discuss its festival form, and in the following its form of symbolic
reversal.

Kwakiutl society, during the 1890s, was marked by a complex
system of social ranking within and among communities, by intense
rivalry and competition to support or to alter such status
distinctions, and by an embryonic system of social stratification.
The centrepiece of competition for status was the well-known
ceremonial institution of the potlatch distribution: here men gave
away or destroyed great quantities of wealth, arduously accumulated
by themselves and their followers, in order to validate those names
of distinction to which they were entitled. All ethnographers,
from Boas on, emphasize the seriousness of these occasions, and the
extent to which the Kwakiutl were obsessed with these activities.

But, spontaneously, when there was 'a feeling that the village
was in the mood for some entertainment' (Codere 1956: 344), a play-
potlatch would be enacted. This event would not be performed at
the same time as serious potlatching. Any family, of high or low
rank, could begin the event by inviting others in the community to
participate: these included all persons, 'from babies to old
people' (1956: 345). The participants took on play-potlatch names;
and they distributed and extolled the worth of items like frying
pans, candies, toilet paper, fruits, pigs, geese, and chickens,
which did not necessarily belong to those distributing this play-
wealth. The event was marked by earthiness, ribaldry, pretense,
and laughter. The emphasis throughout was on the levelling of
everyday divisions of rank, sex and age, which were erased (1956:
346), in a spirit of fun. Codere stresses that this activity was
engaged in also by those same persons who competed with and against
one another in serious potlatching (1956: 347). Participants also
were free to take on roles which not only altered the order of roles
of serious potlatching, but also went beyond common cultural
identities. Thus the women might pretend to be crows, while the
men 'spoke Chinese', until all burst into laughter (1956: 345).
Even items of the greatest value, like the well-known 'coppers',
were mocked: for 'small coppers' were made especially for use in
such play-potlatches, and some of these even were given the names
of famous coppers (1956: 350).

As Codere notes, this play-potlatch was reflexive of all those
divisions, and associated sentiments (rivalry, personal aggrandizement), which marked the serious potlatch, and Kwakiutl society in
general (1956: 348, 350). Distinctions of rank, gender, and age,
were all brought into question, within an affair of community-wide
participation, though play. To my mind, such an event clearly was
a festival, which was defined in terms of play-messages of self-
reflexivity.

That festival which contains messages of play is marked by the
following features: it doubts, questions, and at times erases
external boundaries; and it dissolves the validity of internal
lines. Moreover, it tends to do this in a holistic way. Thus the

festival evokes self-reflexivity on a larger scale and at more
points than any other of the cultural events to be considered.
Within festival, play and ritual messages may alternate, or may be
equilibrated in an unbalanced way (Palio); or the play may dominate
completely (Schembartlauf, play-potlatch). Most important, the
overall or total ordering of the social unit is brought into
question, often through the mass participation of its members.

I have suggested that in festival, through play, there is the
freeing of a self which is highly embedded in social-structural
terms. In other words, there is a transition from a tightly-restricted
self to a relatively free one. I would argue further that the
high-group/high-grid context, in particular, can permit such events,
which site authenticity within pretense, and which question established order on such a grand scale, because both cosmology and
social structure have such a strong everyday hold on the self.
Such systems of very high social and moral control can allow the
self a high degree of reflexivity precisely because the doubts
evoked by festival-play have such a comparatively vast spectrum of
scale and minutiae to question. The active freedom of the self in
festival is complementary to its restriction and incorporation in
everyday life.

MESSAGES OF PLAY IN OTHER CULTURAL EVENTS

Modes of symbolic reversal

These have been called, variously, rituals of reversal (Turner 1969),
dramas of conflict (Norbeck 1967: 209), and rituals of rebellion
(Gluckman 1954), among other appelations. Very widespread, they
tend to be associated with high-group environments. They are only
sometimes events in their own right, and perhaps are often a phase
within ceremony or ritual.

Here let me return to the Kwakiutl. At times, when men held
their large potlatches, the adult women would enact a separate one
of their own. In it they spoofed the men and the customs which so
absorbed men's interest. The women would assume positions of rank,
which accorded with those of their husbands, and 'then proceeded
to mock the business of singing insulting songs and giving insulting
speeches while distributing things like wooden dishes' (Codere 1956:
343). Codere emphasizes that this potlatch was done in fun. Unlike
the festive community-wide potlatch, there was a more restricted
range of commentary in the women's play-potlatch, which pointed
primarily to the relationship between women and men.

Moreoever, within the great Winter ceremonial cycle, of which
potlatch distributions were a part, something similar occurred. At
various points, in these very serious practices, the participants
would put on skits which mocked their own grand speeches and stuffy
postures, in the competition for prestige (Codere 1956: 338-40).
Here again, the band of commentary was more limited. By inverting
their identities temporarily, the participants commented on their
immediate, ongoing ceremonial practices, and on their own roles
within these.

Thus, under the rubric of a single institution of the potlatch, messages of play were permitted a variable measure of commentary on self and society. These events ranged from a festival of mass play-participation (which erased all major distinctions in the community), to a mode of symbolic reversal (which playfully inverted categories of male and female, but in which only those excluded from serious potlatching took part), to symbolic reversals within a ritual frame (in which only the participants of the latter were permitted to comment on themselves).

Symbolic reversals are marked often by the mockery, mimicry, and ridiculing of one category of one person by another, or by a category commenting upon itself. Often this is done in a spirit of play, which may be characterized by more overt expressions of conflict, hostility or aggression. In the context of high group/high grid, reversal is often associated with periods of transition in the calendrical cycle (cf. Phythian-Adams 1972: 67-8; Davis 1972, 1978), with the transfer of office (cf. Phythian-Adams 1972; Vogt 1973; Norbeck 1967), or with both. Although the roles involved here are not ambiguous, the periods in which such reversals occur often are.

In this context, the external boundary of the group rarely is challenged through reversal; nor is the validity of existing roles questioned. In the play the roles remain those of the existing order - only their valencies change, so that access to them temporarily is altered (cf. Renson 1977). Moreover, often only limited segments of a social unit participate in role-reversal at a given time - thus restricting commentary to the roles involved. But it is important to note that reversal and inversion carry unnatural connotations: these are conditions of abnormality. Their correct forms lie in their converse. So ideas of normal order are inherent in temporary modes of reversal (Handelman 1981).

In the high-group/low-grid context the external boundary of the group is defined strongly; while internal lines tend to be ambiguous, but egalitarian. (11) In this context, playful symbolic reversals will tend to comment on the quality of the external boundary and/or on relationships within the group. (12) Take for example the Booger Dance of the Cherokee.

The Eastern Cherokee, as described by Speck and Broom during the 1930s, have a strong sense of group identity; there is comparatively little role-specialization among them; and their ethos is highly egalitarian. During their winter dance series, generally associated with ghosts, the dead, and the defunct, they perform the Booger Dance. This dance is never performed by itself, but is preceded and followed by social and ritual dances. The Boogers mask, dress, and behave like strangers or foreigners, who are often European. Their features are exaggerated; some carry mock-phalli; all have obscene names (e.g. sooty anus, big testicles, making pudenda swell, and so forth); and they speak in whispers and in strange tongues (Speck and Broom 1951: 28ff).

The Boogers burst boisterously into the house where the dance cycle is being held. They are malignant, menacing, and frightening creatures. They act as if mad, fall on the floor, and strike out at onlookers. They are strangers, they want women, and they may want to fight - traits associated with Europeans (Speck and Broom 1951: 31). The name of each Booger is announced, and he does a clumsy solo dance, accompanied by singers who do the Booger dance

song.   Each Booger dances 'as if he were a clumsy white man trying
to imitate Indian dancing.   Each time his name occurs in the song,
the whole company applauds and yells' (Speck and Broom 1951: 32).
The Boogers indulge in exhibitionism, thrusting their buttocks and
mock-phalli at the women and children.

After an interlude the Boogers are joined by an equal number of
women partners, who are nicely dressed in Cherokee style.   As they
dance, the Boogers simulate intercourse with their partners, who
continue to perform with serenity (1951: 34).   At the close, the
Boogers depart noisily, trying to drag some of the laughing women
with them.   The Boogers then unmask and rejoin the others in further
dances.   Throughout their performances, the Boogers 'portray the
Cherokee estimate of the European invaders as awkward, ridiculous,
lewd and menacing, a dramatic perpetuation of the tradition of
hostility and disdain' (1951: 36).   In general the dance is perceived
as warding off harmful alien influences.   It was given to the
Cherokee by the mythical culture-hero, Stone Coat, who, having
foretold the coming of aliens, provided the dance as 'a means of
counteracting the social and physical contamination which their
coming brought upon the natives' (1951: 38).

In the high-group/low-grid context, both culture and nature have
their rotten core;   the external boundary is strong, and internal
lines are ambiguous.   The Boogers represent all that is menacing,
frightful, and evil, beyond the external boundary of the community.
But their presence does not question the validity of the external
boundary.   Instead it objectifies the importance of the vigilant
maintenance of the group.   The Boogers are tangible evidence that
whatever is outside the external boundary is beyond the moral
precepts of the community.   The response of community members is
twofold.   First, they reject the Boogers through laughter and fun,
while these creatures behave in ways which no community member
should emulate.   Second, the behavior of community members is
impeccable.   The women dance serenely and reject the lewd advances
of the Boogers.   In a sense, they tame the wild impulses of the
invading creatures, until the latter leave of their own accord.
The boundary between insider and outsider is drawn with clarity.   The
menace and chaos of the external world is controlled by the community
only so long as its response is one of impeccable morality.   Only
then can these frightful representations be controlled, and
eventually expelled, by the homogeneous response of the community.
Just as the Boogers appear between ritual dances, and are framed by
them, so the final dance of the Boogers, with their female partners,
is also a traditional ritual dance.   Their presence within the
community is framed by the verities of ritual.   And their behavior
is modified by the response of the community: they dance instead
of fight;   they do a ritual dance of importance to the community;
and they leave without the women they came for.

But the Boogers are also masked members of the community: in a
sense, its rotten core is unmasked by their horrible guises.   Hidden
threats, covert hostilities, and a degree of inequality (the Boogers
as representations of power, in the guise of Europeans), are all
exposed to view.   Again the response of the community is twofold:
to laugh at, to mock, to ridicule, and so to control these figures
of evil in their midst, which are normally hidden, and to reassert

the value of moral behavior on the part of a homogeneous community.
In these ways, inner sources of hostility, aggression, lust, and
power, are not permitted to divide persons. Instead, these darker
sides also are expelled, and the community is purged of that menace
which may lurk in every relationship. Thus reflexivity, through
play, is encouraged in two major domains: that of boundary maintenance,
and that of keeping a community with few internal divisions. (13)

The final example of reversal is that of the Kalela Dance, studied
by Mitchell (1959) in the towns of the Central African Copperbelt,
during the early 1950s. Unlike the two previous examples, in which
the reflexivity of the event revalidated its context of occurrence,
the Kalela Dance denies the validity of aspects of everyday
experience.

The Copperbelt was characterized by a rigid class structure,
divided along European and African lines. Within the African sector
there were high rates of labor migration, and men from many different
tribal groups were thrown together as co-workers, in low-status
occupations. As Mitchell (1959: 22) notes, there was little opportunity for the development of community structure in the African
sector, for neighbors and workmates were continually changing. The
overall context of the urban Copperbelt, from the African viewpoint,
could be characterized as high grid (given its class structure) and
low group (given the mobility and ethnic diversity of its populace).
In such a context, Africans were alienated from sources of power,
while they had only limited or intermittent bases for communication
among themselves. (14)

The performance of Kalela was put on by teams which were homogeneous in ethnic-tribal terms. The general organizer of the team,
named the king, dressed in a dark suit and tie. But all the
dancers were garbed in the 'smartest of European wear' (1959: 9).
In addition, the team would include a play doctor dressed in a
white surgical gown, who encouraged the dangers; and also a play
nursing sister, dressed in white, who made certain the dancers were
tidy.

The songs of the dancers were witty and topical: they lampooned,
parodied, and made incisive comments on typical Copperbelt urban
situations (1959: 5, 9). Moreover, the play of the dancing teams
was aimed at tribal groupings. The songs stressed the unity and
virtues of their own ethnic-tribal group, and they derided those
of other tribes (1959: 7-8), whose members were assumed to compose
the spectators. Mitchell notes that, 'except in these dancing
teams, tribalism does not form the basis for the organization of
corporate groups' in the urban situation (1959: 42).

The high-grid attributes of social class, and the low-group
attributes of ethnic diversity, were ever-present features of
Copperbelt daily life. Through the play of the dance, both of these
conditions were altered. The dancers inverted their identities by
donning the attributes of Europeans. Because this was done in
play, these attributes of rank and status were devalued, and the
dancers erased the importance of class distinction. Put otherwise,
through role reversal the dancers held constant the factor of
class within the play-world of Kalela at the same time as they
denied its significance for the messages they communicated. Overall,
they transformed a context of high grid/low group into the reverse -

within the world of the dance. This context was probably more like
the one they had left behind in the rural areas than that of the
urban Copperbelt.

Dyadic joking behavior, among members of different tribal
categories, was prevalent in the urban areas of the Copperbelt.   In
the following section, I will argue that this form of joking
particularly is associated with the context of low grid/ high
group. Mitchell (1959: 41) notes that the Kalela Dance had some of
the attributes of a joking relationship between team members and
their audience: the dancers taunted onlookers and their spoofs and
jokes were not returned with animosity. Instead, the performance
was enjoyed by all. But in Kalela this behavior was embedded in a
group performance, which itself was based on the neutralization of
class distinctions through play. Thus the symbolic neutralization
of class, in the play-world of the dance, gave this medium a much
wider spectrum of commentary about the overall class structure of
the Copperbelt, than did dyadic joking.

But the context created in the Kalela Dance was far removed from
either the ideal or the real experience of much of daily life -
unlike the play-potlatch or the Booger Dance.   Instead, Kalela
messages posed a genuine alternative reality to much of the everyday
context of experience. Messages of ethnic-group primacy, instead
of being denied by the play form, became a reality itself created
by the dance. In a way the dance did overturn everyday life, to
permit the sending of messages about an alternative context of
tribal distinctiveness and unity. Were it not done in play, Kalela
might be akin to a form of millenarian behavior.

When compared with the event of festival, in symbolic reversal
the focus is less on the freeing of the self from all constraints
through play. The reflexive perspective of the self is contained
by the external boundaries of the group. Unlike reflexivity in
'festival', external boundaries rarely are questioned, but often
are reinforced. Within the group the overturning of comparatively
broad internal lines of sex, age, status, or occupation is stressed.
This is true particularly of reversals within the high-group/high-
grid context. Here the self is offered a more limited reflexive
perspective, in terms of those internal categories of person which
become conjoined or opposed. In line with this more limited
perspective, messages of play may appear to be less pervasive and
embracing: and, in place of a mood of gaiety and buoyancy, the
atmosphere may be more hostile and aggressive.

Within the high-group/low-grid context, playful reversals focus
on strengthening the external boundary of the group, and on
reflecting upon ambiguous internal lines which may be confused or
conflicting. Although play-messages allow the temporary rearrange-
ment of these internal lines, the initial categories of discourse
tend to be retained. Therefore the reflexive perspective of the
self is limited to viewing social relationships from the opposite
side of the coin, so to speak. Social categories retain their
validity, for only their relative valencies toward one another are
altered.

Although ethnographic examples were not chosen with this in
mind, within the context of high group/low grid symbolic reversal
often takes the form of play-within-ritual. When this happens,

messages of the dangerous medium of 'make-believe' are encapsulated within the safer integrative medium of rituals. (15) This is in contrast to the organization of festival, within the context of high group/high grid, where there is a greater tendency for messages of play and ritual almost to parallel one another (Palio), or to dominate the event (Schembartlauf, community play-potlatch). Where symbolic reversals stand by themselves, as separate events, there is less emphasis on the emergence of summatory 'truth', for eternal verities are less questioned. Put otherwise, symbolic reversal is generally closer to everyday reality than festival. The same relationship to reality should apply to the self's scope for reflexivity given in different foci of play.

Joking relationships

Joking relationships are forms of routinized interaction, between social categories or between persons, characterized by the exchange of ridicule, by insults, by mockery, or by jokes, at the expense of one another. In its classic formulation (Radcliffe-Brown 1952) such category-routinized joking (Handelman and Kapferer 1972) is obligatory, prescriptive, or privileged; its performance is public; no offense is taken; and it evokes hilarity and enjoyment on the part of participants and audience. Most important, it occurs between categories of persons who stand in potential opposition and conflict to one another, but who need to co-operate with one another and so must avoid open hostility among themselves. In Radcliffe-Brown's terms, such relationships combine elements of conjunction and disjunction, of attachment and separation (1952: 91, 95). The alternative to joking among such categories is mutual avoidance. This is the traditional line of thinking which has dominated inquiry into the subject, with minor modifications.

The societies which Radcliffe-Brown chose to illustrate his thesis, and those to which it has been applied most successfully by others, fall generally within the context of high group/low grid. (16) In other words, these are societies with strong group boundaries, but with ambiguous internal lines. In this context, persons cannot easily escape the strictures of the group; nor can they avoid the ambiguities which pervade certain social relationships. It is this context which tends to be associated with the kind of joking of which Radcliffe-Brown wrote.

In this context joking appears to send the following kind of meta-message: 'Because we joke, we communicate.' In other words, persons joke as the basis for their communication, for serious modes of discourse would highlight the uneasy combination of attachment and separation in their relationship (cf. Handelman 1978b). But, because joking is their communication, there is no serious substance to its content. This kind of message implies distance and formality in their relationship. It suggests an additional message about the content of their actual joking: 'This is not the way we really are. Therefore we really are the obverse of our presentation: that is, distant.' In such joking, the inversion of identity through play permits both the recognition of categorical lines, and communication about their character. Joking brings out the ambiguities of such lines; but, as play, it denies the validity of this lack of clarity in relationships. Therefore the reality of such categorical lines is reaffirmed.

By contrast with the above, for example, Kennedy argues that joking relationships among the Tarahumara of Northern Mexico are indicative of friendship, of a 'special relationship' of intimacy (Kennedy 1970). But I see no contradiction between these two views since the kind of joking they discuss is located in two distinct contexts.

The Tarahumara live in high dispersed ranchos, which consist of from two to five nuclear families. Kennedy states that between the nuclear family and the pueblo (the local Mexican administrative unit) there are no bounded groups, based either on kinship, on residence or on voluntary association. Instead, Tarahumara society is based on household-centred networks, composed of interlocking dyadic relationships. Choice is particularly important for the individual, in deciding with whom to build a relationship which will be dependable and trustworthy; while independence in individuals is valued highly. As Kennedy describes it, Tarahumara society falls within the context of low group/low grid.

Persons also exercise choice in building joking relationships, but joking partners are not required to joke whenever they meet. Joking behavior is associated exclusively with the tesguinada, a beer-drinking party. Between persons of the opposite sex joking is marked by teasing, taunting, and rough horseplay; and between persons of the same sex, by horseplay and by the burlesquing of sexual themes. Such behavior is treated as play, both by the participants and by an appreciative audience, who encourage them. Kennedy emphasizes that there is no basis of structural strain underlying these relationships; and that hostility was rarely evident in them. That is, there is no uneasy combination of conjunctive and disjunctive elements, which may form a basis for joking in the high-group/low-grid context.

In the low-group/low-grid context, joking appears to communicate the following kind of meta-message: 'Because we communicate, we joke.' In other words, since persons do relate, they can pretend to be something else to one another. Then the obverse is true: the joking is not authentic, and the relationship is indeed a friendly one. In contrast to its equivalent meta-message in the high-group/low grid context, here the inauthenticity of joking inversion reflects upon the authenticity of the relationship. It communicates positive sentiment, perhaps through the idiom of 'best friends', or through fictive kinship. Kennedy stresses that, among the Tarahumara, the joking relationship is a strong bond of friendship, between persons who rely upon one another in multiple ways, and who have a high degree of trust in one another. Through the right to pretend truthfully to each other, joking partners signal their mutual intimacy. Thus, although the content of joking relationships may be very similar in both contexts, its meaning is quite distinct in each of them. And I would suggest that conflict-avoidance joking increases as context moves in the direction of high group/low grid; while friendship-joking increases as context moves in the direction of low group/low grid.

One of the advantages of the grid/group formulation is that it

transcends the distinction between complex society and tribal
society. For example, Tarahumara joking may have more in common
with joking in middle-class urban America than it has with this
behavior in the societies discussed by Radcliffe-Brown and others.
Large sectors of middle-class urban America also fall within the
context low group/low grid. Individualism and personal choice are
stressed; while persons are expected to make their way through life
by building a network of friendly and co-operative social relationships.

Here, as Suttles (1970) and others have argued, friendship is a
special relationship: one's friends are those one chooses to
associate and to share things with, rather than those one is
required to interact with for situational reasons. Such relationships, although not institutionalized, are marked by a license to
behave in ways, like joking, which are otherwise unacceptable. Such
behavior characterizes the relationship as one of trust and intimacy.
(17) On the other hand the internal organization of black lower-
class American ghettos moves more in the direction of high group/
low grid. And it is here that the exchange of ritual insults
appears, accompanied by a strict set of semantic rules (Labov 1972).

Compared with festival and with symbolic reversal, in the joking
relationship there is comparatively less emphasis on the freeing
of the self from social constraints. Moreover, the reflexivity
of the self is honed more pointedly to reflect upon one particular
category of other. Therefore the reflexivity of play is restricted
here to particular kinds of relationships: either to those within
a bounded field of ambiguous or ambivalent social categories, or to
personal relationships which are formed by choice within an open
field of competitive social categories. Following the shift away
from a high-group context, reflexivity in play comments correspondingly less on the organization of cosmos and social structure, and
more on relationships between particular individuals. Furthermore,
the play of the joking relationship becomes more restricted in
scope, its range of inversion being limited by the dyadic span of
relationships. So play becomes more mundane in its commentary on
everyday reality. In other words, the joking relationship becomes
even less removed from daily life than symbolic reversal or
festival. It becomes reflexive in more compacted ways; its meta-
messages probably are simpler in structure (i.e. commenting, in the
main, that the overt content of the play-message denies its own
substance).

On the other hand, it is the low-group/grid context which
fosters the growth of 'liminoid' activities (Turner 1974), in which
individual innovation and creativity flourish in different
expressive genres. It is here that audiences are confronted with
the theatre of the absurd, and with happenings. It is here too
that art confronts society, questioning its basic premises, instead
of simply demonstrating its design in yet another medium (cf.
Schwartzman 1977). And it is here that the grotesque and the comic
become conscious creations of an artistic process (cf. Gourevitch
1975: 75) which deliberately challenges social order, in order to
bring out its inner contradictions. But it is in this context that
self-fulfilment comes to be valued above all else, even above the
overall integration and renewal of cosmic and social order.

Spectacle

Spectacle will be discussed cursorily: within it there is the
greatest attenuation of the relationship between the individual and
society. Spectacle connotes the exhibition of a 'specially prepared
or arranged display of a more or less public nature' (OED: 553).
Such a tableau is often grandiose and exaggerated; and it is viewed
at a distance often by choice in both physical and social terms. In
its internal organization the spectacle is somewhat of a world unto
itself: it can function without outside participation, for it
institutionalizes the distinction between the active performer and
the passive spectator (MacAloon 1977: 3). The latter may choose to
view the spectacle more or less on his own terms; conversely the
spectacle can exist virtually without onlookers. Thus the autonomy
of the spectacle is matched by that of the individual viewer. As
MacAloon (1977: 7) points out, the spectacle, unlike the festival,
does not depend on creating a particular mood among participants or
viewers. Instead, the mood of spectacle may be one of diffuse
wonder or awe; so that the spectator can decide for himself, in
large measure, how to interpret the information he receives. This
lack of guidelines for the individual viewer distinguishes the
spectacle from the other events considered and contributes to the
autonomy of both the event and its audience respectively.

Spectacle tends to be associated with the low-group side of the
diagram. When roles are highly insulated passive adaptation is a
common response to everyday life. The socially-reflexive demands,
made on the viewer by the spectacle, are minimal. There is no
requirement that the spectator relate the event to a cosmology
which, at any rate, is hardly developed. Nor need the viewer
relate the event to the boundaries of groups, which may be non-
existent. Instead, the event mirrors the compartmentalization of
roles, in a simplistic manner. In this context would be located
the Roman 'bread and circuses', and similar themes.

The low-group/grid context is an apt site of meeting for the
joking relationship and the spectacle. Through the former,
individuals actively reflect upon one another in a basically dyadic
pattern. The latter involves the mass participation of individual
isolates. The pattern of performer and spectator in the spectacle
is also essentially dyadic; for persons relate as individuals to
what they are viewing, whether these are athletic events (MacAloon
1977; Peacock 1974), or other forms of entertainment. Particularly
in this context, media of mass entertainment encourage the perpetuation of the dyadic relationship between spectator and performer.
Thus, large numbers of persons remain quite individuated, even when
together, while they passively absorb dramatic projections which
themselves do not necessarily reflect upon any reality known to
these spectators. In an important sense, the self-absorbed
individualist and the autonomous spectacle mirror one another within
the context of a weak group/weak grid.

Through spectacle, the self is freed; but its reflexive capacity
is turned largely inward. In the weak-group/strong-grid context,
this involution contributes to the insulation of roles. In the
weak-group/weak-grid context, the reflexivity of this involution
may be closer to that of fantasy than it is to commentary on reality.

Here reflexivity panders to the egoism of the self. This accords
with the freedom and with the passivity with which the self can
react, through play, in a comparatively unstructured context.

Given all of the above attributes, the messages of inter-subjective
play, through spectacle, are weak. They do not challenge the
validity of the cosmos; nor are they addressed directly to real
external boundaries, or to in-the-flesh social relationships.
Instead, spectacle holds up a mirror to the self, which the
spectator may mistake for a model of cosmic or social order.

EVENT AND CONTEXT: CONTINUITY AND CHANGE

Thus far I have suggested the following: that each of the events
discussed tends to be associated with different contexts; and that
these events vary in the degree of scale and the locus of self-
reflexivity which they evoke through play. Festival has the greatest
scale and the most loci of reflexivity: it may bring into question
the character of cosmic and social order, as well as that of the
external boundaries and internal lines of the group. Furthermore,
it may subsume, in its action, both symbolic reversals and joking
activity. Symbolic reversal tends to reinforce the external
boundaries of the group, and to question its internal lines. In
turn it may subsume joking behavior. The joking relationship tends
to question only particular social relationships. It has the least
degree of scale in reflexivity, and its locus tends to become quite
specific. By contrast with the other three events, spectacle
involutes and insulates the reflexivity of the self; and it is the
least concerned with cosmic order or with social groups.

In principle the grid/group scheme suggests that if a context
changes, change also should be expected in the kind of events
which are expressive of that context. Since their association is
not neat, one should not expect the changing relationship between
context and events to be simple: for each has a measure of
independence from the character of the other. None the less, there
is some evidence of the following: an event may help to recreate
that context with which it was previously associated, within a new
context; or the character of an event may alter as its context of
association changes. Examples of these two possibilities will be
discussed.

Davis's studies of the 'Abbeys of Misrule', in sixteenth-century
France, provide the first example (1971, 1978). The Abbeys
originated as organizations of unmarried men in peasant communities.
Through their charivaris and parades they commented continually on
internal lines within the community. (18) Their membership was
widespread, and included the sons of landed peasants as well as
those of the landless. They had a measure of jurisdiction over
persons their own age: for example, they commented on the morality
of village girls, by leaving either may bushes or smelly bushes
before their doors.

But the Abbeys also had some jurisdiction over persons older
than themselves: newly-weds who failed to become pregnant during
the first year, husbands who were dominated by their wives,
adulterers, and second marriages where there was a gross disparity

in age between groom and bride, all came under the 'carnival treatment
of reality' of the Abbeys (Davis 1971: 53). The penalizing of
persons older than themselves involved reversals of status on the
part of the youth (Davis 1971: 54). Such modes of symbolic reversal
were expressed in various ways. For example husbands beaten by their
wives were placed backwards on an ass and, accompanied by a masked
and noisy throng, were paraded through the village. In the charivari
itself, particularly when there were disparities in age between bride
and groom in second marriages the masked youth armed with pots,
tambourines, bells and horns, would clamor outside the house of the
victims, until they paid a fine. (19) In these and other ways the
village was reminded of certain imbalances or ambiguities in actual
social relationships. As Davis puts it, this 'carnival reversal of
status ... was very much in the service of the village community,
clarifying the responsibilities that the youth would have when they
were married men and fathers, and helping to maintain proper order
within marriage' (1971: 54). In their activities the Youth Abbeys
contributed to the defense of community identity, against the
external world (1971: 57).

The foregoing description is of an egalitarian community with
strong external boundaries and falls into the high-group/low-grid
context. Since the activities of the Youth Abbeys are modes of
symbolic reversal, the context and expressive event are associated
here in the expected way.

By the sixteenth century French cities were undergoing fairly
rapid urbanization. When compared to the peasant village, the life
of the city moved up-grid and down-group. Occupational groupings
and social-class distinctions became of increasing importance. The
Youth Abbeys were resurrected in the cities, but their criteria for
membership became more fragmented. To some, only men in certain
occupations could belong. In others, only the sons of the wealthy
were welcome. Still others were organized around a quarter or a
neighborhood. Davis notes that in none of these could men from all
the estates be drawn together (1971: 63).

But, of these various bases of organization, the one most
analogous to the peasant community was that of the quarter or
neighborhood. That is, within the relatively high-grid/low-group
matrix of the city, the neighborhood came closest to the context
of the rural village. As Davis (1971: 64) states: 'A neighborhood
grouping is more coherent and informative than an age grouping on a
busy street.' It is not clear to what extent the neighborhood
Abbeys helped to create a sense of 'community', in a street or
quarter: but some of these Abbeys were given a mandate, by
residents, to 'keep the peace and amity' in a given neighborhood.
Through continued symbolic reversals, these Abbeys commented on
local activities which highlighted ambiguity in the internal lines
of the comparatively homogeneous neighborhood: thus theft, murder,
bizarre marriage, seduction, and the merchant who cheated his
clients, were all commented on in playful ways (1971: 66). Therefore it is likely that in parts of these large cities these Abbeys
contributed both to the strengthening of external boundaries and
to the maintenance of internal lines.

Although some of the Abbeys became defunct in the cities, while
others lost much of their sense of playful misrule, still others

helped to recreate a strong neighborhood context within an urban milieu.   It was on the neighborhood level that the playful reversals of the Abbeys commented constructively on matters of importance.   In this example, the cultural event, with its capacity for playful commentary, helps to recreate a context best suited to its mode of expression.

The second example, that of the pre-Lenten Carnival in Caracas during the nineteenth century (Lavenda 1977, 1978), demonstrates how a change in context affected the kind of event associated with it.   Before 1873 Venezuela was a nation which consisted of a loose federation of states, rent by schism and by local revolts.

According to Lavenda (1977) the Caracas Carnival during this period was a spontaneous expression of symbolic reversal, organized on the basis of small groups.   For three days bands of people took to the streets in wild and rowdy celebration, which often caused injury.   The participants in the main were the poor and the powerless, who fought one another, but more often attacked those with status, as they hurled 'projectiles of barbarism':   paint, urine, eggs, ochre, plaster, and the like.   Lavenda (1977: 5) likens the pre-1873 Carnival to a 'rite of reversal' in which 'those who were usually without power ruled'.   In this period, then, there was the frequently observed association between a context of high group/low grid and a cultural event expressing symbolic reversal.

By 1873 the dictator Guzman Blanco centralized the state by making it a republic and suppressing local revolts and schisms. Determined to turn Venezuela into a Europeanized country, he succeeded in attracting foreign investment, and in the short term the economy of the country went into an upswing.   The nation and the city moved closer to a context of high group/grid.

When the time came for the 1873 Carnival all activities were centralized and highly organized in terms of an opposition between barbarism and civilization.   Costumed celebrants paraded, accompanied by carriages and floats decorated with allegorical motifs.   From houses, women threw down the projectiles of civilization - candies, confetti, streamers, and so forth.   In each parish there were further celebrations: a band played throughout each day, followed by fireworks, a public dance for the lower classes and private balls for the wealthy.   Each morning every parish had a large communal meal;   and on the last night there was a communal singing of the new songs of civilization.   Reports of the time insisted that these changes were very popular, and that most of the city's inhabitants, drawn from all classes and groups, participated together.

The event was organized and controlled from the top, to demonstrate the new centralization of polity and economy, to validate the positions of the old and new elites, and to bring about a measure of intermingling among all social categories, while affirming the class-based internal hierarchy of the city (and of the nation).   In terms of this essay the event began to approach that of a festival of mass participation, which confirmed external boundaries and confused internal lines.   In short, as Caracas moved towards the high-group/grid context, its Carnival began to change from one of symbolic reversal to one which approximated a festival.

By 1897 the economy of the country had plummeted (Lavenda 1978). The national debt was high;   imports and exports were down;   civil

war had become endemic, and the countryside ravaged. Unemployment
was high and the urban poor protested in large numbers. Moreover,
life in the city was divided by even sharper class divisions than
before. The city and the nation were moving up-grid and down-
group - in other words closer to or into a new context of low group/
high grid.
     The formal features of the 1897 Carnival had not changed much
from that of 1873. But the official program was shorter; little
formal entertainment was provided; unifying symbols of progress and
civilization were not invoked; there was neither communal singing
nor parades through each parish to the centre of the city. Moreover,
the problem of law and order again became prominent; while the
activities of the classes became completely separate.
     During the Carnival the main street was invaded by hordes of
starving children, and by others, who fought one another over
cookies and candies tossed from coaches by the wealthy. Later in
the Carnival tension rose to the point where the police were called
out in force, to prevent crowds from gathering. Lavenda writes
that the event had become a masque of degradation (1978: 9). In
terms of this essay, Carnival was moving away from its festival
form, and had come closer to becoming a spectacle. Thus, over a
period of some thirty years, this event termed 'carnival' appeared
to have changed its form from that of a mode of reversal to that of
a festival, and then to that of a spectacle - each time in keeping
with changes in the context of its occurrence.

CONCLUSION

On the limited evidence of these examples it is hard to specify
those conditions under which context and event influence one
another, or the direction such effects may take. I can suggest
only that the associations offered in this essay may hold, in a
general way, in synchronic and diachronic terms: and that there
is sufficient evidence to merit their further investigation. But
let me end on a more questioning note: the likelihood that
reflexivity is evoked, and that it has significance for mundane
existence.
     Throughout this essay I have assumed the following: (1) that
there are cultural events to which messages of play may be integral;
(2) that such messages of play contain commentaries or critiques
about everyday or about other realities; (3) that these commentaries
are reflexive for the self, awakening it momentarily to novel
perspectives on those premises of social order in which it is
ordinarily embedded; and (4) that the self, on its return to the
routine constraints of everyday life, carries such information
with it.
     My initial response to the problem of the evocation of reflexivity
is a systemic one, following from Bateson. There would be little
purpose to other states of reality, whether of play or of ritual,
were these not to carry information about social order which was
otherwise relatively unobtainable. If this view is valid, it
follows that the recipients of such information must be the social
selves of participants. If such information were embedded in the

routine and the mundane, reflexive perspectives would be evoked
only idiosyncratically, and would be dependent on the particular
life situation of each individual, at any given point in time. Such
a set-up could hardly ensure the perpetuation of social order.
Therefore, most of the events discussed tend to ensure that, together,
each member of a collectivity will receive similar information which
is not a part of routine life. Then their experience is reflexive,
and indeed is self-reflexive. This essay has concentrated on
certain organizational conditions of self-reflexivity.

But since such a systemic approach necessarily invokes the
experience of social selves, my further response to the question of
reflexivity would be phenomenological. Experience must have meaning:
and in the events discussed, this meaning must be cultural, in order
for it to be related to the conditions of mundane existence. For
example, Greenwood (1977) describes how a Spanish Basque festival,
the Alarde, which was an epitome of corporate socio-cultural
identity in a town, lost its meaning for participants when elements
of spectacle were introduced to it. Only by understanding how
information is meaningful can we get at its reflexive import in
particular cultural terms. This cultural aspect of self-reflexivity
has barely been touched on in this essay.

Yet a phenomenological perspective necessarily leads back to a
systemic one. If the sentiments evoked in particular events had
meaning only for their own duration, then this would hardly be self-
reflexive: for the experience of the event would be simply different
from that of ordinary life, and so would bear little relation to it.
But the social selves of individuals bridge unordinary and routine
states of collective existence: they are the carriers of information, of experience and of meaning. Therefore it is highly likely
that information which is transmitted to the self in expressive
events also has meaning for it in mundane life. In this regard,
the messages of play are as complementary for routine existence as
are those of other aesthetic modes of communication.

NOTES

1 A preliminary version of this essay was written during the
   tenure of a Mellon Research Fellowship in the Department of
   Anthropology, University of Pittsburgh, 1977-78. This present
   version was written while I was a Fellow of the Institute of
   Social and Economic Research, Memorial University of Newfoundland,
   August-September 1978.
2 Following Bateson (1972a), the epistemological assumption here is
   that all of the information which a viable social unit requires
   for its survival is not communicated through everyday, routine,
   channels of information-transmission. Instead, such information
   may be communicated through the reality and media of myth, ritual,
   art, dance, music, and so forth. Play is one such medium which
   carries reflective messages to the self.
3 Within each category of event, there will be a degree of overlap
   between ethnographic examples. This is necessary to respect the
   cultural validity of each example, while abstracting those of its
   attributes which are relevant to the thesis of this essay.

4   This transformation of ordinary reality occurs in two ways.
First, by changing the valencies of the reality of reference of
play: for example, through reversal, through the abrogation of
otherwise valid social distinctions and forms, and by providing
inverse access to roles (Sutton-Smith 1977: 24). Then such
altered valencies, valid within the world of play, are invalid
within their reality of reference (ordinary reality, ritual
reality, etc.), because their perception is guided by make-believe
and by pretense. Second, such a transformation occurs as an
abstraction, or analogue, of its reality of reference. Here,
attributes of ordinary reality are not necessarily altered, but
the logic of their interrelationship is. Although modelled on a
reality of reference the logic of their play messages are refinements of 'essential versions' of this reality, and hence different
from it (contra Abrahams and Bauman 1978). For, to paraphrase
Bateson and others, the model cannot be that thing which is modelled.

5   The conceptual basis of this argument is given in Handelman (1977a).
There I argue that play is to be distinguished from ritual, with
which it shares similarities, by their respective meta-messages
(see also Rapaport 1971).

6   A brief distinction should be made here between 'play' and
'game'. Forms of play are limited by the representations upon
which they are based, in the phenomenal world. 'Playing at
houses', or at 'being a cowboy' or an 'airplane', is limited by
the meanings and actions inherent in these roles or objects in
the routine phenomenal world. 'Play' is thus 'play-upon-form'.
On the other hand, 'game' is meaningful only in terms of the
arbitrary and conventional form of its rules, however these are
composed. But both are predicated upon the same elementary
meta-message of 'make-believe'; and therefore the messages of
both can comment on other realities.

7   This is in contrast to the intellectualist view adopted, for
example, by Basil Bernstein, who suggests that: 'Reflexiveness
refers to the degree to which an individual is able to make
explicit verbally the principles underlying object and person
relationships' (Bernstein and Henderson 1973).

8   Sienese world view is inward-looking. The concept of the middle
is considered to be life-giving and life-renewing. The race is
held in the centre of Siena, and all contrade face this location.
The race itself is held at twilight, in the middle of day and
night (Dundes and Falassi 1975: 230 ff.).

9   A simplification - only ten horses run in each race, for reasons
not pertinent to this discussion.

10 Before the race, the horse is treated as a creature in a state
of separation. That it is matched with a jockey, who comes from
outside the city, clearly indicates that it has become a vessel
betwixt and between, within which normal boundaries, and the
symbolic domains they separate, have become confounded (see
Dundes and Falassi 1975: 97).

11 In another high-group/low-grid context, the Iatmul of New Guinea,
I argue that the clarification of ambiguity, in the relationship
between the mother's brother and the sister's son, is predicated
on an inversion of identity on the part of the mother's brother.
This inversion, based on messages of play, contains within it the

12 logic of a reversal back to the normal state of the relationship (Handelman 1979).

12 This may be so also where this context itself exists within a different one. Elsewhere (Handelman 1976, 1977b: 154-74; see also Chrisman 1974: 374), I have given examples of playful symbolic reversals within small groups which comment on the state of relationships within them.

13 A very similar analysis can be done also with belsnickling (Christmas mumming), on the La Have Islands off the coast of Nova Scotia (Bauman 1972; Abrahams and Bauman 1978). But I have not the space to go into this here.

14 In terms of the African sector alone, this context could be described as weak group/weak grid. Kalela points up the difficulty of deciding which perspective to adopt in deciding upon the relevant context.

15 When such encapsulation occurs, the following argument by Caillois (1959) has applicability: everyday life controls the sacred through taboos. The ritual frame frees man from everyday reality. In turn, the further inversion of the sacred (through transgression, sacrilege, play) frees man from the sacred - in my terms to reflect upon both ritual messages and everyday reality. Although I think that such arrangements are associated more with contexts in which the group boundary is reified, rather than questioned, the whole subject has hardly been explored. See also Handelman (1977a, 1981).

16 Joking between different tribal categories, outside of Kalela, also invoked a context of strong group/weak grid; but one with a lesser range of commentary than that of the dance itself.

17 The extreme high-group/grid context seems to suggest that the individual is what his presentation or transaction suggests that he is (cf. Marriott 1976). In this context then there would appear to be less of a division between one's public and private selves. On the other hand, the extreme weak-group/grid context would suggest that one is never what he presents himself to be, at least in public (cf. Goffman 1959). Then in the latter context there would be a clear division between the public self intended for most others, and the private self which is reserved for intimacy and trust, and which must be buffered from public presentation. Therefore this latter context is loaded with all kinds of pretense and face-games. And it is because of this that 'special' relationships, like that of friendship, become particularly important to the private self; and that 'special' signs, like that of joking, become hallmarks of intimacy which such friendship requires.

18 Leaders of Abbeys were given names like Abbot of Gaiety, Duke Kickass, Prince of Fools, Grand Patriarch of Syphilitics, and so forth.

19 Here I have not the space to go into the reasons such relations were ambiguous or imbalanced. The reader is referred to Davis's (1971) discussion.

BIBLIOGRAPHY

ABRAHAMS, ROGER D. and RICHARD BAUMAN (1978), Ranges of festival
behavior, in 'The Reversible World', ed. B. Babcock, Ithaca, Cornell
University Press.
BATESON, GREGORY (1972a), 'Steps to an Ecology of Mind', New York,
Ballantine.
BATESON, GREGORY (1972b), Toward a theory of play and fantasy', in
'Steps to an Ecology of Mind', New York, Ballantine.
BAUMAN, RICHARD (1972), Belsnickling in a Nova Scotia island
community, 'Western Folklore' 31: 229-43.
BERNSTEIN, BASIL and E. HENDERSON (1973), Social class difference
in the relevance of language and socialization, ch. 2: 45-6 in
'Class, Codes and Control', vol. 2, 'Applied Studies towards a
Sociology of Language', London, Routledge & Kegan Paul.
CAILLOIS, ROGER (1959), 'Man and the Sacred', Chicago, Free Press.
CHRISMAN, NOEL J. (1974), Middle-class communitas: the fraternal
order of Badgers, 'Ethos' 2: 356-76.
CODERE, HELEN (1956), The amiable side of Kwakiutl life: the
potlatch and the play potlatch, 'American Anthropologist' 58: 334-51.
CSIKZENTMIHALYI, M. and S. BENNETT (1971), An exploratory model of
play, 'American Anthropologist' 73: 45-58.
DAVIS, NATALIE ZEMON (1971), The reasons of misrule: youth groups
and charivaris in sixteenth-century France, 'Past and Present'
50: 41-75.
DAVIS, NATALIE ZEMON (1978), Women on top, in 'The Reversible
World', ed. B. Babcock, Ithaca, Cornell University Press.
DOUGLAS, MARY (1968), The social control of cognition: some factors
in joke perception, 'Man' (NS) 3: 361-76.
DOUGLAS, MARY (1970), 'Natural Symbols', New York, Vintage.
DOUGLAS, MARY (1978), 'Cultural Bias', London, Royal Anthropological
Institute, occasional Paper no. 35.
DUNDES, ALAN and ALESSANDRO FALASSI (1975), 'La Terra in Piazza:
an Interpretation of the Palio of Siena', Berkeley, University of
California Press.
GIRARD, RENE (1977), 'Violence and the Sacred', Baltimore, Johns
Hopkins University Press.
GLUCKMAN, MAX (1954), 'Rituals of Rebellion in South-East Africa',
Manchester University Press.
GOFFMAN, ERVING (1959), 'The Presentation of Self in Everyday Life',
New York, Doubleday Anchor.
GOUREVITCH, ARON I. (1975), The comic and the serious in religious
literature of the Middle Ages, 'Diogenes' no. 90: 56-77.
GREENWOOD, DAVYDD (1977), Culture by the pound: an anthropological
perspective on tourism as cultural commoditization, in 'Hosts and
Guests: The Anthropology of Tourism', ed. Valene L. Smith,
Philadelphia, University of Pennsylvania Press, pp. 129-38.
HANDELMAN, DON (1976), Rethinking 'banana time': symbolic integration
in a work setting, 'Urban Life' 4: 433-48.
HANDELMAN, DON (1977a), Play and ritual: complementary frames of
metacommunication, in 'It's a Funny Thing, Humour', ed. A.J. Chapman
and H. Foot, London, Pergamon.
HANDELMAN, DON (1977b), 'Work and Play Among the Aged', Assen/
Amsterdam, Van Gorcum.

HANDELMAN, DON (1979), Is Naven ludic? Paradox and the communication of identity, 'Social Analysis', 1: 177-91.
HANDELMAN, DON (1981), The ritual clown: attributes and affinities, 'Anthropos', forthcoming.
HANDELMAN, DON and BRUCE KAPFERER (1972), Forms of joking activity: a comparative approach, 'American Anthropologist' 74: 484-517.
HUIZINGA, J. (1970), 'Homo Ludens', London, Palladin.
KAPFERER, BRUCE (1977), 'Rituals, audiences and the problem of reflexivity: exorcism and festival in Sri Lanka', Burg Wartenstein Symposium no. 76 (Cultural Frames and Reflections).
KENNEDY, JOHN G. (1970), Bonds of laughter among the Tarahumara: toward a rethinking of joking relationship theory, in 'The Social Anthropology of Latin America' ed. W. Goldschmidt and H. Hoijer, Berkeley, University of California Press.
LABOV, W. (1972), Rules for ritual insults, in 'Studies in Social Interaction', ed. D. Sudnow, New York, Free Press.
LANGER, SUSANNE K. (1953), 'Feeling and Form', New York, Scribners.
LAVENDA, ROBERT H. (1977), The festival of progress: anthropology, history and the transformation of the Caracas Carnival, 76th Annual Meeting of the American Anthropological Association, Houston.
LAVENDA, ROBERT H. (1978), From festival of progress to masque of degradation: Carnival in Caracas as a changing metaphor for social reality, 4th Annual Meeting of the Association for the Anthropological Study of Play, Notre Dame University.
MACALOON, JOHN J. (1977), Olympic games and the theory of spectacle in modern societies, Burg Wartenstein Symposium no. 76 (Cultural Frames and Reflections).
MARRIOTT, McKIM (1976), Hindu transactions: diversity without dualism, in 'Transaction and Meaning', ed. B. Kapferer, Philadelphia, Institute for the Study of Human Issues.
MILLER, S. (1973), Ends, means, and galumphing: some leitmotifs of play, 'American Anthropologist' 75: 87-98.
MITCHELL, J. CLYDE (1959), 'The Kalela Dance', Manchester University Press.
MOORE, S.F. and B. MYERHOFF (1978), Introduction, in 'Secular Ritual', ed. S.F. Moore and B. Myerhoff, Assen/Amsterdam: Van Gorcum.
NORBECK, EDWARD (1967), African rituals of conflict, in 'Gods and Ritual', ed. J. Middleton, New York, Natural History Press.
PEACOCK, JAMES L. (1974), Secular ritual in archaic but changing society: Java and the American South, Burg Wartenstein Symposium no. 64 (Secular Rituals Reconsidered).
PHYTHIAN-ADAMS, CHARLES (1972), Ceremony and the citizen: the communal year at Coventry, 1450-1550, in 'Crisis and Order in English Towns', ed. P. Clark and P. Slack, London, Routledge & Kegan Paul.
PIERSSENS, MICHEL (1972), Market, fair, and festival, 'Diogenes' no. 78: 1-17.
RADCLIFFE-BROWN, A.R. (1952), On joking relationships, in 'Structure and Function in Primitive Society', London, Cohen & West.
RAPAPORT, R.A. (1971), Ritual, sanctity, and cybernetics, 'American Anthropologist' 73: 59-76.
RENSON, ROLAND (1977), Kings shooting and shooting kings, TAASP Newsletter 4: 15-18.
SCHWARTZMAN, JOHN (1977), Art, science, and change in Western society, 'Ethos' 5: 239-62.

SPECK, FRANK G. and LEONARD BROOM, with the assistance of Will West
Long (1951), 'Cherokee Dance and Drama', Berkeley: University of
California Press.
SUMBERG, SAMUEL L. (1966), 'The Nuremberg Schembart Carnival' (1941,
Columbia University Press), New York, AMS Press.
SUTTON-SMITH, BRIAN (1977), Games of order and disorder,'TAASP
Newsletter' 4: 19-26.
SUTTLES, G. (1970), Friendship as a social institution, in 'Social
Relationships', ed. George McCall et al., Chicago, Aldine.
TURNER, VICTOR (1969), 'The Ritual Process', Chicago, Aldine.
TURNER, VICTOR (1974), Liminal to liminoid in play, flow and ritual,
'Rice University Studies', vol. 60.
VOGT, EVON Z. (1973), Rituals of reversal as a means of rewiring
social structure, IXth ICAES, Chicago.

Chapter 9

POLYHEDRA AND THE ABOMINATIONS OF LEVITICUS: COGNITIVE STYLES IN MATHEMATICS
David Bloor

How are social and institutional circumstances linked to the
knowledge that scientists produce? To answer this question it is
necessary to take risks: speculative but testable theories must be
proposed. It will be my aim to explain and then apply one such
theory. This will enable me to propose an hypothesis about the
connexion between social processes and the style and content of
mathematical knowledge.

To do this I shall bring together the ideas of two books. One
of these is Imré Lakatos's 'Proofs and Refutations' (1976); (1)
this describes the history of a mathematical dispute, and it is
also a piece of advocacy in the philosophy of mathematics. The
other is Mary Douglas's 'Natural Symbols' (1973), (2) which contains
an anthropological theory about pollution, ritual, dietary
restrictions, and religious cosmologies. The books have a common
theme: they deal with the way men respond to things which do not
fit into the boxes and boundaries of accepted ways of thinking;
they are about anomalies to publicly-accepted schemes of classification. Whether it be a counterexample to a proof; an animal
which does not fit into the local taxonomy; or a deviant who violates
the current moral norms, the same range of reactions is generated.
Both writers have, in their own way and unknown to one another,
charted and illustrated this range.

Once the similarity of their conclusions has been spotted,
insights can be transferred from one account to the other. The
crucial point is that Mary Douglas has an explanation of why there
are different responses to things which break the orderly boundaries
of our thinking: these responses are characteristic of different
social structures. Her theory spells out why this will be so, and
describes some of the mechanisms linking the social and the cognitive.
This means we should be able to predict the social circumstances
which lie behind the different responses which mathematicians make
to the troubles in their proofs. The first thing will be to look at
Lakatos's philosophy of mathematics in some detail.

I

Everyone remembers the mathematical textbook which begins with long
and complicated definitions, announces a surprising theorem, and
then develops an austerely compelling proof. Definition; theorem;
proof; QED. No, says Lakatos; this is all upside down. What
really come at the beginning are not definitions, but problems and
conjectured solutions to them. Theorems are conjectures. Like all
conjectures they need testing, and proofs, odd though this may
sound, are attempts to test them. (3) In opposition to the usual
dogmatic and 'formalist' ideas about mathematics Lakatos favours a
'fallibilist' approach. He presents himself as a follower of both
Popper and Hegel. (4)
     Proofs start with a 'thought-experiment', or exploit some quasi-
empirical procedure to break down the problematic conjecture,
embedding it into what may be a quite distinct body of knowledge.
Each step in this decomposition of the theorem becomes a possible
source of error. It will fail if exceptions are found to it.
Exceptions to the steps of the proof Lakatos calls 'local' counterexamples; exceptions to the original conjecture are 'global'
counterexamples. Once a proof has been advanced, the original
conjecture is even more vulnerable than it was before, for now it
risks local objections as well as the global ones.
     The main example Lakatos uses to illustrate this idea is Euler's
theorem: that for polyhedra the number of faces (F), edges (E),
and vertices (V) are related by the formula $V-E+F=2$. This guess,
first put forward in 1758, can easily be verified for cubes and
prisms and pyramids, but does it work for all polyhedra? The
history of the conjecture is a history of attempted proofs, counterexamples and revised proofs. The argument lasted until Poincaré's
work in 1899 seemed to stop the squabbles. (5)
     Lakatos starts the story with a proof based on the work of
Cauchy, Crelle and Cayley. Imagine that the polyhedron is hollow
and made of rubber - this is the quasi-experiment. One face is
then removed so that now $V-E+F=1$, provided that the original
conjecture is true. The polyhedron is then stretched flat and extra
lines are drawn joining the vertices so that the faces turn into
sets of (perhaps curvilinear) triangles. Every new edge produces a
new face so that the equation $V-E+F=1$ is not disturbed. The triangles
are then removed one by one. This can be done so that the number of
edges, faces and vertices that disappear with each removal of a
triangle still leaves the equation the same. Finally one triangle
is left for which, trivially, $V=3$, $E=3$ and $F=1$, so the equation
$V-E+F=1$ still balances. The condition for it holding was that the
original conjecture is true; nothing in the proof procedure has
altered the value of V, E, and F; so the original conjecture is
true.
     Or is it? First Euler's theorem is attacked with local counter-
examples. Can all polyhedra be stretched flat? What about a
picture-frame shape? Even if they can be flattened, can the faces
always be triangulated without disturbing the equation? What about
a cube with another cube sitting on top of it in the middle of one
of its faces (6) - a 'crested cube'? A line joining an inner and an
outer vertex of the rectangular border around the top cube does not

increase the number of faces, so triangulation breaks down here.
Criticisms and exceptions like this lead to refinements and
qualifications to the proof procedure: it has to be restricted to
'simple' polyhedra that are topologically equivalent to a sphere
so that they can be stretched flat when one face has been removed.
And it has to be limited to polyhedra with 'simply connected' faces
to exclude the ring-shaped areas for which triangulation fails. (7)

Global objections are considered next. These invariably spark
off definitional controversies. For example, what about a cube
with another cube hollowed out of the middle? For these 'nested
cubes', V−E+F=4.   They were first spotted by Lhuilier in 1812 and
rediscovered by Hessel in 1832; both men had been looking at
crystals which sometimes take this form. (8) Again, what about two
tetrahedra joined at a vertex? Each one singly satisfies the
theorem, but the Siamese twin does not: V1E+F=3. (9) Or what about
a cylinder? Here there are no vertices, only 2 edges and 3 faces,
so V−E+F=1. The problem is whether these are really counterexamples,
or whether they are not exceptions which refute the theorem because
they are not the kind of thing the conjecture was meant to cover.
After all, what is a polyhedron? At first it may have seemed obvious
what it meant for a shape to be 'like' a cube and a prism. Of course
a cylinder is not a polyhedron, but why not? The counterexamples
make the boundaries of the species look problematic.

This is the origin of those complicated definitions. It emerges
that a polyhedron is not to be thought of as a solid, it is a system
of polygonal surfaces; and exactly two faces have to meet at every
edge; and it must be possible to get from any face to any other
without crossing a vertex; and through any arbitrary point it must
be possible to draw a plane that will slice the polyhedron into
only one polygonal cross section, etc., etc. (10) These qualifications trace the history of the struggle between those who support
the conjecture and those who propose the counterexamples. As
Lakatos says, they do not precede the proof, but really come at the
end.

So far this could all be accepted without much change in the
usual dogmatic view of mathematics. Everyone knows that argument
helps to uncover the holes in our reasoning. Won't mathematicians
argue until somebody has hit upon a real proof, then the argument
has to stop? This misses Lakatos's point. To see why, we must
look further into what he says, particularly at what he calls
'concept-stretching'.

II

We have seen that a proof begins with the invention of a technique
or procedure, like stretching or triangulating. This can be carried
out on a limited number of familiar figures, but everything
surrounding this narrow area of accomplishment is, at first, simply
darkness. The accomplishment is mute about its own scope and about
the broader range of contingencies to which it may come to be
related. It says nothing about whether such things as nested cubes
or twin tetrahedra do, or even can, exist; or whether they have any
relevance to the study of polyhedra.

This approach to proofs may be called 'finitist'. (11)   The point is that a proof procedure does not have a set of preordained implications outside the immediate context of use.   How it comes to be accorded these implications as that context of use is extended is precisely what Lakatos is investigating.   He is not saying that the implications pre-exist but we do not know what they are: the implications await our creation.   In particular, the question of whether there are counterexamples to a proof procedure is not settled in advance.

Our normal habits of thought do not allow us to entertain such a striking idea.   Suppose there are no counterexamples to a conjecture: surely there are only two possible explanations?   There really are counterexamples, but no-one has noticed them;   or the range of cases that could be cited as counterexamples has been exhausted.   Is reality not a kind of store-house of all possible cases, and does this not determine whether a theorem is correct or not?   Variants of this compelling view are usually dubbed 'Platonism'.   Most of us, most of the time, are Platonists.   We usually think that mathematical objects or structures fall into a unique, natural set of kinds or sorts, as if there are specially privileged 'real' boundaries which demarcate different kinds of thing.   In short we assume a limited stock of Essences or Forms.

This is what Lakatos rejects.   He treats mathematical 'kinds' as being our creations.   We draw the boundary lines.   Classification is our achievement and our problem.   Nothing is to be gained by seeing different boundary lines as more or less corresponding to the 'real' ones.   But this is not all.   For Lakatos the world is so densely populated by objects of all shapes and sizes, and there are so many imaginable procedures that can be based on them, that there is an indefinitely large number of different boundaries that we might reasonably draw.   Unlike the sparser, pre-packaged picture of the world suggested by Platonism, where there are clear gaps on the shelves between the different kinds of thing, for Lakatos the world is more densely stocked.   There will always be some equivalent to that surprising stream of nested cubes, crested cubes, twin-tetrahedra and picture frames which gushed forth and threatened to swamp Euler's conjecture.

Can we escape this difficulty by using very simple principles of classification?   Even if we cannot decide what should count as a polyhedron we can surely decide once and for all what is to count as, say, a vertex, or an edge, or a plane?   If we retreated into using absolutely simple and perfectly understood terms we might build up the more complicated classifications out of these.   Then our reasoning would be so clear that everyone would always know exactly what was being said.   Decisive proof or decisive disproof would be possible.   There might be some verbal differences but at least there would be a nucleus of achievement that would be perfectly secure against further counterexamples or disagreement.

No, says Lakatos again: simple ideas can always be turned into complex ones and the whole problem started again.   The belief in a fixed basic vocabulary of perfectly understood terms is an illusion created by our verbal habits.   We become habituated to a certain usage in a particular context;   it becomes 'obvious', transparent, and direct.   We think that we will know exactly how to use the word in all future cases, as if there were a unique and natural way of extending it outside its old range. This is wrong, because new proof procedures can decompose any idea, however simple. They bring to it a new context, suggest new connotations and hence endow it with a new, inner complexity. What the Cauchy proof-procedure did for our idea of polyhedra could be done for any concept including point and line. Our concepts can always be 'stretched'.

Is Lakatos saying that there always will be counterexamples to theorems? In one sense, yes he is: there will always be objects that could be used to make a mockery of our classifications. But potentiality is not actuality; for something to be actually a counterexample requires another step: it depends on its being accorded this status. Being a counterexample is a role which is conferred upon something, and this depends on how it is used. When we say that we 'recognize' things as counterexamples we ought not to mean that we directly apprehend the intrinsic and permanent character of the thing; the visual metaphor, with its usual platonizing connotations, is wrong. We should use the word 'recognize' as we do when we say a man achieves recognition by being honoured. Conferring a knighthood is not revealing that a man was, all along, a knight. Because 'counterexamplehood' is likewise a social achievement, men are incessently pushing and pulling at the boundaries of their concepts, trying to achieve a better or a different order, and of course, using different conceptions of order to suit their different aims. As order is achieved in one place, so it will be disturbed in others. More anomalies will be created, and previous achievements will be thrown out of joint. For example Cauchy used the concept of 'polyhedron' to cover roughly what we would call 'convex polyhedron'. (12) On his usage Euler's conjecture looked like a general theorem that covered all things properly called 'polyhedra'. When this class was stretched to include previously ignored figures, the proof procedure ceased to be generally applicable and the original conjecture was frequently violated. This is not an isolated case; a similar thing happened with the idea of a 'function'. (13)

On the one hand, then, Lakatos uses his finitist idea of a proof procedure to remove guarantees against counterexamples, and on the other he introduces his assumption of complexity and his picture of concept-stretching, which between them guarantee that there always will be things which could be used as counterexamples. Before looking at the great significance of this conclusion we had better consider and answer some objections to how it was reached.

III

It may be said that Lakatos is making a trivial, purely verbal point: when the meaning of a word is changed then of course sentences that were previously true become false. If the word 'bachelor' is 'stretched' to cover men who merely behave like bachelors then of course it will be false that all bachelors are unmarried men - though in terms of the original meaning it is as true as ever.

This fails to meet Lakatos's point. He is saying that concept-stretching and the redrawing of classificatory boundaries is an integral part of mathematical reasoning. Trying out wider and different applications of concepts, and making the consequent adjustments to theorems and definitions is something that is going on all the time. Changing the meaning of concepts in this way is not a subterfuge to be shrugged off, as if the counterexamples it created were unimportant. (14) This is because our intellectual judgments are guided by the properties of our overall system of thought, not by its isolated elements. In the interests of overall coherence any particular achievement may be subverted and any theorem may have to be modified: 'You cannot separate refutations and proofs on the one hand and changes in the conceptual, taxonomical, linguistic framework on the other.' (15)

The Platonist will not be at a loss for an argument to express his distaste for this conclusion. Surely, he will say, if concept-stretching is to be plausible a term cannot be stretched at will. (16)   A theorem about polyhedra could not really be refuted by citing one of the properties of a cylinder as a counterexample. If the term 'polyhedra' were stretched to cover cylinders it would simply create an ambiguity in the meaning of the word. It would be using it to refer to two different kinds of thing. If we are not to lapse into confusion, then our words must respect the natural boundaries between different sorts of thing. Once this constraint is acknowledged, the Platonist will continue, then Lakatos's claim fails: there is no guarantee that genuine or unambiguous counter-examples can be produced merely by reclassification or concept-stretching.

Of course this is precisely what is at issue: are there any boundaries which our words must respect? This is what divides Lakatos from the Platonist in the first place. What gives Platonism its plausibility, and what is correct about the objection in the previous paragraph, is that at any given time there are limits to the amount and direction of concept-stretching and reclassification. The exact character of these constraints is indeed an unsolved problem, but one thing is clear; the constraints can be seen as relative, not absolute. They may be explained by pragmatic considerations related to the difficulties of evolving a shared and workable form of knowledge out of the vested interests and habits of the past. They need not be explained by the alleged need of our words to reflect the ultimately real demarcations between things. We must remember the extensive freedom we have exercised in the past in redrawing the accepted boundaries between different sorts of thing. In the history of science, model has been piled on model, metaphor upon metaphor. Add to this the varied interests which knowledge has served, and the constraints felt by the Platonist seem more like historical contingencies than timeless necessities.

We can now leave behind the trivializing idea that criticism in mathematics merely removes error and reveals truth; the situation is more complicated and more interesting than that. Lakatos is saying that the stability and scope of every theorem is precarious: critical argument and adjustment is in principle endless; there is no final truth to reveal, only a ramified and interlocking network of claims and counterclaims to be balanced and stabilized. (17)

There is, however, a further step which Lakatos does not take but

which is suggested by his picture. If the stream of potential counterexamples is endless, then the processes whereby we accord, or fail to
accord, recognition of them must also be endlessly at work. Without
their remorseless operation and that of the forces which govern them,
there would be neither order nor coherence in mathematical knowledge.
Its classifications, its counterexamples and its theorems would have
no agreed relations to one another. The great significance of
Lakatos's work is that it makes the forces which govern the response
to anomaly constitutive of mathematical knowledge: they are a
necessary part of that knowledge.

A metaphor may help. We can say that Lakatos has shown us that
mathematics is something that has to be 'negotiated'. Logically it
is totally underdetermined, but if it is to be real knowledge,
something objective rather than a confusion of subjective opinion,
then it must be determined somehow. The answer is that it is
socially determined in the course of negotiations: mathematics is
whatever is the outcome, and nothing more. Lakatos, however, has
given us only an abstract account of these negotiations. Put
bluntly, things are at stake, but Lakatos does not tell us what, so
we only have half the story. To get the whole story we need to
know if there are any general patterns in these endlessly necessary
negotiations, and what the currency is in terms of which profits
and losses are calculated. What investments do men have in changing
or in maintaining the boundaries of mathematical concepts?

As to the patterns themselves Lakatos is both informative and
ingenious. He plays out the history of Euler's theorem in the form
of an imaginary classroom debate between a teacher and a number of
terrifyingly precocious pupils called Alpha, Beta and so on. The
pupils adopt different methodological strategies: Alpha throws
counterexamples at the theorem and declares it refuted, while Delta
defends it by expedient redefinitions and other ploys. The pupils
are the spokesmen for the real mathematicians who struggled over
the theorem, and the classroom arguments have all been culled from
the historical record of this and similar events. Unfortunately
this form of presentation has its snags, for again it is abstract.
It makes the pattern of debate look as if it depends on nothing
more than the personal preferences or the 'intellectual needs' of
individuals. (18) It should in fact be placed in a social framework, and this is where Mary Douglas's theory comes in.

IV

Anthropologists have given us detailed studies of how different
social groups endow their world with intellectual coherence. They
have found systematically different conceptions of pollution and
dirt, edibility and misdemeanour. The proper ordering of social
behaviour and relationships, of household space, the passage of
time, and the division of labour are all, in their own way,
classifications that must be protected against violation. Since
Durkheim, anthropologists have argued that the patterns of domestic
and common-place life can often be detected in a group's wider
system of classifications: those that range over the animal and
plant world, and ultimately over the whole of the natural order.

Squabbles over wives and neighbours and illnesses and gifts and
contracts find counterparts in beliefs about God and Nature and the
great forces that discipline the world. (19)

Why is this? One theory is that men use their ideas about Nature
and Divinity to legitimate their institutions. It is put around that
deviation is unnatural, displeasing to the gods, unhealthy, expensive,
and time consuming. These instinctive ruses map nature onto society.
Nature becomes a code for talking about society, a language in which
justifications and challenges can be expressed. It is a medium of
social interaction.

Social arrangements can also be used as models with which to
grasp the physical or metaphysical order of things. They are a deep
well of metaphorical resources, although the conditions which prompt
their use in this way are not yet fully understood. But again, the
effect is to produce a structural identity between the social and
natural orders. (20) Either way, it is easy to see that classificatory anomalies may take on a moral significance. By these hidden
routes they acquire the connotations of irregular social behaviour,
which makes a response to them all the more urgent.

One response is to 'taboo' the anomaly which violates the
classification, declaring it an abomination and seeing it as a
symbol of threat and disorder. What were the abominations of
Leviticus, asks Mary Douglas, but a list of anomalies to the animal
classification so carefully laid down in the Pentateuch. The pig,
for example, fails to satisfy all the proper conditions for being
a ruminant: it does not both cleave the hoof and chew the cud. This
principle also explains why the list includes eels, rock badgers,
and others whose status as abominations has always perplexed biblical
commentators. Their common characteristic is that they all clumsily
straddle the boundary lines of God's demarcations. We shall
understand why the Jews did not eat pork when we see the social
significance attached to this classificatory scheme. (21)

Pollution-conscious societies are usually small, and often rent
by competition and conflicting loyalties. They survive by the
threat of expulsion, or suffer repeated schism. They are frequently
subject to outside threat and consequently their whole system of
classification is pervaded by the dichotomy between the good inside
and the evil and perverted outside. They need to exercise and
symbolize high group control. Strict observance of the group's
system of classification distinguishes loyal insiders from traitors
and strangers - hence the use of animal taxonomies to impose dietary
restrictions. Internal discord is construed in terms of penetration
and pollution by outside forces. Among the best examples of such
groups are the villages of central Africa which conduct their
politics through the idiom of witchcraft accusations. (22)

What an interesting jolt to turn to Lakatos and see that this is
exactly how Delta responds to anomalies like the cube with another
cube cut out of its middle: 'It is a *monster*, a pathological case,
not a counterexample', he cries. (23) The same boundary-drawing
rhetoric of exclusion is found in Jonquières who says of the picture
frame that it is merely a 'polyhedral complex' not a polyhedron
'in the ordinary sense of the word'. (24) Similarly, Schläfli says
of the small stellated dodecahedron that it is not 'a genuine
polyhedron' (25) and Baltzer goes so far as to say 'It would be more

appropriate to find a special name for non-genuine (uneigentliche)
polyhedra' (i.e. for those in which V-E+F does not =2. (26))
   This whole style of response, which seems to have been very
prominent in the history of mathematics, Lakatos dubs 'monster-
barring'. (27) He could not have hit on a better name. Lakatos
further shows his grasp of this consciousness of pollution when he
has Delta declare: 'I am gradually losing interest in your monsters.
I turn in disgust from your lamentable "polyhedra", for which
Euler's beautiful theorem doesn't hold. I look for order and harmony
in mathematics, but you only propogate anarchy and chaos.' (28)
Again, this rhetoric is not mere fancy on Lakatos's part: he is
making Delta paraphrase a letter of Hermite's to Stieltjes, although
the topic there is the theory of real functions. (29)
   It is easy to see how a mathematical counterexample could provoke
monster-barring. Imagine a closed group of practitioners with a
leadership whose authority derives, say, from the discovery of a
theorem. A counterexample becomes the basis for a revolution.
Rivals can use it as a justification for a take-over. Attitudes
towards the counterexample will have to polarize. From one point
of view it is indeed the symbol of a monstrous threat. Only the
ensuing power struggle will decide whether the anomaly really is,
say, a polyhedron or not. Reality has no other basis here. Personal
preferences have little role in all this. Suppose a compromiser
spoke out. As long as total victory were possible, to adopt the
compromise would mean that one side or the other would lose ground;
nobody could afford to listen, so polarity and exclusive boundaries
would be the form of the knowledge. When the dust settled this is
how it would be passed on to others. Explicit propositions about
polyhedra will be implicit propositions about society: platonic
essences will mirror social power.
   Now let us look at a more elaborate response to anomaly. Imagine
a large, diverse but stable system of institutions. Many interests
have been accommodated in it and complex relations have emerged
between the different segments of society. Correspondingly complex
conceptual accommodations are needed to justify them and render
them intelligible. It is here that elaborate theologies and
metaphysics are generated. There will be little anxiety about
pollution because there is no simple social dichotomy for it to
symbolize. It will be the internal structure of boundaries that
will be the focus of concern. The salient feature will be the
automatic response to those who disturb the complex equilibrium.
The efficacy of received forms and symbols, ritual rather than
pollution, will be the theme. Nature will be seen in a way that
upholds this pattern; institutional boundaries will be seen as the
boundaries between the powers or parts of nature. All this suggests
an extensive repertoire of methods for responding to anomaly and
for their reclassification. They will be fitted in somewhere, or
the classificatory scheme will be expanded. Complicated rites of
atonement; promotions and demotions; special exceptions;
distinctions, assimilations and legal fictions will abound. And
pervading the use of all these expedients there will be a vague
sense of overriding unity.
   Here again there is the shock of recognition on moving from
'Natural Symbols' to 'Proofs and Refutations'. These techniques are

described in detail in Lakatos's account of what he calls the 'monster-adjustment' (30) and the 'exception-barring' (31) methods. Monster-adjustment is practised by the casuistical Rho who shows that we can learn to see many of the counterexamples in a way which makes them fit Euler's theorem after all. We have to realize that polyhedra have 'hidden' edges. As Matthiessen put it: 'any polyhedron can be analyzed in such a way that it corroborates Euler's theorem.... In each such case we can show that the polyhedron has hidden faces and edges, which, if counted, leave the theorem V-E+F=2 untarnished even for these seemingly recalcitrant cases'. (32)

Exception-barring is equally 'scholastic', accommodating the anomaly by drawing more subdivisions. A boundary can be drawn between the theorem and the acknowledged exceptions to it. All that a counterexample does is to restrict the scope of the theorem: its truth is untouched but the span of its authority, as it were, is narrower than had been thought. It was in this vein that Cauchy, in 1821, said that we were never to 'attribute to formulae an undetermined domain of validity. In reality most of the formulae [in his 'Cours d'analyse'] are true only if certain conditions are fulfilled'. (33) And Bérard in 1818 insisted that 'One should not confuse false theorems with theorems subject to some restriction'. (34) (Cf. also Gergonne's description of the way in which Euler's theorem and its exceptions are to be found in separate parts of Lhuilier's memoir, and Zacharias's description of similar widespread compartmentalization. (35))

Exception-barring like monster-adjustment also leads to an especially characteristic form of mathematical generality. Here knowledge is additive and segmented - at least in the eyes of its critics. In the case of Euler's theorem the formula V-E+F=2 is supplemented by additional terms which accommodate case after case of polyhedra which were exceptions to the original formula. First it becomes V-E+F=2(n-1) for n-spheroidal polyhedra, the original formula standing for the special case of monospheroidal polyhedra. Then it becomes:

$$V - E + F = 2 - 2\left(n-1\right) + \sum_{K=1}^{F} e_K$$

for n-spheroidal or n-tuply-connected polyhedra with e_K edges that can be deleted without reduction of the numbers of faces. Then to allow for polyhedra with cavities, the formula blossoms into:

$$V - E + F = \sum_{j=1}^{K}\left\{ 2 - 2\left(nj-1\right) + \sum_{K=1}^{F} e_{Kj}\right\}$$

To many of the mathematicians who struggled over Euler's theorem this last formula - or variants of it - represented a supreme achievement. It was, they hoped, truly general. (36) To these men this sequence of formulae revealed the unfolding of a single principle of order: 'Isn't this a miraculous unfolding of the hidden riches of the trivial starting-point?' asks the later Alpha, marvelling with Plato at the way that 'a single axiom might suffice to generate a whole system'. (37)

To explain exception-barring and monster-adjustment we need only

imagine mathematicians employed in a number of stable but independent
institutions. There would be no chance of drumming up support for
exclusive boundaries. However loudly the advocates of the counterexample might proclaim that the theorem was refuted, and however
vehemently the inventor of the theorem might declare the counterexample to be a monster, their two achievements would live side by
side, insulated from one another by an institutional boundary. The
public form of the knowledge would reflect the relations between
their institutions, not their individual states of mind. Gradually
others would accept this coexistence as a fact of life. Since neither
achievement could be banished, the favoured way of advancing the field
would be to invent a device for adding them together. No prizes
here for the mathematician who invented an entirely new approach or
novel proof procedure. This would not solve the problem of the co-
existence of the theorem and counterexample, it would only introduce
yet another result to live alongside them. So knowledge will grow
in the ad hoc way illustrated above: the diversified pattern of
power will leave its mark in formula and method.

Lakatos's own position is that we should reject and improve upon
all of the mathematical styles that we have seen so far. Anomalies
are to be publicly embraced. Classificatory schemes are expedients
which can be discarded, and change opens the way to progress. Of
course it may be necessary to take risks like ignoring a few initial
refuting instances. Better to set out to prove a conjecture that
is already known to be refuted than prematurely abandon it. Only
by living on credit for a while can new conceptual resources emerge
for future use.(38) Now images of social irregularity begin to
look attractive:

> if you want to learn about anything really deep, we have to
> study it not in its 'normal', regular, usual form, but in its
> critical state.... If you want to know functions, study their
> singularities. If you want to know ordinary polyhedra, study
> their lunatic fringe. (39)

Gone is the old 'horror of counterexamples' with its dogma and
conventions and 'monotonous increase in truth'. (40)

One should always be ready, as Zeta says 'to abandon one's
original problem in the course of solution and replace it by
another'. (41) After all, who ever said that the term 'Eulerian'
occurred in God's blueprint of the universe? (42) On the other
hand, even if we stay with the same problem, our approach should
be to establish 'a unity, a real interaction, between proofs and
counterexamples'. (43) New forms of classification should put
theorem and counterexample in a new light. This method of using
counterexamples to deepen a proof Lakatos calls 'the method of
proofs and refutations'; it is, he says, a 'dialectical' method.

Is there a social organization which can be seen to generate
this style? We must ask what social forms exert a pressure towards
innovation and novelty, and encourage transactions across the
boundaries of existing classificatory schemes, dissolving them in
change? Where is discontinuity more desired than regularity? Where
can mistakes be tolerated and risks taken? Where is the tension
most acutely felt between the missing of opportunities due to a
reluctance to change, and missing them because of lack of sustained
application? Which societies embody this contradiction in their

very structure? The answer is: individualistic, pluralistic, competitive, and pragmatic social forms.

Here there can be neither the hope of total and permanent victory nor stable compromise. Now the prizes will indeed go to those who can invent new perspectives rather than preserve the achievements of the past. Knowledge will no longer be fashioned with an eye to the particular and concrete; it will reflect a striving to be universal - or at least as general as the competitive structure that provides its motor. In this competitive environment the question: where is the boundary which separates off 'real' polyhedra? cannot be asked. It has no intellectual meaning because it has no social meaning; there are no stable platonic essences because there are no stable social essences.

V

Mary Douglas offers a simple way of bringing out the orderly character of the connexions that have just been illustrated. In 'Natural Symbols' she shows how these patterns can be expressed in terms of two theoretical dimensions called 'grid' and 'group'. (44)

The boundary which separates the members of a social group from strangers is called simply the group boundary, and its strength is said to vary from low group to high group. A very high position on the group axis represents a social group in which the same people work together, take their leisure together, inter-marry, and live in the same neighbourhood. Where it is possible to evade personal pressures by changing jobs, houses, or friends, the group rating is lower.

The pattern of roles and statuses is thought of as a grid of internal boundaries. Recognizing high grid means looking for extended gradations of rank, of a kind associated with varying rights and duties and expected kinds of behaviour. An army or a bureaucracy is high grid. Open competition, where the only rules are abstract principles of fair comparison, is low grid.

The grid/group theory applied to Lakatos's data then yields an hypothesis connecting mathematical knowledge, with social structure. The pollution-conscious, monster-barring societies have been described in a way that makes them low on the grid axis but high on the group axis: they are low grid and high group. The more static, complex and diversified societies, preserving continuity by monster-adjustment and exception-barring are high grid and high group. The mere co-existence of theorems and counterexamples, with no effort at all towards synthesis, indicates high insulating boundaries without much group pressure i.e. high grid, low group. Competitive and individualistic societies, where there is always room for innovation and mobility, where the rules of the competitive game are the only accepted social forms, are obviously low grid, low group. The unifying idea of the theory is that the response to anomaly, and hence the drawing of intellectual boundaries, will be negotiated into alignment with the pattern of social boundaries. The full hypothesis is summarized in Figure 9.1.

One observation about this diagram is worth stressing. It should not be supposed that the low grid, low group corner is, in any

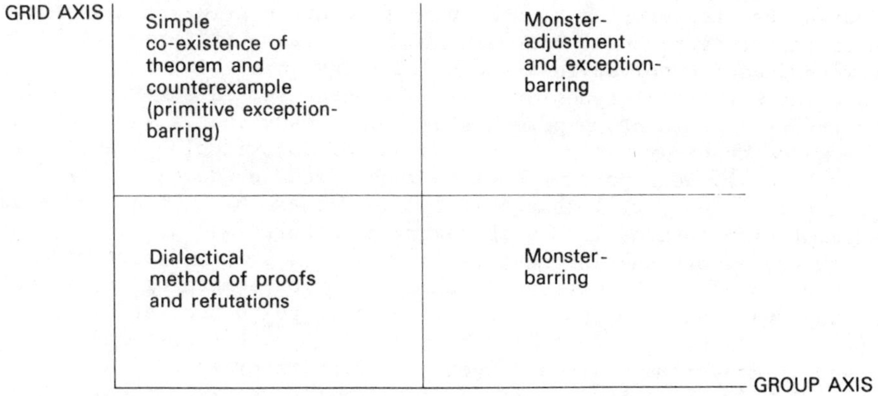

GRID AXIS

Simple co-existence of theorem and counterexample (primitive exception-barring)	Monster-adjustment and exception-barring
Dialectical method of proofs and refutations	Monster-barring

GROUP AXIS

FIGURE 9.1   The predicted relation between mathematical knowledge and social structure, derived from Lakatos and Douglas

general sense, an area of low 'social pressure'. It might be tempting to assume that here both knowledge and the individual will be 'free' from society. This is wrong. All that changes is the form of the social pressure, perhaps from personal to impersonal pressure. It would be better to say that the burden of social meaning carried by knowledge is the same everywhere, but even this formulation can be improved upon. Take the pupils in Lakatos's classroom: what they are doing is rehearsing styles of life, and patterns of social interaction, as well as moves in the game of mathematics. But in doing this they are not doing two different things, nor are they doing sometimes the one and sometimes the

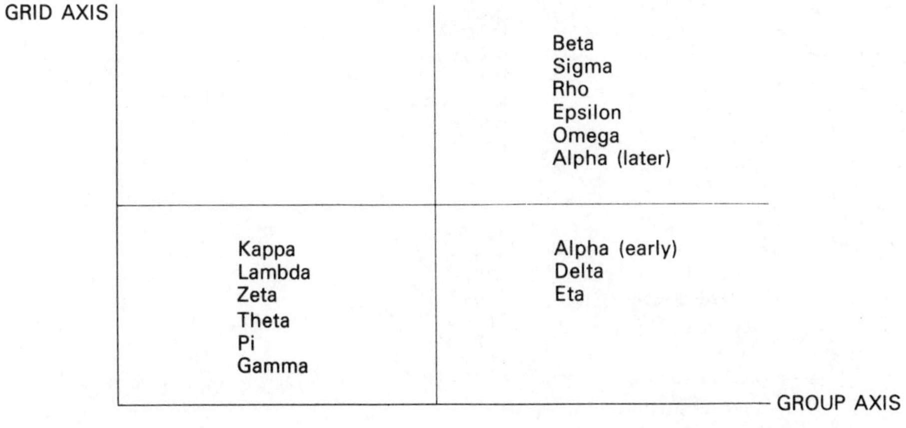

GRID AXIS

	Beta Sigma Rho Epsilon Omega Alpha (later)
Kappa Lambda Zeta Theta Pi Gamma	Alpha (early) Delta Eta

GROUP AXIS

FIGURE 9.2   The social style implicit in the pupils' response to anomaly

other;   knowledge being what it is, in doing the one they are doing
the other. See Figure 9.2.
   Now for the problem of testing the theory. I shall take it for
granted that the problem of assigning a relative grid/group position
to an institution, and the problem of recognizing different styles of
knowledge can be solved in a rough and ready way. Exhibiting
analogies with ideal types or exemplary cases should suffice to test
the theory's explanatory power. (45)   The issue that I shall discuss
is how the theory relates to expressions of individual belief. This
will obviously be important because much of the evidence for or
against the theory will take this form. For example, if an individual
mathematician engages in monster-barring rhetoric and practices, does
the theory assert that he must be located in a small, disorganized,
or threatened group? Or suppose that we notice something odd about
the way that Cauchy responded to star-shaped polyhedra, and we
conclude with Lakatos that 'Cauchy knew of them, but his mind was
strangely compartmentalized; when he had an interesting idea about
star-polyhedra he published it; but he ignored star-polyhedra when
presenting counterexamples to his general theorems about polyhedra'.
(46) Does the theory predict that this strange compartmentalization
must be a reflection of a compartmentalized high grid/high group
environment, and that this is where Cauchy must be socially located?
   There is a clear rationale behind individual predictions of this
kind. Within a given social setting only certain forms of persuasion
and justification will be effective; the rest will fall on deaf
ears. It is of no use appealing to group loyalty to put pressure on
people if mobility in and out of the group is easy, nor of appealing
to what is proper for occupants of a certain role, if everyone else
is chopping and changing. Nor, in the case of Cauchy, can one
expect more than a collection of disconnected results, if the
relevance and meaning of each result is closely tied to one of a
number of strongly demarcated roles that he has occupied. By a

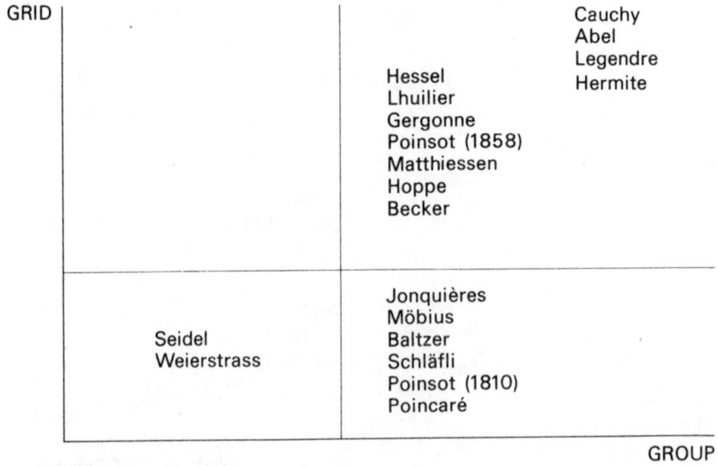

FIGURE 9.3 Probable location of individual mathematicians estimated
from Lakatos's text (for explanation see below)

process of selective reinforcement, characteristic forms of argument
will emerge in a social setting, standing out by their frequency.
This will give each social structure its dominant repertoire of
explicit legitimations and its characteristic style of knowledge.
The inference to individual behaviour is then justified because of
the high probability that individuals will exhibit the characteristic
form.

On this basis the claims in Figure 9.3 about the social location
of individual mathematicians would appear to be probable, given the
descriptions of their methodological biases in 'Proofs and Refutations'.   Men like Poinsot are interesting here.   In 1810 he was
urging counterexamples against the theorem;   by 1858 he was engaged
in monster-adjustment.   The individualistic version of the theory
predicts some relevant change in his social milieu to account for
this.

Unfortunately, it is easy to see how the basis upon which these
predictions are made can be challenged.   The problem can be illustrated by appealing once more to Lakatos's pupils in Figure 9.2.
On the basis of their professed beliefs I gave the individual
pupils widely different positions on the grid/group diagram,
assigning them to different social milieus.   But is this not wrong,
because the pupils were all allegedly interacting together in a
classroom, sharing and creating the same social milieu?   Lakatos's
own presentation must make the pupils belong together in the low
grid/low group, competitive corner of the diagram.   Looked at in
this way, 'Proofs and Refutations' goes against the predicted
correlations, and refutes 'Natural Symbols' rather than supports
it.

Of course Lakatos's classroom is a piece of fiction.   Perhaps
the mathematicians that the pupils represent really were spread
out on the diagram in the predicted way.   This reply only ducks
the issue.   The problem is that, in putting pressure on one another,
people may try out arguments, use idealized social images, make
claims and propose values which taken in isolation 'belong' to
other social milieus than the one they occupy.   Their utterances
may depend more on their goals and aspirations than on their
present location.

It is easy to see how this might happen in a low grid/low group
environment.   There will always be attempts to evade the rigours
of competition and secure past achievements, establish monopolies,
close group boundaries or reach stable accommodations and under-
standings.   Other positions on the grid/group diagram will, so to
speak, all find their advocates.   And perhaps this is not peculiar
to a competitive social structure.   In all social positions men
will be trying to push their institutions into other shapes, some
wanting to increase mobility and competition, others trying to
diminish it.   If this is correct, it could destroy any neat
correlation between isolated individual utterances and social
location.

Obviously this question is an empirical one, but even if the
individualistic predictions of the theory turn out to be wrong,
the information amassed in refuting them would still be valuable.
It would be useful to know if there is any systematic variation in
the extent to which individual beliefs cluster around the predicted

characteristic style. Does it vary across the grid/group diagram,
or change in response to other identifiable circumstances? Perhaps
it falls into step with periods of normal or revolutionary science.
Or it may be possible to isolate the features of those individuals
who do, and those who do not, conform to the predictions of the
theory, either socially or psychologically.

There is, however, a less individualistic way of understanding
the theory which would survive the failure of predictions of the
kind just considered. In this more explicitly sociological version,
the theory is to be seen as connecting public, objective forms of
knowledge with social structure, and not commenting directly on
the beliefs of individuals. After all, society is not a set of
individuals, it is a system through which individuals pass, and the
theory can be pitched at this structural level. For instance we
have seen that if two mathematicians, who are both individually
monster-barrers, are forced to coexist the overall style of
mathematics is not monster-barring but, say, monster-adjusting.
A direct inference to the structure of public knowledge from their
isolated individual beliefs would be a mistake, and vice-versa.
Individual evidence is always to be treated by putting it in a
context where its typicality and its contribution to the overall
pattern can be assessed. This overall pattern is precisely the
system of boundaries and classifications - it is the style of
knowledge - and this is what the theory is about. (47)

At first this approach seems to have its dangers. It seems to
say that a style of knowledge might be created by a set of individual works, none of which in itself contains or expresses that
style through its own make-up. This would mean that the theory
would never be informative about individual pieces of work, and
could never be invoked to explain them. It would make the style
of knowledge merely an aggregative effect that was divorced from
the content of knowledge. The example of two monster-barrers that
I have just used shows that this may be true for a while, but only
for a while. The overall style, the 'aggregative style', is itself
something that can be perceived and known by social actors. It
can be taken for granted and accepted as the basis for further
work by a third practitioner alongside the two whose works contributed to it. Once this has happened, style in the aggregative
sense becomes embodied in individual productions or beliefs. It
becomes 'intrinsic style', that is, style which can be detected
and exhibited in individual works, comprising perhaps their
unspoken assumptions, or their mode of using established results
and resources.

Continuing with the same simplified example we can see that,
taken in isolation, the individual works would now amount to two
in monster-barring style, and one in monster-adjusting style;
what is more, the latter style may have to be read into the implicit
structure of knowledge rather than supported by direct and recorded
claims. If this evidence is interpreted individualistically, it
would seem but weak support for the grid/group theory: two cases
definitely negative, one perhaps positive. Put in context, however,
the three cases are mutually supporting and they all contribute to
the same picture of a body of knowledge evolving in a way which
bears the predicted mark of its social setting. Even in its

strictly sociological form, then, there is still an intimate
connexion between the theory and individual belief, only now the
connexion is more complicated than before, and is itself a matter
for detailed enquiry and theoretical interpretation.

VI

In this section I shall outline and then assess a sociological
answer to one of the main historical problems posed by Lakatos's
text: why was there a methodological revolution in mathematics
in the 1840s? He insists that before the 1840s, mathematicians
had just not thought of using counterexamples dialectically to
squeeze out hidden assumptions and improve their proofs. It 'was
virtually unknown in the informal mathematics of the early nineteenth
century.' (48) 'It never occurred to [Cauchy or Abel] that if they
discover an exception, they should have another look at their
proof.' (49) Well into the nineteenth century, (50) monster-barrers,
monster-adjusters, and exception-barrers ruled the roost. For
instance Cauchy thought that he had proved that the limit function
of any convergent series of continuous functions was itself
continuous; Abel and Fourier knew of exceptions and cited certain
series of trigonometric functions. Between 1821 and 1847, there
the matter rested. Not until Seidel invented the concept of
uniform convergence was it clear what further restrictions had to
be imposed on functions before they obeyed Cauchy's theorem, and
what it was about Abel's series that made them exceptions. (51)
Seidel's discovery was, at the same time a quite self-conscious
announcement of the new dialectical method of proofs and refutations.
    First of all, though, we need to make sure that the question of
the mathematical revolution of the 1840s is construed as one about
objective knowledge, rather than one of individual thought
processes. It is implausible to suggest that a new method of
human thought was discovered and exercised by Seidel. What must
be at issue is why the natural capability to think dialectically
was, allegedly, idiosyncratically rather than routinely deployed
in mathematics before the 1840s. Lakatos talks of a methodological
discovery made by an individual. (52) We should talk rather of
the inhibiting or the encouraging of public exercises or displays
of this methodological style.
    Lakatos's own explanation is weak. In effect he says that men
failed to make this methodological discovery because they were in
the grip of the wrong methodology. (53) To move out of this trivial
circle of ideas being used to explain ideas, we need to ask about
the dispositions and purposes of those who use them, and these in
turn are to be related to the social context. What overriding
social preoccupations gripped mathematicians around 1840?
    Much of the answer to this question is provided by R.S. Turner's
fascinating studies of the growth of professorial research in
Prussia. (54) He sets out to explain how making discoveries
became part of the role of being an academic in Germany. He
begins by describing the closed, collegiate character of most
eighteenth-century German universities: they retained some ancient
guild privileges, whilst being constrained by mercantilist limitations

on the mobility of students and professors. Above all, they
controlled their own appointments, which assured that group loyalties
were dominant. As would be expected, these small groups were riven
with internal conflict, and charges of corruption and immorality
were rife. To this the early years of the nineteenth century added
the threat of falling enrolments. The reform ministries which
followed the Prussian defeat by Napoleon in 1806 set to work to
produce a new school and university system. Spiritually, the
universities were to be symbols of regeneration and unity; more
practically they were to provide competent schoolteachers and
bureaucrats: loyal men of culture and moral probity. This was to
be the task of the revived philosophical faculty. Those who taught
there were to be of the best: intellectuals of wide appeal and
renown. To achieve this goal the government bureaucracy took over
the control of appointments to university chairs. Ignoring protests,
and untouched by the criteria of collegiate acceptability, the
bureaucrats used standards that they could understand and manipulate.
They read an applicant's publications and they consulted his fellow
practitioners throughout Europe. Disciplinary accomplishments
were the new criteria, and all the universities had to compete
with one another for students, competent professors, and intellectual renown.

The aim was not to produce innovation but merely to achieve
excellence, which could derive either from esoteric scholarship or
from grand synthesizing achievements. The growth of detailed
learning in particular areas was to be combined with an overriding
sense of the organic unity of knowledge. Hence the explicit
encouragement given to the specialist seminars in history and
philology, as well as the great synthesis of German Idealism.

The result, however, was that competitive specialization
prevailed over harmonious accumulation and organic synthesis. The
divisive forces of detailed research and the endless pursuit of
discovery outweighed the more static group loyalties and the vague
philosophical systems which symbolized them. The reason was that
making discoveries became a necessity for those who aspired to
chairs; the mere compilation, transmission, or refinement of
established knowledge in handbooks, translations and encyclopaedias,
was now a thing of the past.

This movement did not come about merely by universities
'reflecting' a general European movement towards competitive
individualism, although this was its effect. It was the result of
direct administrative intervention, which ironically was largely a
reaction against the values of liberalism. Nor, on Turner's
account, is the growth of competition in German universities to be
explained teleologically by appeal to the institutional requirements
of science. Specialization, in fact, occurred in the humanities
first, and it was the desire to ape these prestigious and accepted
academic forms, and to rid the sciences of the taint of mere utility,
that led to their adoption in mathematics and science. The competitive, innovative outcome, which gave Germany her leading role in
nineteenth-century science, was the unintended result of the
introduction of centralized, bureaucratic appointments criteria.

One can see Turner's work as a description of the shifting grid
and group characteristics of the Prussian universities. It is easy

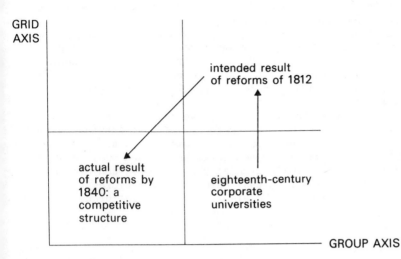

FIGURE 9.4   Grid/group rendering of Turner's account of Prussian
university reform

to read his work as a detailed account of small, low grid, high
group corporations being reformed with the aim of making them part
of a larger high grid, high group system. The consequence, as we
have seen, was in fact to create a low grid, low group structure.
This sequence is presented in Figure 9.4.

Turner provides precisely the kind of detailed institutional
description which could explain the dating of Lakatos's methodological revolution. Notice that the institutional environment with
which he deals is the one that impinges directly on the mathematician
qua mathematician. The wider society only has an effect in as far
as it impinges on that role. It was precisely by the 1840s that a
competitive environment was firmly established in at least one part
of the institutional setting of European mathematics. And this
environment, of course, is just the one that encourages a dialectical attitude towards proofs and counterexamples. (55)

We need to move with caution, however, for Turner's data deals
only with Prussia, and Lakatos's hero Seidel, for instance, was
based in Munich. (56) Turner's findings should be cited in the
present context as an example of a type of explanation. Equally
detailed accounts of, say, the academic scene in France would
perhaps produce a different picture. There would be nothing
surprising in finding that certain institutions maintained a closed,
elitist, and exclusive structure, successfully swimming against the
tide of European social change. What is to be made of this? The
most immediate consequence is that we should expect the institutionalized employment of the dialectical method to be patchy. But there
is also a more interesting conclusion: that we should resist the
temptation to see history as a relentless drift towards low grid,
low group, i.e. putting the dialectical method in the vanguard of
progress and seeing exceptions as 'cultural lags'.

In the place of this naive progressivist assumption we could put a steady state theory, or some equivalent of geological uniformitarianism. Perhaps we should expect as a general rule that organized groups will circulate round the grid/group diagram: being pushed into competitive relations; hauling themselves back up the group axis; finding themselves hedged in by a grid of bargains and obligations, and so forth. After all, competitive individualism is a very old social form. There are primitive non-technological cultures which are like us in being secular, pragmatic and individualistic. Our world-view is not new; we have been here before. (57)

We should not expect that the emergence of a dialectical method in mathematics is a once-and-for-all phenomenon - a sort of methodological 'big bang'. We may expect it to have faded away in some circumstances after Lakatos's crucial year of 1847, and also to have been present well before that date. Earlier cycles through competitive social forms should also reveal mathematicians thinking dialectically.

VII

I hope that enough has been said to show the utility of taking grid/group theory out of its anthropological context and extending it into scientific knowledge. Clearly the approach is not confined to mathematical examples but should illuminate the workings of the natural sciences too. For instance, it should help to show when and why an anomaly is turned into a crisis-provoking anomaly in Kuhn's sense, or why in Lakatos's terms a research programme can be said to be degenerating. (58) Of course this approach does not deal with all aspects of knowledge. For instance, in the present case it does not illuminate the origin of proof procedures nor the original perception that an object might be deployed as a counter-example. (59) But it is hardly a criticism of a theory that it falls short of being a total account of knowledge. In any case, no theory could ever show that knowledge was 'purely social', for our psychological and physical make-up can never be ignored.

One final point is important when assessing the grid/group theory. It is no good having ideas like 'interest' or 'resource' or 'negotiation' or 'image', if they are unco-ordinated by a unifying theoretical scheme. At the moment these ideas are typically used in an entirely ad hoc way. (50) Grid/group theory deserves our attention because it helps to repair this defect. This does not mean that its use will be straightforward or unproblematic; quite the opposite: it will in fact immediately increase the number of problems, for example by throwing into prominence issues that it was previously possible to ignore. But the generation of problems is as much an argument in favour of a theory as an argument against it; it is bound to happen when a diversity of empirical findings and an existing repertoire of concepts are related to a new theoretical idea. Just as Lakatos said that new proof ideas in mathematics actually increase the scope for criticism, so we must expect an explanatory theory to have the same effect in the sociology of knowledge. (61)

APPENDIX: HOW RADICAL IS LAKATOS?

There is a striking oddity to be found between the covers of 'Proofs
and Refutations', which needs to be made explicit lest it should
bias the way the book is understood.   I am referring to the content
of the editorial interventions.   Everyone has cause to be grateful
to the editors, John Worrall and Elie Zahar, for undertaking the
work of publishing 'Proofs and Refutations' after Lakatos's death
in 1974.   But in one way they have discharged their duty oddly:
they have inserted a number of editorial footnotes, indicated by
an asterisk, in which they hasten to reassure the reader that
Lakatos had changed, or would have changed, his mind on certain
topics.   They stress the achievements of modern logic and emphasize
how different it is from the cases which fit Lakatos's approach.
It is not difficult to see what prompts these flurries of editorial
activity: they happen whenever Lakatos is becoming too radical.

    For example, at one point Lakatos makes pupil Kappa say 'concept-
stretching will refute any statement' (p.99). (62) Any instance of
a concept however central or stable it may seem can always be
glossed afresh.   We have already seen that this is the reason why
no theorem ever has a perfectly stable scope or status.   Kappa's
statement sums up the central thrust of Lakatos's argument.   The
editors, however, step in to reassure the readers that Kappa 'is
wrong to think that ... one can always produce counterexamples by
"concept-stretching"' (p.100n).   Clearly if the editors are right,
Lakatos is wrong.   Let us examine the matter.

    Their argument is that:

    By definition, a valid proof is one in which, no matter how one
    interprets the descriptive terms, one never produces a counter-
    example - i.e. its validity does not depend on the meaning of
    the descriptive terms, which can thus be stretched however one
    likes (p.100n).

The nub of their claim can easily be illustrated.   The form of the
argument 'If all A is B, and C is A, then C is B', does not depend
on the meaning of A, B, or C.   Their meaning can be altered at will
without touching the validity of the inference.   So the editors are
claiming that a proof is really an inferential step, a movement
from 'if' to 'then', and it is the validity of the step, not the
content of the premise or the content of the conclusion, that
matters.   This concern with form rather than content is what Russell
had in mind in his famous quip that 'mathematics may be defined as
the subject in which we never know what we are talking about, nor
whether what we are saying is true'. (63)

    The obvious way to reply is to notice that the editors' argument
depends on the tacit assumption that only descriptive terms can be
stretched and that the logical words in an inference are immune
from stretching.   A determined Kappa ought to insist that even
valid, formal, logical arguments can be made to have counterexamples
by stretching the meaning of the terms they contain - why should
'all' and 'some' and 'if' and 'then' be any different from the rest
of our language?   If Lakatos's position is a really general one, if
it is not to be arbitrarily truncated, this is one way that it
could go.   After all, no one has yet succeeded in separating the
'logical' words in our language from the others and showing that

they are special in being unstretchable. No principle of an
absolute and abstract kind has been found which demarcates them:
the existing division is a convention. (64)

There is, however, a much simpler answer which avoids the need
to fight the logician on his own ground. This is that it is false
to portray mathematics as if it were essentially a contentless web
of inferences. The whole point of Lakatos's material is to remind
us of the subtle and substantial character of the concepts A, B,
and C that the logician ignores as he slots them into his
stereotyped inferential steps. Why does Lakatos's account of
mathematics feel more like the mathematics that we have encountered
in lecture halls, despite all the shortcomings of pedagogy, than
does the work of the logicians? The answer is because he has
reversed the order of priority that has dominated the more
philosophical accounts. They have let the substance recede into
the background and have high-lighted the relations between things;
Lakatos has reversed the figure and the ground, and highlights the
substance of the proofs. He is saying that the important part of
mathematics is precisely the content that is left out of account
in focusing on the formal, logical relations. How can the relations
of conjunction and disjunction, of negation and material implication
do justice to processes like imagining that a polyhedron is made
of rubber, stretching it flat, constructing the triangulated
network, and then removing the triangles one by one? They do not
and cannot capture these things, and yet all proofs have some such
steps.

There might appear to be a decisive objection to all this. What
is it that provides the alleged 'substance' of mathematics? The
more we argue that it is not the steps of inference between the
premise and conclusion that counts, but the premises and conclusions
themselves, the more we need to say what these propositions refer
to. If the truths of mathematics are not just true inferences,
true 'if thens', they must be true claims about something – but
about what? We need to specify an ontology. Are we perhaps forced
back into Platonism, into postulating a world of mathematical
objects for the theorems to be about? Perhaps Euler's theorem is
about a seraphic Ideal Polyhedron after all. It would be sad to
have to admit that, because Lakatos rejects 'if thenism', he was
after all a tacit Platonist. (65)

Fortunately there is another possibility. We do not have to
choose between Platonism and 'if thenism'. The substance of
mathematical ideas can be traced back to the material world, to
our psychological dispositions, and to a structure of metaphors
built upon our experience. We get the idea of what polyhedra are,
of what numbers are, of area, distances, rotations, translations,
mappings, and of the patterns that can be made with them, all from
our experience. Hence the importance of 'quasi-experiments' in
Lakatos's account. Of course much more needs to be said, but
however unfashionable 'psychologistic' theories of mathematics
might be, and however odd it may seem to associate them with
Lakatos's name, they provide the answer to the objection we are
considering. (66)

Another editorial intervention occurs when Lakatos says that we
must 'give up the idea that our deductive, inferential intuition is

infallible' (p.138n). The editors announce that this 'passage seems
to us mistaken and we have no doubt that Lakatos, who came to have
the highest regard for formal deductive logic, would himself have
changed it' (p.138n). This exercise in impression-management has
some amusing consequences. On p.52 one of the pupils quotes
Poincaré's claim that 'Today absolute rigour is attained'. Lakatos
greets this proud boast by 'giggles in the classroom', and in a
footnote slyly reminds us that the class is a very advanced one.
Directly opposite this (p.53n) the editors solemnly announce that
'modern logic' has provided us with a precise characterization of
validity and that therefore 'logic certainly can make us believe
in an argument'. Later they add that once mathematical proofs have
been cast into the 'systems' of Russell and Frege, 'There is no
serious sense in which such proofs are fallible' (p.57n). So the
editors, at least, did not join in the giggles.

In fact Lakatos provides his own answer to his editors. He has
his own reason for rejecting the idea that proofs are to be equated
with formal structures of inference from 'if' to 'then'. He says
that before the quasi-experiments of informal mathematics can be
put into formal logic, they will have to be carefully dismantled
and rebuilt in the new, simpler logical material. To change the
metaphor: they will have to be re-encoded or translated. All the
troubles to which mathematics is heir to will not be avoided by casting
them into 'infallible' logic, they will only be shifted. Squeezed
out of one place they will crop up in another: in arguments about
the translation process (p.123). Worrall and Zahar mention in
passing the relevant fact that the translation of mathematics into
'infallible' logic is acknowledged to be fallible, but they make
nothing of it. Indeed their position would imply that arguments
about this translation process are not arguments about the proof
as such, because for them the proof is only the formal structure
of the inferences *once they have been translated*. But this is an
evasion; it simply rests on changing the meaning of the word
'proof'. The trend of these editorial interventions is clear. It
represents the intrusion of that very philosophy of formalism that
Lakatos's book is devoted to outflanking.

How could this strange situation have come about? It surely
deserves some explanation. One hypothesis is that the retreat into
formalism is the result of anxiety about the uses to which Lakatos's
work may be put, for example in sociologically oriented papers such
as this. Perhaps it stems from a desire to preserve some small
area of unnegotiable objectivity from the relativism which threatens
to engulf knowledge. (67) If this is so, then the historian and
the sociologist would do well to ignore the editorial blandishments,
for they are nought but a strategy for protecting disciplinary
boundaries. In terms of the grid/group theory we can suggest that
the editors find themselves further up the group axis than did
Lakatos, or they are trying to move up that axis by closing ranks.
They obviously do not care to take the risks associated with a
lower grid/lower group intellectual environment. It would involve
them in transactions across established academic demarcations. In
short, we can see their retreat into formalism as another case of
monster-barring. Perhaps it represents an awareness that Lakatos's
work on mathematics is potentially disruptive, at least from the

standpoint of the usual philosophical procedures and competences. Such anxiety would be well founded, for 'Proofs and Refutations' opens the door to a sociological approach to mathematics. (68)

NOTES

*   This paper first appeared in the 'British Journal for the History of Science', vol.11 November 1978, pp.245-72 and is reproduced here by kind permission of the editor.

   This paper started life as an essay review of Imré Lakatos's 'Proofs and Refutations: the Logic of Mathematical Discovery', Cambridge, Cambridge University Press, 1976. I am extremely grateful to the editor of this journal for his patience and understanding in allowing a review to metamorphose in this way.

   I am especially indebted to Professor Mary Douglas for her generous   encouragement and help. I have also benefited enormously from the critical and constructive comments of Barry Barns, Alex Bellamy, Celia Bloor, Ken Caneva, Nicholas Fisher, Donald MacKenzie, Martin Rudwick, Steven Shapin, Fran Wasoff and Peter Whittingham. I am aware that I have only been able to answer some, rather than all, of the questions that they have raised.

1   Imré Lakatos, 'Proofs and Refutations: the Logic of Mathematical Discovery', Cambridge, 1976.

2   Mary Douglas, 'Natural Symbols: Explorations in Cosmology', Harmondsworth, 1973.

3   Op.cit. (1), pp.74-5.

4   Ibid., pp.139, 144-6.

5   Ibid., chapter II.

6   Op.cit. (1), p.34.

7   Ibid., p.36.

8   Ibid., p.13.

9   Ibid., p.15.,

10   Ibid., pp.15-21.

11   This technical term is used here in the sense given it by Mary Hesse in her 'The Structure of Scientific Inference', London, 1974, chapter VIII.

12   Op.cit. (1), p.87.

13   Ibid., p.151.

14   Ibid., p.86.

15   Ibid., p.93.

16   Ibid., p.102.

17   My interpretation of Lakatos's ideas has been influenced by the similarity that they bear to Mary Hesse's general account of scientific concepts given in her op.cit. (11). The negotiability of all predicates or classifications is central to her 'network model'. Lakatos's rejection of a perfectly understood vocabulary of simple terms is essentially the same as Hesse's rejection of the pure 'observation language' of empiricism. The general structural features of our network of knowledge, Hesse's 'coherence conditions', are at least in part provided by Lakatos's strategies for responding to counterexamples.

   To see Lakatos as arguing that all classifications and hence

all theorems and proofs are negotiable is a reading of Lakatos
that has been challenged by, of all people, his own editors.
This important matter is discussed in the appendix at the end
of this paper.

18 Op.cit. (1), p.29.

19 The classic statement is E. Durkheim amd M. Mauss, 'Primitive
Classification', London, 1963 (first published 1903). For two
detailed studies in this tradition see R. Bulmer, Why is the
cassowary not a bird? A problem of zoological taxonomy among
the Karam of the New Guinea highlands, 'Man', 1967, 2, 5-25,
and S.J. Tambiah, Animals are good to think and good to
prohibit, 'Ethnology', 1969, 8, 424-59.

20 R. Horton argues that in primitive societies social structures
provide models for nature because social knowledge is the most
stable intellectual resource available. See his African
traditional thought and western science, 'Africa', 1967, 37,
50-71, 155-87. For a mathematical example in which the social
is appealed to as a metaphor, see Paul Forman, Weimar culture,
causality, and quantum theory, 1918-1927: adaptation by German
physicists and mathematicians to a hostile intellectual
environment, 'Historical Studies in the Physical Sciences',
1971, 3, 1-115. Section II.4 on intuitionism vividly illustrates
the way images of a cultural crisis were used to characterize
and create a sense of mathematical crisis. This episode can
also be read as an example of concept-stretching, where a
deliberate restriction in the scope of accepted mathematical
procedures is advocated in order to produce counterexamples
and anomalies where previously none had existed.

21 The original theory, that the abominations were category-
violators was proposed by Mary Douglas in 'Purity and Danger:
an Analysis of Concepts of Pollution and Taboo', London, 1966.
A developed version of the theory which describes the historical
circumstances which gave special significance to eating pork
is to be found in her 'Implicit Meanings: Essays in Anthropology',
London, 1975, chapter XVII.

22 See Douglas, op.cit. (2), p.87.

23 Op.cit. (1), p.14.

24 Ibid., p.21.

25 Ibid., p.17.

26 Ibid., p.16.

27 Ibid., p.14.

28 Ibid., p.19.

29 Ibid.

30 Ibid., p.30.

31 Ibid., p.24.

32 Ibid., p.39.

33 Ibid., p.26.

34 Ibid., p.24.

35 Ibid., p.36.

36 Ibid., pp.79, 97.

37 Ibid., p.81.

38 Ibid., p.75.

39 Ibid., p.23.

40 Ibid., pp.4, 5, 37.

41 Ibid., p.68.
42 Ibid.
43 Ibid., pp.30, 37.
44 These dimensions were first introduced in Douglas, op.cit. (2), chapters IV and VI. The form of the diagram used on p.129 will be followed here rather than the earlier, somewhat more complicated, figures.
45 This theory has been applied to interview data from contemporary scientists by C. Bloor and D. Bloor (this volume).
46 Op. cit. (1), p.84.
47 The biologist Bateson used to say that plants were not matter, but systems through which matter passed; cf. W. Coleman, Bateson and chromosomes: conservative thought in science, 'Centaurus', 1970, 15, 228-314. I have used this striking idea in the above paragraph. For a valuable discussion of 'structural' explanations in sociology, and a comparison with such explanations in other branches of science, see S.B. Barnes, 'Interests and the Growth of Knowledge', London, 1977, chapter III.
48 Op.cit. (1), p.48.
49 Ibid., p.55.
50 Ibid., p.81.
51 Ibid., p.131.
52 Ibid., p.136.
53 Ibid.
54 R. Steven Turner, The growth of professorial research in Prussia, 1818-1848 - causes and context, 'Historical Studies in the Physical Sciences', 1971, 3, 137-82; University reformers and professorial scholarship in Germany, 1760-1806, in L. Stone (ed.), 'The University in Society', Oxford, 1975, ii, 495-531.
55 Turner's account may be compared with J. Ben-David's earlier treatments of the same episode, summarized in 'The Scientist's Role in Society: a Comparative Study', Englewood Cliffs, 1971, chapter VII. The two accounts agree on the main point that a competitive system was established around the middle of the nineteenth century.
56 J.C. Poggendorff (ed.), 'Biographisch - Literarisches Handwörterbuch zur Geschichte der exakten Wissenschaften', Leipzig, 1863, ii, 896-7.
57 See for example the description of the 'Big-men' societies of New Guinea in Mary Douglas, op.cit. (2).
58 For example Eugene Frankel in Corpuscular optics and the wave theory of light: the science and politics of a revolution in physics, 'Social Studies of Science', 1976, 6, 141-84, describes how a power struggle between supporters and opponents of Laplace in the Paris Académie des Sciences precipitated a crisis in the corpuscular theory of optics. His account would appear to fit well with the description of monster-barring versus theorem-barring in high group, low grid communities. Another example is provided by the same institution a little later, only this time the monster-barrers won. This was when Pasteur disposed of the 'incompetent' experiments of Pouchet who believed in spontaneous generation. See J. Farley and G. Geison, Science, politics and spontaneous generation in nineteenth-century France: the Pasteur-Pouchet debate, 'Bulletin of the History of Medicine', 1974, 48, 161-98.

59 This does not mean that the theory can never contribute towards
    such an understanding, or that such subjects fall outside the
    scope of sociology; far from it. Proof procedures may often
    arise by an extension of existing ones that have become customary,
    or they may be explained by social interests highlighting
    empirical processes which may be made the basis of new procedures.
    For example see the accounts of how eugenic concerns influenced
    the growth of Galton's and Pearson's statistical ideas in Ruth
    S. Cowan, Francis Galton's statistical ideas: the influence of
    eugenics, 'Isis', 1972, 63, 509-28, and D. MacKenzie, The
    development of statistical theory in Britain, 1865-1925: a
    historical and sociological perspective, University of Edinburgh
    PhD thesis, 1978.
60 Notice for instance the lack of unifying theory in S.B. Barnes,
    'Scientific Knowledge and Sociological Theory', London, 1974,
    and D. Bloor, 'Knowledge and Social Imagery', London, 1976.
61 The problems I have in mind are, for example: how do the
    concepts of grid and group relate to the idea of role? Can
    there really be a unique grid/group rating for an individual as
    he moves from role to role? Or take the case of the followers
    of Weierstrass represented as low grid, low group. They were
    put here because of their dialectical methodology and their
    initial rejection of monster-barring, etc. But their attitude
    to counterexamples produced later by Cantor's work was precisely
    to resort to monster-barring (Lakatos, op.cit. (1), p.50).
    This subtle pattern of different methodologies being adopted in
    different circumstances, governed by the varying demands of
    expediency, is a problem which awaits the theory. Cf. also the
    way Jonquières used 'monster-barring against cavities and
    tunnels but monster-adjustment against crested cubes and star-
    polyhedra', (ibid., p.38). But only those who want to see the
    theory fail will assume at this stage that these problems are
    refuting instances.
62 All page references in the appendix are to Lakatos, op.cit.(1).
63 Bertrand Russell, 'Mysticism and Logic', London, 1963 (first
    published 1910), p.59.
64 In 1935 Tarski posed the problem of how to demarcate logical
    words from others. Popper thought that he had solved the
    problem in 1947, but is now of the opinion that he failed, and
    is sceptical about future success. Cf. Karl Popper, Logic
    without assumptions, 'Proceedings of the Aristotelian Society',
    1947, 47, 251-92, and Replies to my critics, in P.A. Schilpp
    (ed.), 'The Philosophy of Karl Popper', La Salle, 1974, p.1096.
    The fact is that logical words are stretchable. For example
    they had to be stretched to cope with the introduction of the
    truth table method.
65 For a clear description of 'if-thenism' see Alan Musgrave,
    Logicism revisited, 'British Journal for the Philosophy of
    Science', 1977, 28, 99-127. On p.123 Musgrave suggests that
    Lakatos's account of mathematics rests on a naive Platonism.
66 J.S. Mill's despised 'psychologistic' theory of mathematics
    has recently been defended and developed in D. Bloor, op.cit.
    (60), chapter V.
67 For Popperian rhetoric against the threatening 'tide of

subjectivist relativism' see Alan Musgrave, The objectivism of
Popper's epistemology, in P.A. Schilpp (ed.) op.cit. (64),
p.588.

68   Instead of retreating back into formalism the editors might
have helped rather than hindered the development of Lakatos's
research programme by drawing attention to other work in logic
and mathematics of a similar tendency. For instance, those
impressed by Lakatos's achievement would have much to learn from
Alfred Sidgwick's direct and forceful attack on formal logic
in his 'The Use of Words in Reasoning', London, 1901. He too
had reached the conclusion that 'To offer proof is to offer
definite points of attack' (p.82). Sidgwick shares Lakatos's
attitude to counterexamples: 'The difference of method proposed
is not that between attending only to rules and attending only
to exceptions, but between avoiding and welcoming the discovery
of exceptions to rules' (p.130). But if there is any book that
deserves detailed comparison with 'Proofs and Refutations' it is
Wittengstein's 'Remarks on the Foundations of Mathematics',
Oxford, 1964. Both writers reject the usual view of mathematics
having its 'foundations' in a trivial logical starting point;
both are aware of the contrived and distorted effect of
translating living and growing concepts into the impoverished
apparatus of formal logic; both are masters of the art of
spotting alternatives to steps in reasoning which look
'compelling', or conclusions which look 'inevitable'; both have,
in one sense of the word, a 'finitist' picture of mathematical
proof; both are profound critics of the glib 'Platonism' or
'Realism' so prevalent in logic and mathematics. Indeed, what
gives their work its force is the fact that both men are deeply
responsive to the social dimension of knowledge.

Chapter 10

COGNITIVE STYLES IN GEOLOGY
Martin Rudwick

INTRODUCTION

The most difficult task currently facing historians of the natural
sciences is to find an adequate way of analysing the relation
between scientific knowledge and the social environments in which
it has been - and still is - constructed. Mary Douglas's theory of
grid/group analysis offers a promising heuristic tool for this
purpose. It suggests features of both cosmologies and social
environments that may be expected to be found in regular conjunction
with each other. Earlier statements of the theory (Douglas 1970,
1975) were in some respects confusing and the terminology was
inconsistent; but a coherent formulation can be derived from more
recent descriptions (Douglas 1978), enabling the theory to be
applied to, and tested on, the cosmologies of scientific knowledge.
   Grid/group analysis is concerned in the first place with a four-
fold classification of the social environments of individuals and
with the cosmologies that they construct, or at least find plausible.
Each correlation between an individual's social environment and an
expected set of characteristic world views or cosmologies may be
tested on empirical material drawn not only from primitive peoples
or the everyday common-sense reality of advanced societies, but
also from the relatively esoteric bodies of knowledge that are the
modern natural sciences.
   This paper presents a brief preliminary interpretation of
cognitive styles in one particular branch of science, namely
geology, in terms of grid/group analysis. Most examples will be
from the classic period of geology in the early nineteenth century,
not only because my own historical research has been mainly in that
period, but also because all the styles I want to distinguish can
be clearly found in the debates of that time. I shall also allude
briefly to their manifestations in the present century, drawing
partly on my own earlier experience as a geologist. I deliberately
used the well-worn term style in order to emphasise that what is
being characterised is not only - or even mainly - the theories and
concepts elaborated in explicit reflection by participants in
geological debate, but also the attitudes and assumptions that
remain implicit in unreflective geological practice. Style is

preferable to tradition, because it does not prejudge the question
of intellectual lineages between historically or socially separate
manifestations of a given style;   it is also preferable to paradigm,
because it does not imply any necessary cognitive or social
coherence among those who have worked in a given style.   I shall
illustrate the various styles mainly by reference to the work of
individuals who are well known to historians of science.   More
detailed studies of larger numbers of lesser figures would fill out
the collective aspect of the different styles, but would not, I
believe, greatly alter their character.

I shall outline four broadly distinct styles of geological work
which I shall term abstract, concrete, agnostic and binary;   their
validity deserves to be judged quite apart from their putative
social correlations.   Then I shall consider how far the four styles
of work, and the social environments of those who have used them,
correspond to Douglas's grid/group typology.

FOUR STYLES OF GEOLOGICAL WORK

The abstract style

The first of the four styles of geological practice I shall term
'abstract'. Examples of those working in this style include the
paradigmatic 'uniformitarian' of the mid nineteenth century, Charles
Lyell, together with those who have traditionally been seen as his
intellectual ancestors, James Hutton and John Playfair. But I
also include here several of Lyell's near-contemporaries who were
not uniformitarians in the strictest sense, such as Constant
Prévost, George Scrope, John Phillips and Charles Darwin (the last
being much more a geologist than a biologist at the period I am
considering).   I see the abstract style as continuing - or, more
precisely, reappearing - in much of modern geology, particularly
those branches that have been most influenced by physics or biology.
I shall characterise this style in terms of seven related features.
(Not all features are equally prominent in the work of all those
with this style: like a modern biological taxonomy, my classification of style is polythetic.)

(i)   The treatment of geological time is dimensional. By this I
mean that the earth's history is described in terms of events that
are - or in principle could be - plotted against an independent or
neutral dimension of physical time (Fig.10.1). Time itself is
treated in the classic Newtonian manner as (in the words of the
'Principia') that which 'of itself, and from its own nature, flows
equably without regard to anything external'.

This usage shows itself in geological work in various ways.
Obviously it is most explicit where, as in modern geology, there is
a fairly reliable quantitative time-scale available for the dating
of at least some events. But any attempt to construct such a time-
scale, however approximate or uncalibrated, is evidence of the
dimensional style: examples include Lyell's abortive scale based
on the rate of organic change (Rudwick 1978), Scrope's and Darwin's
on the rate of erosion (Rudwick 1974;   Burchfield 1974), and
Phillips's on the rate of deposition.   It makes no difference

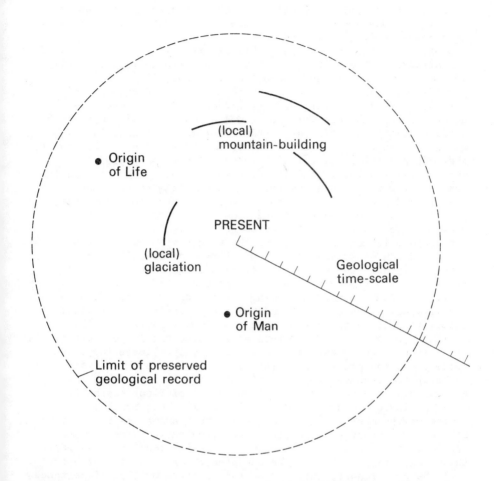

FIGURE 10.1 Diagrammatic representation of the abstract style of
earth-history, showing absence of universal boundaries, and diverse
local events that can (in principle) be dated against a dimensional
time-scale. The centre represents the present, with the past
extending outwards; the circumferential dimension represents
spatial distribution. The form of the diagram is intended to bring
out the analogy with the astronomer's exploration into space.

whether the time-scale proposed was shorter than the modern one
(e.g. Phillips) or longer (e.g. Darwin): it is the qualitative
dimensionality that matters.

    This dimensionality is also revealed in the use of the analogy
between time in geology and space in astronomy, as in the work of
Lyell, and before him in that of Playfair. They clearly regarded
the geologist as one who peers back into the past to interpret the
obscure traces of distant geological events, just as the astronomer
peers into space to interpret the faint traces of distant celestial
objects. Geological events are evidently at different 'distances'

from the present, just as celestial objects are from the earth,
even if the measurement of those distances remains difficult or
even impossible.

(ii)   The treatment of earth-history is only weakly classified.
The history of the earth is relatively undifferentiated; the
temporal dimension is not sharply divided into distinct 'natural'
periods.   In earlier writers such as Hutton and Playfair, this
follows from an image of earth-history as endlessly cyclic but
unphased: a continent will be eroded on one part of the earth's
surface at the same time as another (future) continent is being
formed elsewhere on the ocean floor, so there are no global events
that could provide natural limits for a series of periods.
Geologists of a later generation, such as Lyell, acknowledged the
reality of more or less distinctive phases in earth-history.   But
they regarded any periodisation as merely a practical convenience;
geological periods and the boundaries between them were merely
pragmatic conventions, not natural entities.   The same attitude
can be seen in modern geology in the attempts to base the (necessary)
periodisation of earth-history on a series of so-called 'golden
spikes' fixed in the succession of strata at convenient and
agreed - but ultimately arbitrary - points.

(iii)   When theories are being elaborated, anomalies are
assimilated.   They are welcomed and their reality is accepted;
but it is confidently anticipated that in due course it will be
possible to assimilate them into an improved theoretical structure.
This reaction to anomaly (which is not peculiar to geology)
corresponds to 'proofs and refutations' in Lakatos's analysis of
mathematical argument (Bloor, ch.9 of this volume) and to 'monster-
assimilating' in Caneva's (1981) extension of Bloor's scheme.
For a geological example I will only mention here Lyell's response
to one of the most important and refractory anomalies in early
nineteenth-century geology, the Devon problem (Rudwick 1979).
Lyell did not try to explain away the fossils found in apparently
the wrong strata in Devon; he accepted the reliability of Henry
De la Beche's report, insisted on the great theoretical importance
of the anomaly, and simply waited until eventually the observation
could be fitted into an enlarged theoretical explanation.

(iv)   The apparent complexity of the earth is reduced programmatically to an underlying simplicity.   The analysis of earth-
history is directed to the discovery of the basic abstract
principles that are believed to underlie whole classes of events.
Hutton envisaged a single pair of counteracting causes underlying
the cyclic rhythm of the earth.   Lyell elaborated this into several
pairs of complementary processes, elevation and subsidence, erosion
and deposition, extinction and the 'birth' of species, and so on
(Rudwick 1970a).   Darwin wrote with sublime confidence in one of
his notebooks, 'Geology of whole world will turn out simple'
(Herbert 1977).   Such confidence in the ultimate simplicity of
underlying abstract principles is related to what Popperians would
term 'bold conjecture'.   This is all the more striking when it is
found in a generation - that of Lyell and Darwin - in which such
conjectures were widely frowned on as 'unscientific'.   Yet Darwin
conjectured boldly throughout his scientific career (Ghiselin
1969);   while Lyell took his 'strong' belief in the abstract

principle of the uniformity of nature so far that he almost isolated
himself in a theoretical sense (Bartholomew 1976).

(v)   The analysis of earth-history is strongly hermeneutic in
method.   Since the geologist, like the astronomer, is barred from
direct contact with many of his objects of study (in the geologist's
case, the past events) their observable traces must always be
interpreted.   There can be no question of unmediated plain facts;
all observations are theory-laden.   This viewpoint is quite explicit
in Lyell's work, not only in his metaphor of deciphering the
languages of nature (Rudwick 1977), but above all in his thorough
use of observable present processes as an interpretative key for
understanding unobservable past events.   He did not invent this
'actualistic method', nor did contemporaries working in other styles
deny its validity;   but Lyell did apply it with far greater
consistency and confidence than most other geologists.   In modern
geology the same hermeneutic method is apparent in the large-scale
theorising that has led to the concept of plate tectonics: a
wide variety of phenomena - some of them long familiar - have been
interpreted to yield a new meaning (Hallam 1973).   Though usually
less self-conscious and articulate, the same concept of the
hermeneutic task of the geologist can also be found in other work
in the abstract style.   A good early example is Hutton's scorn
for 'mere' fieldwork, and his emphasis on the reflective task of
the 'natural philosopher' considering such matters.

(vi)   The analysis of earth-history is strongly causal in
orientation.   The goal of analysis is to discover the physical or
organic causes of past geological events, however puzzling their
preserved traces may be.   Once again Lyell is a crucial example,
not because his work was unique in this respect - Prévost gave him
an important precedent - but because it was so extensive, coherent
and articulate.   William Whewell showed a perceptive appreciation
of this: in his classification of the sciences he distinguished
a family of 'palaetiological' sciences concerned with the causal
interpretation of past events, and chose Lyell's style of geology
as the type example to illustrate what he meant.

(vii)   The interpretation of earth-history is open to ideas
from outside the discipline of geology.   Concepts and metaphors
are transposed freely from other sciences and other human enterprises,
and put to work in novel contexts for the explanation of strictly
geological problems.   This openness is most obvious in earlier
periods when by any standards a discipline of geology scarcely
existed anyway;   but Hutton, for example, rejected even the less
restrictive limitation of natural history in favour of a wider-
ranging natural philosophy.   Lyell made wide and creative use of
analogies from contemporary historiography, linguistics and
demography (Rudwick 1977), not to mention his extensive borrowing
from physical geography, meteorology and other natural sciences.
Scrope used an implicit analogy between geological time and money
as a medium of exchange (Rudwick 1974).   Darwin's use of alien
concepts in his more biological conjectures needs no emphasis.
A similar openness can be seen in modern geology wherever the
abstract style is apparent: traditional geological problems are
tackled by welcoming concepts and techniques from a wide range of
other disciplines, physical, chemical and biological.

The abstract style, as characterised above, may seem so self-
evidently modern and therefore correct, particularly to geologists,
that it must be emphasised that it has generally been the style of
a small minority of geologists in any generation. This assertion
may seem less implausible in the light of a characterisation of the
second of my four styles of geology.

The concrete style

The style I shall term 'concrete' has been displayed by most
geologists in most periods since the emergence of a self-conscious
science of geology. In characteristing it I shall cite as examples
such prominent geologists as Abraham Werner in the late eighteenth
century; Alexandre Brongniart, Léonce Elie de Beaumont, Alcide
d'Orbigny, William Buckland, William Conybeare, Adam Sedgwick and
Roderick Murchison in the early nineteenth; together with scientists
such as Alexander von Humboldt and William Whewell whose work covered
many other fields besides geology. But the real locus of the
concrete style lies in the ordinary books, memoirs and articles on
geology by lesser known figures, particularly in the nineteenth
century but also well into the twentieth. It is still prominent
in the work of many ordinary modern geologists. I shall characterise
it by means of seven features contrasted with those of the abstract
style.
    (i) The focuse of attention is the concrete order of strata and
other rocks, rather than the temporal earth-history that they
represent. It is of course acknowledged in principle that this order
represents a temporal sequence of depositional events or periods,
but in practice the concrete language of strata, formations and
systems is far more common than the overtly temporal language of
epochs and periods. In practice time is not treated as an independent continuum outside the (literally) solid structures of geological data; it inheres in the sequence of the strata themselves.
Time is not Newtonian but 'Nuerian': as the perception of time for
the Nuer inhered in the sequential pattern of their daily tasks
(Evans-Pritchard 1940), so for geology in the concrete style it
inheres in the sequential pattern of the successive formations and
systems. This is not a matter of the lack of an adequate time-piece,
but of a different concept of time itself. The concept of time
displayed in practice in the concrete style of stratigraphical
geology has not been necessarily eliminated by the availability of
radiometric dating, any more than the Nuer perception of time would
(perhaps) have been affected by the import of wristwatches.
    The pervasive effects of a non-dimensional treatment of time in
geology has only been overlooked, I believe, because geologists and
historians of science have been bemused by the programmatic
statements of those working in the abstract style, to the effect
that geology is intrinsically a historical science concerned with
matters of time-scale (or, in my terms, that the abstract style is
the natural one for the science to adopt). I would claim, on the
contrary, that the concrete style has been a mainstream tradition
(perhaps even 'the' mainstream tradition) ever since geology emerged
as a recognisable science, and has remained so to the present day.

In a recent analysis of the so-called geognosy or descriptive geology
of Werner and his followers, Albury and Oldroyd (1977) correctly note
that 'a formation was *essentially* defined by its relative position',
and that geognosy was conceptually analogous to contemporary sciences
such as crystallography and comparative anatomy; but they fail to
draw the conclusion that, like those other sciences, geognosy was
also concrete, not historical, in its cognitive orientation.   A
striking symptom of this was Von Humboldt's proposal for a purely
algebraic notation (pasigraphie) to represent just the order of
formations, stripped of all other 'accidental' features.   And far

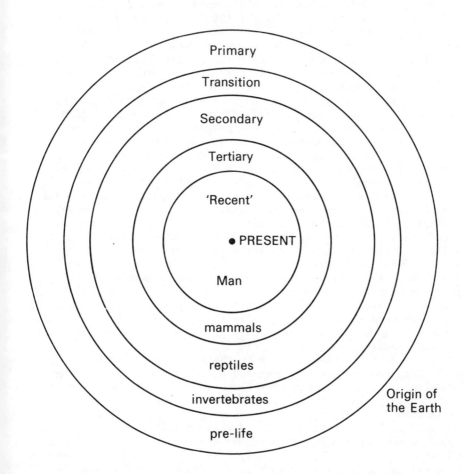

FIGURE 10.2 Diagrammatic representation of the concrete style of
earth-history (drawn on the same basis as Fig. 10.1), showing many
equally-emphasised real boundaries between stratigraphical systems/
periods with distinctive organisms (for the sake of simplicity, only
the main divisions and organisms are drawn here, as understood in
the early nineteenth century). The analogy with diagrams of the
Ptolemaic universe is intentional. (Note that this and the similar
diagram for the binary style (Fig. 10.3) are not Venn diagrams.)

from dying out with the demise of some of Werner's particular theories
the geognostic description of the order of the strata developed
without a break into the stratigraphy of the later nineteenth and
twentieth centuries.

(ii)   The structural order of formations is subjected to strong
classification (Fig. 10.2). The correct assignment of strata to
formations, and of formations to systems, is a central concern; and
'classification' is itself a favourite word. The whole stratigraphical series is thus strongly differentiated; each part has its own
concrete individuality, whether this is seen primarily in terms of
distinctive kinds of rock or distinctive assemblages of fossils.
Boundaries between systems and their subdivisions are strongly
emphasised; and their correct location often gives rise to heated
controversy, because they are considered to be real natural
divisions and are not regarded merely as pragmatic conventions.
The vehement controversy between Sedgwick and Murchison over their
Cambrian and Silurian systems is just one well-known historical
example. Even when the usual structural language is replaced by
more temporal terminology, the same orientation merely acquires a
new gloss: the treatment of earth-history is strongly periodised,
and much attention is given to the correct classification into
periods and their subdivisions, and to the correct placing of
boundaries between them: the long-standing modern controversy
over the Siluro-Devonian boundary is a characteristic example.

This concrete orientation became vividly apparent when, during
the early nineteenth century, geology developed its own conventional
visual language of maps and sections. Illustrations accompanying
geological texts generally remained within a cognitive zone of
visual forms that were adapted to concrete or structural cognitive
goals (Rudwick 1976). The construction of geological maps and
sections was facilitated by, and reciprocally encouraged, an
emphasis on the distinctiveness of adjacent formations and the
sharp boundaries between them. More openly theoretical ideal
sections simply adapted the concrete iconography of real sections:
what they summarised was not really the history of the earth and
its inhabitants, but the supposedly global order of the formations
and their fossils.

(iii)   Anomalies that appear in the course of elaborating
geological conclusions are adjusted out of the status of being
anomalies (cf. Bloor, ch.9 of this volume). Using the Devon problem
again as an example, Murchison's rejection of De la Beche's
apparently 'factual' report - because it did not fit his own
'classification' of the strata and their fossils - drove him to
find a way to eliminate it, which he did eventually by reclassifying
the offending strata so that their fossils were no longer anomalous.

(iv)   The apparent confusion of the features of the earth's
surface is regarded as reflecting a real underlying complexity.
This is closely related to the belief in the concrete individuality
of every part of the stratigraphical series (or of the corresponding
periods of earth-history). Reduction to a few simple abstract
principles is regarded as illusory, generalisations are suspect,
and the rich diversity of geological phenomena is highly valued.
The dynamic behind the enterprise of stratigraphical description is
that of extracting order out of confusion and 'chaos', by revealing

new diversity in the form of new systems or periods. Buckland
referred to the (literally!) epoch-making work of Sedgwick and
Murchison on the Cambrian and Silurian in terms of the progressive
'enclosure' of 'the great common field of geology', because they
had carved new well-defined and sharply-boundaried systems out of
the remaining undifferentiated 'chaos' of the oldest strata.

(v) In the concrete style the methodological emphasis is
empirical. Facts are treated as plain and unambiguous for any right-
minded and unprejudiced observer; theory-building is regarded as a
quite separate activity, proper if kept in its place but logically
and normatively posterior to observation. Conybeare's long and well-
argued informal critique of Lyell's geology is a good example
(Rudwick 1967).

(vi) The concrete style has order rather than cause as its
primary cognitive goal; causal explanation is a much lower priority
than the unravelling of the correct order and structure of the
rocks. Causal explanation is often regarded as a desirable but
distant goal, to be reached only after the consolidation of
descriptive work. Whewell's treatment of causal explanation in
geology, in his works on the classification of the sciences, is a
good example. When geologists working in the concrete style do
discuss causal explanations, it is often only in response to, and
in criticism of, those proposed by geologists working in the
abstract style; their own causal explanations are often almost
empty. For example most of the 'catastrophists', as Whewell dubbed
the critics of 'uniformitarians' like Lyell, had no substantive
causal explanations of phenomena such as valley erosion, mountain
elevation and species extinction; they merely argued that actual
causes were inadequate, and that the real causes were not (yet)
known.

(vii) Geologists working in the concrete style are relatively
closed to ideas from outside what they self-consciously regard as
a 'discipline' with clear cognitive boundaries. Even within the
discipline, they readily accept or deliberately create further
boundaries, welcoming the division of specialist labour as the
most effective way to advance the science. Admittedly, this
characteristic hardly fits the broad interests of some of the
individuals I have mentioned here, but it does increasingly fit the
geologists who came to dominate the science as it became more
professionalised during the nineteenth century. If they had other
interests and concerns outside geology, they increasingly kept
them apart from their geological work.

The agnostic style

Not all geological work falls clearly into the abstract and concrete
styles. Two other styles can be distinguished, comprising work that
is less well-known or less valued in traditional histories of the
science, but none the less significant for my general argument.
The first I shall call agnostic, though the term is intended to
refer to geological, not religious, scepticism. Only a few of the
more prominent geologists of the classic period seem to belong here,
but they include George Greenough, first president of the first

geological society, and Henry De la Beche, first director of one of
the first state geological surveys. However it is possible that
many less well-known figures should also be placed here: for example
the many local amateur collectors of rocks and fossils in the
nineteenth century (cf. Allen 1976), the subordinate 'officers' of
geological surveys and, in the present century, the subordinate
members of the geological research and exploration teams of mining
and oil companies. I shall try to characterise the agnostic style
in terms of the seven related aspects I have already used.

(i) The attitudes towards the construction of any major synthesis
of the stratigraphical series or of earth-history is agnostic. By
this I mean that there is either great scepticism about the possibility of such syntheses, or simply a lack of interest in making
them. Much detailed research may be performed, but it is not
integrated into any coherent overall theory. Greenough for example
was notorious for his extreme scepticism about the possibility of
any reliable theoretical generalisations in geology. De la Beche
issued the first official regional report of the new Geological
Survey in Britain without committing himself on the relation of its
stratigraphy to the would-be universal categories being formulated
by others. This set the tone for later official survey memoirs on
particular regions, at least in the sense that their authors were
not encouraged to theorise, or anyway rarely did so, beyond the
limits of the area assigned to them for investigation. Likewise
most local amateurs have collected fossils from their home area or
studied its local strata with little concern for the high theoretical debates taking place elsewhere (the exceptions are, not un-
naturally, those who have attracted the attention of historians).

(ii) The phenomena of geology, for example the formations of
strata, are subjected to what can best be described as incoherent
classification. Greenough for example insisted in an almost
scholastic manner on the precise definition of terminological
categories, and his detailed geological map of England and Wales
sharply distinguished many different formations. Yet he denied –
or was extremely reluctant to admit – that many of these formations
lay in an invariable orderly sequence. Survey geologists and local
amateurs have often been the most concerned to detect and define
the most minute (and often merely local) subdivisions of the strata.
Yet classifications in the agnostic style tend to remain 'incoherent'
in the sense that they remain local and are not integrated into
programmatically more universal systems.

(iii) Anomalies to theoretical generalisations are embraced
(Caneva 1981). This follows naturally, since such theories are not
highly valued and have generally been propounded by others anyway.
A stand is taken on the facticity of the facts, and if they upset
a theory, 'so much the worse for the theory'. Once again the Devon
controversy provides a fine example of this response to anomaly:
De la Beche continued in a spirited manner to insist on the obstinate
reality of the fossil plants he had found in the 'wrong' strata,
whatever their effect on the high-level stratigraphical theories of
Murchison and others. Significantly, those who supported him were
Greenough and some of the local geologists in Devon.

(iv) The whole cognitive field of geology is seen as one of
irreducible complexity, as in the concrete style. This is obviously

related to the emphasis on the sheer facticity of local details, and
to a suspicion of sweeping generalisations that are seen as submerging
those details out of sight.

(v) The attitude to geological method is strongly empirical, even
more so than in the concrete style. Greenough's scepticism was
directed to exposing the theory-laden character of the most ordinary
geological terms, not in order to advance a more sophisticated view
of the relation between observation and theory, but in order to make
the science more rigorously factual. De la Beche, although one of
his books was entitled 'Researches in Theoretical Geology', was in
practice an extreme empiricist (McCartney 1977). The reaction of
amateurs and survey geologists with local expertise, when confronted
by geologists propounding sweeping theoretical interpretations, is
often to emphasise 'the brute facts' and tell the theoreticians
that they can keep their theories!

(vi) The cognitive goals of those working in the agnostic style
are directed to the uncovering of order rather than cause, however
local the order remains. Description of the facts is valued above
causal interpretation and analysis. This again is similar to the
concrete style, but perhaps even more marked here; and it is
obviously related to the preceding points.

(vii) The attitude is open to the reception of information from
outside the ranks of qualified geologists, either because the
individuals working in this style are themselves outside those
ranks, or because they value highly the knowledge of local experts,
whatever their 'status'. Greenough for example compiled his map
to a considerable extent through such a use of local informants.
However, unlike the use of similar informants by those working in
the other styles so far described, the knowledge is not critically
assessed in the light of the adjudged qualifications of each
informant, but accepted more or less at face value. This atomistic
compilative strategy is clearly related to the extreme empiricism
characteristic of the agnostic style.

The binary style

The last style of geological work that I shall distinguish may be
termed binary. The clearest examples are the scriptural geologists
of the early nineteenth century (Millhauser 1954) and their modern
creationist counterparts; the followers of Velikovsky also perhaps
belong here. In a less pure form the style can also be seen within
the mainstream geology of the late eighteenth and early nineteenth
centuries in the work of diluvialists and glacialists such as
Jean-André Deluc, Georges Cuvier, William Buckland and Louis
Agassiz; their work can be regarded as intermediate between the
'pure' binary style and the concrete style. Once again, seven
related aspects can be used to characterise the style.

(i) The concept of geological time is strongly dimensional, but
only from the present back to a unique boundary-event in the past,
beyond which it can best be described as incoherent or chaotic.
Deluc pioneered the construction of 'natural chronometers', based
on the observed present rates of geological processes, in order to
calibrate earth-history back to this boundary-event - but no further.

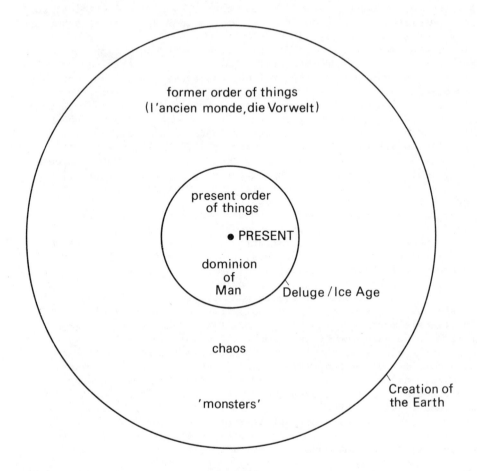

FIGURE 10.3 Diagrammatic representation of the binary style of
earth-history (drawn on the same basis as Figs. 10.1 and 10.2),
showing the single unique boundary separating qualitatively distinct
portions of time. In some binary theories the Creation is merged
into the main boundary-event, so that the 'outside' becomes the
'chaos' before the Creation.

His methods were adopted later by Cuvier and Buckland for the same
purpose. Scriptural geologists and modern creationists were and are
prepared to use conventional methods of dating past events in recent
pre-history - but only to a certain point.
     (ii) Earth-history is strongly classified, but (unlike the
concrete style) in a simple binary manner. There is one unique
boundary in time, which divides earth-history into two sharply
contrasted periods (Fig.10.3). In the early nineteenth century the
more recent period was termed historical, human or post-diluvial,
or - most revealingly - the present order of things. The earlier
period remained relatively undifferentiated; it was the prehistoric
or pre-diluvial period before the dominion of Man, or it was termed

'die Vorwelt', 'die Urwelt', 'l'ancient monde', or the former order
of things.

The boundary-event itself was of course commonly identified with
the biblical flood or Deluge. This has tended to lead to the
dismissal of diluvial theories as unworthy of serious attention;
but it might be more fruitful to regard diluvialism as a historically
contingent manifestation of a binary style that has no necessary
connection with biblical literalism. In fact diluvialists such as
Cuvier and Buckland were widely regarded by both their conservative
and their liberal critics as playing 'fast and loose' with the
Genesis narrative; and when Agassiz later proposed an 'Ice Age'
as an equally drastic boundary-event, Buckland shifted to that
explanation with no apparent difficulty, although it was still
further from any biblical literalism (Rudwick 1970b). The drastic
reordering of the solar system postulated by Velikovsky is an
analogous alleged boundary-event in recent earth-history, yet
entirely divorced from any pretensions of supporting biblical
literalism. What all these boundary-events have in common is not
biblical literalism at all, but a specific relation to Man's place
in earth-history. Although the pre-diluvial existence of mankind
remained a theoretical probability for diluvialists, in practice
both the Deluge-event and the Ice Age were used to demarcate the
human world from the pre-human. In practice, therefore, the binary
pair present/past tends to merge with human/non-human. The pre-
boundary world tends to be regarded as undifferentiated, only
describable in vague or incoherent terms, or even chaotic. In
Deluc's work there is a striking contrast between his clear analysis
of post-diluvial processes and history, and a nebulous treatment of
the pre-diluvial world. Even when his followers Cuvier and Buckland
became aware from stratigraphical research - some of it their own -
that the pre-diluvial world could be divided into many distinctive
periods, their rhetoric tended to remain binary although their
practice became more concrete in style.

(iii) Anomalies to the main interpretative scheme are barred
(cf. Bloor, ch.9 in this volume); they are rejected out of hand as
monstrous and their existence is denied. The best example is
perhaps the rejection of the organic origin of fossils by some
nineteenth-century scriptural geologists and modern creationists;
or at least, the rejection of evidence suggesting that the organisms
lived and died where they are found, over far longer periods than
a few thousand years. This is a far more drastic treatment of
anomaly than the monster-adjustment found in the concrete style.

Appropriately weaker examples of the 'barring' of anomalies can
be found in the work of the mainstream diluvialists: for example
Buckland argued that a human skeleton found in a cave in association
with the bones of pre-diluvial animals was really a later burial
from the Roman period, and thus denied that early Man had co-existed
with these extinct species (North 1942).

(iv) The image of earth-history is characterised by its
simplicity; not the simplicity of underlying abstract causal
principles as in the abstract style, but the simplicity of the
binary scheme of earth-history itself. This is often linked to an
appeal to common sense, as when the scriptural geologist William
Cockburn attacked the mainstream geologists of the mid nineteenth

century: any sane, right-minded ordinary man, he argued, should
be able to see that talk of millions of years of earth-history is
mere fantasy. Similar rhetoric pervades the writing and public
lecturing of modern creationists. But on a more sophisticated level,
much of the mainstream diluvialism of the early nineteenth century
was sustained by a not unreasonable appeal to the 'manifest' dichotomy
of pre- and post-diluvial features on the earth's surface (cf.
Rudwick 1970b).

(v)   The method adopted is as hermeneutic as in the abstract
style. Explicit stress is placed on interpretation: observations
will only yield their true meaning if rightly interpreted. Deluc
interpreted the Lake of Geneva, for example, as evidence for the
recent date of the diluvial event;   Cuvier interpreted fossil bones
to infer that the event had been sudden;   Buckland interpreted
similar bones in caves to reconstruct the pre-diluvial scene in
detail.   The scriptural geologists insisted that the evidence of
the strata, correctly interpreted, was compatible with a traditional
interpretation of Genesis;   and their modern creationist counterparts take the same line.

(vi)   The explanatory goals are strongly causal, as in the
abstract style, but only for the boundary-event and the subsequent
history of the earth.   Present causal processes are of much interest,
not (as in the abstract style) as a key to all past earth-history,
but in order to highlight the contrast between the present and
former 'orders of things'.   They demonstrate the inadequacy of
ordinary causal explanations of the 'ancient world' and - still
more - of the boundary-event itself.   But proximate ('secondary')
causes of that event are sought with great zeal - recourse to
supernatural explanations has rarely been favoured - even though a
satisfactory causal explanation may tend in practice to be regarded
as a long-term aim (as for some work in the concrete style).   Thus
Buckland long intended to write a sequel to his book on the
geological evidence of the Deluge, dealing with its cause;   he
never did so, but only because he became convinced that the physical
cause of most of the supposed diluvial effects had been the global
Ice Age postulated by Agassiz.

(vii)   Geology in the binary style tends to be closed to outside
influences in the sense that information from sources that do not
share the same presuppositions and goals is often regarded with
suspicion.   This is clearly linked to the stress on interpretation:
the witness of self-styled experts is considered of dubious value
compared to that of the 'honnête homme' or the true believer.
This is obviously less applicable to the transitional binary/
concrete style of men like Buckland, who were quite prepared to
argue their diluvial case before their fellow scientists, than it
is of the pure binary style of the more marginal groups I have
mentioned.

A GRID/GROUP ANALYSIS OF THE FOUR STYLES

It will already be obvious that my four proposed styles of
geological work are intended to serve as examples of Douglas's
four main types of cosmology, within the specific field of geology.

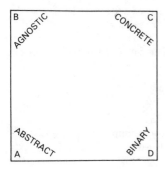

(a) geological styles

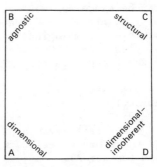

(b) attitudes to time

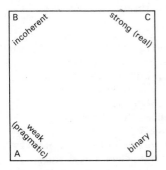

(c) classification of
    time or strata

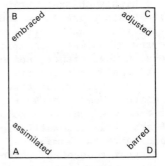

(d) responses to anomaly

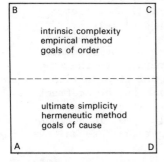

(e) high- and low-grid
    characters

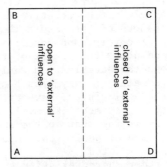

(f) high- and low-group
    characters

FIGURE 10.4

I believe that they also exhibit a reasonably good fit with the social environments anticipated on the grid/group theory.

The proposed identification of the four styles in terms of grid and group can be expressed most economically in diagrammatic form (Fig. 10.4a). Figure 10.4b-d indicates the corresponding positions of the first three cosmological features that I traced through successive styles. The other features can then be related to either the grid or the group parameter (Fig. 10.4e-f).

The abstract style

I identify the abstract style as a low-grid/low-group cosmology, which should therefore correlate with a social environment of individualism (corner A).

The abstract style clearly belongs to the stable diagonal A-C, since it has been one locus of stable and enduring cosmologies or cognitive traditions in geology (e.g. uniformitarianism). It embodies a highly elaborated symbolic system of geological interpretation: primary observations are elaborated to form subordinate components of highly abstract principles, in terms of which the earth and its history are to be understood.

In social terms the abstract style is very clearly that of competitive individualists, the Big Men of geology. They consciously build careers in the science, not necessarily in the sense of securing fixed employment and rising salaries, but primarily in the sense of securing their reputations among other members of the scientific elite. They achieve this through the quality and quantity of the work that they complete and publish. They demand the highest standards of excellence from themselves, and judge others according to the same standards. They value bold originality and versatility of conceptual invention. Because they have many or large projects continually on hand, they are constantly aware of the shortage of time in which to carry them out. They therefore restrict their obligations to other scientists as far as possible to those that are likely to yield tangible benefits to themselves (cf. Morrell 1976, on Lyell). Because they are continually assessing their own work competitively in relation to that of others, they are often secretive about their still uncompleted projects, jealous of the credit that is due to them for their priority of discovery, and concerned about the size of their following and about the extent of the influence of their ideas.

This broad characterisation would apply generally to the individualist elite in any branch of science, but it also fits very well the geologists I have cited as working in the abstract style, particularly men like Lyell and Darwin. It could be summarised by saying that in the abstract style symbolic action - the construction of geological theories - is personalised and the goals are ego-oriented.

Several other characteristics suggested by Douglas (1978) for low grid/low group (A) can also be recognised in those who work in the abstract style in geology. They show a critical attitude to history - in this case the history of the earth - in the sense that great emphasis is given to the need for correct interpretation

of the raw data of that history. Travel is highly esteemed, because
it liberates the geologist from the provincialism of the familiar
features of his home region and gives him first-hand experience of
a wider range of phenomena. Tolerance of diverse metaphysical
beliefs is also noticeable, for example, in Lyell's extreme discretion
in public on the (then) vexed relation of geology to Genesis (cf.
Rudwick 1975), and in his concern to establish an autonomous science
in which the metaphysical beliefs of individuals would be seen as
irrelevant. Whether the abstract style also embodies a contrast
between nature and society is more difficult to assess: on the
face of it, this would seem to be the case with Lyell, for example
(cf. Bartholomew 1973), but not with Darwin.

Another problem with the present grid/group interpretation is
that the geologist who perhaps embodies most perfectly the individualist social style of the Big Man - namely Murchison - did work
that is more in the concrete than the abstract cognitive style.
But this is the kind of anomaly that any case-study of this kind
must - following the individualist style! - accept and seek to
assimilate, by improving the interpretation.

The concrete style

I identify the concrete style as a high-grid/high-group cosmology,
which should therefore correlate with a social environment of
ascribed hierarchy (corner C).

The concrete style clearly belongs to the stable diagonal A-C,
since, like the abstract style, it has been the locus of the stable
and enduring cognitive tradition of stratigraphy. It too embodies
a highly elaborated symbolic system in the sense that local details
of strata are integrated into an extended and programmatically
universal scheme of stratigraphical order. But in social terms
the concrete style belongs at the opposite end of the diagonal
from the abstract. Those who work in the concrete style have
goals that are group-oriented, and their symbolic action - their
geological practice - is 'routinised' (Ostrander, ch.1 of this
volume). They form the backbone of geological societies and other
voluntary organisations, thereby involving themselves in a web of
obligations for the benefit of the group. They willingly or even
eagerly submit to the restrictions implicit in the division of
the scientific labour. They are content to become experts in some
small corner of their field and to receive the credit due to them
for that limited expertise, because they see that achievement as
a contribution to a wider collective endeavour. Within a general
loyalty to the geological community, their specific loyalty is
bestowed on their own 'invisible college' of specialists, and most
of their scientific interactions take place within the boundaries
of that group. Their sense of the propriety of boundaries is as
strong in their perception of the subdivisions of the field of
research as it is in their perception of the 'natural' divisions
of their objects of research.

Perceptions of hierarchy are as strong in interpersonal relations
as in the ordering of the entities under study: the special
expertise of other experts, and the superior expertise of those with

longer experience, tend to be accepted readily. Other characteristics
suggested by Douglas (1978) for this type of cosmology can also be
recognised in the concrete style. Geology in this style is highly
historical, but in the special sense that attention is focused on the
sequential order of strata and periods, rather than their causal
interpretation. The earlier emphasis on the natural-theological
concepts of harmony and design in nature, which was prominent in
the work of men like Sedgwick and Buckland, can be regarded as a
special example of an inclination towards natural-law theories in
general.

It should be noted that practitioners in the concrete style were
and are generally lodged firmly in the often hierarchical institutional structures of mining schools, geological surveys and
universities. The 'profession' of geology is the primary locus of
the concrete style.

The agnostic style

I identify the agnostic style as a high-grid/low-group cosmology,
which should therefore correlate with a social environment of
atomised subordination (corner B).

The agnostic style fits the unstable diagonal B-D, in that it
has never produced an enduring tradition; it also fits the B end
of that diagonal reasonably well. Douglas (1978) characterises
the B position in terms of social insulation and exclusion. This
applies well to the rare examples of relatively prominent
geologists working in the agnostic style. Greenough, although a
highly active member of the Geological Society he had helped to
found, seems to have felt increasingly excluded and isolated
intellectually, as the Society abandoned the extreme empiricist
norms he had tried to impose on it (cf. Rudwick 1963, Laudan,
1977). Certainly the correspondence of other prominent members
is full of scornful remarks about Greenough's 'reactionary'
emphasis on uninterpreted fact-collecting. Greenough's great
wealth should have given him the economic freedom to move across
the social map; but if as I suggest it was cognitive pressures
that forced him into isolated exclusion, that serves to emphasise
how far grid/group analysis must be expected to cut across simple
categories of economic position. De la Beche, on the other hand,
was forced into a similar isolation partly by economic pressures:
having lost his inherited fortune he was excluded from the freedom
of action of the 'gentlemen-amateurs' who formed the rest of the
English geological elite, and was often physically isolated from
their debates by his official Survey duties in remote areas (cf.
McCartney 1977).

Such individuals as Greenough and De la Beche may be thrust into
the B position by unusual sets of circumstances, but others find
themselves there for more structural reasons. I have suggested
that subordinate members of official or company survey teams are
a case in point: they are assigned specific limited tasks and may
be given little insight into the broader strategy to which these
tasks are to contribute. This can be correlated with a cosmology
that is not so much eclectic (Douglas 1978) as just incoherent;

Douglas's suggestion that people in this position tend to lack any
rational sense of history can perhaps be matched here in the failure
of the agnostic style to generate any coherent conception of earth-
history.

The binary style

I identify the binary style as a low-grid/high-group cosmology,
which should therefore correlate with a social environment of
factionalism (corner D).

The binary style, unlike the agnostic, might seem to have been
the locus of an enduring tradition, namely that of scriptural
geology, which seeks to reconcile geology with Genesis by
reinterpreting the former. But in reality the scriptural tradition
was not a stable tradition in the sense that, for example, uniformitarian and stratigraphical geology have been. It was a series of
more or less isolated projects by individuals who frequently
criticised each other for not being sufficiently faithful to
scripture (or to geology). It shows all the fissiparous sect-like
tendencies that are characteristic of factionalism. Geology in
the binary style represents an 'unelaborated symbolic system'
(Ostrander, ch.1 of this volume), in that a very simple scheme of
earth-history is imposed on the complex data presented by expert
geologists. The very short time-scale of this scheme needs no
emphasis. Resistance to innovation is also clearly characteristic
of those using the binary style. Their work is strongly group-
oriented, in that the scriptural interpretations of geology are
put forward for the edification of other members of the same group
of true believers - a group which tends to be strongly boundaried
by criteria of strict orthodoxy.

The characteristics just summarised for the earlier scriptural
geologists are equally applicable to the modern creationist
geologists. They may also apply to the followers of Velikovsky,
although their cosmology is not so obviously sustained by religious
aspirations. It might however be more fruitful to see all those
groups as united more by their social position than by the cognitive
context of their cosmologies: they all seem to be small groups
that were or are consciously on the defensive against the threatening power of the expert knowledge of mainstream scientists. How
far, then, can the tendency towards the binary style be matched
with the environment of factionalism, when it is found among the
mainstream geologists themselves? The brief rise and fall of
diluvialism in early nineteenth-century geology does in fact seem
to correlate rather well with a transitory conflict between
geology and religious orthodoxy. In the reaction that followed
the excesses of the French Revolution, geology was for a time
suspected of encouraging infidelity. For geologists who valued
orthodoxy as much as geology, this created a confusing ambiguity
of roles; and it was in the small group characterised by that
ambiguity that diluvialist theories briefly flourished, within the
larger community of geologists. It is worth noting in conclusion
that this small group - men such as Buckland and Sedgwick - attacked
the scriptural geologists as vehemently as they were attacked in
return; factionalism was operative here too.

CONCLUSION

In the space of this paper I have only been able to point out a few
features of geological work, past and present, which at least suggest
that the theory of grid/group analysis may be valid in this area of
natural-scientific cosmologies. To make the case more persuasive
would need much more detailed illustration and documentation than
is feasible here; but I consider that the distinguishable cognitive
styles in geology fit the anticipated grid/group characteristics
well enough to justify a further search for evidence. In the course
of that search, it will be important not to apply the grid/group
theory in a Procrustean manner to the historical or sociological
data, as was so widely done with Kuhn's notion of paradigms in
the 1960s. The characterisation of the parameters of grid and
group, and of the spaces on the field that they generate, must
themselves be subjected to modification and improvement in the light
of concrete case-studies of all kinds.

I have analysed geological work in terms of four fairly distinct
cognitive styles; but it is important in conclusion to reiterate
that this is a simplification for purposes of exposition. I have
deliberately used an open-square design for my grid/group diagrams,
precisely in order to emphasise visually that the four grid/group
types represent extremes of a two-dimensional continuum. Such a
design should encourage us to consider what movements in any
direction across the grid/group field would mean, both socially
and cognitively, whether in the life of an individual or as a
broader historical trend, without being tempted to think that any
such movement must necessarily involve a kind of quantum leap. I
have indicated briefly at least a few examples of intermediate
positions and movements across the grid/group field. The mainstream
diluvialists, for example, seem to be intermediate between the
concrete and binary style; and Buckland moved only temporarily
into that intermediate (and perhaps unstable) position, from a
base that was more clearly in the concrete style. Lyell seems to
have moved from the concrete style of his early training (under
Buckland), along the stable diagonal to the abstract style of his
mature work. De la Beche perhaps moved from the same corner
towards the agnostic style. All such suggestions need more
intensive and critical study; but the important point is that the
correlations between cosmology and social environment are plausible
enough at a first approximation to justify that more detailed study.

Staunch 'defenders of the faith' in scientific truth may be
disturbed at my lack of reference to the truth-value of the
geological work that was and is achieved within these cognitive
styles. This omission does not in fact betray a rabid relativist;
the reason for the omission is that the scarcely deniable
cumulative element in geological knowledge has no simple historical
association with any one style. The mythology of the science gives
special credit to the traditions (e.g. uniformitarianism) that I
identify with the abstract style - but perhaps because those with
power to control the mythology are generally the Big Men who
themselves work in that style.

It is doubtful, however, whether the modern synthesis of earth-
history could have been achieved if the emphasis on causal analysis

in the abstract style had not been in continual interaction with
the emphasis on a unique sequence in the concrete style. Even the
agnostic style was probably valuable at one period of history, to
counteract the over-extravagant proliferation of theory in disregard
to attainable observation. And the binary style was correct, at one
period of history, to insist on the reality of an extraordinary event
in the recent past, even though that event was later identified as
a series of glacial periods and not as a single Deluge.

It seems therefore more fruitful to regard the grid/group field
simply as the formalisation of a field of variation in possible
social environments, any part of which is likely to support
cosmologies of a particular kind. To use a biological metaphor,
the cosmologies are adapted to their social environment. But to
assert the fact of adaptation is, as all historians of evolutionary
theory are well aware, to say nothing at all about its cause.
Likewise, the establishment of cultural bias (Douglas 1978), or of
correlations between cosmologies and social environments, tells us
nothing about the causation of these correlations. It certainly
does not immediately justify the naive determinism that would
reduce the cosmologies - in the present case the geological theories
and the research from which they grow - to nothing but the products
of particular social environments.

ACKNOWLEDGMENTS

Earlier versions of this paper were given to the Institutionen
fÜr idé- och lardomshistoria, University of Uppsala, Sweden, and
as the John Joly Memorial Lecture at Trinity College, Dublin,
Ireland: I am much indebted to the historians and geologists
present on these occasions for their many helpful comments on my
argument. I am very grateful to Dr David Bloor (University of
Edinburgh) and Dr Kenneth Caneva (University of North Carolina)
for valuable discussions about the adaptation of grid/group analysis
to deal with material from the natural sciences.

I am also indebted to Dr Caneva for allowing me to use his article
(1981) before it was published; with that exception, I have not been
able to refer here to work that appeared after 1978, when this essay
was written and accepted for publication.

BIBLIOGRAPHY

I have not thought it appropriate, in this short essay, to give
references to primary sources, or even to attempt a full documentation of modern historical studies. I have however referred to a
number of my own articles, because the theme of the present essay
has been consciously though implicitly present in my recent work.

ALBURY, W.R. and OLDROYD, D.R. (1977), From Renaissance mineral
studies to historical geology, in the light of Michel Foucault's
'The Order of Things', 'British Journal for the History of Science',
vol.10: 187-215.
ALLEN, D.E. (1976), 'The naturalist in Britain. A social history',
London, Allen Lane.

BARTHOLOMEW, M. (1973), Lyell and evolution: an account of Lyell's
response to the prospect of an evolutionary ancestry for Man,
'British Journal for the History of Science', vol.6: 261-303.
BARTHOLOMEW, M. (1976), The non-progress of non-progression: two
responses to Lyell's doctrine, 'British Journal for the History of
Science', vol.9: 166-74.
BLOOR, D.C. (1978), Polyhedra and the abominations of Leviticus,
'British Journal for the History of Science', vol.11: 245-72 (re-
printed in this volume).
BURCHFIELD, J.D. (1974), Darwin and the dilemma of geological time,
'Isis', vol.65: 300-21.
CANEVA, K.L. (1981), What should we do with the monster? Electro-
magnetism and the Psychosociology of Knowledge, in Everett
Mendelsohn and Yehuda Elkana (eds), 'Sciences and Cultures:
Anthropological Studies of the Sciences' (Sociology of Science: A
Yearbook, vol.5), Dordrecht and Boston, D. Reidel, pp.101-31.
DOUGLAS, M. (1970), 'Natural Symbols', London, Barrie & Rockcliff.
DOUGLAS, M. (1975), In the nature of things, in 'Implicit Meanings.
Essays in Anthropology', London, Routledge & Kegan Paul, pp.210-29.
DOUGLAS, M. (1978), 'Cultural Bias', London, Royal Anthropological
Institute.
EVANS-PRICHARD, E. (1940), 'The Nuer', Oxford, Clarendon Press.
GHISELIN, M.T. (1969), 'The Triumph of the Darwinian Method',
Berkeley and Los Angeles, University of California Press.
HALLAM, A. (1973), 'A Revolution in the Earth Sciences. From
Continental Drift to Plate Tectonics', Oxford, Clarendon Press.
HERBERT, S. (1977), The place of Man in the development of Darwin's
theory of transmutation, part II, 'Journal of the History of
Biology', vol.10, pp.155-227.
LAUDAN, R. (1977), Ideas and organizations in British geology: a
case study in institutional history, 'Isis', vol.68, pp.527-38.
McCARTNEY, P.J. (1977), 'Henry de la Beche: Observations on an
Observer', Cardiff, National Museum of Wales.
MILLHAUSER, M. (1954), The scriptural geologists. An episode in
the history of opinion, 'Osiris', vol.11, pp.65-86.
MORRELL, J.B. (1976), London institutions and Lyell's career,
1820-41, 'British Journal for the History of Science', vol.9,
pp.132-46.
NORTH, F.J. (1942), Paviland Cave, the 'Red Lady', the Deluge,
and William Buckland, 'Annals of Science', vol.5, pp.91-128.
RUDWICK, M.J.S. (1963), The foundation of the Geological Society
of London: its scheme for co-operative research and its struggle
for independence, 'British Journal for the History of Science',
vol.1, pp.325-55.
RUDWICK, M.J.S. (1967), A critique of uniformitarian geology: a
letter from W.D. Conybeare to Charles Lyell, 1841, 'Proceedings of
the American Philosophical Society', vol.111, pp.272-87.
RUDWICK, M.J.S. (1970a), The strategy of Lyell's 'Principles of
Geology', 'Isis', vol.61, pp.5-33.
RUDWICK, M.J.S. (1970b), The glacial theory, 'History of Science',
vol.8, pp.136-57.
RUDWICK, M.J.S. (1974), Poulett Scrope on the volcanoes of Auvergne:
Lyellian time and political economy, 'British Journal for the
History of Science', vol.7, pp.205-42.

RUDWICK, M.J.S. (1975), Charles Lyell F.R.S. (1797–1875) and his London lectures on geology, 1832–33, 'Notes and Records of the Royal Society of London', vol.29, pp.231–63.
RUDWICK, M.J.S. (1976), The emergence of a visual language for geological science, 1760–1840, 'History of Science', vol.14, pp.149–95.
RUDWICK, M.J.S. (1977), Historical analogies in the geological work of Charles Lyell, 'Janus', vol.64, pp.89–107.
RUDWICK, M.J.S. (1978), Charles Lyell's dream of a statistical palaeontology, 'Palaeontology', vol.21, pp.225–44.
RUDWICK, M.J.S. (1979), The Devonian: a System born from Conflict, in M.R. House et al. (eds), 'The Devonian System', London, Palaeontological Association (also, 'Special Papers in Palaeontology', no.23), pp.9–21.

Part Three

CLOSE FOCUS ON SELECTED COSMOLOGIES

INTRODUCTION
Mary Douglas

Now I come to introduce the last section. Already we have had many
examples of how people come to think alike when they are in a like
situation, defined in grid/group terms. Three concluding essays
illustrate how the internal consciousness is structured in a
particular social environment. Steve Rayner gives the example of a
homogenized and shrunken perception of time and space which is
encouraged by choosing to live in small strongly bounded egalitarian
groups. If his ideas are substantiated by further research, it must
be extremely interesting to have a precise account of the grid/group
conditions which make credible millenarian claims that doomsday or
paradise will occur next week. In the preceding section Martin
Rudwick has related similar conceptions of geological time to the
same sector of the grid/group scheme. Michael Thompson suggests
in this section not only a parallel insight but also describes the
mechanisms by which people cut off their consciousness of a long
time-perspective as part of their commitment to a society which
does not allow claims to be made in the name of the ancestors or
of posterity. With these three independent suggestions converging
on the same point, I hope that future research will take up the
effect of grid/group positioning on consciousness of temporal
structure.
   Steve Rayner's work in the Workers' Institute is particularly
interesting because he places it on our diagram further to the
bottom right-hand corner than any religious sect that has been
described. Its organization realizes perfect fraternal equality.
Most religious sects which endure long enough to be recorded are
authoritative, and delegate distinctive roles, usually a marked
difference between the sexes, a grade of elders and a leader. But
they endure, while the line of ancestry from which the Workers'
Institute is descended is hard to trace because dissolutions and
new starts occur so frequently. Sects are famous for their
schismatic tendencies, but they are stable compared with the
ephemeral life histories of the progenitors of the Workers' Institute.
Steve Rayner notes the costs which attend the realization of the
fraternal ideal: information about the outside society is severely
distorted. No growth of knowledge occurs within, there is no
arguing and no concluding at the discussion meetings. Time and

space are shrunk to fit the aspirations of the group. The cost of
keeping the aspirations alive and nurturing the group's existence
upon them is the loss of political effectiveness for ever achieving
the stated goals.

Dennis Owen shows further how intense preoccupation with the
unity of a village, Salem, in the 1690s drastically reduced the
individual's ability to apply the normal critical canons of the time.
Spectral evidence was not legally recognized by the courts. Yet
accused witches were convicted mainly upon this inadmissible
evidence. The Puritan preachers narrowly reduced the pool of
available religious metaphors to those few about infectious disease
and demonology which resonated with the passionate political conflicts
uppermost in the minds of their hearers. If he were to develop
further the argument that religious metaphors draw on dominant
political concerns, he would have to make an equivalent analysis
of the sermons of the preachers of the Anglican Communion in Boston
in the same period. These would afford an appropriate contrast
since the Anglicans' message of toleration particularly angered the
Puritans. If Dennis Owen has chosen and understood his own material
well, their sermons should say much less about purity, poisoning
and Satan's infiltrations and use more hopeful, perhaps horticul-
tural, metaphors.

Michael Thompson's first chapter (ch.2 of this volume) is densely
argued. His second chapter (ch.13) gives an illustration of a whole
culture sustained for generations at this fifth, still point. He
finds not a single hermit but a whole society of live-and-let-live
philosophers, Sherpa Buddhists poised always in the present, leaving
all exits open at all times, a challenge to existing sociological
paradigms but assimilable within his own. This is the ethnographic
illustration of the theoretical proposals he makes in the section
on method.

Our theory, spelt out with its assumptions, starts with
individuals creating their social conditions by the bargaining and
argumentation which sets up social categories or breaks them down.
We assume that they choose how they deal with each other, but the
choice for a certain kind of social relationship unwittingly
involves the chooser in a particular constrictive social environment.
All the more reason to understand the further cognitive and psychic
consequences of decisions about how families or institutions shall
be run; all the more vital to know the range of possibilities and
to understand what kinds of shackles are forged by decisions to
escape from or enter in society of one sort or another. This
exercise relativizes individual judgment within a steady framework.
It offers several different positions from which to judge the
reasonableness of excuses and blame. The theory helps the historian
to lift the perceptual veil which made obviously hard choices harder
at the time. It foretells the perceptual shifts that accompany
the tightening of a group's boundaries or the weakening of its
strength. We can assess those pressures of personal wills upon
personal intentions in the light of cultural theory. The biggest
claim of this approach could be that it encourages us to choose how
we deal with one another with awareness of the particular distorted
and restricted visions of social reality entailed in each choice.

Chapter 11

THE PERCEPTION OF TIME AND SPACE IN EGALITARIAN SECTS: A MILLENARIAN COSMOLOGY

Steve Rayner

> All men have stood for freedom ... and those of the richer
> sort of you that see it are ashamed and afraid to own it,
> because it comes clothed in a clownish garment .... Freedom
> is the man that will turn the world upside down, therefore
> no wonder he hath enemies .... True freedom lies in the
> community in spirit and community in the earthly treasury,
> and this is Christ the true manchild spread abroad in the
> creation, restoring all things unto himself. (Gerrard
> Winstanley, 1649)

Attempts at providing a general explanation of millenarianism have
hitherto addressed themselves to the question: Why does millenarianism occur? The answers offered to this question almost
invariably amount to relative deprivation theories which have many
shortcomings. This paper rests on the contention that the question
why millenarianism occurs can only be answered by a specific
historical account. Such an account may well include instances of
relative deprivation, but that is not sufficient justification to
raise this one aspect of the phenomenon to the level of a general
explanation.

The argument in this paper is that the interesting question at
the level of general explanation must be: How is millenarianism
possible? The answer exploits the prediction made by grid and group
classification that each social environment must have its own
distinctive cosmology. I argue that it is only possible collectively
to maintain millenarian beliefs in a social environment in which it
is possible collectively to foreshorten historical time and compress
geographical space. (These are seen as logical conditions of
millenarianism.) In terms of grid and group, these conditions can
only exist within a strong group boundary and increase in likelihood
as the grid weakens and provides fewer points of historical and
spatial differentiation.

MILLENARIANISM AND UTOPIANISM

Although the term millenarianism originally designated belief in

the biblical prophecy of the thousand-year reign of Christ on Earth
(Revelation XX) it has come to be indiscriminately applied to any
ideology which envisages a collective earthly salvation. Thus,
orthodox Marxism-Leninism is sometimes described as millenarian
because of its declared aim of creating a classless society (Cohn
1957, Ling 1966).

This is casting the net too wide. If every optimistic political
and religious viewpoint is designated as millenarian, then the term
ceases to tell us very much about the movements it is applied to.
I prefer to reserve the term millenarian to describe movements which
organise their activity around the belief that the world will be
turned upside down by the imminent intervention of an external
agency, which will exalt the weak and humble the powerful.

In the sense that it is used in this essay, millenarianism is
distinguished from other sorts of utopian prophecy, including the
prophecy of the millennium as it is accepted by the orthodox
Christian denominations. The point is that while Anglicans,
Catholics, Methodists, etc. may accept the prophecy as more or less
significant, they do not expect its fulfilment at any particular
date, let alone do they act on the belief that it is imminent.

Similarly, one would be hard pressed to find a Communist Party
member today who will hazard to guess the date of the triumph of
world socialism. Marxism like Christianity is an optimistic
ideology, and like Christianity it contains millenarian movements,
one of which - the Workers' Institute of Marxism-Leninism Mao Xedong
Thought - will be examined in this essay. However, neither Marxism
nor Christianity in their established forms would be considered to
be millenarian by the standards of the present paper. I am clearly
at odds with Cohn (1957: 309-11) on this point, for he equates
twentieth-century Nazism and Communism with medieval millenarianism.

There seem to be three basic predicates for the definition of
millenarianism adopted here. They are respectively temporal,
spatial and ethical in character:

1 The conviction that the present epoch is finite and known to
be ending shortly.
2 The conviction that the new epoch will be established by the
external intervention of some powerful agency.
3 The conviction that all men ought to be recognised as moral
equals.

These three themes have consistently occurred in the history of
European millenarianism. Early Christians, like the Jehovah's
Witnesses of the nineteenth century, looked for the imminent second
coming of Christ. But in both cases the failure of the advent led
to a reluctance to fix a specific date and eventually to its long-
term postponement. The Jehovah's Witnesses have variously specified
1847 and 1914 respectively as dates for the second advent. They no
longer commit themselves to dates, although 1925 and 1975 have been
unofficial favourites (Wilson 1970: 110-17).

In Britain the belief in the imminence of the second advent of
Christ became most widespread during the social upheavals of the
mid seventeenth century and affected all classes of society.
Christopher Hill (1975: 97) reports the concern expressed by a
Bristol Baptist in 1654 upon hearing that two Frenchmen had
predicted the end of the world for 1656. John Tillinghast declared

in 1654 that 'This generation shall not pass until the millennium
has arrived' ('Generation-work' quoted in Hill 1975: 97). Alas,
he died the following year and was not able to hear John Bunyan
confirm in 1658 that 'the judgment day is at hand' ('Works', III,
quoted in Hill 1975: 97).

The theme of moral equality was at the forefront of the Diggers'
movement. Their leader, Gerrard Winstanley, was convinced that the
old dispensation was 'running up like parchment in the fire', and
preached that 'the Earth is a common treasury to all'. Norman Cohn
(1957: 316) has described Winstanley's vision as a 'primitivist
millennium in which private property, class distinction, and human
authority would have no place'. The Diggers' preparations for the
advent took the form of co-operative farming on common land at
St George's Hill in Surrey in the hope that their example would
lead mankind back into a 'virgin state', ready for Christ's
return. Alas, not all millenarians have confined themselves to
such preparations by example. At various times elsewhere in
Europe they have attempted to achieve a state of equality by the
physical annihilation of the powerful, the wealthy, and any other
usurpers of true spirituality (especially priests) who might
oppose them. This was certainly the path followed by the sixteenth
century Anabaptists of Münster under the leadership of John of
Leyden (Cohn 1957: 283ff).

The modern heirs to the millenarian tradition in Britain include
the Workers' Institute of Marxism-Leninism Mao Xedong Thought, a
tiny political sect which predicted the liberation of the world
from tyranny by the end of 1977.

In the United States millenarianism reached its zenith in the
nineteenth century. William Miller, who predicted the coming of
Christ by March 1844, received widespread support until the
postponed date of October 1844 (an adjustment to the Jewish
calendar) failed to yield results (Wilson 1970: 97-9). Those who
did not give up adventism in the face of this disappointment formed
such sects as the Jehovah's Witnesses, Christadelphians, and
Seventh-Day Adventists.

Possibly the most dramatic instances of millenarianism in the
anthropologists' catalogue are the Melanesian cargo cults. In
these cases, all of the three basic themes of our definition are
clearly present. Cargo movements are characterised by the
abandonment of productive activity (and in many cases the destruction
of the traditional means of production) in favour of the co-operative
construction of an airstrip or jetty to receive the cargo which is
expected imminently to arrive from the ancestors. To the participants in cargo movements, the arrival of such a cargo consisting
of the commodities enjoyed by Europeans would place the black man
on an equal moral basis with the white man, who presently exerts
his moral superiority (in defiance of the fierce egalitarianism
of the Melanesians) through his control over cargo (Burridge 1960).

All of the movements I have described in this introduction
exhibit the temporal, spatial, and ethical features which I have
identified as basic predicates of millenarianism. These features
have been observed by most commentators. However, in formulating
general explanations of millenarianism, they have concentrated on
the ethical theme (in the form of relative deprivation theories) to

the virtual exclusion of the temporal and spatial themes. This
paper is intended as a first step in restoring these themes to a
central position in our understanding of millenarian phenomena.

RELATIVE DEPRIVATION THEORIES

In their most tangible form, relative deprivation theories have been
concerned with cathartic responses to social tension arising out
of the unequal distribution of material resources. Peter Worsley's
study of cargo cults in 'The Trumpet Shall Sound' (1970) is one of
the best examples of this version of the theory.

Worsley points out the drastic impact of colonialisation on
Melanesian society, the consequent economic disruption, and the
overthrow of traditional normative and political systems. He
describes how the supression of indigenous culture by missionaries
of various denominations gave rise to a syncretist mythology based
on Christian eschatology and the Melanesian tradition of the return
of the ancestors. The picture emerges of cargo cults as a means of
adapting to alienation under colonialism. Loss of tribal lands,
fluctuating copra prices, and the consequent insecurity of the
labour market, were all seen by the native population as aspects
of an irrational economic system. Successive changes in governing
colonial powers and different religious denominations compounded
the appalling conditions and dispossession of the indigenes,
whilst the message of Christianity appeared inconsistent with
the behaviour of the colonists.

According to Worsley, the upshot of all this is a conflicting
desire for the end of foreign rule and for ownership of the white
man's cargo, which is seen as rightfully belonging to the ancestors.
Seen in this light, cargo cults serve a rational integrative
function by overcoming contradictory aspirations through the
destruction of traditional culture and by pulling people into a
nationalist phase in which the catharsis of millenarian activity
(in the form of the replacing of the traditional productive
process of individual gardeners by collective preparation for the
arrival of cargo) compensates for the natives' actual inability
to control their world.

Worsley's account is detailed and coherent: its major fault is
that there is nothing in it to explain why relative deprivation in
this case, or in general, should produce a specifically millenarian
response rather than any other form of revolutionary activity, or
even a non-revolutionary response such as a nativist cult, like
the Navaho Peyote religion which David Aberle (1966) attributes to
relative deprivation.

There have been attempts to come to grips with the problem of
theoretical analysis of millenarianism through an expanded notion
of relative deprivation. Aberle (1962) has suggested expanding
the concept to cover any negative discrepancy between legitimate
expectation and reality, whilst Burridge says in 'New Heaven: New
Earth' (1971) that by enlarging the traditional definition of
religion to include all concerns with human redemption and by, in
effect, expanding the concept of relative deprivation from concerns
with mere material disadvantage to cover any denial, or supposed

denial, of access to the means of salvation, we have the basis of a general explanation of millenarian activity.

These examples raise the question of whether we are stretching the explanatory concepts (religion and relative deprivation) beyond the point where they are really meaningful. For example, the tiny Brixton-based political sect, The Workers' Institute of Marxism-Leninism Mao Xedong Thought, would have to be included as a religious organisation according to Burridge's wider definition. Although we might speak of political convictions being held with religious fervour, I doubt if many of us would be happy to push this usage far beyond the metaphorical. Politics and religion may both be concerned with human redemption, but as sociological categories they must be allowed to refer to different areas of activity, though they be polythetically defined. In any case, I hope to show by the example of the Workers' Institute that millenarianism need not be considered as a primarily religious phenomenon, but may occur in a wholly secular context.

However, the real point is that the net of relative deprivation is being cast so wide as to render it logically vacuous as a general explanation of millenarianism.   The scope of its many definitions is such that it is hardly possible to conceive of a society which does not experience it according to one or another of these definitions. Relative deprivation does not stand the test of the negative case where it exists without producing millenarian activity. In this case, relative deprivation may produce a variety of non-millenarian responses such as the revitalisation movements discussed by Wallace (1956), those movements which Linton (1943) described as nativist or ecstatic cults such as the Zar cults of the northern Sudan which Lewis (1971) ascribes to the exclusion of women from mainstream Islam. On the other hand, relative deprivation may produce no coherent movement at all, whilst some forms of utopian activity may appeal to members of a society who cannot be usefully or sympathetically described as relatively deprived in any distinct sense.   One such was Thomas Muntzer, an egalitarian millennialist of the sixteenth century who 'appears neither as a victim nor as an enemy of social injustice but rather as an "eternal student", extraordinarily learned and intensely intellectual' (Cohn 1957: 251).

Relative deprivation theories attempt to trace a direct route from the social experience of deprivation to the construction of a millenarian world view. But the route is too direct to be theoretically informative. The theory accounts for millenarianism in terms of compensation for lack of political or economic justice, but it does not explain why any particular response to relative deprivation should be specifically millenarian. The most that can be said is that relative deprivation is frequently a factor in the historical accounts of a variety of cults of revolt or withdrawal. But this tells us nothing specifically about millenarianism because the role of relative deprivation cannot be understood independently of a different sort of question: What kind of social environment enables people to maintain millenarian beliefs? Or more specifically: What are the social conditions which give rise to the following basic temporal and spatial predicates of a millenarian world view?

1 The conviction that the present epoch is finite and known
   to be ending shortly.
2 The conviction that the new epoch will be established by the
   external intervention of some powerful agency.

It is only in this context that we can examine what role relative
deprivation might play in creating the sort of environment which
supports millenarian beliefs. If we are to avoid reducing the
concrete histories of movements to special pleas for relative
deprivation theory, then we are required to locate the social
environment characteristic of millennialists in a general typology
of social relations and corresponding structures of world outlook.

The approach which I am proposing here would achieve what
Kaminsky (1962) sought in what he called 'an analytical approach
to the problem of explaining millenarianism'. That is, one that
takes the evidence of the movement itself as grounds for inference
about the relationship of the movement to society. Kaminsky has
suggested relating the movement to the society in which it has its
being, by constructing a typology of alienation and withdrawal.
Unfortunately, Kaminsky himself was unable to make this approach
workable because of his concept of what such a typology would be.
For example, he offers as one type, 'the man so neurotic that he
cannot find adequate pleasure in the ordinary sources of delight.
Another might be a man belonging to a persecuted race or religion.'
In other words, Kaminsky's concept of a typology is an essentialist
one, and the result is that his explanations are simply circular.

it must be conceded that analysis of movements cannot by itself
tell us why particular movements erupt into being ... except
in circular terms: the movement includes or presupposes X;
therefore when we find a movement we can be sure of the presence
of X. (Kaminsky 1962: 209)

A further criticism of Kaminsky's view of a social typology is
that he constructs his categories in terms of individual psychology
rather than in terms of social structure. What we require is an
analytic typology which relates the ideological and social structural
aspects of millenarian groups to the society in which they have their
being, without forcing us into mere circularity. Grid and group
offers us just such a typology. The Workers' Institute of Marxism-
Leninism Mao Xedong Thought offers us a test case.

The reader will recall that grid/group analysis claims that
individuals and social units located in different parts of this
typology of social experience will develop different cosmologies
(types of ideology), because the premises involved in defining the
social environment in terms of grid and group place certain
distinctive constraints on the structure of the beliefs which can
be used to legitimate actions taken within it. Thus the typology
reflects the logical possibilities of different structures of
thought and behaviour characteristic of a social system according to
the relative strengths of its grid and group. Our first task is to
identify which of these logical possibilities most nearly represents
the type of social environment and corresponding cosmology
characteristic of millenarian movements. Fortunately, the three
basic predicates of our definition of millenarianism provide a
strong lead.

The first theme is the imminent end of the present epoch. The

second theme is the spatial theme of external intervention. This
points to an experience of clear distinctions between outside and
inside, characteristic of high group.   Theme number three is the
egalitarian ethical imperative which is translated into action
within the boundaries of the group by, for example, the abolition
of money in Münster by Jan Matthys (Cohn 1957: 28), the renunciation
of private property by the Diggers and Levellers (Hill 1975: ch.4),
and the destruction of traditional capital in cargo cults (Wilson
1975: 199-206). This theme therefore points to a low-grid condition.
      The short future envisaged by the temporal theme of an imminently
ending finite epoch reinforces the second and third themes, for as
Douglas (1978: 29) points out, the experience of the past at low
grid/high group is relatively undifferentiated. 'Correspondingly
the perception of the future is also less discriminated. This
means that the sudden arrival of the millennium is more credible
here....'
      It should be clear from our definition of millenarianism, that
such movements exhibit at least some of both the social
structural and cosmological characteristics of a low-grid/high-
group condition. So let us look more closely at the constraints
which the social relations of such an environment will place on
the cosmology of individuals located within it, and then see how
our chosen example matches up.
      In strongly bounded egalitarian groups the social experience of
the individual is constrained first and foremost by the external
boundary maintained by the group against outsiders. Individual
behaviour will be subject to controls exercised in the name of the
whole group. The extreme case would be a monastic type of community
in which the total life support of individuals could be derived
from the group. There will be few internal divisions and an
absence of specialised roles, which will inevitably lead to
difficulties in determining who should adjudicate in disputes.
Adjudicating roles will therefore remain implicit. The only
sanctions available to the group will be expulsion, and when major
disagreements arise they will result in fission. Hence the short
life-expectancy of groups located here. However, as a rule
disagreement will be driven underground and, if the group is large
enough, covert factions might develop. There will be few constraints
from a publicly received system of classification. Buffered by the
strong group boundary, such a social unit will be able to maintain
its own order of the universe independently of any contradiction
between its views and the received views of the outside world.

THE WORKERS' INSTITUTE OF MARXISM-LENINISM MAO XEDONG THOUGHT

So far we have dealt only with the formal conditions for a social
unit to be located at low grid/high group, and the constraints which
the social environment can be expected to exert upon the cosmology.
It behoves us to look in some detail at a millenarian organisation
to see if it fulfils our expectations.
      The Workers' Institute of Marxism-Leninism Mao Xedong Thought is
a tiny Maoist sect centered in the Brixton area of south-west
London, which in 1977 confidently predicted that the world would be

liberated from capitalist oppression by the Chinese People's Liberation
Army before the end of the year.

The Institute was founded in 1974 by a minute faction led out of
the tiny Communist Party of England (Marxist-Leninist) by a Malaysian
called Balakrishnan. The breakaway group claimed that the CPE (M-L)
leadership had renounced the leadership of the 'great, glorious and
correct Communist Party of China', and had joined the service of the
'International Fascist Bourgeoisie'. The CPE (M-L) itself had only
been formed in 1972 out of the English Communist Movement (M-L),
which was itself the successor to the Internationalists group of the
late 1960s.

The central core of the Workers' Institute is a 'communist
collective', numbering about thirteen people, who live at the Mao
Xedong Memorial Centre in Brixton. Some members of this collective
have jobs outside of the group in order to support the centre and
the remaining members of the collective who devote themselves to
full-time political activity. The group is fiercely self-supporting
and refuses any contributions to its funds from non-members.

The main political task of the group is seen as 'building a stable
revolutionary base in and around Brixton', which was chosen for the
Institute's location 'because it is the worst place in the world'.
The Mao Memorial Centre is the focus for the activity of the whole
of the Workers' Institute, whose total membership is less than
double the number in the core. Political co-operation with other
groups is rejected because the latter 'do not uphold the line of
the Communist Party of China'. Similarly work in the trades unions
is rejected by the Institute because they are simply 'organs of
Fascism'.

Although the Institute appears to have an irregular periphery
of 'supporters' who turn up for occasional meetings, they do not
regularly attend the Centre's prized Political Evening School.
The Workers' Institute appears as a case of very strong group, with
its periphery of supporters acting as part of the buffer between
the group proper and the outside world.

In respect of grid factors, there are no discernible insulating
social classifications operating within the Workers' Institute.
There is no emphasis on formal office-holding. Although Balakrishnan
is the titular secretary of the organisation he does not occupy
separate office facilities. There is no discernible division of
labour in the political sphere, and no separation of members and
cadres, or of theoretical and activist cadres.

In addition to the lack of internal differentiation, there is
an absence of disagreement within the group. 'Discussion' in the
Political Evening School is a stilted procedure in which each
cadre in turn will reiterate a non-controversial piece of the
collective wisdom of the group. There are no adjudicators. The
lecturer in charge of the meeting makes no comment on the discussion
contributions, but nods dispassionately at various points in each
contribution. At the end he makes no attempt to summate the
contributions, or expose any possible controversy which might
require him to adopt an adjudicating role. Disagreement is not
merely driven underground but actually goes unrecognised in the
Workers' Institute. Members frequently express contradictory
interpretations of the group's collective wisdom, but any attempt

an outsider may make to expose these inconsistencies meets with
total resistance. The outsider simply does not understand because
of his failure to 'think dialectically'.

We have noted that the characteristic absence of specialised
adjudicating roles may lead to the formation of covert factions
and frequent fission. The Workers' Institute does not seem to be
large enough for this to have happened yet, but the fact that the
Institute itself is the product of a series of schisms over less
than ten years seems to confirm the view, based on the relevant
factors considered above, that the social environment of the
Workers' Institute fulfils our expectations.

TIME AND SPACE

The object of this essay is to establish that perceptions of time
and space have a central role to play in millenarian movements.
The next step must be to see how the temporal and spatial predicates
of millenarianism may be generated by this environment in contrast
with time and space perception over the typology as a whole.

Western European thought has traditionally regarded time as an
ontological continuum. The first departure from this view in
modern times was Kant's (1959 edn). He postulated that our
perceptions of time are functions of innate structures of thought
which order events according to sequence, duration and spatial
location. Kant's view challenged the Newtonian assumption that
time exists apart from the ordering of events and is an absolute
which flows equably without regard to anything external (Newton
1962 edn). Although Leibniz had argued that time is formed by
events and relations among them, constituting the universal order
of succession, Kant went further. He said that time only existed
in virtue of our experience of the succession of events with
regard to duration in space. His view also established that time
and space are inextricably related as the primary ordering concepts
of human existence.

The grid and group typology suggests that time and space should
be considered as socially variable aspects of the cosmology,
subject to the same structural constraints from the social environment as other aspects of an individual's world view (Douglas 1978:
25-30). Here I wish to argue that time and space are not merely
aspects of the cosmology, but, as primary ordering concepts, they
may exert their own constraints on the other aspects of the
cosmology in turn, thus reinforcing it. For example, time and
space may influence ideas about ornamental gardening but gardening
(except where it is a means of subsistence) is unlikely to
dominate the formation of temporal and spatial concepts in the
same way.

Time I

In approaching the social mediation of time, anthropologists have
cut different slices into the topic. For example; Evans-Pritchard
in his celebrated study of the Nuer distinguished between ecological

time and structural time (1940: ch.III); Lévi-Strauss has been more
interested in what he calls reversible and irreversible time (1966:
ch.8); whilst Leach has given us a whole range of time categories
to play with, including ritual time, abnormal time and sacred time
(1961: ch.6).

The central issue affecting all of these distinctions is the
relative strength of social and natural constraints upon time
perception. For example, Evans-Pritchard's category of ecological
time is determined by seasonal variations etc., whilst structural
time is determined purely by social activities.

This distinction is echoed by Maurice Bloch (1977), who reminds
us that anthropologists should not lose sight of the fact that there
are natural as well as social constraints on human concepts. Bloch
claims that societies have two cognitive systems, and therefore
two ways of structuring time. One of these is based on natural
constraints, and is concerned with the organisation of production,
etc., whilst the other is a socially determined 'ritual' time.

I want to make a different sort of distinction between two
types of time - historical time and operational time - both of
which are subject to both natural and social constraints, forming
a single cognitive system.

Historical time is concerned with the ordering of events or periods
in the life of an individual or a society, which are of contemporary
significance. Historical time is non-repetitive, marked by epochs,
and is learned or remembered. An example of this learned historical
dimension is the ordering of genealogies among the Nuer, where the
lineages are carefully remembered for as far back as they affect
the cattle rights of the living, and then may be tagged onto the
end of the local legendary ancestral lineage.

Operational time is repetitive, marked by regular intervals
concerned with the job in hand and/or repeated operations, and it
is experienced rather than learned about. An example of the Nuer
use of operational ordering concepts is the phrase, 'I shall return
at the milking'.

Both of these categories overlap with both of Evans-Pritchard's,
but unlike his structural and ecological time, both historical and
operational time are socially structured and both link their
respective concerns with the appropriate cycles of ecological
events which impose natural constraints upon the social structuring
of time. Rather than enforcing a dichotomy between knowledge
derived from nature and knowledge derived from social life, the
distinction between historical and operational time emphasises the
social mediation of the categories which we use to organise our
knowledge of the natural world and firmly establishes both sorts
of time as subject to grid/group constraints.

There is, however, an important distinction between operational
time and historical time which clearly emerges from our two Nuer
examples. The ecological constraints on historical time are
weaker in relation to the social constraints than is the case with
operational time. Consequently we may reasonably expect greater
variation in the patterns of historical time around the grid/group
typology than we may expect to find in patterns of operational

time. Epochs of historical time may be of different length in terms
of ecological cycles. Certainly important periods will seem to have
been longer than insignificant ones which may be compressed or even
missed out altogether. Such was the fate of the generations of
Nuer which must have passed between the clan founders and the founder
of the minimal lineages (Evans-Pritchard 1940: ch.V).

On the other hand, operational time is a resource in the tasks
and affairs of living men. Sleeping, milking, sowing and reaping
are ordered by the constancy of factors such as the rotation of the
earth, seasonal variation, etc. The social significance of these
activities is not likely to vary so greatly from day to day as to
introduce apparent differences in the duration of successive days
on anything like the spectacular scale we can observe between
successive epochs of historical time. There may be minor differences,
for example if a particular task is difficult or boring, but
generally speaking the ecological constraints on operational time will
tend to outweigh the social constraints. Operational time is
unlikely to be collapsed or extended in the same way as historical
time. However, we shall shortly see that the way in which a society
divides up its operational time, for example whether it is a
collective or an individual resource, will have its own reverbera-
tions on other parts of the cosmology.

Time II

We must now turn to the question of how lack of internal differentiation within a high-group environment constrains the use and perception of operational and historical time, in such a way as to
support the basic temporal and spatial predicates of millenarianism.

In this case operational time is not a resource in short supply.
The boundaries around the group, which constrain the social
experience of individuals within it, will set the limits of its
uses, whilst the lack of classificatory insulations within the
group means that time should not be compartmentalised. Operational
time in such an environment should therefore be a flexible community
resource, with no rules about when it is appropriate to promote
group concerns or witness to beliefs. There should be no formal
separation of work and play, entertainment and politics, business
or religion, such as we would expect to find in strong-grid
environments, where business personnel, friends, political associates,
etc. would all be classified into separate compartments, each having
a different call on the operational time resources of the individual.

This prognosis from the formal definition of the low-grid/high-
group environment seems to be fully borne out by the Workers'
Institute, for whom operational time is entirely a community resource.
Time spent outside the group working for money is time spent working
for the community, since all of the income of the working residents
of the Mao Xedong Memorial Centre is channelled into its funds. The
Institute's political activity is community activity involving all
of its members. The Workers' Institute are scathing of 'so-called
revolutionaries who spend their time talking in pubs'. Whilst
heated political discussion over a pie and a pint is commonplace
amongst the groups of the British far left, the Workers' Institute

carry this non-separation of leisure and politics much further. Leisure and politics are integrated into 'revolutionary socials' at the Mao Memorial Centre. These may be attended by members of the periphery who are treated to speeches and refreshments. These are strictly community events involving all the members of the Institute, and unlike time spent in a pub, the revolutionary social is a legitimate use of operational time resources.

The strict community control over operational time is clearly a means by which the Workers' Institute maintains its internal egalitarianism. Individuals do not have the time to have experiences outside of the group which may alter their internal standing; in particular they do not have time for individual learning which might equip them to cause or resolve disputes and thus emerge as potential leaders. Thus we are able to establish that the characteristic organisation of operational time supports the internal egalitarianism which we have identified as one of the three basic predicates of our definition of millenarianism.

We now turn to examine another of the three themes present in our definition of millenarianism. The reader will recall that the first of our basic predicates is the conviction that the present epoch is finite and known to be ending shortly. This is an expectation of historical time which compresses the past and the future into the present in much the same way as the Nuer compress their entire history into eleven or so generations. The Nuer compress their past in this way at the point where social differentiation of the dead ceases to bear on the living. This is a point around five generations back, at which the clan ancestors take over the mantle of history from the dead of the minor lineage. But the Nuer are stronger grid than our millenarians. In the Workers' Institute, as we have seen, social differentiation is absent from the present. In an unbounded individualist environment the pressures of competition and consequent scarcity of operational time resources stabilise historical time perception. But where operational time is constrained only by the group boundary, the historical dimension, the past and the future, literally collapses into the present. The group boundary becomes the deciding factor in historical perception. How is this possible?

The historical time dimension in this kind of unit will be severely constrained by the group's tendency to frequent fission. The record of its own history from its foundation to the present is liable to be briefer than the history of groups with more differentiated relationships. In societies with strong internal social classifications, disputes may be settled by demotion, promotion, or other reclassification of individuals. In egalitarian groups, the only solutions to serious disputes are expulsion or fission. The Workers' Institute for example has only been in existence for four years and is the outcome of a series of splits away from larger groups. Thus it is but a few small steps from the founding ancestor to the recent schisms that have given rise to the group. For example the writings of Marx, Engels, Lenin, Stalin and Mao are as valid today as when they were written, and so far as the Workers' Institute is concerned the world has not changed in any fundamental respect since these writings were first conceived by their authors.

Modelled on the past, the perception of the future is also less differentiated in this kind of social environment than elsewhere in the typology. The political demands of the Workers' Institute are all posed as immediate - with the minimum discrimination between short- and long-term aspirations. They speak of the old world as already passing away, and the achievement of world socialism is on their immediate agenda. This is in marked contrast with the view expressed by more orthodox groups on the British left who distinguish between the struggle to maintain working-class living standards during the present crisis of capitalism and the longer-term aim of achieving socialism. I suggest that this distinction is possible because these groups are more internally differentiated and have a weaker group boundary than the Workers' Institute. And indeed, the Communist and Labour Parties, which are relatively strong grid and certainly weaker group than the Trotskyist and Maoist left, are frequently criticised by the latter for losing sight of the long-term aim of socialism altogether.

The nearness of the foundation of the low-grid sect and the strength of its external boundary will permit the movement to justify its consequent smallness by reference to its historic importance as the repository of urgent revolutionary truth or of divine revelation in the present epoch. Hence, group members are likely to have a strong sense of the past as a charter for their present activities. The Workers' Institute, for example, draws an explicit parallel between the surrender of Peking after the defeat of Tientsin during the Chinese People's War of Liberation and their own millenarian scenario for 1977, according to which the People's Liberation Army of China was to break the back of the United States defence forces in Taiwan. This victory would have left the American mainland defenceless against the Liberation Forces. With the military defeat of the United States (Tientsin), the Soviet Union (Peking) would have collapsed internally, and its peoples embraced the INTERNATIONAL DICTATORSHIP OF THE PROLETARIAT. Finding itself surrounded, European Capitalism was to have almost incidentally capitulated to the new order.

Hence we can see how, based on self-consciousness of an historic mission, knowledge of the future in low-grid sects is likely to be as certain and as immediate as knowledge of the past. This compression of past and future into the present supports the temporal predicate of our definition of millenarianism - the conviction that the present epoch is finite and known to be ending shortly. The arrival of the millennium is consequently more credible here than in any of the other environments defined by grid and group:

1   At low grid/low group, competitive pressures on operational time will stabilise the historical dimension. Douglas (1978: 30) observes of this social environment: 'Its future is recognised as full of uncertainty (as indeed it is) but this realistic acceptance of a high-risk short-term future does not make it susceptible to millennial prophesies. Prophets of doom must make good their claims like any other people or ideas.'

2   At high grid/low group, the insulated individual 'has no

special selective principle from which to construct its history' (Douglas 1978: 30), whilst his experience of operational time will be highly compartmentalised and under the control of others. History here is likely to be a mere continuation of the experience of repetitious operational time, stretching endlessly into both the past and the future. The perception of historical time is therefore extended in this environment and is the opposite of the compressed historical perception of low grid/high group. The prospects for imminent radical social change will seem negligible in this environment. The only sources of salvation will be individual, whether in this world or the next.

3   At high grid/high group, disputes are less likely to be so destructive as in strongly bounded societies at low grid. High grid/high group is therefore likely to be a long-lived stable society. The careful classification of personnel here will provide a model for chronological segmentation. Just as there will be great men, there will be important historical epochs which will provide charters for present group activities. This sense of differentiated historical time will be inimical to collapsing the past and the future into the present, so millenarian expectations are unlikely to arise here.

FROM TIME TO SPACE

The concept of the 'epoch' seems to be a feature of high group. High grid/low group does not have any selective principle according to which the historical dimension could be divided into fixed periods, whilst low grid/low group is constantly subjecting the historical dimension to re-evaluation and therefore does not maintain a consistent conception of historical periods because history is being constantly redefined. On the other hand, history at high grid/high group may be organised into a number of epochs of varying significance, whilst in the high-group egalitarian type the finite character of the all-important present epoch is emphasised.

The conception of history as consisting of epochs is an invitation to compress selected periods of historical time. But the stronger the grid constraints on the perception of historical time, the further back in past history this compression is likely to occur and there is less likelihood of millenarianism occurring.

For example, we know that the Nuer compress historical epochs beyond the fifth ascending generation of their genealogies, and that the time-span of their remembered history is limited to about fifty years. The Nuer are certainly high grid/high group. They live in discrete wet-season villages and concentrate in large dry-season cattle camps. They have a strong sense of local community and of bounded social units. The Nuer are certainly stronger grid than the Workers' Institute. Although there are no great individuals of rank exercising political authority, the Nuer are nevertheless strongly classified by their age-set system, and their exceptionally complex lineage system, which has more orders of segmentation than, for example, their close neighbours the Dinka. Nuer do compete for cattle, but the movement of cattle is controlled by kinship

obligations. The Nuer are therefore subject to classificatory
constraints on exogamy, ceremonial, cattle rights, etc., which
derive from the kinship system. There is a degree of institutionalised
classification which is absent from the Workers' Institute.

We may reasonably suppose that this is a significant factor in
determining the point (five generations back) at which the Nuer
compress historical epochs. Time cannot be compressed before this
point because the classification of living people is determined by
their kinship classification of the preceding generations. The
classification of the dead by the living constrains the social life
of the living in choice of marriage partners, ceremonial, cattle
rights, etc. However, beyond the minimal lineage, only the names
of the founders of the important lineage branches need be placed in
a determinate order of ascent, from the founder of the minimal
lineage to the clan founder, because these are the only individuals
from so far back in history who are still important reference-points
for the living. The generations which passed between these various
individuals are ignored, and the history of each of their epochs
is collapsed into a single ancestral generation.

> It is evident ... there has been a telescoping of the agnatic
> line from the founder of the minimal lineage further up the
> line of ascent to the founder of the clan. (Evans-Pritchard
> 1940: 199)

What is of especial interest to us is that Nuer are fully conversant
with the full range of their genealogical relationships up to a
specific point. Beyond this point they reckon kinship solely in
terms of lineages because it is necessary to know what lineage a
man belongs to in deciding questions of exogamy and ceremonial.
But the relation between clan lineages is not determined by straightforward descent. Particular lineages may be reckoned to be closer
to each other if they are co-resident in the same community than
lineages which may be closely linked by descent, but are not co-
resident. Evans-Pritchard comments on the Nuer view of their
lineage system:

> They see it primarily as actual relations between groups of
> kinsmen within local communities, rather than as a tree of
> descent, for the persons after whom the lineages are called do
> not proceed from a single individual. (Evans-Pritchard 1940: 202)

Outside of certain ritual situations, Nuer evaluate clan and
lineage in terms of their local relations. It even happens that
genealogical fictions are created by which the founders of the
various ascending branches of a lineage are incorporated into the
lineage which has given its name to the local community. Hence,
where the influence of grid weakens historically and epochs are
compressed by the Nuer, their understanding of history is dominated
by spatial rather than temporal idioms. To put it another way,
group constraints may dominate the understanding of history in high-
group societies, when historical epochs are compressed. For the
Nuer, grid constraints from the lineage system enforce a chronological
conception of history for five generations back, after which
consciousness of their own bounded group becomes more important in
explaining how the past has made them what they are today. If the
understanding of history when epochs are compressed is dominated
by the group boundary and concepts of space derived from it (as we

have suggested is the case with the Nuer past), then we should
expect spatial constraints to figure largely in the Workers' Institute's understanding of the present epoch.

This brings us to consider the spatial predicate of our definition
of millenarianism - the conviction that the new epoch will be
established by the external intervention of some powerful agency.

Space I

In considering space, I want to follow the distinction we have
already made between two types of time and look at two types of
space; geographical space and operational space. Geographical
space is concerned with the ordering of places beyond the daily
experience of an individual or a community. It is generally learned
or remembered, and, also like historical time, geographical distance
may be perceived as socially compressed or extended in relation to
its ecological limitations. For example, Evans-Pritchard tells us
that a Nuer tribe forty miles from another perceives itself as being
structurally closer to it than to a Dinka tribe only twenty miles
away.

Operational space is concerned with the ordering of space within
which people live out their daily lives. It is directly experienced
rather than learned about or remembered, and (as with its counterpart
operational time) the perception of operational distance is subject
to more direct constraints from nature than geographical space. The
perception of operational distance relative to conventional
ecological measurements may vary between societies, depending upon
whether or not they possess mechanised transport and upon the
ecological constraints of terrain. But operational space will not
be selectively variable in the way geographical space is. However,
the way a society divides up its operational space, for example
whether it is a collective resource with few boundaries, or a
fiercely guarded individual resource, is a social variable of
critical importance to our grid/group analysis.

Space II

In high-group societies we should expect recursive patterning of
the group boundary at all levels, internal and external. The
limitations of operational space should coincide with the boundary,
whilst geographical space should lie outside it. The degree of
internal differentiation significantly alters the expectations we
should have of the distribution of recursive boundary patterns.

We can expect the high classification of operational space to
be a logical accompaniment to the strong classification of persons.
How better can the social classification of individuals be more
visibly enforced at high grid than by limiting their access to
specified areas of rigidly demarcated space? We can recognise
such constraints in the forms of first- and second-class travel,
saloon and public bars, separate toilets for managerial and manual
workers, etc. Hence at high grid/high group we can reasonably
expect the rigid division of operational space to follow the

recursive patterning of the group boundary which provides a
convenient model for internal differentiation of the group. Here
hierarchies may be represented spatially as a series of concentric
circles, representing decreasing status moving from the centre,
rather than in linear fashion representing decreasing status moving
from top to bottom. Outsiders, and outside geographical space, will
not be so susceptible to a high level of differentiation modelled
on the group boundary simply because outsiders are not particularly
relevant to the activities of the group. Hence we may expect a
predominance of internal recursive patterning of the group boundary
from high-grid/high-group environments.

This is in marked contrast to our expectations in respect of low
grid/high group. Here operational space must be a community
resource with few restrictions about who can go where, and use what
space, within the boundaries of the group. Operational space,
largely within the group boundary, will therefore be relatively
undifferentiated by recursive boundary patterns. The creation of
internal spatial divisions would threaten the egalitarianism of
the group by providing individuals with opportunities to control
small units of space and possibly to develop expertise and control
over the activity carried on in that area. However, the history
of schisms makes the movement susceptible to external threats to
the cohesion of the group. It is important to identify and
discriminate between a large variety of threatening outsiders.
Hence we may expect the group boundary pattern to be frequently
repeated externally, dividing geographical space outside of the
group, rather than dividing operational space inside.

These formally derived differences between spatial perception
at opposite ends of the grid dimension at high group are well
illustrated by comparing the geograms of the socio-spatial
categories of the Nuer and the Workers' Institute (Fig. 11.1).
The Nuer, who are relatively high grid, have a hierarchy of five
levels of spatial discrimination within their daily face-to-face
communities (i.e. the cattle camps and smaller units). There are
six divisions of Nuer outside of that boundary, but still within
range of kinship classifications, and only two categories of
unambiguously external geographical space. The Workers' Institute
have only two internal distinctions, which depend upon residence.
They have a single category of supporters who provide a spatial
buffer between themselves and the outside world, which consists of
five concentric categories of hostile space, surrounded by a single
all-embracing socio-spatial category.

The Nuer geogram is Evans-Pritchard's summary of the values
Nuer give to spatial distributions. I have constructed the geogram
of the Workers' Institute from the spatial categories I have known
members to use during my fieldwork. The contrast between the two
geograms is a crucial clue to the way in which a strongly bounded
egalitarian environment can support the spatial predicate of our
definition of millenarianism.

The Nuer maintain six divisions of geographical space between
the village, or cattle camp, and the boundary of Nuerland. This
is because their local communities are linked by shared grid
constraints emanating from the kinship and age-set systems. Most
relevant spatial discrimination is within Nuerland. Geographical

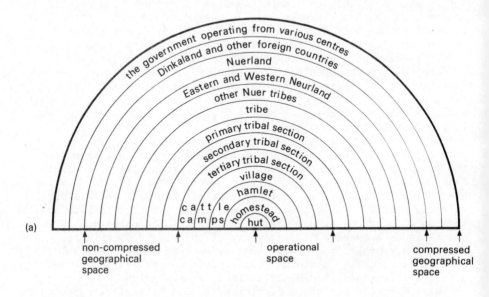

(a)

non-compressed
geographical
space

operational
space

compressed
geographical
space

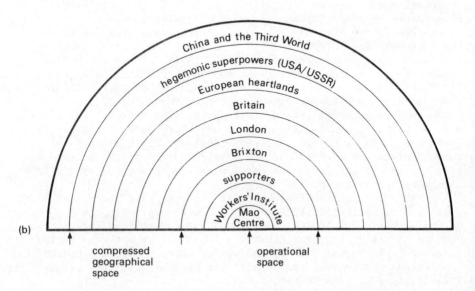

(b)

compressed
geographical
space

operational
space

FIGURE 11.1 (a) Nuer socio-spatial categories, (b) socio-spatial
categories of the Workers' Institute.

space beyond is relatively undifferentiated. The grid distinctions
which Nuer make among themselves are not applied to outsiders because
it is not important for Nuer to accurately discriminate between
outsiders. We may suppose that the world beyond Nuerland was
compressed into a single category (i.e. Dinka and other foreigners)
before colonialism imposed a further level of discrimination upon
the Nuer. As with the compression of historical time, we can see
that the existence of strong social discriminations prevent the
group from compressing geographical space before a point some
considerable distance away from the focus of their own daily
activities - the village or cattle camp.

On the other hand, the strongly bounded group at low grid does
not see itself sharing the same classificatory constraints as its
neighbours; rather it distinguishes itself from its neighbours
by the very absence of grid distinctions within its boundary and
stands alone against outsiders. This is certainly the case with
the Workers' Institute who see themselves as the 'sole upholders
of chairman Mao's revolutionary banner in the imperialist heartlands'.
However, the Workers' Institute cannot afford to ignore the world
beyond its boundaries because it is this world, dominated by the
'International Fascist Bourgeoisie' which both threatens the
Institute's existence and provides the rationale for its being.
Hence, the Institute discriminates between five categories of
potentially dangerous geographical space commencing directly outside
the group boundary and a single benign category which encompasses
the whole system.

The Workers' Institute is organised in London because 'it is
the worst place in the world'. Its role is not to organise a
revolution but to prepare for the period of socialist reconstruction
which will follow the liberation of the world by the People's
Republic of China - 'THE BRIGHT RED BASTION OF WORLD REVOLUTION'.
The liberation was confidently predicted to be completed by the end
of 1977, and was to have been achieved through the agency of the
'Three Magic Weapons', which are (1) The People's Liberation Army
of China, (2) Invincible Marxism-Leninism Mao Xedong Thought, and
(3) The Popular Front of Third World Countries led by People's
China. The Institute's justification for fixing the date of the
liberation for the end of 1977 relied upon Chairman Hua's address
to the Eleventh Congress of the Communist Party of China, in which
he promised that with the defeat of the Gang of Four, 1977 would
see that 'Order will be brought throughout the land'. The Institute
interpreted this promise to include Taiwan, and we have seen how
the rest of the liberation scenario follows inevitably from the
restoration of Taiwan to China. This is strong evidence to suggest
that the Workers' Institute do see the Republic of China and its
allies as encompassing all other socio-spatial concepts as represented in the geogram.

The Institute's conception of the Three Magic Weapons gives us
an indication of the way in which its members perceive the recursive
boundaries of geographical space which they discriminate between
their own operational space and China, as the source of their
millenarian hopes. When challenged about the use of the term
'magic', the self-styled scientific socialists of the Institute
defend the term because they claim that there is no other way to

convey to the oppressed masses the speed and invincibility of the
liberation. I have been told that the People's Liberation Army will
move so quickly that they will be in London and Washington before
the Imperialists wake up to what has happened. The same informant
compared the liberation to the 1977 New York blackout both in its
speed and its dramatic effects. Based on their own limited
experience of operational space, we find that members of the Workers'
Institute perceive geographical distances as being quite minor
obstacles to the path of their liberators. The creation of recursive
geographical boundaries, unsupported by strong-grid constraints to
provide experience of operational boundaries, is an invitation to
weak-grid/strong-group movements like the Workers' Institute to
compress geographical space around themselves in much the same way
as they compress historical time.

Further evidence for this assumption is that the threat of
nuclear reprisals by the United States or the Soviet Union is
dismissed by Institute members with the argument that the Chinese
have developed electronic weapons which would prevent enemy missiles
from even taking off. It is also believed that the Chinese can
interfere with the operation of all manner of electronic equipment
in the Imperialist Heartlands by remote control. I have been told
that the infamous translation error on President Carter's visit to
Poland, which represented the President as 'desiring the Poles
carnally', was due to the Chinese exercising their remote control
weaponry as a warning to the super-powers! The description of the
liberator's weapons as magic is more appropriate than the members
of the Workers' Institute are aware. Action at a distance, which
is the basis of their belief in the capacity of Chinese electronic
weaponry, is characteristic of the sort of magical beliefs which
are present in millenarianism. It seems that this magical element
is supported by the compression of geographical space. All of
these beliefs in Chinese electronic weaponry are justified by the
historical charter of an article in the 'Peking Review' in which
Mao was reported to have expressed a belief in the infinite
divisibility of matter in 1955. My informants were adamant that
subsequent research had justified Mao's belief and that this in
turn justified their own faith in the world leadership of China
in the field of electronics.

The use of the Peking-Tientsin campaign as an historical charter
for the liberation scenario is not only evidence for the smallness
of the steps between the founding ancestor and the present. It has
important implications for understanding the Institute's manipulation of socio-spatial categories. The Workers' Institute reproduces
the history of the macrocosm in the microcosm. The history of the
People's Republic provides a model for the rest of world history.
Nowhere is this more clearly shown than in their creation of the
West's own 'Gang of Four in the Imperialist Heartlands', consisting
of the leaders of the Communist Party of England M-L (from which
Balakrishnan broke away in 1974) and of its fraternal parties in
Ireland and Canada. Hence, we can see how the Workers' Institute's
understanding of the present epoch, in which historical time is
compressed into a few short years, is dominated by concepts of
geographical space derived from the group's own boundary. For the
Workers' Institute, the course of the historical present is under-

stood through historical charters which originate in geographical
concepts derived from the group boundary. This is because temporal
differentiation of history which is derived from grid constraints
is at its minimum in the compressed present epoch. It should come
as no surprise to discover that societies such as the Workers'
Institute live in a shrunken world surrounded by enemies, in which
the source of radical social change has to be a benign outsider
reaching across a hostile wasteland to the faithful within the
movement.

From the definition of the grid and group dimensions, we have
logically generated a model of time and space experiences. This
is a model of a shrunken world with a foreshortened perception of
historical time and compressed geographical space, modelled on the
structure of the group itself and buffered from external contradiction by its group boundary. We have seen that the Workers'
Institute fulfils our expectations in these respects. The crux of
my argument is that the three basic predicates of our definition
of millenarianism can all only be supported within a shrunken
world of this sort. Hence, low grid/high group should prove to
be a necessary condition of millenarianism. It is not however a
sufficient condition. I have not set out to explain why particular
groups of people turn to millenarianism. Rather I have confined
myself so far to the more modest question of what kind of social
environment, defined in terms of grid and group, is capable of
supporting millenarian ideas. I believe that we have made worthwhile progress with this approach and have succeeded in restoring
the temporal and spatial themes to a central place in the explanation of millenarian phenomena.

RELATIVE DEPRIVATION IN GRID/GROUP PERSPECTIVE

The starting-point for our extensive discussion of time and space
was the contention that the role of relative deprivation in
millenarian movements cannot be understood independently of the
question: What kind of social environment enables people to maintain
the temporal and spatial concepts which are characteristic of
millenarianism? We have established that the low-grid/high-group
social environment supports all three basic predicates of our
definition of millenarianism:
1   The conviction that the present epoch is finite and known
    to be ending shortly.
2   The conviction that the new epoch will be established by the
    external intervention of some powerful agency.
3   The conviction that all men ought to be recognised as moral
    equals.
We are now in a position to re-examine the role relative
deprivation might play in the process by which millenarian movements
develop within a weak-grid/strong-group environment.

In 'Mambu' (1960) Kenelm Burridge suggests that there is evidence
that millenarian cults of some sort occurred among the Tangu of New
Guinea before the coming of the Europeans and that cargo cults are
syncratic versions of traditional revitalisation movements. During
the Tangu cults, individual productive activity in the scattered

gardens and competitive feasting are abandoned in favour of collective
ritual activity, the adoption of white man's dress, and the co-
operative construction of temples, triumphal arches, or storage huts
to contain the cargo which is expected to come from the ancestors.
Douglas (1973) supports Burridge's suggestion that the origins of
this sort of activity pre-date colonial contact because she identifies
a contradiction inherent in all low-grid/low-group environments.
This is a contradiction between the ideology of equality necessary to
maintain open big-man competition and the benefits of scale which
will accrue to successful competitors:

> One would anticipate an ego-focused grid system to swing between
> the glorification of successful leaders and the celebration of
> the right of the masses to enjoy success. Thus the cargo cult
> and its prototypes would be cults of revolt against the way the
> social structure seems to be working, but not of revolution
> against the traditional structure itself. (Douglas 1973: 168)

It might be said that the contradiction, which in the Tangu
example counterposes expected equality to actual inequality, is
merely a case of what Aberle calls 'a negative discrepancy between
an anticipated state of affairs and a less agreeable actuality'.
If this is so, grid and group has produced yet another version of
the relative deprivation thesis. In fact, the presentation of the
grid dimension in 'Natural Symbols' would support this view because
it does not adequately distinguish between culture and social
relations. However, in 'Cultural Bias', the contradiction is not
one between ideology and actuality, but a structural contradiction
in the actual social relations, between relations being conducted
on the basis of an absence of explicit public social classifications,
and the presence of private classificatory filters being operated
by those individuals who are seeking to develop benefits of scale
in their social transactions. As Marx (1964: 84) said of processes
of social change such as the abolition of slavery, introduction of
a monetary economy, and other upheavals which promise to enlarge
the sphere of political and economic competition: 'Individuals may
appear to be great. But free and full development of individual
or society is inconceivable here, for such evolution stands in
contradiction to the original relationship.'

The periodic crisis which besets the Tangu is one of both the
socio-economic and cultural spheres. It is likely to produce real
structural conflict in the social relations, both between big-men
and between big-men and less successful managers. In the cultural
sphere, there is a growing conflict between the traditional
egalitarian indices of man and the growing dominance of successful
entrepreneurs. In this environment there is a proliferation of
sorcery accusations arising from the pressures of competition
between big-men, and from their fear of revenge being taken upon
them by the less successful (Burridge 1960: 84).

The contradiction between the traditional egalitarian indices
of man among the Tangu, and the growing dominance of successful
big-men, may well be what Aberle and Burridge are seeking to
describe in their extended relative deprivation theses. However,
we can see that rather than being the first cause of Tangu cults,
their experience of relative deprivation is itself the result of a
contradiction in the social structure which produces, in the first
instance. sorcery accusations rather than millenarianism.

Of course, relative deprivation may be experienced for a variety of other reasons which have nothing to do with the contradiction in the social relations experienced by the Tangu. I am not claiming that this contradiction is a general cause of all instances of relative deprivation. I do hope to show how millenarianism offers a genuine solution to the pressures of competitive inequality and consequent sorcery accusations which may be produced by the contra- diction experienced by the Tangu and is not merely a catharsis for lack of power to change the system.

An effective immediate response to the low-grid contradiction would be a movement to form a high-group environment to counter the effects of unrestrained competition. This is an obvious point illustrated by the formation of pressure groups, preservation societies, etc. in opposition to large corporate interests or motorway developments. Such a group will be able to confront the state or a large corporation more effectively than a number of disparate householders who can be filtered out one by one. This response to the low-grid contradiction strengthens group and holds the key to the development of millenarianism.

Burridge tells us that group identifications in Tangu are generally determined by neighbourhood, and rather less by kinship. During this century, both territorial and kinship identifications have been in a state of flux. Whereas warfare used to unite communities within Tangu, the suppression of warfare by colonial governments has brought about a changed situation. Community identity has been lost, leaving Tangu to identify most strongly with small individual households at the local level, and more generally to see themselves as Tangu and as Black Men.

Present-day Tangu activities provide little opportunity for strengthening the communities which lie between these extremes. Tangu households spend their days working independently in the scattered gardens or hunting further afield. The community rarely gathers as a whole, except for feasting and dancing, when in any case one half of the community will act in competitive reciprocal opposition to the other.

> Tangu are egalitarians, aggressively so. Their moral order is characterised by a fierce insistence on equivalent reciprocities and by a minimum of delegated responsibilities. But while much time and energy are spent in coping with and containing expressions of self-willedness and the non-reciprocal in others, there are many who covet that reserve of self-willed and non- reciprocal power which will enable them to assert themselves against their fellows. Highly competitive, Tangu egalitarianism is maintained by competition ... (Burridge 1969: xxii)

This classic description of the competitive individualist environment is the background to a recurring series of cargo cults which have stressed communal entities to check the competitive division of the community. Burridge (1954: 241) records that 'In the cult situation no food exchanges take place between one half the community and the other, households become merged in a larger whole and all act together.'

In 'Natural Symbols' Douglas speaks of a swing between Tangu glorification of successful leaders and the right of the masses to enjoy success. I suggest replacing the metaphor of the swing with

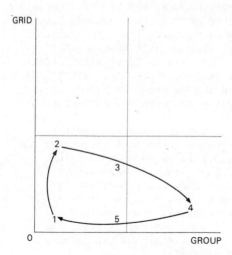

FIGURE 11.2 The Tangu Cycle
1 Highly competitive social environment maintained by fierce
   egalitarianism. However, successful managers operate implicit
   filters against less successful individuals.
2 As inequality becomes more visible less successful individuals
   are actually forced up the grid in contravention of the
   ideology of equality. Recognition of the increasingly unequal
   basis of competition leads to increasing fears of sorcery
   being used by competitors.
3 In order to counteract the effects of strengthening grid
   constraints and in pursuance of traditional egalitarian values
   Tangu adopt a high-group strategy which emphasises communal
   activity and the abandonment of traditional productive
   activity.
4 At low grid/high group the cult's perception of time and
   space facilitates millenarian beliefs which would be untenable
   elsewhere.
5 The millennium fails to arrive so the members of the cult
   drift back into traditional competitive individual activities.
   But each individual has to rebuild his productive capacity
   more or less from scratch because the gardens have been
   neglected and capital may have been destroyed in the creation
   of the low-grid/high-group environment.

a cyclical one (Fig. 11.2). According to this model, the Tangu
response to the uncertainties posed by the low-grid contradiction
is to develop a high-group environment in pursuance of traditional
egalitarian values. The abandonment of individual gardens, and in
some cases the wholesale destruction of capital, which is characteristic of cargo cults, occurs in the creation of the low-grid/high-
group environment, within which all resources are collectively
exploited. It is not only the relatively deprived who participate
in these cults. A successful manager might calculate that participation in the cult would reduce the chances of his life being termina-

ted through the sorcery of other individuals whom he has pushed out
of the competition in the past. When the grid contradiction becomes
too acute, and the whole system of competition is threatened, the
creation of a low-grid/high-group environment is a way of redistribu-
ting finite resources in preparation for another round of competitive
activity. Millenarianism is not the only way in which this could be
achieved, for example warfare could fulfil the same ends through the
destruction of capital and the bringing together of local communities
for a common purpose. However, the banning of warfare by colonial
governments seems to have created a vacuum which can be conveniently
filled by the cargo movements.

The strategy of developing a high-group environment itself
ensures the failure of the cult as a revolutionary movement. By
choosing this strategy, Tangu place themselves in a position where
revolutionary change could only be imposed from the outside, i.e.
by the actual arrival of the millennium. This will always be the
case in an extreme low-grid/high-group environment because the
dominant ideology of equality and the group constraints will
militate against the emergence of a coherent leadership capable of
controlling sufficient resources to force through a revolutionary
transformation of society, without splitting the group. We have
seen how groups such as the Workers' Institute are organised to
discourage the emergence of strong leaders. Anyone attempting to
exert themselves in such a role will find themselves subject to
accusations of being outside infiltrators. Amongst the Tangu,
cargo cultists are likely to regard such figures as being sorcerers
from the outside competitive environment which they are attempting
to remedy. Furthermore, the millenarian sect cannot become an
effective revolutionary organisation without obtaining a mass
following. In this case, the sect's cosmology, normally buffered
against the social classifications of the wider society by its own
boundary, would be untenable to people not so protected. The group
could only become a viable popular force by shedding both its
ideology and its protective boundary. An example of a British
political group undergoing such a change is the Socialist Workers'
Party.

In an egalitarian sect, revolutionary change could only occur
with its transformation, or in the cases of sects which do not
transform themselves, with the intervention of some external agency
such as the cargo-bearing ancestors in the case of the Tangu, or
the People's Liberation Army in the case of the Workers' Institute.
Tangu cargo cults do not transform themselves, and when the millennium fails to arrive the cult is simply abandoned and Tangu once
more pursue personal gain and attempt to compete in much the same
way as before. However, the levelling off which has occurred
during the millenarian phase allows them to start again as equal
competitors without benefits of scale. The cycle thus begins anew.

The high-group strategy is not the only one available to those
who experience the weak-grid/weak-group contradiction. There are
three possible strategies available to an individual in this
predicament:

1   To renounce his own perspectives, accept the filters that
    others are operating against him, and move up the grid
    dimension, possibly as a long-term investment with a view to

building up resources which will facilitate later competitive success - for example, the student who accepts his own lack of control over his undergraduate studies in the hope of a PhD place later.

2   To move up the grid dimension and shift to high group, accepting a limited individual role in world affairs, but as part of an historic movement which will prevail over those who pushed him up grid - for example, the small shopkeepers who turned to the Nazis in pre-war Germany.

3   To shift into high group, maintaining an egalitarian world view, independently of the prevailing system of thought about the order of the universe and buffered by the strong-group boundary from competitive pressures.

The Workers' Institute seems to be composed of individuals who have adopted the third strategy. The membership of the Institute is principally of overseas origin. For example, of the ten cadres at one session of the evening school which I attended at the Centre, three were of European racial origin, one was of West Indian origin, two were of Malay origin, and the remaining four were of Chinese racial origin (although I believe that several of these are Malaysian). With two possible exceptions, all of the members present were also ex-students who had given up their studies in order to 'integrate with the working class'.

The contradiction between ideal equality and real competitiveness is particularly acute for university students who live in an environment which encourages competition and claims to be training students to think for themselves. The reality, especially in the natural sciences, is that students are denied any real control over the organisation of their studies but are subject to apparently arbitrary limitations of disciplines and the imposition of curricula drawn up by their teachers.

In general, immigrants to the United Kingdom are also likely to experience strong insulation and impersonal controls. Unless located in an established community, they are also likely to have little group reference as individuals. If they are also students, the pressures forcing them up grid are likely to be even stronger than those acting on indigenous students. The subjective experience of the contradiction between their aspirations to benefits of successful competition, and the implicit filters operating in that environment to push them up grid, is likely to be stronger for students from the Third World than is the case with indigenous students. This is all the more likely where the overseas student has already had the experience of being part of an educational or economic elite, whose talents are more in demand and whose status is much higher than students enjoy in Britain. It is therefore hardly surprising that ex-students from overseas make up the backbone of the Workers' Institute.

Only a concrete account of the historical circumstances specific to each case can explain which of the three strategies for resolving the low-grid/low-group contradiction will be adopted by an individual or society. Grid and group does not therefore provide us with a causal explanation of why a particular group choose the strategy which leads to millenarianism. However, we have shown that it can do two other things to significantly advance our understanding of millenarian phenomena.

Firstly, it enables us to identify the sort of social environment that will support the characteristic spatial, temporal, and ethical predicates of millenarianism and enables us to restore the temporal and spatial themes to a central place in the explanation of millenarianism.

Secondly, it shows us why relative deprivation in the form of the grid contradiction can be an important factor in some cases of millenarianism, and not in others, since the grid contradiction is not the only possible explanation of why individuals gather in egalitarian groups behind strong-group boundaries. Furthermore, it is important to be clear that there are three possible strategies for dealing with the grid contradiction. This accounts for the fact that there are cases in which the contradiction is perceived as relative deprivation but does not give rise to millenarianism.

ACKNOWLEDGMENTS

My thanks are due to Mary Douglas, Phil Burnham, William Shack, David Ostrander, Doug Clark, and Jan Zvaifler for their encouragement and their invaluable criticisms of earlier drafts of this paper. This research is part of a longer project financed by the Social Science Research Council of Great Britain, and the Central Research Fund of the University of London.

BIBLIOGRAPHY

ABERLE, D. (1962), A note on relative deprivation theory as applied to millenarian and other cult movements, in S. Thrupp (ed.), 1962: 209-14.
ABERLE, D. (1966), 'The Peyote Religion among the Navaho', Chicago, Aldine.
BLOCH, M. (1977), The past and the present in the present, 'Man' (NS) 12: 278-93.
BURRIDGE, K. (1954), Cargo cult activity in Tangu, 'Oceania' xxiv: 241-53.
BURRIDGE, K. (1960), 'Mambu', London, Methuen.
BURRIDGE, K. (1969), 'Tangu traditions', Oxford, Clarendon.
BURRIDGE, K. (1971), 'New Heaven: New Earth', Oxford, Blackwell.
COHN, N. (1957), 'The Pursuit of the Millennium', London, Secker & Warburg.
DOUGLAS, M. (1973), 'Natural Symbols', Harmondsworth, Penguin.
DOUGLAS, M. (1978), 'Cultural Bias', London, Royal Anthropological Institute, occasional paper no.35.
EVANS-PRITCHARD, E.E. (1940), 'The Nuer', Oxford University Press.
HILL, C. (1975), 'The World Turned Upside Down', Harmondsworth, Penguin.
KAMINSKY, J. (1962), Problems of explanation, in S. Thrupp (ed.), 1962: 215-17.
KANT, I. (1969), 'Critique of Pure Reason', London, Dent.
LEACH, E. (1961), Two essays concerning the symbolic representation of time, in 'Rethinking Anthropology', London, Athlone.
LÉVI-STRAUSS, C. (1966), Time regained, in 'The Savage Mind', London, Weidenfeld & Nicolson.

LEWIS, I. (1971), 'Ecstatic Religion', Harmondsworth, Penguin.
LINTON, R. (1943), Nativistic movements, 'American Anthropologist' 45, April-June: 230-40.
LING, T. (1966), 'Buddha, Marx, and God', London, Macmillan.
MARX, K. (1964), 'Pre-capitalist Economic Formations', London, Lawrence & Wishart.
NEWTON, I. (1962), 'Mathematical Principles of Pure Philosophy', Berkeley, University of California Press.
THRUPP, S. (1962), 'Millennial Dreams in Action: Essays in Comparative Study', The Hague, Mouton; NY, Humanities Press.
WALLACE, A. (1956), Revitalisation movements: some theoretical considerations for their comparative study, 'American Anthropologist', 58: 264-81.
WILSON, B. (1970), 'Religious Sects', London, Weidenfeld & Nicolson.
WILSON, B. (1975), 'Magic and the Millennium', St Albans, Paladin.
WINSTANLEY, G. (1649), A Watch-word to the City of London, in G. Sabine (ed.), 'The works of Gerrard Winstanley', New York, Cornell University Press (1941).
WORSLEY, P. (1970), 'The Trumpet Shall Sound', St Albans, Paladin.

Chapter 12

SPECTRAL EVIDENCE: THE WITCHCRAFT COSMOLOGY OF SALEM VILLAGE IN 1692
Dennis E. Owen

Like a magnet, the Salem witchcraft trials have continually drawn the attention of historians back to the drab and terrifying events of 1692. There is perhaps a fascination with the demonic or at least with the uncanny which might account for this. Additionally there has been an embarrassment that our Puritan forebears should have been so overwhelmed by the apparently irrational. Consequently progress in our understanding of the witchcraft trials has been rather slow and painful. Much analysis has concerned itself with laying blame as if designating those responsible could somehow remove the stain of Salem from the record of colonial history. As late as 1949 Marion Starkey, who claimed the insight and objectivity of psychological method, attributed the entire episode to 'the childish fantasies of some very little girls', and to a general craving for 'Dionysiac mysteries'. (1) A more fruitful approach appeared in 1969 with Chadwick Hansen's 'Witchcraft at Salem' which, apparently informed by the sociology of knowledge, made the point that people could honestly believe in witchcraft and that such belief could indeed affect their perceptions and experiences of reality.

The greatest contribution to our understanding of the witchcraft trials came in 1974 with the publication of 'Salem Possessed: The Social Origins of Witchcraft'. In an admirable application of careful historiographical method, Paul Boyer and Stephen Nissenbaum have laid open the underlying social conflicts which produced the witchcraft accusations of 1692. After 'Salem Possessed' there may well be little left to be said beyond some restructuring of Boyer and Nissenbaum's work which will be the case in this essay. I have only a few criticisms of their effort: the scope of their inquiry is ultimately too narrow, focusing entirely on Salem Village and ignoring connections to rather momentous colony-wide events; there is a need for a theoretical orientation which will allow one to move from the social conditions so patiently uncovered to the outbreak of witchcraft accusations without assuming self-evidence; the direction of the witchcraft accusations up the social scale is explained through weak and unnecessary psychologizing. It is my intention to offer a correction for these deficiencies while at the same time supporting the fundamental accuracy of the approach taken in 'Salem Possessed'.

One of the issues which has yet to receive satisfactory attention is that of the central role played by spectral evidence in the witchcraft trials. The term 'spectral evidence' derives from testimony offered during the trials which purported to tell of the activities of the 'spectre', a ghost-like double, of an accused witch. Persons making witchcraft accusations, particularly those who formed the core group of accusers, claimed literally to have been assaulted by the spectre of the accused. They were bitten, pinched, scratched, choked and pressured to write in a book (sometimes 'The Devil's Book') by their invisible assailants. A contemporary observer described the scene during the examination of Rebecca Nurse.

> her [Nurse's] Motions did produce ... effects as to biting, pinching, bruising, tormenting, at their breasts, by her leaning, and when, bended, bended back, were as if their backs were broken. The afflicted persons said, the Black Man [presumably the devil] whispered to her in the assembly.... Thomas Putnam's wife had a grievous fit, in the time of the examination, to the very great impairing of her strength, and wasting of her spirits.... Others also were there grievously afflicted, so that there was one such an hideous screetch and noise, (which I had heard as I walked, at a little distance from the Meeting house,) as did amaze me.... (2)

Assistants Hathorne and Corwin who presided at the examinations described the meeting of Sara Good and her accusers, a scene which was repeated with each of the accused.

> All the abovesaid children when present accused her face to face upon which they were all dreadfully tortured and tormented for a short space of time, and the affliction and tortures being over, they charged said Sara Good again that she had then so tortured them, and came to them and did it, although she was personally then kept at a considerable distance from them. (3)

Since only the records of the preliminary investigations have survived, we shall probably never know for certain the precise role played by spectral evidence in the trials before the Court of Oyer and Terminer. Nevertheless there are ample grounds, even without those records, to conclude that the role must have been a formidable one indeed. Boyer and Nissenbaum point out that the magistrates presiding at the preliminary investigations and presumably also those presiding at the trials attempted to 'buttress' the spectral evidence 'with other, more empirical, forms of evidence'. (4) While their judgment is accurate, it does not tell the whole story. The court did indeed seek other evidence. The records are filled with testimony referring to quarrels, odd behavior, arguments closely followed by mysterious illnesses either to persons or animals. However, except in the cases of Bridget Bishop and George Bouroughs, it is clear that without the admission of spectral evidence, not simply as grounds for suspicion as was counseled by Puritan divines such as Perkins, but as substantive evidence for conviction, verdicts of guilt could not have been returned if indeed the accused could even have been brought to trial. (5) In the first place, spectral evidence dominates the

questioning of the accused by the court during its investigation,
and in the second place, spectral evidence did not serve as grounds
for suspicion in the mind of the court, but as presumption of guilt.
Consider, for example, the interrogation of Sara Good.

Question: Why do You hurt these children?
Answer: I do not hurt them I scorn it.
Q: Who do you employ, then, to do it?
A: I employ nobody.
Q: What creature do you employ then?
A: No creature. But I am falsely accused.

A little later, after Hathorne had the girls look at Good with the
result that they were afflicted with fits, the record continues:

Question: Sara Good, do you not see now what you have done?
             Why do you not tell us the truth? Why do you thus
             torment these poor children?
Answer: I do not torment them.
Q: Who do you employ then?
A: I employ nobody. I scorn it. (6)

It is evident here as well as in the questioning of other
suspects that the examiners presumed guilt on the basis of spectral
evidence.   Thus the line of questioning assumes that Good is
afflicting the children, and in good Ramist fashion, assumes that
she does it either directly or through an agent, and if through an
agent then either through a human agent or a creature. The case
against Rebecca Nurse was almost entirely spectral with only one
incident of an argument followed by a mysterious death. (7) Very
likely this was a factor in Nurse's initially being found innocent
at her trial. However, according to Calef, when 'the Jury brought
in a verdict of not guilty, immediately all the Accusers in the
Court, and suddenly after all the afflicted out of Court, made an
hideous outcry...'. (8)   The judges, dissatisfied with the verdict,
remanded the jury on the basis of a single ambiguous statement
which Nurse had made, without taking pains to allow her further
to explain herself. Although Calef does not say so, it seems safe
to assume that the 'hideous outcry' involved further spectral
attacks, a judgment supported by his report that when the governor
later granted Nurse a reprieve, spectral assaults attributed to
her began anew and 'the Governor was by some Salem Gentlemen
prevailed with to recall the reprieve, and she was executed with
the rest'. (9)

The cases against Sara Good and Rebecca Nurse are not atypical.
From the records of the preliminary investigations and the second-
hand accounts of the trials, it seems evident that we must draw
the conclusion that spectral evidence formed the basis upon which
convictions for the crime of witchcraft were obtained. The Salem
witchcraft trials thus inverted the proper relationship between
spectral and 'empirical' evidence. Further, let us note that when
Increase Mather finally denounced spectral evidence of all kinds
in 'Cases of Conscience Concerning Evil Spirits Personating Man',
and when Governor Phips accordingly ended the Court of Oyer and
Terminer and called a special session of the Superior Court which
did not allow spectral evidence, the trials quickly ground to a
halt. The Salem witchcraft trials were thus largely a matter of
spectral evidence, and no account of the trials can be complete

without solving the problem of why New England broke with the
established guidelines for trying suspected witches - guidelines
of which the clergy were well aware - and was willing to execute
persons on the basis of such evidence.

It is at this point that an analysis of the witchcraft trials
must be extended beyond the confines of Salem Village and Salem
Town. Persons could not have been executed without at least the
passive consent of the rest of the colony, and at the outset of
the trials that consent was far more than passive. Additionally
the issues of spectral evidence had been raised with the clergy
of Eastern Massachusetts, and although they counseled caution,
there was no decisive action comparable to 'Cases of Conscience'.
(10)   Further, a letter from Cotton Mather to John Richards, one
of the judges on the Court of Oyer and Terminer, although suggesting
that the devil could impersonate the innocent thereby casting grave
doubt upon the use of spectral evidence, also goes on to deliver
the opinion that

>   there is cause enough to think that it is a horrible witchcraft
>   which has given rise to the troubles wherewith Salem Village is
>   at this day harassed, and the indefatigable pains that are used
>   for the tracing this witchcraft are to be thankfully accepted
>   and applauded among all the people of God. (11)

In this mixture of caution and applause, it was the latter which
carried the day until witchcraft accusations got totally out of
hand and included, so rumor had it, even the wife of the new
governor. It seems reasonable to assume that spectral evidence,
despite the doubts surrounding it, struck enough of a responsive
chord in the colony as a whole, and certainly in its leading
figures, to warrant its acceptance. Cotton Mather was clearly
ambivalent; he was concerned, even disapproving, but unwilling
to act, and the same was true among his colleagues. This is the
problematic remainder which I shall attempt to clarify in the rest
of this essay by constructing a perspective from which the issue
of spectral evidence and hence of the trials themselves becomes
intelligible as an expression of a malaise which underlay not only
Salem Village but also the entire Bay Colony during the second
half of the seventeenth century.

Such a perspective, I believe, can be derived from Mary Douglas's
controversial but seminal book, 'Natural Symbols'. Douglas argues
here that witchcraft cosmologies and accusations are endemic to a
particular kind of social experience. Working primarily with
African examples, she finds witchcraft societies to be characterized
by a strong sense of group-identity and strong pressure to conform
to group norms (high group) on the one hand, and by confusion and
disjointedness in its internal systems of classifications and
patterns of public roles (low grid) on the other. High group, as
Douglas intends the term, is not a free-floating theoretical
abstraction, it bears direct implications for the quality of everyday social experience. Individual and collective action will be
justified in the name of group interest. Legitimations for the
suppression of deviance and dissent will similarly be constructed
upon the foundation of collective well-being. The flow of daily
activity will be largely between members of the group. One will
work, trade, worship, attend marriages and bury dead with group

members. The more this is the case the higher up the group dimension
the society is placed. (12) What Douglas is calling 'grid' likewise
bears directly upon the quality of one's experience of the world.
Where grid is high individuals have available to them coherent,
comprehensive and clearly articulated patterns of status and role
which help insulate them from conflict and help resolve it when it
occurs. As grid is reduced the internal structure of the society
becomes confused and hence confusing, the likelihood of conflict
increases and the possibility of its resolution decreases.

The generation of witchcraft cosmologies by high-group/low-grid
contexts is a function of what Douglas calls a 'drive to achieve
consonance in all levels of experience', which 'produces concordance
among the means of expression'. (13) She argues: 'Just as the
experience of cognitive dissonance is disturbing, so the experience
of consonance in layer after layer of experience and context after
context is satisfying.' (14) If Douglas is right about this it
becomes possible to make some useful correlations between social
organization and cosmology. We can expect to find what might be
called a 'goodness of fit' between the two. Each of the four
extreme types of social structures (high group and grid, high group/
low grid, etc.) (15) will be accompanied by a particular cosmological style, or by what may be better designated particular
cosmological clusters with varying attitudes towards things such
as purity, magic, the physical body, trance and suffering. Body-
symbolism will be particularly useful in connecting cosmologies
and social organizations for, since the human body itself is a
complex organization, it is capable of furnishing metaphors for
other complex bounded systems. The physical body, however, is
also a social construct; its relationship to society is dialectical.

The social body constrains the way the physical body is
perceived. The physical experience of the body, always modified
by the social categories through which it is known, sustains a
particular view of society. There is a continual exchange of
meanings between the two kinds of bodily experience so that
each reinforces the categories of the other. As a result of
this interaction the body itself is a highly restricted medium
of expression. The forms it adopts in movement and response
express social pressures in manifold ways.... All the cultural
categories in which [the body] is perceived, must correlate
closely with the categories in which society is seen in so far
as these also draw upon the same culturally processed idea of
the body. (16)

The suggestion that one can find layers of congruence between
various forms of bodily experience is itself an invitation to
expand both the metaphor and its application. If we take 'body'
to indicate a complex bounded unit, it becomes apparent that we
live in a number of bodies at one time. We are or have physical
bodies, we distribute power in social and political bodies, we
worship in ecclesiastical bodies, and we understand ourselves
through bodies of thought. We ought, then, to expect to find
congruence among all of these bodies; the basic structural patterns
of one ought to be evident in the others. This is precisely what
Douglas finds occurring in witchcraft societies which have a strong
sense of group identity but which are internally confused and

dissonant. The body of the witch is itself a microcosm of the
society.

A closer look at the symbolism of witchcraft shows the dominance
of symbols of inside and outside. The witch himself is someone
whose inside is corrupt; he works harm on his victims by
attacking their pure, innocent insides. Sometimes he sucks out
their soul and leaves them with empty husks, sometimes he
poisons their food, sometimes he throws darts which pierce
their bodies. And then again, sometimes he needs access to
their inner bodily juices, faeces, semen, spittle, before he
can hurt them. (17)

Witchcraft symbolism represents the experience of what Douglas
is calling the high-group/low-grid society. The individual here
is under considerable pressure to conform to public norms, but
finds such norms confused and in conflict. No longer capable of
gaining security and identity through the internalization of well-
articulated and co-ordinated social roles, the individual is secure
only in his identification with group boundaries. In the absence
of a coherent system of internal classifications, deviance becomes
difficult both to define and to contain within the group.
Definition is problematic because one cannot be certain which
behavioral patterns are acceptable and hence the range of potential
deviants becomes very wide. One is under a great deal of pressure
to conform, but to conform to what? to roles which are ill-defined
and only serve to intensify conflict? to group boundaries which
only either include or exclude? The latter seems to be the only
available choice, but the employment of group boundaries as the
mode of social control means that deviants will be ridden out of
the social body and that witchcraft accusations will flourish.
Further, the lack of a coherent and comprehensive system of internal
classifications deprives individuals of the insulation afforded by
ascribed status and role, introduces ambiguity and competition into
social relationships, increasing the likelihood of conflict. The
same weakness in the classification system also makes it difficult
to deal with conflict, for it affords no publicly legitimated
channels through which it can flow toward resolution. Consequently
conflict tends to be driven underground where it is likely to
continue to smolder, and the social group tends to divide into
warring factions which lack mechanisms of reconciliation.

The use of bodily metaphors to describe social experience would
also seem to play a significant role here, for a social body would
appear to be something other than any social group. The term
'social body' implies a kind of organic solidarity and a particular
kind of susceptibility to threat. Social bodies will experience
social diseases where social groups experience deviance. In the
case of social bodies, social ills will parallel physical ills.
Deviants in this view can become tumors - cancerous growths on or
within the social body. Their removal through expulsion becomes a
matter of primary importance, for left untreated there is the
likelihood that they will infect the entire body. The power of
the bodily-disease metaphor will become apparent in my discussion
of Salem. For the moment, suffice it to say that the social disease
par excellence is witchcraft, for here numerous levels of bodily
symbolism and experience can be seen to merge.

My approach to the problem of spectral evidence in the Salem witchcraft trials will be to correlate it with the experiences of Massachusetts' various bodies. My argument will ultimately attempt to show that the spectral evidence witnessed at the witchcraft trials represented in dramatic form significant underlying theological, ecclesiastical, political and social conditions in the colony as a whole and in Salem Village which came to fruition in 1692.

The argument begins with a well-established theme: the sense of purpose which informed the Puritan settlement of New England, and the metaphors through which they understood themselves and their experience. The Puritan understanding of their adventure involved strong social pressure and expressed itself largely through bodily images. John Winthrop, in his ship-board sermon, 'A Model of Christian Charity', gave the theme its definitive shape. The venturesome souls aboard the Arabella, according to Winthrop, were not a heterogenous group seeking to carve individual fortunes out of the New England wilderness. They were, instead, a church, and in Winthrop's Biblical imagery, the body of Christ.

All the parts of this body being thus united are made so contiguous in a special relation and they must needs partake of each others strength and infirmity, joy and sorrow, weal and woe. If one member suffers, all suffer with it. (18)

Winthrop's congregation was not a church among other churches. It was 'the' church, the true body of Christ. The life of that body depended upon the success of the Puritan mission. The church therefore could not afford dissent; it had to be one, else it was no church at all, for the body of Christ could not be divided against itself. Each individual member could find his identity only in terms of his participation in the whole. Individualism meant disembodiment and ultimate failure for both the individual and the community. If New England were to keep its corporate convenant, it must, according to Winthrop, 'be knit together in this work as one man...'. (19) The twin themes of unity and destiny cannot be separated; each entails the other. New England could not be divided and still be the body of Christ, and only as the body of Christ could New England justify its existence.

Membership in the body of Christ, however, entailed sharing in the sin of other members. The deviance of one person endangered the entire community by shattering the oneness of the political and ecclesiastical bodies, and violating the terms of the covenant. Thus the Puritan doctrine of sin bears the imprint of Puritan social experience. Sin in New England was no mere deviance occurring within the boundaries of the community. It was, more seriously, an attack upon the integrity of group identity and the prospects for group fortune. Consequently the sin of the individual was as much a matter of public concern as it was of private anguish. As in most Christian traditions, sin for the New England Puritans basically involved a deviation from the ways of God, or from the ways in which God had decreed that men live out their lives. As such, sin was an arrogant denial and rejection of one's God-given identity and purpose, and hence a rejection of membership in the body of the church. (20) In addition to this rather unitary view of sin, the Puritans held a second view which allows us to draw some parallels between the relationship of sin to the individual, of the

individual sinner to the social body and ultimately of the witch
to society. Sin in this view was a foreign invader, an alien presence
in the self. Joshua Moody employed a metaphor of invasion, preaching,
'You feel the body of sin in you, fighting and disturbing you'. (21)
Samuel Willard called sin a 'traitor' lodged within us, for it was
'in league with satan', seeking to betray us to the power of the
devil at every opportunity. (22) Similarly, Urian Oakes suggested,
'There is a traitor in our own bowels that is ready to open our
parts and let in the adversary'. (23)

The view of sin as an unwelcome invader which draws heavily upon
images of inside and outside, itself stands in tension with the more
unitary theological view. The Puritans in their theologically self-
conscious language invariably spoke of the sinfulness of human
nature. The stain was ubiquitous, and the saints were as Luther
had us all, at once sinful and justified. A condensed expression
of the prevailing opinion was offered by Cotton Mather who claimed
that all human beings had a corrupt nature inherited from Adam
and Eve which held within itself the possibility of performing any
particular evil. More importantly, our nature was also inclined
to evil. (24) Thus our characters tended toward sin and inexorably
found the necessary media of expression. Although Puritan theology
acknowledged the traditional utter depravity of human nature as one
of its central pivots, it none the less hedged against its own
doctrine. A sinful nature was ultimately an unnatural state of
affairs, running counter to God's revealed demands and intentions
for human life. A pure inside could thus be maintained, but it
meant dividing the cosmos up into warring forces of good and evil.
Samuel Willard, for example, held men accountable for their sinfulness, but attributed the fall largely to the activity of Satan who
became, as it were, the prime mover of evil. (25) Because our
primal mother was seduced into sin, and our primal father duped,
the real fault lay on the outside, and our God-given nature, it
could be claimed, was corrupted but not erased. Corruption was
viewed as a disease from which one might recover given grace and
vigilance, but which, in the absence of either, was sure to be fatal.

As we might expect, the relationship of the sinner to the
community parallels that of the sin to the individual sinner, and
again expresses itself in bodily metaphors heavy with images of
pollution, invasion, and disease. This is also a view which readily
lends itself to concerns of witchcraft. Those who chose to sin also
chose to enter into a covenant with Satan and to submit themselves
to his control. The more a man sinned, the more he reaffirmed his
choice, and the more power Satan gained over him. (26) He became,
according to Urian Oakes, a soldier of evil wearing the 'full
armor of the devil'. (27)   Increase Mather sought to remove the
sinner from the body of Christ in writing in his 'Angelographia':

He that committeth sin, is of the devil, for the devil sinneth
from the beginning. As children are of their father, so are
they that commit sin, of the devil; his image they bear, and
him they imitate.... (28)

Thomas Walley constructed the same boundaries using images of the
body diseased. New England, he claimed, suffered from a 'cold,
sleepy disease' when it came to attempting to please God. In
Walley's words, 'New England is sick, the country is a sickly

country, the country is full of healthy bodies, but sick souls'.
(29)   Within such a perspective, there seem to be two likely
choices: gradual healing, perhaps through ritual integration, or,
in the absence of a coherent set of publicly articulated patterns
of reconciliation, surgical removal of the invader through some
form of expulsion.

In a society whose internal system of classifications and behavioral
patterns lack coherence and comprehensiveness, one should expect the
boundaries between normalcy and deviance to become both unclear and
an object of great concern.   The Puritans' understanding of how
Satan waged his war against the saints provides us with a theological
expression of such an experience.   Satan was powerful but not
omnipotent;   he was a creature and as such had no choice but to
obey God's will even in his rebellion.   Men, as a result, found
themselves living in a world in which Satan had to acknowledge their
freedom.   They could be tempted, but they could not be forced into
sin.   Satan had to operate by guile to gain their trust and seduce
them into his power.   For example, men were dependent upon their
senses to perform what Samuel Willard called 'experiments' upon the
external world, and to report back on the desirability of various
objects and options.   Since Satan possessed a vast knowledge of the
workings of the material world, he was capable of being cognizant
of how a man's senses were operating at any moment, and could adjust
his temptations accordingly.   Every particular temperament and
nuance of mood could be taken into account so that the temptation
could be delivered precisely at that point where men were already
closest to sinning. (30)

One of Satan's most dangerous advantages in his never-ending
battle against the saints was his ability to appear other than he
was.   It was universally agreed that the devil was capable of
appearing as an angel of light with a radiance that gave no hint
of his true nature.   Satan was therefore unlikely to provide his
human followers with horns and cloven hooves.   Flamboyance would
clearly have been counter-productive.   Instead, he would attempt to
employ the apparently good man for the purpose of leading others
astray.   The more impressive the person, the more godly the
appearance, the greater became the chance that Satan's ally would
be effective.   Samuel Willard, for example, warned his congregation
that whenever Satan found people who were 'singularly witty', he
would attempt to recruit them into his service. (31)

In order to divert even a New England Puritan from the path to
salvation, Satan would offer all the pleasures of the world:
wealth, honor, ease, success.   The problem was compounded by the
fact that the world and its pleasures were good when held in the
proper perspective.   The trick, as Perry Miller put it, was that
men were to 'labor in the vineyard without acquiring an inordinate
love of the grape'. (32)   Satan's task was simply to destroy the
vigilance which maintained everything in its place and to forge
demonic ensnarements from the bounty of the world.   If a man would
but love his wealth more than God, Satan's purpose would be
accomplished.   When anything other than God held the place of
God, men were, in effect if not by intention, worshippers of the
devil.

One point to be emphasized here because of its compatibility with

witchcraft cosmologies, is the invisibility of demonic activity.
In this respect evil is much like an internal tumor which, because
it produces no immediately visible symptoms, is far more dangerous
than a more painful but obvious wound. Hence, the person who
faithfully attended worship and lectures, whose visible self performed
the right behavior at the right times but whose heart was elsewhere
posed a most serious threat to the community. In the Puritan view,
worship not inspired by proper motivation counted as no worship at
all, or worse, as idolatry. Properly motivated worship, of course,
would be Biblical (Puritan) worship since God would only accept those
patterns of faith delineated in the Puritan understanding of the
Scriptures. Improper (non-Puritan) worship, Samuel Mather cautioned,
'Provokes the Lord to jealousy against his people, and pulls down ...
the desolating judgments and wrath of God upon them'. (33) When
Satan could not persuade people to be 'downright atheists', Mather
claimed, 'he tempts them to worship God in the wrong way'. (34)

   Purity concerns over matters of worship naturally informed New
England's opposition to religious toleration. In his farewell
sermon to the Dorchester congregation in 1657, Richard Mather set out
the theological foundations upon which the Puritan position on
toleration was based.

   Therefore believe not them that think a man may be saved in any
   religion, and that it were good to have all religions free,
   and that opinions have no great danger in them. These are but
   the devices of Satan, that so pernicious errors might be more
   easily entertained.... (35)

From Mather's perspective, toleration was nothing more nor less
than the most subtle of Satan's stratagems for destroying true
religion in New England. If Satan could convince people that a
variety of religious forms might safely be allowed, the result
would be the practice of plausible yet false faiths which would
doom New England to failure. Thomas Shepard preaching in 1672
agreed that it was 'Satan's policy to plead for an indefinite and
boundless toleration', so that 'Christ may have his kingdom and he
will let Satan alone with his, and so both of them live lovingly
and quietly together'. (36)

   Such benign co-existence was obviously impossible according to
Puritan theology. Those who were tolerant in matters of faith
were by definition not Christians, and ought not to expect divine
favor. Shepard warned that the 'host of superstitious and anti-
christian forms of worship' which could inevitably accompany
toleration 'would provoke the Lord most severely'. (37) Samuel
Mather, preaching against Anglicanism in 1670, made it clear that
the problem was not a 'boundless toleration', but any toleration
at all.

   If you do but wear a surplice for peace sake, why not as well
   admit the sign of the cross in baptism, or bow to an altar,
   and in a little time you will find that the same reason is as
   strong for bowing to an image, to a crucifix, and why not as
   well say Mass too, for the peace of the church, and then at
   last swallow down everything, submit to the Pope, worship the
   Beast, and so be damned and go to hell.... Oh there is no end
   here, when a man is going down the hill in a way of carnal
   compliance and superstition, he will never cease. (38)

Again the controlling metaphor, lying just beneath the surface,
is one of a body attacked internally by an apparently benign but
in reality malignant disease which requires surgery before the whole
becomes infected. Those whose clarity of vision enabled them to
discern the worms at the core were obligated to make the danger
explicit. Although every individual was ultimately responsible
for his own damnation, the truth of Puritanism being self-evident
to all who did not choose to resist it, the New England saints
were not about to permit a wide range of choices and allow the
responsibility to fall upon those who chose wrongly. Such a policy
would have damned New England itself, for it was to be judged as
one man. Puritan accommodation to inauthentic Christianity would
constitute a renunciation of the covenant and would invite upon
New England the divine judgments prepared for those being tolerated.
Satan was too powerful and devious and God too jealous of his
covenanted people to leave men to their own devices. To guarantee
oneself, it was also necessary to keep one's brother.

We have thus seen in seventeenth-century Massachusetts what I
have called a 'latent witchcraft cosmology' of the type which
Douglas has found endemic to the strong-group society. The cosmology
is highly dualistic, split between warring forces of good and evil.
There is an attempt to claim cosmic forces of good for the inside
of the group and to assimilate the dangerous outside to cosmic
forces of evil. To the extent to which strong grid accompanies
strong group and the society is capable of maintaining internal
coherence and cohesion, one will find a relatively controlled
cosmic dualism. Evil will be held in check by good, Satan's
chain will be rather short, the cosmos will ultimately be stable.
Since strong grid also implies effective mechanisms of power
capable of protecting the classification system from either internal
or external threats, when witchcraft accusations do occur, they
will be directed down the social scale as in the English cases
described by Alan Macfarlane and Keith Thomas. (39) However as
grid weakens and a society's internal relationships begin to generate
increasing amounts of irresolvable conflict, the stability of the
strong group and grid cosmology also begins to weaken. The cosmic
struggle between good and evil becomes more problematic, Satan's
chain is lengthened, dangers on the outside are seen penetrating
into the pure insides of the group. In this situation, because it
is likely that power will be ineffective in maintaining or clarifying
the system of internal classifications, witchcraft accusations have
a tendency to be directed up the social scale as those who find
themselves violated by new and seemingly chaotic powers they can
neither control nor understand seek to protect their dwindling
resources through a process of expulsion which both classifies the
threats they experience and tightens group boundaries. (40) This,
as we shall see, was the experience of Salem Village.

I have at several points alluded to weaknesses in Massachusetts'
internal systems of classification. In attempting to make good this
promissory note, I will argue that the witchcraft trials are related
to a series of events whose significance for understanding Salem
has largely been underestimated. There is an abundance of material
here, more than can be handled within the space of an essay, and
therefore I must beg indulgence for the use of explanation sketches

at some points where more detailed analysis would have been fruitful. With reference to the problem of spectral evidence, I will show that the devastating events of the second half of the seventeenth century display striking structural similarities to the symbolism of witchcraft as well as to what we have just seen in the Puritan concept of sin. We will find Massachusetts suffering politically, socially and ecclesiastically the kinds of invasions it feared theologically. The underlying structure will not change as we move from cosmology to social experience. It is still one of the pure inside body being invaded by forces connected to the evil outside. Experience and expression will remain in close congruence.

As long as Massachusetts maintained possession of its charter which granted the colony virtual autonomy, it had available the resources to resist invasions of the social and political bodies. The traditional election-day sermons continually appealed to the magistrates to guard New England's spiritual purity. Political power was to guarantee it that all conformed to the rules of godliness and that no impure forms of worship polluted the social body. England's growing interest in overseeing colonial affairs during the seventeenth century brought forth increasingly passionate pleas for the defense of the charter. Such pleas, however, were ultimately in vain. The revocation of Massachusetts' charter in 1684 and the subsequent establishment of the Dominion of New England under Sir Edmund Andros marked the end of Puritan autonomy and was a blow from which New England Puritanism never recovered. (41)   Its charter gone, Massachusetts watched helplessly as political power was removed from the hands of the godly and given to a royally appointed governor and council having the right to make laws, collect taxes, control the military and create courts. New England's laws could henceforth be reviewed in England, and court decisions involving sums over £300 could be appealed to the king's courts in England. (42) Puritan hopes for renewed autonomy flickered briefly after the Glorious Revolution of 1688, but the charter was not restored. The invasion of Massachusetts' body was permanent, and the Puritans found themselves infiltrated by watchful eyes rather unsympathetic to the task of building the perfect Christian state in the wilderness.

The response of the Puritan orthodoxy to these unpleasant affairs took several directions. The argument was made that the Dominion violated their rights as Englishmen in so far as it collected taxes without the consent of an elected assembly in New England. (43) Less modestly, some Puritans interpreted the revocation of the charter and the establishment of the Dominion as nothing less than a popish plot against the whole of New England. In justifying their overthrow and imprisonment of Andros after the Glorious Revolution, they claimed that Andros was engaged in a treacherous conspiracy to surrender New England to the French. A number of residents of Salem testified to this, asserting that Andros had invited the French to send a fleet of warships to New England to accept his surrender. (44)

One of the more ominous aspects of the Dominion of New England was its imposition of religious toleration upon Massachusetts and the establishment of an Anglican Communion in Boston in 1686 under the leadership of Parson Ratcliffe. The Anglicans met for a while

in the Boston Town House, but needing more suitable accommodations,
appealed to the Congregational churches for the loan of a meeting-
house. When the appeal was denied, Andros was forced to order the
loan of Samuel Willard's Third Church, Boston, until the Anglican
congregation could construct a building of its own, a project
initiated in 1688. (45) Unhappy over the necessity of toleration,
the Puritans were infuriated by what they took to be the usurpation
of their meeting-house. Although Ratcliffe's congregation was
careful to avoid conflicts with scheduled Puritan meetings, the
hosts saw it quite differently. Increase Mather virtually
experienced rape. In his version, the Anglicans 'thrust themselves
into that meeting-house, and there continued until interrupting
the people of the south congregation, often in their times, sometimes
in the very parts of their worship the whole town cried shame on
them'. (46)

Since the political situation rendered traditional appeals to the
magistrates useless, the Puritan clergy shifted its attention to
interior concerns. The danger was no longer to be found on the
outside, that level of violation already a fait accompli, but on
the inside. Anti-Anglican sermons after 1687 consequently did not
denounce toleration (religious toleration after all meant that
Anglicanism would not replace Puritanism as New England's established
religion), but instead castigated impure, obviously still Anglican
forms of worship. John Allen, in 1687, offered a timely sermon
entitled 'The Neglect of Supporting and Maintaining the Pure Worship
of God'. Allen warned that if men did not display sufficient
respect for 'God's Holy and Pure Institutions' they would likely
fall prey to the institutions of men in matters of worship. 'The
greatness of this sin', according to Allen, was that it grew 'from
an evil root, an heart of unbelief ... where there is a forsaking
of God and undervaluing him, and overvaluing the creature'. (47)
Cotton Mather, among others, issued a similar warning:

But let us keep close to the word of God in our building.
Are there any materials which we would build the church
by admission of? Let them all be of God's constitution.
Let us not willingly lay the rotten timber of either heretics
or hypocrites in the fields of our Ark. (48)

Other sermons identified Anglican worship as sinful and as no better
than 'rank atheism', for it expressed the human desire to create a
God in the image of sinful man. (49) Joshua Moody, preaching in
1691, argued that a man's concept of God matches the type of worship
offered. False worship, or to be more exact, non-Biblical and hence
non-Puritan worship, necessarily entailed a false concept of God
which, from the Puritan perspective, equalled idolatry and atheism.
(50) Unfortunately, Anglican atheism, unlike its Roman Catholic
mentor, was not immediately recognizable to all as atheism. On the
contrary, it appeared to be most devout, spiritual, and pleasing to
God. Here, of course, lay its gravest danger, and, we should note,
a danger identical to that presented by the witch. Because
Anglicanism superficially matched men's expectations of what
religion ought to be, the unwary would be likely to assume that
salvation could be found therein, and consequently if unintentionally
offer themselves for damnation. We are now witnessing a situation
in which social experience, classification systems and behavioral

norms are becoming ambiguous, confused, and ridden with anxiety.
There are a number of other layers in this process.

The Puritans' understanding of Anglicanism bears a number of
similarities to their fears about the apparently diminishing
religiosity of the latter generations. As perceived by the clergy,
the once pure religious body of New England was showing alarming
indications of a growing internal decay. Joshua Scottow, in a
sermon appropriately entitled 'Old Men's Tears', asked, 'What is
become of the primitive zeal, piety, and holy heart found in our
parents?' (51) According to Samuel Danforth, those virtues had
nearly been forgotten:

> But who is there left among you, that saw these churches in
> their first glory, and how do you see them now? Are they not
> in your eyes in comparison thereof, as nothing? How is the
> Gold become dim? (52)

When it came to diagnosing the reasons for this unhappy state of
affairs, the clergy was not lacking in explanations. The underlying
problem however, seems to be that such explanations never formed a
coherent analysis, and never set out clear behavioral norms capable
of resolving the conflict. Laments about moral profligacy and
indecent dress were common, particularly during times of stress.
For Joshua Scottow, the lost lustre of New England's gold was making
a dangerous reappearance in its women:

> Our spot is not the spot of God's children; the old Puritan
> garb, and gravity of heart, and habit lost and ridiculed into
> strange and fantastic fashions and attire, naked backs and
> bare breasts and forehead, if not of whorish woman yet too like
> unto it as would require a more than ordinary spirit of
> discerning to distinguish. (53)

Numerous sermons cautioned against social dissension, arguing
that open hostility between the Saints was one more weapon in
Satan's arsenal. Other sermons focused upon New England's spiritual
purity, claiming that people had grown weary of God's service and
were setting easier but ultimately disastrous goals for themselves.
What was once a vibrant religion had degenerated into an empty
performance - clear Anglican tendencies. New Englanders had not
revolted directly against God; they still served him, but did so
'very dully'. 'They do all', Urian Oakes complained, 'as a task
in a slavish way. They have no delight ... no joy, no alacrity in
their obedience'. (54) The problem here has been reduced to the
private recesses of the inner self, a very elusive quarry indeed.
Suggested remedies for New England's ills were similarly elusive
and, I would argue, incapable of providing clearly defined and
co-ordinated behavioral norms. To cite some typical examples:
Josiah Flint called upon the unconverted souls of Massachusetts
not to 'resist' the gospel; William Adams enjoined his congregation,
'get the spirit of God in you'; Eleazer Mather warned his flock to
stop quarreling; Urian Oakes suggested that New England required
a religious revival whose distinguishing mark would be 'humble
submission'. (55)

I think it is fair to conclude that exhortations such as these
were unlikely to provide established channels through which social
conflict could be mediated. Instead these sermons and others of
similar hue which form the jeremiad tradition are clearly expressions

of the colony's social experience. The consonance to be found in
various layers of experience and expression should give added
weight to Perry Miller's claim that the jeremiads became an
instance of 'the tyranny of form over thought'. (56) The form,
however, is more than literary. It is social, political,
ecclesiastical, economic. The jeremiads in raising and attempting
to answer the question, 'How is New England in danger of being lost
even in New England?' (57) give expression to the experience of a
diversifying society incapable of integrating change through its
old system of classifications and unable to insulate itself from
the pressures of a polluting external world. With regard to
economic activity, Bernard Bailyn contends that the basic problem
was one 'of containing the merchants at all within the structure
of Puritan society'. (58) An acquaintance with the symbolic
patterns expressed in the clergy's understanding of New England's
experience reinforces Bailyn's analysis. The jeremiad sermons
represent an attempt to reaffirm and tighten group identity in the
face of growing internal heterogeneity. Massachusetts had indeed
been invaded by subtle and dangerous enemies, and had found traitors
lodged within its own heart. Social and economic diversification,
the loss of the charter and Massachusetts' subsequent failure to
regain it, the imposition of the Dominion of New England and the
arrival of the Anglican congregation are all experiences describable
in the structural metaphors we found in the Puritan concepts of
sin. Incapable of repelling the onslaught through a direct
application of legitimated power, the Puritans' only recourses
were increased vigilance within and symbolic resistance.
    Although the Salem witchcraft trials could not have taken place
without the consent of the colony as a whole, their generation was
immediately a function of the experiences of the troubled community
of Salem Village. The history of the Village forms a microcosm of
the history of Massachusetts, displaying the same patterns of inside
and outside, of attack and invasion. From its first attempts to
establish a church in 1671 to the outbreak of witchcraft accusations
in 1692, Salem Village found itself embroiled in continuous and
irresolvable conflicts. Such a lengthy period of conflict set
Salem Village strongly at odds with traditional concepts and
expectations that a Puritan community ought to be marked by
harmony and unanimity in all things. Michael Zuckerman's persuasive
analysis of Puritan mechanisms for dealing with conflict in
'Peaceable Kingdoms' indicates that there was a weakness inherent
in Puritan classification systems which made social conflict
especially disturbing. There is simply a limit to the effectiveness
of appeals to goodwill and to ideals of harmony in the face of
sustained social discord. Classification systems based on the
assumption that conflict must and need not exist will be incapable
of channeling it once it occurs.
    Contention did occur, and when it did it confronted the
    communities of the province with a cruel dilemma. They could
    neither acknowledge the conflict nor ignore it. They could not
    avow it because they lacked both the intellectual and the
    institutional implements for its acceptance; yet they could not
    neglect it because it broke the unanimity on which effective
    action in the society rested....

> Disputes were consistently seen as unnatural and undesirable
> deviations from the norm.   In the absence of any socially
> sanctioned role for opposition, the dissent that did occur was
> generally surreptitious .... And when antagonism endured for
> any considerable length of time the effectiveness of the community
> collapsed or declined sharply. (59)

The special problem of Salem Village was that it was unable to heal
its dissensions and was forced to live with them for an exceedingly
long time. Ultimately the witchcraft trials provided the only
socially legitimated mechanism for resolving the antagonism.

The parallels between Salem Village and the Bay Colony as a
whole become explicit when one looks at the actual patterns of
witchcraft accusations. Here I should again express my debt to
Paul Boyer and Stephen Nissenbaum for the careful historiography
accomplished in 'Salem Possessed'. My selective summary of their
findings should in no way be taken as an adequate substitute for a
first-hand acquaintance with their work. The accomplishment of
'Salem Possessed' has been to uncover the warring factions in Salem
Village who played out the witchcraft trials and to delineate with
a great deal of clarity the fields of their struggle. The factions
involved in the trials remained relatively constant for over twenty
years although they occasionally reversed their positions on some
of the issues through which the struggle was being waged. We shall
see here on a highly empirical plane the same basic structures we
have already found in Puritan cosmology and in the political and
ecclesiastical experience of Massachusetts as a whole. Since the
factions remained constant over time, and since one faction
eventually leveled witchcraft accusations against the other I shall
designate them 'the accusers' and 'the accused'.

Most of the accusers lived in the western part of Salem Village,
farthest away from Salem Town, Boston, and hence from links to the
outside world. They lacked easy access to the roads and waterways
which led to the markets of the Town and Boston. Further, their
land, which was their only source of wealth, was bounded on all
sides, on the north, east and south by other towns, and on the west
by hilly, swampy land and a greater danger of Indian attack. (60)
Such physical confinement not only limited wealth, but focused
the daily activity of the accusers within the boundaries of their
own group. Lacking the ability to expand or even maintain their
landholdings, the accusers watched their wealth diminish. They
not only lacked the best land in the Village but they had to divide
it into increasingly smaller parcels as the second, third, and
fourth generations came of age. The accusers' continual boundary
disputes with neighboring towns gives further indication of their
concern with protecting their single limited resource. (61)

The nucleus of the group of accusers was the family of Thomas
Putnam Jr, which supplied a number of significant participants.
Thomas, his brother Edward, and a brother-in-law, actively testified
against accused witches. Thomas's wife Ann Sr, his daughter Ann Jr,
and a servant-girl Mercy Lewis held center stage as members of the
afflicted group by whom virtually all the accusations were generated.
(62) The history of the Putnam family can in some respects be taken
as paradigmatic of the history of the accusing group. Once the
pre-eminent family in the Village, the Putnams had seen their wealth

and power fade. Their lands were hemmed in, particularly by the
holdings of the Porter family which rivaled and ultimately surpassed
them. They were unable to avail themselves of the Town markets,
incapable of achieving economic diversification. (63) The Village,
the agrarian Village, was their life, their identity.

The most devastating blow to the Putnam family occurred when
Thomas Sr, one of the pre-eminent figures of the second generation,
took Mary Veren, a woman of Salem Town, as his second wife. Mary
bore one son, Joseph, in 1669, and when Thomas Sr died in 1686,
the bulk of his estate went to her and her son. A bitter suit to
overthrow the will was pursued by Thomas Putnam Jr, his brother
and two brothers-in-law, but proved unsuccessful. A final coup de
grace fell when Joseph Putnam married into the Porter clan, thus
cementing his connections with the interests of Salem Town, further
confirming his status as an outsider, and making it clear that a
substantial portion of Putnam wealth had been lost through what
amounted to betrayal and invasion. (64)

The people against whom witchcraft accusations were directed
lived in the eastern part of Salem Village, and in surrounding towns.
The location of the accused placed them closer to Salem Town and to
Boston and to the commercial routes which linked them to the markets
of the outside world. (65) Salem Town had become a burgeoning
commercial center, one of Massachusetts' two ports of entry, and
had spawned a wealthy merchant class which dominated Town politics
after 1655. (66) The Porter family into which Joseph Putnam married
provides a paradigm and a focus for those accused of witchcraft.
The Porters' eastern location allowed them access to outside commerce
and permitted an economic diversification unavailable to the Putnams.
Unlike the Putnams, they did not join the village church and
actively opposed the ordination of Samuel Parris which made that
church possible. The Porters' connections to Salem Town were forged
of the chains of economic interest, political allegience, church
membership and marriage. (67)

A perceptive and significant characterization of the Porters
provided by Boyer and Nissenbaum is that they were 'behind the
scenes' men, working efficiently for their interest, but seldom
openly. (68) One Porter attempted to discredit the least creditable
of the afflicted girls and Israel Porter, the second generation
counterpart of Thomas Putnam Sr supported Rebecca Nurse, the least
likely of all the accused witches. (69) Boyer and Nissenbaum
speculate that the invisible hand of Israel Porter may well have
been instrumental in arranging the marriage of his daughter
Elizabeth to Joseph Putnam. Although none who were Porters by blood
were accused of witchcraft, accusations did swirl through their
immediate circle. Boyer and Nissenbaum find that no less than
seventeen accused witches were related to Israel Porter through bonds
of friendship, marriage, or business. (70)

The Porters and the accused villagers in general had formed a
natural allegiance to the interests of the Town and were able to
avail themselves of the opportunities afforded by Town commerce.
It was in the interest of the Town to maintain control over its
outlying farming areas which included most particularly Salem Village.
In the political relationship of the Town and Village it was
ultimately the Town which had control over such vital areas as the

setting of prices for farm products, the construction of new roads and the allotment of lands. (71) Consequently the issue of Salem Village achieving political independence from the Town loomed large for more than twenty years before the witchcraft trials and served as a continual source of conflict between the accusers and the accused, the former perceiving their best interests in independence, the latter in continuing the relationship with the Town.

In the peculiar world of New England politics, however, an issue of political independence necessarily involved questions regarding the establishment of a church, for a community could not attain legitimate political status without first forming a duly covenanted church. Because this was the case, the political and economic conflicts within Salem Village inevitably spilled over into church politics and hence, I would suggest, directly into the labyrinths of Puritan cosmology. From 1672 until well after the witchcraft trials, the factions in Salem Village battled each other through either supporting or attacking the various clergy who tried to lead the Salem Village parish. Oddly enough, at the beginning of this dimension of their struggle, it was the accused, whose interests lay in maintaining connections with the Town, who supported the clergy (Bayley and Borroughs), and it was the accusers whose interests lay in separation and consequently in the establishment of a Village church, who formed the opposition. The issue at this time, however, seems not to have been the possibilities for independence inherent in a Village church, but a question of church control, the accused arguing for wide suffrage in the selection of a minister (which was in fact granted) and the accusers arguing for a limitation of suffrage to church members. (72) The positions taken by the factions here were thus compatible with their underlying self-interest. With the arrival of Deodat Lawson in 1683 and the decision of the accusers to push for ordination and full church status for the Village parish, the factions reversed their relative positions, the accusers now supporting the minister and the accused forming the opposition. With help from Salem Town, which was looking after its own interests, the accused were able to block the ordination of Lawson, prevent the establishment of the church, and thwart the move for independence. (73)

I cannot do justice here to the rich and intricate detail of these events provided by Boyer and Nissenbaum. The entire episode is a classic example of weak-grid politics: underhanded maneuvers, covert plotting, packed meetings, false issues and so on. Much of this is attributable to the highly ambiguous position of Salem Village during this time. As Boyer and Nissenbaum describe it

> Salem Village was virtually the first Massachusetts community to
> enter for a protracted period this gray area in which its
> separate existence was given legal recognition, but in such a
> way as to deny it any real autonomy. (74)

The political status of the village was ambiguous in that although it had its own meetinghouse and Village committee, it was still a part of Salem Town. The political organ of the Village, the committee, lacked any real power as far as the accusers were concerned, for all it could do was to levy and collect the ministerial tax. (75) This relatively insignificant power in the hands of the accused, however, could be turned into a significant weapon, as

we shall see, while in the hands of the accusers it was rendered
impotent. The Village church likewise suffered a long period of
ambiguous status, for it was not really a church. Its official
status was that of a 'parish', which meant that the word could be
preached but communion and church membership could not be offered.
(76)

Taking advantage of the general political turmoil produced by
the Glorious Revolution, the group of accusers, led by the Putnam
family, covenanted the Village church and ordained Samuel Parris
minister on 19 November 1689. (77) This successful move was
accompanied by yet another unsuccessful attempt at independence,
rendering the accusers' victory a pyrrhic one. When members of the
other faction refused to pay the ministerial tax, there was little
that could be done, for the power to deal with such problems lay
not with the Village committee, but with Salem Town, which refused
to take any action. When the accused gained control of the Village
committee, they were able to use its limited power effectively
simply by refusing to levy a tax to pay Parris's salary. (78) Thus
by the time of the witchcraft trials the two factions each had
established a power-base, the accusers in the church and the accused
in the Village committee. In addition, it is important to point
out that as far as effective power was concerned, given the fields
of factional strife, the group of accusers was in the inferior
position because of their ultimate dependence upon Salem Town.
The church, therefore, could provide only symbolic refuge for the
beleagured group of accusers. Besides this, it should also be
pointed out that those villagers who were accused of witchcraft in
1692 by and large did not join the Village church. Some worshipped
with the Village congregation while maintaining membership elsewhere,
while other accused villagers worshipped elsewhere, primarily with
the Salem Town congregation. It is not surprising then that Boyer
and Nissenbaum have been able to trace a growing anxiety about the
security afforded by the Village church in the sermons of Samuel
Parris. His initial view of the church as a secure barrier against
evils lying on the outside gave way, as the trials progressed, to
a view in which the boundaries of the ecclesiastical body had been
penetrated and danger in the form of traitors and aliens lurked on
the inside, until finally Parris sought refuge in a vision of a
spiritual congregation which was no longer of this world. (79)
However mistaken Samuel Parris may have been about the presence of
witches in his congregation, the theme of invasion in his sermons
was no mere paranoid delusion. The point is that Salem Village,
taken as a discrete entity with rights to territorial integrity
at cultural-symbolic levels as well as at a geographic level, had
in fact been violated. There were persons living within the larger
body of the Village who were aligned with outside forces which did
not acknowledge the integrity nor even the legitimate existence of
the Village body. There were persons within the Village who
belonged to external churches, worshippers in the Village congregation who owed allegiance even to the God of another church, to put
it in the extreme. Samuel Parris was merely describing the reality
of the situation. He was, however, describing it in the metaphors
of the Puritan cosmology, and he was not adding anything new.

Witchcraft accusations thus radiated out from the western Salem

Village toward the east and directed themselves geographically, economically, and socially against very real dangers. The movement of the accusations up the social scale cannot, therefore, be attributed, as Boyer and Nissenbaum suggest, to the need of the Putnams to find cathartic substitutes for Mary Veren Putnam and Israel Porter, both of whom held high status. (80) That explanation will not bear the weight and, furthermore, no substitution theory is necessary. Witchcraft accusations made by a relatively poor and weak group whose wealthiest members have seen their resources severely diminished will go up the social scale if they are to identify the source of their problems. That Mary Veren Putnam and Israel Porter were not accused is certainly psychologically interesting and may, as Boyer and Nissenbaum suggest, have something to do with deep-running 'habits of deference'. (81) However, those who were subjected to witchcraft accusations had good claims to that distinction in their own right. Before returning to the problem of spectral evidence, let us consider the symbolism involved in first the figure of the witch, the position of the accused relative to their accusers, and finally the position and experience of the colony as a whole.

The figure of the witch involves connections to cosmic forces of evil, to the 'outside' of the socially legitimating cosmos. The witch works his or her malevolence through supernatural agency. The connections between malevolent activity, charms, spells, pins inserted into dolls and their effects such as illness are mysterious, invisible, outside the usual connections between things. Witches are surreptitious, underground 'behind the scenes' figures, gathering in clandestine meetings, conspiring against their victims. Even to the trained observer, witches are virtually indistinguishable from ordinary persons, their malevolence of spirit is concealed beneath a normal exterior. Occasionally their bodies belie them through the presence of a witches' teat, in effect a breast created by the devil used to suckle the witches' pets (known as 'familiars') who do their malevolent bidding. But the discovery of a witch's teat requires careful scrutiny of the body and even then the results may be inconclusive. (82) Witches are thus difficult to 'discover'. One must find a way of penetrating the veneer of normalcy to lay bare the internal corruption. The symbolism of witchcraft points to the invasion of the social body by dangerous but ambiguous forces. The witch himself is one such force; going about his business in apparently normal fashion, he spreads poison on the inside of the social body. The body of the witch with its normal exterior and degenerate interior can thus serve as a thinly-veiled social metaphor. In accusing and in one way or another eliminating a witch, a community has both a language for its experience and a way of stripping away the appearance of normality, of uncovering the evil lurking within the witch and hence within the social body itself.

When we look at the social body of Salem Village we find patterns which are strikingly similar to the figure of the witch. The integrity of the social body was continually violated by the exercise of power from Salem Town. The Village was also violated by aliens: new arrivals, persons taking advantage of the economic possibilities of the Town and hence of an alien style of life, persons owing allegience to the Town instead of the Village, persons belonging to other churches, persons consorting with outsiders along the Ipswich Road. The Putnam family had even found traitors within their own ranks. The effects of the outsiders' activity upon those who identified themselves with the social body of the Village was a steady sapping of wealth and strength. Meanwhile those who had violated the Village were growing wealthier, more powerful and were moving up the social scale. Yet none of these were grossly deviant. Their economic activity, their associations, their style of life, even their rather underhanded ways of fighting were all dangerous to the social body, yet because of the weak grid in the larger situation, none were decisively outside the range of acceptable activity, certainly not as far as official and effective power was concerned. They were danger wearing the guise of normality, and they could not be eliminated.

When we look at the experience of the colony as a whole the same patterns are again evident. The integrity of Massachusetts had been violated. It had been stripped of its charter and invaded by royal governors. What Massachusetts took to be its own internal economic and political affairs had suffered interference from the crown. Devil-worshippers in the form of pious Anglicans had established a foothold in Boston and it was certain that there would be others. Like Salem, Massachusetts had grown diverse and had seen substantial power shift into the hands of the merchant class. The lack of compatibility which Bailyn saw between Puritan society and the merchant class heightened the danger of this turn of events and intensified the sense of violation and invasion. Boyer and Nissenbaum's description of Salem Village could also apply to the entire colony:

> what was going on was not simply a personal quarrel, an
> economic dispute, or even a struggle for power, but a moral
> conflict involving the very nature of the community itself.
> The fundamental issue was not who was to control the Village,
> but what its essential character was to be. (83)

All of these events which severely threatened both the colony and Salem Village took place within the context of the Puritan cosmology. The metaphors, the symbol-systems, which were available to the New England Puritans and which both interpreted and shaped their experience, were largely images of invasion by cosmic forces of evil, consequent internal decay, and ultimate doom. As the events leading up to and surrounding the witchcraft trials have been uncovered, layer after layer has shown the same basic structural patterns. The witchcraft trials and the issue of spectral evidence are a result of a piling up of these congruent patterns of experience and meaning. Let us look briefly at the general patterns involved in spectral evidence before drawing the matter to a close.

In most of the testimony there seems to be an imbalance between the terror provoked by spectral attacks and the actual malevolent activity involved. The constant repetition of certain formulas makes it clear that the transcripts are not verbatim, but that would not seem to make them inaccurate. Throughout the records of the preliminary investigations it is repeatedly stated that spectres of suspected witches 'did most grievously afflict', or 'did most grievously torment', or 'did most dreadfully afflict'. These

formulas hardly vary from witness to witness. When it came to
stating how the spectres attacked their victims, the complaints
are again very regular: pinching and pricking probably head the
list, followed by biting, choking and tempting the victim to write
in a book. Occasionally, but far less frequently, the victims would
claim to have been thrown down and wrenched about. One is led to
wonder why the legions of hell engaged in such trivial assaults.
The degree of fear provoked by these attacks is not a problem, for
we can well imagine that any assault by a spectral figure, regardless
of the particulars of the attack, would indeed be terrifying.

     However, regarding the rather mild nature of the assaults, we can
recall that those who were accused of witchcraft, while posing a
real and fundamental danger to the accusers and their way of life,
were not grossly deviant. They afflicted the social body, to be
sure, but like Anglicanism, they were on the margins of legitimate
activity. Regarding charges of choking, which often appear in the
formula 'almost choking me to death', let us recall that the
accusers had literally been cut off from the possibilities of
economic growth, and had seen their wealth slowly but inexorably
waste away. The problem of the temptation to sign a book, sometimes
the 'devil's book', has virtually been solved by Boyer and
Nissenbaum. Since few if any of the afflicted girls and women
could write (they did not sign pieces of testimony and complaints
but instead made their mark), the only thing we can reasonably
expect that they could have written in the book would be their
names, or their marks which were equivalent to signing their names.
Thus writing in the book suggests enlisting oneself in the legions
of hell, covenanting with Satan and writing oneself down in his
ledger. The afflicted reported that they were urged to write in
the book, and often that spectres tempted them to write. Boyer
and Nissenbaum's analysis of Ann Putnam Sr's anguish at the hands
of the spectre of Rebecca Nurse (whom Ann had accused of witchcraft)
is much to the point.

     Ann's frantic monologues reveal a great deal about the nature
of her obsession: 'I know what you would have ..., but it is
out of your reach' '[We] judged she meant her soul', interpolated
Deodat Lawson (a little defensively?).... It is Rebecca's
death ... which obsessed her. 'Be gone! Be gone!' she cries....
She insists that Rebecca's name has been blotted out of God's
mind forever....

     But there is guilt as well as rage in all of this: for
[the Putnam family had been] ... forced openly and perhaps even
consciously to confront the fact that it cared, and cared
profoundly about money and status.

     The apparition which ... urged Ann Putnam to 'yield to her
hellish temptations' and which denied, as Ann put it, 'the power
of the Lord Jesus to save my soul', was after all the mind of
Mrs Putnam herself. Did she fear that ... she had indeed lost
her soul? that it was she and her husband, with ... their ...
pursuit of money ... who were the real witches? (84)

     It seems reasonable to generalize from the torments of Ann Putnam
and to suggest that the accusers in general felt deep psychic
ambivalence. Those whom they accused were both threatening and
tempting. Their increasing wealth and status were certainly cause

for envy, and yet such envy was inevitably tinged with guilt, for Puritanism itself condemned covetousness and called into question the things which were being coveted.   But such psychic ambivalence would seem to be endemic to what Douglas has called the weak-grid society.   Here behavioral norms are in confusion, relationships are fraught with competition, conflict and ambiguity.   Ranges of activity become liminal, to borrow from Van Gennep via Turner: they lack goodness of fit with the old system of classifications, but they are not easily demonstrated to be grossly deviant.   Their threat is hidden, difficult to name.   There should be little doubt that those making, those supporting and those allowing witchcraft accusations experienced something of this.   In addition, their inner anguish was indeed connected to external states of affairs. The temptations were actually there, and there were real persons to tempt them.

Those who suffered spectral attacks seemed indeed to be in genuine anguish.   To contemporary observers, the victims of spectral assaults appeared as if their bodies were literally being torn apart.   What was happening to the victims of witchcraft, however, had actually happened to Salem Village and to the Massachusetts Bay Colony.   In the face of the events of the second half of the seventeenth century, the Puritans turned their attention inward, attempting to reassert the identity of the corporate body.   Weak grid coupled with strong group, to return to Douglas's terms, produces an extremely difficult situation, for when the inner life of the social body is riddled with ambiguity and conflict, what is called into question is the identity of the group as a whole, for external boundaries become the coin of identity.   Consequently all were called upon to introspect, to discover their inner evils and to cast them out, and not only as individuals.   The fate of the individual and social bodies was one.   The witchcraft trials were a part of this process, for they allowed the society to unmask the alien presences within itself and expel them to make the body once again pure and whole.   Those who were accused of witchcraft were in fact in league with outside powers, and posed a real threat to a way of life which was inexorably losing its resources.   Spectral evidence solved a very complex problem.   It allowed the stripping away of the guise of normalcy, the exposure of the hidden internal danger, a danger which at that time had no other name, and finally its elimination. Far from being an embarrassing erruption of the irrational into New England's history, the spectral character of the Salem witchcraft trials points directly to the depths of New England's social experience at numerous levels, and itself is an expression of that experience.

NOTES

1   Marion L. Starkey, 'The Devil in Massachusetts', New York, 1949: 14, 46-7.
2   Deodat Lawson, 'A Brief and True Narrative' (1692), in Boyer and Nissenbaum (eds), 'Salem Village Witchcraft, A Documentary Record of Local Conflict in Colonial New England', Belmont, 1972: 111.

3 'Summary of the examination of Sara Good' by John Hathorne and
   Jonathan Corwin in ibid.: 6.
4 Paul Boyer and Stephen Nissenbaum, 'Salem Possessed: The Social
   Origins of Witchcraft', Cambridge, Mass., 1974: 18.
5 In the case of Bishop there was physical evidence - dolls stuck
   with pins - and in the case of Bouroughs there were persons
   who claimed to be eye-witnesses who testified to acts of super-
   human strength.
6 'Salem Village Witchcraft': 5.
7 Ibid.: 29-30.
8 Calef, 'More Wonders of the Invisible World' in 'Salem Village
   Witchcraft': 104.
9 Ibid.: 104-5. The others were Sara Good, Susannah Martin,
   Elizabeth Howe, and Sara Wildes.
10 'The Return of Several Ministers Consulted' drawn up by Cotton
   Mather in June of 1692 argued that demons could appear in the
   guise of innocent persons to foster the devil's 'ill purposes'.
   However the same document began with a word of approval and
   thanks to those responsible for the discovery of 'abominable
   witchcrafts' ('Salem Village Witchcraft': 118).
11 Cited in Chadwick Hansen, 'Witchcraft at Salem', New York,
   1969: 97.
12 Mary Douglas, 'Natural Symbols', Harmondsworth, Penguin, 1973:
   ch.4, 7; 'Cultural Bias', London, Royal Anthropological
   Institute, occasional paper no.35, 1978: 15-16.
13 Douglas 1973: 95.
14 Douglas 1973: 98. It is not my intention to ignore the
   importance of this claim. Douglas is attempting here to unpack
   the mechanisms through which the Durkheimian equation of God
   and society can be made, and to deliver some of structural
   anthropology's promissory notes. Much of this essay is an
   effort to demonstrate how one particular social organization
   generated an active witchcraft cosmology.
14 For a breakdown of these types, see Sheldon R. Isenberg and
   Dennis E. Owen, Bodies, natural and contrived: the work of Mary
   Douglas, 'Religious Studies Review', vol.3, no.1, January 1977.
   In addition see Douglas 1978.
16 Douglas 1973: 93.
17 Douglas 1973: 139.
18 John Winthrop, 'Papers', vol.III, Boston, 1931: 289.
19 Ibid.: 295.
20 Samuel Willard, 'A Compleat Body of Divinity', Boston, 1726:
   4-5 is a good orthodox summary.
21 Joshua Moody, 'Souldiery Spiritualized', Cambridge, Mass.
   1674: 14.
22 Willard, 'The Christian's Exercise by Satan's Temptation',
   Boston, 1701: 84. Hereafter cited as 'Christian's Exercise'.
23 Urian Oakes, 'The Unconquerable, All Conquering and More than
   Conquering Soldier', Cambridge, Mass., 1674: 5. Hereafter cited
   as 'Unconquerable Soldier'.
24 Cotton Mather, 'Advice from the Watchtower', Boston, 1713: 6.
25 Willard, 'Christian's Exercise': 58-9.
26 Joshua Moody, 'Souldiery Spiritualized', Cambridge, Mass.
   1674: 22.

27 Oakes, 'Unconquerable Soldier': 5.
28 Increase Mather, 'Angelographia', Boston, 1696: 84.
29 Thomas Walley, 'Balm in Gilead to Heal Sion's Wounds', Cambridge, Mass., 1669: 8.
30 Willard, 'All Plots Against God and his People Detected and Defeated', Boston, 1682: 205. Hereafter cited as 'All Plots'.
31 Ibid.
32 Perry Miller, 'The New England Mind: the Seventeenth Century', Boston, 1954: 43.
33 Samuel Mather, 'A Testimony from Scripture Against Idolatry and Superstition' Cambridge, Mass., 1670: 22. Hereafter cited as 'Testimony'.
34 Ibid.: 26.
35 Richard Mather, 'A Farewell Exhortation to the Church and People of Dorchester in New England', Cambridge, Mass., 1657: A-4.
36 Thomas Shepard, 'Eye-Salve: Or a Watchword from our Lord Jesus Christ to His Churches', Cambridge, Mass., 1673: 14.
37 Ibid.: 38.
38 Samuel Mather, 'Testimony': 25.
39 Mary Douglas, 'Cultural Bias': 30-1. Macfarlane and Thomas both attribute witchcraft accusations in Tudor-Stuart England to a change in the system of social classifications which rendered the status of beggars ambiguous for a time. The relationships and responsibilities of the upper classes to those who begged door to door were consequently also rendered ambiguous and anxiety-producing, a situation which produced witchcraft accusations as a temporary means of social control. When working mechanisms for dealing with the poor were finally established, witchcraft accusations ceased. See Alan Macfarlane, 'Witchcraft in Tudor and Stuart England', New York, 1970; and Keith Thomas, 'Religion and the Decline of Magic', New York, 1971.
40 Mary Douglas, 'Cultural Bias': 30-1.
41 The question as to whether Puritanism in New England was in a state of decline prior to this time is moot. Perry Miller, Darrett Rutman, Bernard Bailyn and others have argued that it was. However Robert G. Pope has counterattacked arguing that traditional indices of religiosity such as baptismal records and the percentage of church members in the total population warrant no such conclusion. If anything, Pope sees New England experiencing a revival during the years 1675-90. (See 'The Half-Way Covenant: Church Membership in Puritan New England', Princeton, 1969; also The Myth of Declension in John Mulder and John Wilson (eds), 'Religion in American History', Englewood Cliffs, NJ, 1978: 45-56.) Nevertheless the material of the 'Jeremiad Tradition' establishes that leading clerical voices at least believed that New England's faith was in decline, and the work of Rutman ('Winthrop's Boston', New York, 1965) and Bailyn ('The New England Merchants in the Seventeenth Century', New York, 1955) shows an increasing and formidable heterogeneity in Massachusetts society.
42 Viola Barnes, 'The Dominion of New England', New Haven, 1923: 53.
43 Wesley Craven, 'The Colonies in Transition', New York, 1968: 219-20.

44 W.H. Whitmore (ed.), 'The Andros Tracts', Prince Society, Publications 5-7, 1868-74, I, 119.
45 Massachusetts Historical Society Collections 3, Series 1: 84.
46 'The Andros Tracts', II: 44-5.
47 John Allen, 'The Neglect of Supporting and Maintaining the Pure Worship of God', Boston, 1687: 10.
48 Cotton Mather, 'Work Upon the Ark', Boston, 1689: 7.
49 Joshua Moody, 'The Great Sin of Formality in the Worship of God', Boston, 1691: 27.
50 Ibid.: 27.
51 Joshua Scottow, 'Old Men's Tears', Boston, 1691: 4.
52 Samuel Danforth, 'A Brief Recognition of New England's Errand Into the Wilderness', Cambridge, Mass., 1671: 18.
53 Scottow, 'Old Men's Tears': 5.
54 Urian Oakes, 'Seasonable Discourse Wherein Sincerity and Delight in the Service of God is Earnestly Pressed Upon Professors of Religion', Cambridge, Mass., 1682: 17.
55 Josiah Flint, Introduction to William Adams, 'The Necessity of the Pouring Out of the Spirit from on High Upon an Apostatizing People', Boston, 1679; William Adams, 'The Necessity of the Pouring Out of the Spirit', : 40; Eleazer Mather, 'A Serious Exhortation to the Present and Succeeding Generations in New England', Cambridge, Mass., 1671: 10; Urian Oakes, 'New England Pleaded With', Cambridge, Mass., 1673: 25.
56 Perry Miller, 'The New England Mind', vol.2: From Colony to Province, Boston, 1953: 31.
57 William Stoughton, 'New England's True Interest Not to Lie', Boston, 1663: 21.
58 Bailyn, 'New England Merchants': 76.
59 Michael Zuckerman, 'Peaceable Kingdoms: New England Towns in the Eighteenth Century', New York, 1970: 124.
60 'Salem Possessed': 35, 38 (map), 83, 84-5 (maps), 91.
61 Ibid.: 44, 90, 94.
62 Ibid.: 145.
63 Ibid.: 114, 115, 117, 126, 128.
64 Ibid.: 136-8.
65 Ibid.: 33.
66 Ibid.: 87-9.
67 Ibid.: 114, 117, 119, 120.
68 Ibid.: 115.
69 Ibid.: 116.
70 Ibid.: 141, 185.
71 Ibid.: 41-2.
72 Ibid.: 40-1, 45-8, 92.
73 Ibid.: 57, 58.
74 Ibid.: 51.
75 Ibid.: 50-1.
76 Ibid.: 43.
77 Ibid.: 61.
78 Ibid.: 65-6, 77.
79 Ibid.: 171-4.
80 Ibid.: 144-7.
81 Ibid.: 188.
82 Some of the accused were so scrutinized during the Salem Witchcraft

trials, and in some cases there were suspicious findings.
However none of these were ever conclusively identified as
witches' teats, and the findings seem not to have played a
significant role in the trials.

83   'Salem Possessed': 103.
84   Ibid.: 149-50.

Chapter 13

THE PROBLEM OF THE CENTRE:
AN AUTONOMOUS COSMOLOGY
Michael Thompson

INTRODUCTION

The two-dimensional picture that has been widely used in applications
of grid/group analysis is often treated as if it were static. The
four compartments obtained by the intersection of the lines dividing
weak and strong grid and group describe four kinds of social context
with each of which is associated a distinctive kind of cosmology or
cultural bias. The picture simply says, four times over, 'With
this kind of social context you can expect to find this kind of
cosmology'. This originally speculative statement has now, through
applications and testings in a variety of fields, received some
validation but, at the same time, those investigations have revealed
a serious problem: what happens at the centre - at the crossover
point between the four contexts?
  One way of approaching this problem is to ask what the two
crossed lines represent. Douglas is quite explicit about this:
they separate extremes of social context. The trouble arises from
using lines to represent this separation. We all learned at school
that lines have no thickness, but these may have! Because grid and
group are measured on ordinal scales, there is no way of knowing how
extreme these four extremes are - there is no way of telling whether
these crossed lines have no thickness or are incredibly fat. So
when you draw

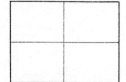 you may, in fact, have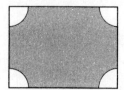

FIGURE 13.1

If the lines were infinitely thin, then the transition from one
cosmology to another would be instantaneous; if they were incredibly
fat, the transition would take place gradually. In the thin-line
case the grid/group analyst's separation separates all possible

contexts; in the fat-line case it separates a few of them. So the
very success - the intuitive rightness - of grid/group theory has
served to emphasise a huge hole right in the middle of it. It is in
the hope of doing something about this hole that I have produced
my three-dimensional picture.

The idea behind the three-dimensional picture is to extend the
familiar two-dimensional picture so that it displays its own
dynamism and becomes capable of handling power and social action.
But it is not simply a matter of adding a third dimension to the
original two. The way the three-dimensional picture develops suggests
that the two-dimensional picture is inadequate in certain respects
over and above those inadequacies that result from its relatively
static nature. At the same time, it suggests that certain modifications could be made to the two-dimensional picture to improve the
description that it furnishes. Turning the argument around, we can
put the three-dimensional picture to the test, in an economical and
convincing way, by listing these suggested inadequacies of the two-
dimensional picture (and the corresponding modifications indicated
by the three-dimensional picture) and then going out and looking in
the sort of social contexts where the three-dimensional picture
predicts that we will find these inadequacies. To avoid these sorts
of contexts would be to avoid a proper testing of the three-dimensional picture and to run the risk of establishing it merely as a
valid but trivial extension of the two-dimensional picture.

The sorts of social contexts chosen for this non-trivial application and testing are those occupied by the Sherpas of Nepal, in
particular those of them who have become involved in mountaineering
and tourism. Consequently a report on this fieldwork (1) falls
quite naturally into three stages. First, a full explanation of
the three-dimensional picture (this has already been provided in
chapter 2: my essay 'A Three-Dimensional Model). Second, the
listing of these suggested inadequacies in the two-dimensional
picture and the modifications indicated by the three-dimensional
picture. Third, an investigation of these suggested inadequacies
drawing upon both fieldwork and existing ethnography.

INADEQUACIES AND MODIFICATIONS

These can be summarised under five heads:

1 Fifth equilibrium state: the autonomous strategy ideal

Four of the equilibrium states (the flattish regions of the surface)
in the three-dimensional picture correspond quite well (geometrical
niceties apart) to the four compartments of the two-dimensional
picture. However, the geometry insists (2) that there is a fifth
equilibrium state, the autonomous strategy ideal, for social contexts
at or near zero group and zero grid. I will argue that the contexts
of the individual Sherpas who, residing in the Khumbu region,
comprise the 'traditional' Sherpa society described in the ethnography are all close enough to zero group and zero grid for them to
be attracted to this equilibrium state. I will further argue that
their cosmology expresses this ideal and that its bias is quite

distinct from those found in association with the other four
equilibrium states.

2   Centrality of autonomy

This fifth equilibrium state was, at one time, included by Douglas
in the two-dimensional picture (though not in a central position).
She later decided to exclude it on the grounds that it was 'off the
social map', as indeed it is in the sense that it displays little,
if any, of the involvements with group dynamics and network-building
that are often held to be necessary conditions for the social bond.
If, as I will argue, the 'traditional' Sherpa society holds together
without any of this supposedly vital social glue, we are faced with
a serious problem which is that our social map is not much use if
an entire society is off it! The three-dimensional picture shows
how autonomy can be included on the social map and, at the same
time, explains why it is that we should be tempted to leave it out.
It is, in fact, absolutely central on the social map, not just
literally, but also in the sense that it differs from the other four
equilibrium states in a way quite other than that in which they differ
from one another. The other four states correspond to the four
possible extremes of involvement: autonomy corresponds to the
absence of involvement. If our notions of society assume involvement,
then we will be tempted to leave autonomy off the social map. The
three-dimensional picture suggests that autonomy is central, that
the four extreme types of involvement can only be fully understood
in relation to it, and that the investigation of the rather strange
properties that result from non-involvement may well modify our
ideas of what society is. One might draw an analogy with the idea
of heat: taking autonomy off the social map is rather like taking
absolute zero off the thermometer.

    This centrality of autonomy is apparent in the Sherpa example in
relation to two of the other equilibrium states (bottom left and
bottom right) towards which individual Sherpas tend to move once
they leave the rather unique confines of their homeland: the Khumbu
region beneath Mount Everest. I have not come across any cases of
Sherpas moving towards the other two equilibrium states (top left
and top right) but examples of similar people making these moves
do exist in the literature and may be drawn upon to support the
argument.

3 The separation of cosmologies

In the two-dimensional picture the assumption is that there is the
possibility of transition from one cosmology to another but, since
we cannot know whether the lines are fat or thin, we have no way of
telling whether such transitions are gradual or sudden. This,
combined with the difficulties of measuring accurately an individual's group and grid co-ordinates, undoubtedly leads to difficulties
when one tries to describe what is happening in the cases of those
many individuals whose social contexts are not very extreme. One
of the attractions of the three-dimensional picture is the way it

tidies up these confusions by suggesting that cosmologies are
associated with equilibrium states and that, since there are clear
separations between the five equilibrium states, there will be clear
separations between the five associated cosmologies. This pictorial
distinction between the flattish regions (the equilibrium states)
and the steeply sloping regions that separate them (the disequilibrium states) does away with the unsatisfactory convention of the
two crossed lines with their associated squares in the two-dimensional picture. It also gives a clearer description of what is
involved in an individual's transition from one equilibrium state
to another (see 4 and 5 below).

I will make use of this picture of clear separation in my argument
that there in fact is a fifth equilibrium state, autonomy, and that
the Khumbu Sherpas are in it. It is very important for the credibility and for the usefulness of grid/group analysis that the
distinctions between the five types of cosmology are drawn in terms
of differences in kind rather than just of degree, and the three-
dimensional picture with its clear separations enables us to do
this.

4 Bimodality of cosmologies

These clear separations between equilibrium states, and hence
between cosmologies, are laid out in three dimensions and they can
overlap when projected downwards onto the two-dimensional base.
These areas of overlap are outlined by the two cusp catastrophes
and, over the range of social contexts that lie inside these limits,
there are two equilibrium states and therefore two likely
cosmologies. It is this suggested inadequacy in the two-dimensional
picture that is likely to provide the best means of testing the
three-dimensional picture, for it is in their prediction of what
is likely to happen in these regions that the two-dimensional and
three-dimensional pictures are at their most contradictory.

The two-dimensional picture says that individuals in the same
social context should have the same cultural bias. The three-
dimensional picture says that individuals in the same social context
can (as long as that context is inside one or other of the cusps)
have very different cultural biases. They can't have just any
cultural bias, but they can have one or other of the two biases
associated with the two overlapping equilibrium states involved in
a cusp. The discovery of such bimodal pairs of individuals would
cast serious doubt on the validity of the two-dimensional picture,
but (provided that, when plotted on the group/grid space, their
shared contexts all lie within the cusps) that same discovery would
give powerful support to the three-dimensional picture.

One of the most exciting results of the Sherpa fieldwork is that
it reveals the existence of such bimodal pairs. Sherpas, on leaving
Khumbu to seek work in tourism and mountaineering in Kathmandu,
often move into one of these cusp regions with the result that there
are, among these diasporic Sherpas, two remarkably different modes
of adjustment in response to very much the same sort of shifts in
social context.

5   Gradual and sudden transition

The discontinuous changes from one equilibrium state to another that may be expected if cusp catastrophes are present have no counterpart in the two-dimensional picture which, because of the thin-line/fat-line problem, contains no theory of change beyond the assumption that it is possible.

The three-dimensional picture provides a description of gradual change along certain routes from one equilibrium state to another but, at the same time, it provides a description of quite sudden and discontinuous change along those routes that happen to pass through a cusp. This pictorial distinction between gradual and sudden conversion from one type of cosmology to another, and the prediction that all sudden conversions will occur in contexts on or near the cusp lines, suggests an excellent way of testing the three-dimensional picture. Sudden conversions are very clear-cut and noticeable phenomena, and the requirement that they should occur only on or near clearly specified lines in the group/grid plane is very stringent even when we make allowance for the difficulties in measuring social context.

Unfortunately, most of the routes taken by Sherpas do not cross the cusp catastrophies and so involve only gradual change. However, some individual Sherpas on leaving Khumbu for Kathmandu have fallen on bad times and, feeling they have little to lose, have taken dangerous and not particularly well-paid or promising employment with mountaineering expeditions. To their astonishment some of those who survived this, often literally, dead-end employment have found that it has led them to fame, fortune and central positions in remarkable financial empires. By eliciting their biographies it is possible to reconstruct the routes they have taken and to pinpoint the catastrophic moment – the lucky break – when they suddenly moved from one of the bimodal adjustments to the other.

THE INVESTIGATION

These five inadequacies are serious and their investigation is, unfortunately, a lengthy business. I propose here largely to ignore the last two, which require for their exposition the biographies of individual Sherpas, and to concentrate on the first three in such a way that they illuminate what is probably, at present, the biggest single objection to grid/group theory: the problem of the centre.

Hampton (3) has defined this problem by pinpointing two awkward questions concerning the point in the two-dimensional picture where the four contexts meet: 'How do you know where it is?' and 'How do you understand what happens there?'.

In the two-dimensional picture the centre is not the origin of the context graph but the point half way along each of its axes. If the grid and group scales were cardinal this would present no problem but, as Hampton points out, they are inevitably ordinal: just an ordering, not an accurate measure, of contexts. Half way along a cardinal scale is an exact spot, but half way along an ordering can (depending on the basis chosen for the ordering) be anywhere between its two extremes: the crossover point can be almost anywhere and, in consequence, the picture is really only capable of handling the four extremes.

The advantage of the three-dimensional picture is that 'the centre' now appears at the origin. The scales are still ordinal but they have both positive and negative values. If, in relation to groups, you are neither actively included nor excluded you will be plotted at the origin no matter what ordinal measures for positive and negative group are used. The same is true of grid. The three-dimensional picture can, with ordinal scales, handle the four extremes and also the centre. This still, of course, leaves a large 'grey area' but the charm of the three-dimensional picture is that its grey area no longer obscures what is happening at the centre.

Hampton's fear that only those people near the four extremes will have clear-cut cosmologies and that all those in his grey central area will just have a mishmash of eclectic, loosely integrated cosmologies turns out to be groundless. At the centre there is, not a mishmash, but a fifth clear-cut cosmology. All the problems raised in the two-dimensional picture by the crossover point for the four cosmologies are now resolved: there is in fact no cross-over point. Ordinal scales will now allow us to handle all five stabilisable conjunctions of social context and world view, and the grey area now corresponds (quite appropriately) to the unstable zones that separate them.

The fifth context

The Khumbu Sherpas came in a roundabout way to the area where they now live. The first influx from Tibet, after reaching Nepal down one of the deeply-cut valleys north of Kathmandu, turned east and settled in the fertile uplands of Solu, purchasing them very cheaply from the Rai owners who preferred to live at lower and warmer altitudes. Only later, when Solu was well established, did some of its more marginal inhabitants move even further east to settle in the higher and harsher Khumbu region, the disadvantages of which could be offset by rewarding but difficult trade into Tibet across a nineteen-thousand foot pass, the Nangpa La. (4)

'Sherpa' is the Tibetan word for 'easterner' and so contradicts, rather than reflects, this remote history. Whilst one should not make too much of such historical contortions, it is clear that they must have started off well to the west of most easterners (and not a few westerners) in Tibet and this, combined with the fact that they now live well to the south of both easterners and westerners, somehow typifies the easy tolerance that has endeared the Sherpas to generations of European mountaineers and, more recently, anthro-pologists.

My early involvement with Sherpas was as a mountaineer, on expeditions to Annapurna in 1970 and to Everest in 1975, and only on my third visit in 1978 was my role as anthropologist uppermost. Even so, the time-perspective conferred by my mountaineering visits helped me in my anthropological aim which was to apply gird/group analysis in a rather unusual setting. A specialised approach such as this, seeking answers to those specific questions that are thrown

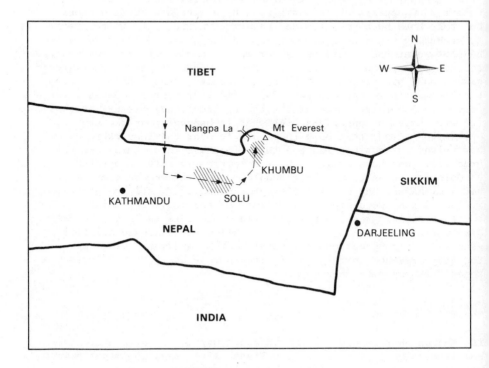

FIGURE 13.2

into sharp relief by a particular theory, might be described as
second-generation fieldwork and, in so far as it has been successful,
this success is very largely thanks to the high quality of the
first-generation fieldwork. It is not just mountaineers who climb
on the shoulders of those who go before and, in locating the
'traditional' Sherpa society on the gird/group map, I have, in
particular, relied heavily upon Haimendorf's general ethnography
of the Sherpas and upon his later study of Himalayan trade. (5)

My own limited fieldwork in this area has served the minor but
useful role of assuring me that this reliance is not misplaced.
That said, I hasten to add that the way I have chosen to interpret
this first-generation fieldwork is my responsibility alone and that
it should in no way be seen as implying that the ethnographers
whose work I have drawn upon would place the Sherpas where I place
them, nor indeed that they would consider such an exercise desirable
or even possible.

The easy tolerance of the Sherpas, so noticeable to the outside
observer and so different from the impressions he gains of their
neighbours, is a generalised (and inferred) quality embedded in
their actions - in their social style. Social style implies certain
recurrent regularities in social action, and recurrent regularities

in social action imply some common strategy for action. I have
argued that viable strategies vary systematically with social
context and that they provide the linking mechanism that systematically confers credibility upon one world view and withholds it
from others. In this way social context and cosmology (shareable
world view) are related. It follows that an appropriate starting-
point for this investigation is the question: 'What sort of social
context does one find associated with easy tolerance?'
    The investigation has both negative and positive sides. Taking
the negative first, one can eliminate some contexts where the Sherpas
definitely cannot be: those involving strongly positive group.

> Anyone who has travelled in rural Nepal has experienced the
> difference in the attitudes of Buddhist and Hindu communities.
> In the former it is easy to gain entrance to houses and offers
> of hospitality are usually freely forthcoming while in Hindu
> villages no stranger is admitted to a private house and even
> his attempts to purchase victuals often meet with difficulty. (6)

Haimendorf equates these polar attitudes with two sorts of social
system: the Hindu, characterised by the strong control exercised by
the joint family over its individual members and by the high level
of prescription imposed upon an individual by the rules of his
caste; and the Buddhist, characterised by the independence of the
individual and his freedom from prescription.

> Unlike the member of any of the Hindu castes of Nepal, the Sherpa
> is a free agent from a relatively early age. There is no
> obligation to, or control by, a joint family in which even adult
> sons with wives and children of their own are subject to the
> authority of an elderly head of the family. (7)

> The Sherpa ... enjoys a freedom from crippling restrictions which
> might impede relations with trading partners. Not bound by
> dietary taboos or the ban on inter-dining with persons classed as
> socially inferior, he can accept hospitality wherever he goes and
> entertain in his own house anyone whose custom may be economically
> advantageous. (8)

Khumbu society is individualistic, egalitarian, open and expansive.
It is free from the fears of pollution that characterise the strongly
positive group/strongly positive grid social context and it suffers
none of the xenophobia and witchcraft worries that characterise the
strongly positive group/strongly negative grid social context. Like
the White Horse in the whisky advertisement, you can take a Sherpa
anywhere.
    These two strongly positive group contexts are so emphatically
absent from Khumbu society that one is tempted to look to the
remaining two of the four contexts in the two-dimensional picture,
and it is indeed true that the Sherpa emphasis on individual freedom
and economic opportunism carries a familiar western ring. And yet,
within the confines of Khumbu society, these two contexts are
scarcely to be recognised.
    In the west these two contexts are always found in association.
This is because the elaboration of personal networks that characterises the strongly negative group/strongly negative grid context
inevitably results (once the networks have worked their way through
the society) in the exclusion of some individuals who, finding their

lives largely prescribed by the ramifications of the networks of others, are forced into the last remaining context in the two-dimensional picture: strongly negative group/strongly positive grid. This context appears so unattractive that even some of the protagonists of grid/group analysis have been puzzled as to why anyone should stay there. This network-building process provides the answer: they stay there because they are unable to move away.

In particular it is the entrepreneurial context (strongly negative group/strongly negative grid) that, at first glance, would seem to fit the Sherpas. After all, it is to the eager mobility of the occupants of this context that the glossy whisky advertisement is directed, and it is here that the tolerant stance demanded by liberal philosophy finds its most ardent proponents. But, on closer inspection, such an assignment does not appear valid. First of all, this entrepreneurial context is normally found in association with the counterpart, the strongly negative group/strongly positive grid context, and this latter just does not seem to be occupied in Khumbu society (even by the women, who are its most frequent occupants in the west). Secondly, the fact that in the west liberal philosophy tends, most intolerantly, to demand tolerance from its adherents reveals that the tolerance associated with the bottom left context in the two-dimensional picture is essentially uneasy. The characteristics of this latter context: the concealed screening operated by the overtly egalitarian 'big man', the frequent scandalous contraventions of the ideal of fair play, and the invisible pedagogies that operate behind the seemingly progressive educational facade: are nowhere exhibited in Khumbu. The Khumbu Sherpa never finds himself in the predicament of the Hampstead liberal: nicely summed up in the passionate and contradictory assertion 'If there's one thing I can't stand, it's intolerance!'

If Haimendorf's Buddhists occupy none of these four contexts then grid/group theory is in trouble. Here I argue that they are in the fifth context, revealed by the three-dimensional picture: that at or near zero group/zero grid. In such a context one would expect both a high degree of individual freedom and the absence of prescription but, at the same time, networks could not be developed beyond the point at which an individual might begin to put the squeeze on others nor, conversely, beyond the point where he himself might begin to be squeezed by others. Such a context, emphasising egalitarianism and individualism but excluding exploitation, sounds too good to be true. How could it possibly be stabilised?

Stability and the fifth context

Whilst I would not claim to list all the necessary conditions for the stability of this fifty context, there are four features of Khumbu society that would appear to operate in such a way as to increase the likelihood of its being maintained. First, the natural environment (in relation to Sherpa technology, at least) favours exploitation by small family units. (9) That is, there have until recently been few opportunities for economies of scale. Second, the opportunities for individual enterprise arise only in relation to trade (and more recently tourism and mountaineering) and this, by its very nature,

ensures that the networks essential to its conduct lie largely
outside the community. Third, there has always been a means of
escape from the community for those individuals whose social
contexts may begin to threaten its quite delicate equilibrium. In
the old days the individual who stepped out of the autonomous line
could seek work in Darjeeling. Nowadays he goes to Kathmandu. Fourth,
the Sherpas have a distinctive cosmology that insists on the desirability of such an equilibrium. This cosmology enters into an
individual's decision-making (and his subsequent actions) in such a
way as to benefit those who by their actions bring their contexts
closer to zero group/zero grid and to penalise those who either do
not or cannot take such actions. In other words, it acts as an
attracter to those who are sufficiently close to zero group/zero grid
and it acts as a repeller to those whose contexts have strayed
outside these limits. This subtle switch from benefit to penalty
provides the necessary incentive for an individual to decide to take
the escape route to Kathmandu rather than stay behind and rock the
autonomous boat.

Morality and social action

In terms of the picture, the centre is a rather complicated saddle-
point (not unlike the South Col with heavily corniced Everest and
Lhotse Ridges). At zero group and zero grid the surface is flat and
the level of manipulation is zero. Move away from the centre, in
any direction, and you will find yourself on an increasingly steep
slope: either steeply uphill (manipulating) or steeply downhill
(being manipulated). This fifth context differs from the other four
in that it alone enjoys zero (or very low) manipulation. It is
precisely this lack of squeezing that makes for the quality of easy
tolerance and sets it in such sharp contrast to the uneasy tolerance
associated with the entrepreneurial context with its high level of
manipulation. The centre is the only one of the five stabilisable
contexts that forms a saddle-point and, in consequence, the conditions
for its stability are particularly stringent. The other four contexts
are essentially either hilltops, in which case stability is maintained
by avoiding downhill movement, or basins, in which case stability is
maintained by avoiding uphill movement. At a saddle-point both
uphill and downhill movement have to be resisted.
  Now it might appear that an equilibrium dependent upon such
contradictory avoidances is bound to be unstable. This is not so.
Both uphill and downhill movement can be resisted by following one
simple rule: 'always pull back from steepening slopes'. Easy
tolerance can only be sustained in the absence of squeezing and both
strong groups and extensive networks inevitably, in their different
ways, exert strong social pressures; as they develop, they give rise
to ever higher levels of manipulation. This means that the fifth
context will only remain stable if neither groups nor networks are
much developed, that is, if the level of manipulation (both positive
and negative) remains low. Since the vertical dimension in the
three-dimensional picture depicts manipulation, the golden rule
'always pull back from steepening slopes' translates directly into
the social imperative : 'avoid social involvements that lead to high

levels of manipulation'. So, when we come across such a stabilised
context, we should expect to find cut-out mechanisms that intervene
in group and network processes in such a way as to prevent them from
developing beyond very low thresholds. (10) This is indeed the
Sherpa case.

There is little in the way of group formation and such groups as
do exist remain remarkably open. Clans have no ritual, residential
or property significance, (11) and serve only to prohibit marriage
between their members. Since there are between eighteen and twenty-
five of these clans, and since many Khumbu inhabitants do not belong
to any of them, (12) this group rule places little restriction on
individual freedom. Haimendorf says that the rule is strictly
adhered to but some Sherpas told me that this was not so, adding
with a smile that 'fifty per cent of what Haimendorf says is wrong'.
Similarly they said that, though Haimendorf says they don't mention
the names of the dead, they do it all the time. Since many Sherpas
are well read, fieldwork conversations often take this seminar form
and my impression is, not that half the time Haimendorf is wrong,
but that his Sherpa critics are really emphasising their independence
and tolerance by claiming the right to marry clan members and to
mention the names of dead though, in fact, they seldom do. Also
there can be no doubt that, since Haimendorf carried out his fieldwork, the development of tourism has resulted in many a Sherpa's
context shifting further towards negative grid, and Haimendorf's
more voluble critics tend to be the 'biggish men' (who are also
prone to killing yaks and walking round 'mani' walls the wrong way:
acts no autonomous Sherpa would lightly undertake).

One of these genial critics, Dawa Norbu (who is Executive Director
of an hotel and trekking business, the Sherpa Co-operative) has
himself carried out some fieldwork in Darjeeling and discovered
that, though most of the migration there from the Everest Region
must have happened within the last sixty years or so, very few
Darjeeling Sherpas knew where their parents or grandparents came
from. The results of his own research tend to contradict his
assertion that Sherpas do not avoid mentioning the names of the
dead. This is because the effect of such an observance is to make
it difficult to remember much 'real' history. Such deliberately
cultivated ignorance produces the truncated time-perspective predicted
for autonomy and a corresponding inhibition (or cut-out mechanism)
on the formation of lineage groupings, ancestor cults, memorialism
and nationalistic histories. (13) On several occasions I have seen
Sherpas struggling to express to me their regret at the news of the
death of a mutual friend without, if possible, having to come out
with his name.

One level at which group is undoubtedly present is the village.
Villages are agglomerations of houses and potato fields rather than
formally organised settlements but, even so, they form ritual units
(sometimes with one or more other villages) and they have a temple,
various festivals and certain offices for the seasonal control of
livestock and for safeguarding the resources of the forest. The
cut-out mechanism for the grid threat implicit in such obligations
and offices is provided by their rotation. Each family, for instance,
takes it in turn to provide the food and drink for the main annual
festival and the fact that everyone except the hosts can freeload,

and that even they can look forward to many a free binge in the
future, helps to ensure the conviviality without coercion which is
so marked a feature of Sherpa entertainment.

The cut-out mechanism along the group dimension is provided by
the openness of the village community, and even this party-giving
obligation is ultimately voluntary. Haimendorf recounts how, when
a quite recently settled Khampa family decamped rather than fulfil
its obligations, the other villagers, far from saying 'good riddance'
(the strong group response), were filled with remorse at having
inadvertently exposed the family to such extreme economic pressures.
It is a fairly onerous obligation, and families start organising
their finances some years in advance, but the general feeling is that
it should be an equal burden and that the lavishness of the entertainment should be proportional to the resources of the host. Every
family, rich and poor, takes its turn but the real 'blow-outs' occur
only when the hosts happen to be large yak-breeders or prosperous
traders.

The same sort of open boundary exists in those other group
situations in Khumbu, the monasteries and the nunneries. Monks and
nuns are self-sufficient, either on the modest proceeds of their
investments or thanks to the support of a relative or patron (who
receives merit in return for this generosity). They live and eat
separately in their own small houses irregularly grouped around the
main building and there is nothing comparable to the refectory
commensality so basic to the life of western monasteries. Monks
and nuns in some of their orders take vows of chastity but if they
break them, or wish to break them, they simply leave the order and
return to secular life. Since monasteries and nunneries are almost
next door to one another such occurrences are not uncommon. Some
orders permit marriage and all inmates can, if they choose, leave
their institution and live and work within the lay population. Even
those within the institutions are constantly being called upon to
perform services of various kinds for the villagers. The result is
that, though some inmates remain for life, there exists a continuous
and easy flow between religious and secular spheres not unlike that
which some contemporary British critics long to see between academia
and the wider world of industry and government.

Even the basic economic unit, the nuclear family, has an inbuilt
cut-out mechanism and could never, for instance, become the locus of
amoral familism in the Mediterranean manner.

> The marital relationship ... is a freely entered and terminable
> association between two equal partners, each of whom retains the
> right over the property he or she contributed to the association.
> (14)

Sexual equality and sexual freedom are so marked that concepts such
as honour and shame can gain no toehold in Sherpa society.

The status of women in Khumbu society provides perhaps the most
persuasive element in my argument for the fifth context. It is
probably no exaggeration to say that Khumbu women enjoy all those
conditions that are the aim of the women's rights movements in the
west. Sons and daughters share equally in the inheritance of their
parents' property and receive their shares about the time they get
married and set up their independent households. Before marriage
they enjoy equal (and considerable) opportunities in education, in

not necessarily balanced, but any imbalances are not predominantly
in favour of one sex over the other. Sometimes the wife contributes
more land and moveable property, sometimes the husband. Sometimes
it is the wife who is the forceful trader: travelling, establishing
personal networks and accumulating wealth while the husband stays at
home. Sometimes it is the other way round.

A Sherpa marriage entails a number of stages, the first of which
sometimes does not occur until after the birth of the first child
(or children). Such children, even though they may not be by the
husband-to-be, do not suffer any disadvantageous illegitimate status.
The easy-going permissiveness towards the human elements in the
marriage stands in marked contrast to the treatment accorded the
animate and inanimate elements: the wealth that each of the human
elements contributes. Despite the smoke and the alcoholic haze of
these wedding feasts, scrupulously accurate lists of all the
contributions are drawn up (usually by monks, whose literacy and
vows of abstinence render them particularly suited to this important
task).

Such precision in the midst of such casualness is rather surprising
until one realises that the precision is actually what makes its
surrounding casualness possible. The parties to a Sherpa marriage
are able to enter freely into the relationship because they know
that, if it turns sour, they can easily terminate it by dividing up
their property along the lines that existed at the time it was
merged. The more this line is blurred the less easy the termination
will become. Since animals give birth and die, household goods
suffer wear and tear, and land may be brought into and pass out of
cultivation, blurring can easily happen. At least initially, the
precise and public listing of the contributions to the marital
property is an essential part of the cut-out mechanism, for without
it marriage would not be nearly so freely enterable a state. 'Keep
your exits clear' might well be adopted as the motto of anyone
anxious to maintain the stability of the fifth context.

Conversely, the clogged exits associated with social contexts far
removed from zero group/zero grid often frustrate the aspirations of
the women's rights movements in the west and subvert them from what
I take to be their true aims. Instead of seeking the clearing of
the exits (a general shift in the social contexts of both women and
men towards zero group/zero grid) the campaigners, all too often,
find themselves struggling for the equal right to clog them (for
equal female representation in the high manipulation context,
strongly negative group/strongly negative grid).

This argument for the existence of a fifth stabilisable context,
and for the Khumbu Sherpas being in it, can perhaps be best
concluded by reference to Ostrander's essay (chapter 1 in this
volume). It is always a sly pleasure to be able to chide a colleague
for the ethnocentric shortcomings of his universal scheme and I must
point out that, in his otherwise admirable round-up of the four
context picture, he has excluded the Sherpas.

One of his conclusions is that a context and its associated
cosmology can never characterise an entire social system.
Egalitarianism (bottom left) he insists exists among males in the
system. Females he holds are always subject to the control of

fathers, uncles, brothers, husbands and the like. This puts them
in the top left context even when their husbands are in the bottom
left. He is quite right in insisting that these two contexts are
always found in association: quite wrong in assuming that women are
never equal.

Sherpa women are equal. Yet, though there are many activities
which they share with men, there are others that are fairly
exclusive to one sex or the other. Women mostly cultivate, whilst
animal husbandry is largely a masculine preserve. Only men go above
Base Camp on expeditions (though this may be the result of European
prejudice): (15) only women, dare I say it, bear children. In any
of the other four contexts such an occupational distinction is
immediately pounced upon as the basis for a status distinction. If
women knit and men hunt, then hunting becomes a high-status activity
and knitting a low-status activity. If women menstruate and men do
not, then it is women who are polluting and threaten to drive away
the game. No such status differentials attach to sexual specialisms
among the Sherpas. Women can look after yaks and they are not
believed to present any threat to their well-being (in fact, women
often acquire expertise in the treatment of sick livestock).
Similarly, Sherpa men can, and quite often do, turn their hand to
cooking, sewing and child care. The absence of such status differentials means that the Sherpa woman does not have to emulate the male
to assert her equality. Sherpa women wear their Tibetan-style
dresses and multicoloured aprons, the men wear down jackets,
corduroy breeches and Italian climbing boots: but the one ensemble
is simply different from, not better than, the other. The Sherpa
woman, pace Ostrander, does not have to wear the trousers to be up
there in the saddle.

Toeing the invisible line

Both the two-dimensional picture and the three-dimensional picture
insist that a social context and a world view can only be stabilised
if there is a shared commitment to that world view by the occupants
of that context. Such a shared world view constitutes a cosmology
and the three-dimensional picture offers an hypothesis as to why,
as Douglas insists, there should be only a limited number of
cosmologies. You can only have a cosmology - a shared commitment to
a world view - if that world view is shareable and, in the three-
dimensional picture, world views are in general not shareable. They
only exhibit shareability at or near the flat parts of the surface
and, since there are only five of these flat parts, there are, the
hypothesis suggests, only five possible cosmologies.

The shareability of the world view associated with the fifth flat
part, that at the centre, is particularly problematical. The world
view appropriate to this context is summarised in the ideal of
autonomy: the desirability of non-involvement. At first sight, the
proposition that you draw nearer to this atomised social state by
means of a shared commitment to it appears contradictory. How can
the moral imperative to avoid any coercive involvement with others
give rise to judgments that coerce others? And how, if by some
means or other it does end up exerting such coercion, can it possibly

maintain the stability of a regime dedicated to the avoidance of coercion? How does a community force its members not to force its members to do anything?

The resolution of these paradoxes has two related parts. First of all, it is not involvement per se that the autonomous ideal rejects but coercive involvement. Non-involvement, the exact saddle-point, can be attained only by the hermit, and Sherpas are no more all hermits than Scotsmen are all Rob Roys. As you move further away from the hermit's absolute zero so your involvement increases, but to start with this venturing into group and/or network involvement brings with it little in the way of manipulation. Depending on whether you have moved upwards or downwards from the col so you will find yourself manipulated by others or manipulating others, but such coercion is slight and the reconciliation of ideal and real is still quite easily achieved. (By 'reconciliation' I mean that an individual is more likely to maximise his goals by pursuing the autonomous strategy then he is by switching to any one of the other four strategies.)

This region of Sherpa involvement, wherein a real but low level of squeezing remains reconcilable with the ideal of no squeezing, presents a clear working example of the jurisprudential principle: 'your fist's freedom ends where my nose begins'. Now it is regrettably true that, from time to time, one Sherpa's fist does not stop short of another Sherpa's nose and it is by observing what happens on these occasions that the anthropologist gains an insight into just how a shared commitment to the non-squeezing ideal operates in such a way as to stabilise this fifth context.

Haimendorf has summarised the Sherpa idea of the good life in terms of two principles: the acquisition of wealth and its proper utilisation, and the cultivation of courtesy, gentleness and a spirit of compromise and peacefulness. The first principle ensures that prestige and admiration are accorded to those who exhibit generosity in the expenditure of the wealth they have acquired. The second principle depresses the social standing of the strong and ruthless man (the admired man in terms of the manipulative individualist ideology associated with the entrepreneurial context) and elevates that of the reasonable and considerate man: the peacemaker. Such a person, in the contexts prevalent in western society, only gets his reward in heaven: the Sherpa gets his in heaven and on earth.

Haimendorf goes on to describe how such generally admired individuals may, at an appropriate stage in their lives, come to undertake the occasional role of peacemaker. When one Sherpa's fist, literally or metaphorically, strays beyond its legitimate range the smooth surface of the autonomous life is alarmingly ruffled. In some cases the dispute may be so serious or so one-sided that one of those involved decides to take the escape route to Darjeeling or Kathmandu, but in other less severe or more balanced disputes there remains the possibility of restoring calm without such extreme resort. Haimendorf describes a reconciliation party that was held by two peacemakers to heal a whole complex of rifts that had occurred between some of the most prominent men in the community. Such a party begins with formal expressions of apology by the disputants and is followed by a lavish and increasingly informal distribution of 'chang', the rice beer that in all probability was a major contributing factor in the original dispute.

I have myself watched the landlord of a Kathmandu chang-house
follow exactly the same procedure with two of his customers who had
come to rather befuddled blows. Peacemaking procedures of this
type occur, of course, in other social contexts but it seems to me
that in the context occupied by the Sherpas there is a much deeper
shared commitment to the healing of rifts and peacemaking is successful in situations where it would not even be contemplated elsewhere.
A British landlord would never have gone to the lengths taken by his
Nepalese counterpart. Had those two belligerent expedition porters
been in a British pub, they would have found themselves forcibly
ejected and barred!

The openness - the continual clearing of exits - of Khumbu
society is crucial to its stability. Some individuals have started
off outside it, entered it and stayed; others have stayed a while
and then moved on; still others have started off inside and have
left, and of these some have stayed away and others have returned.
The peacemaker does not hold any office nor is his role in any way
permanent. Those that he mediates between are not coerced by him
in the sense that they find their exits blocked by the peacemaker.
No one would dream of standing in the way of an individual who was
convinced that he should go to Kathmandu, and the peacemaker's
activities are confined to those people who do not wish to leave but
find themselves drawing perilously close to the situation where they
will have to seriously consider this possibility.

The early career of Ang Phu (now one of the great mountaineering
Sherpas and a member of that select band who have stood on the
summit of Mount Everest) provides an example of the other possible
outcome of unpleasantness in Khumbu: rapid departure through a
clear exit with ne'er a peacemaker in sight. After graduating from
Sir Edmund Hillary's school in the village of Khumjung, be became
assistant teacher at a similar school in Thami and after a year
moved on to become headmaster of a new school in Phortse. A year
or so later some new and, in theory, better qualified teachers were
brought in from Darjeeling to improve the quality of the rapidly
expanding educational system. The news that these Darjeeling
teachers were to be paid more than the local teachers sparked off
a first-class row: Sherpas do not take kindly to the idea of
differentials.

Accounts differ as to whether Ang Phu resigned or was dismissed
but whichever it was the outcome was the same: he suddenly found
himself without employment. Twenty-one years old, single, one of
five children in a poor family and oppressed on all sides by the
ill-feelings that the row over the Darjeeling teachers had generated,
he could see few immediate prospects for himself in Khumbu. Sherpas,
like hippies, have an aversion to heavy scenes and for Ang Phu the
Khumbu scene was by this time very heavy indeed. He left for
Kathmandu, clear in his own mind that he wanted to get away from
Khumbu but with little idea of what Kathmandu would be like or of
what he would do when, after ten days of walking, he got there.
After a miserable four months, sustained on his not-very-golden
handshake, he managed, by a bit of a fiddle, to get himself taken
on as an Ice Fall Porter on the ill-fated International Everest
Expedition. It is from this inauspicious beginning that his
impressive mountaineering career has developed.

Ang Phu's example illuminates several characteristic features of the fifth context. First, there is the strong Sherpa sense of independence and of economic individualism. Second, there is the distaste for being coerced and for the scenes by which coercion manifests itself. Third, economic individualism ensures that the exits are kept clear and that there are no obstacles to rapid departure in the event of any scene becoming too heavy. Fourth, Ang Phu, by acting in what he perceives to be his best interest, is also acting in the best interest of the entire community in the sense that his departure helps calm the dangerously ruffled surface of Khumbu life. Nor is he permanently alienated by his actions. That he decides to leave is itself proof that he still shares the autonomous ideals of those he is leaving; both he and they feel that it is right that he should leave and, once things have quietened down, there will be few obstacles to his return. Time is a very rapid healer in Sherpa life (it is staying away in the alien context of Kathmandu for too long that, as many Sherpas are now discovering, makes it difficult to return).

Perhaps less obvious is the way the cultural bias of this fifth context actually enters into Ang Phu's decision-making process. The cosmology of this context emphasises the present: the past is systematically demolished rather than systematically preserved (as happens, for instance, in Ireland where Drogheda and the Boyne are remembered more clearly than yesterday). Ang Phu's appreciation of his situation is consistent with this truncated time-perspective. The short term looms large in his considerations: he knows how bad things are at present, he knows pretty accurately what his assets are and what his inheritance is likely to be, he knows he has no ties so tight that he cannot escape them and he knows that he has no particularly pressing obligations to discharge. If he considers the long term at all it is only to satisfy himself that he need not take it into his calculations. His inheritance will remain unchanged whether he stays or goes and he knows that though things look pretty black they will sort themselves out sooner or later: later if he stays, sooner if he leaves. Whether he considers the morrow or not, the outcome of his deliberations remains the same. Once he has escaped from beneath his dark Khumbu cloud he is quite prepared to enjoy himself and this, perhaps surprisingly, is just what he does on his first expedition.

The cultural bias associated with the fifth context encourages economic individualism whilst at the same time discouraging long-term considerations. The hypothesis predicts that this combination will promote a strategy of risk acceptance whilst discouraging too much awareness of risk. To those in other social contexts, the rational Sherpa behaviour based on this strategy is likely to present a quite horrifying picture: the cheerful and casual acceptance of appalling risks. For many, this represents the unacceptable face of autonomy. Even experienced High Altitude Porters will pause for a smoke, a bar of chocolate and a chat half way through the Khumbu Ice Fall choosing, as likely as not, the shelter of a tottering hundred-foot tower of ice. Left to themselves, instead of choosing the safer period before the morning sun has reached the three-thousand-foot wall of Nuptse, loosening the festoons of ice and snow that all too often detach themselves and

thunder down into the narrow valley below, they will set off much
later up the Western Cwm in a happy crocodile. Every year there
occur the seemingly avoidable tragedies of Sherpas, long used to a
cold and harsh environment, lying down in the snow to sleep off an
excess of chang.

Ang Phu accepted the risks of his first Everest expedition, not
in a mood of grim determination, but with casual exuberance; he
enjoyed the adventure enormously. He was one of a hundred Sherpas
on the mountain and so lowly was his position that he did not even
meet any of the western climbers. On looking back, he was, he said,
aware that it was dangerous but he did not know what was dangerous.
Far from being dismayed, he was elated; in his own words, he
'didn't care about avalanches'.

The stability of the fifth context, unlike that of the other four
contexts, cannot be achieved simply by resisting a single tendency:
to stay on a hilltop you need only resist downward movement and to
stay in a basin you need only resist upward movement, but to stay at
a saddle-point, you must resist both these tendencies. The South
Col of Everest is quite spacious and, provided you do not stray too
far, it is not difficult to return to your tent. But stray outside
these limits and you are likely to fall under the influence of other
powerfully attractive forces, just at the moment when return to the
tent is beginning to become quite difficult. If you move away from
the saddle-point in an upward direction, this displacement may well
make the lure of standing on the summit of Everest or of Lhotse more
attractive than the return to the tent. And if you move away from
the saddle-point in a downward direction, there will come a point
where Base Camp, or even gravity, becomes more attractive. (16)

The Khumbu Sherpas handle the social equivalent of this topo-
graphical predicament very effectively with the help of their two
different kinds of admired person: the hermit and the peacemaker.
The hermit sits on the exact saddle-point, totally uninvolved. The
rest of the Sherpas, as they spread out on the col, become in their
different ways increasingly involved with one another. The peacemaker
acts like some oriental Catcher in the Rye, helping those who have
inadvertently ventured onto the steeper slopes to return to more
level terrain. At the same time, he knows that there is no point in
stretching out his hand to those who by their momentum are already
firmly committed to uphill or downhill movement. In the west the
hermit's voice is always raucous. Sitting on his col in the wilderness, his cries, if they are to be heard, will have to carry to those
distant peaks and valleys where most of his fellow men are clustered.
The Sherpa hermit's voice need scarcely rise above a whisper, for all
his fellows are well within earshot.

COSMOLOGY, CREDIBILITY AND THE STABILITY OF INSTITUTIONS

The second part of the resolution of the paradox entailed in the idea
of coercing by avoiding coercing has to do with the roundabout way
in which the coercion comes to be exerted. A brief discussion of
this will serve the double purpose of completing the present argument
and of pointing the way in which grid/group analysis may be able to
offer a fresh, and perhaps useful, view of the nature of institutions.

In general, the more links there are in a causal chain the more
likely it is that the connectedness of the two ends will be overlooked. This is particularly so in the Sherpa case for here the
time perspective is so truncated that any causal chain has only to
disappear for a moment across the nearby horizon for the connection
between its two ends to be irrevocably snapped: the connection, of
course, still exists – it is the means of perceiving it that does
not. It is thanks to this cultivated myopia that the Khumbu Sherpa
is able to go through life shrewdly assessing and gambling on those
risks that happen to swim into his short-term ken, all the while
blissfully unaware that the world beyond his field of vision is
filled with all kinds of ravening beasts that would scare the living
daylights out of those who, by virtue of their occupancy of other
social contexts, enjoy the mixed blessing of longer sight.

Trying to extract a Sherpa world view direct from a Sherpa is an
unrewarding exercise. To begin with, one may obtain a few disjointed
bits and pieces but press him further and the Sherpa will give up
his struggle to make explicit his personal view of how the world is
and will begin to recite a general, and often rather inaccurate,
account of Buddhist belief. Instead, it is in many ways better to
deduce his strategy by watching what he does – the options that he
considers and the way in which he arrives at his decisions as to
which of these options to choose – than to mount a direct frontal
assault to capture his ideas about the nature of the world and of
man's place within it: ideas which, one assumes, make the adoption
of his chosen strategy possible. But this devious approach leaves
an awkward question unanswered.

The hypothesis suggests that a strategy is shaped and made viable
by a cosmology: by a shared commitment to a shareable world view.
How can a Sherpa be committed to a world view, and how can he commit
himself to the sharing of that world view, if he has only the
vaguest idea of what it is? For instance, the outside observer can
see that Khumbu society everywhere conforms to the principle 'always
pull back from steepening slopes' but, at the same time, he is aware
that this principle is not all the time on every lip. There is in
Khumbu nothing remotely like a rallying cry: there is no hint of
the moral fervour of a crusade to resist the erosion of autonomy.
How, then, is stability maintained and erosion resisted?

Sherpa actions conform to this principle, not because it is
directly and consciously applied, but because certain Sherpa
institutions (such as the accurate listing of the private property
brought into a marriage, and the avoidance of mentioning the names
of the dead) are widely adhered to. The first, by ensuring the
clear and unambiguous delineation of private property, keeps the
exits clear. The second, by continually dismantling the past, brings
the horizon of causation very close indeed. These (and other)
institutions, by systematically imposing clarity here and fuzziness
there, create conditions ideally suited to the adoption of a
strategy based upon the eager acceptance of myopically-perceived
risk. When it comes to decision-making, the Sherpa does not have to
make explicit his entire moral framework before he can decide what
course of action he should follow. Sherpa institutions constitute a
sort of automatic pilot: all he has to do is act in accordance with
them and they will make sure that he does the right thing. Though he

may have a firm conscious grasp of the moral principles by which he
and others operate, it is not essential for him to have such a grasp
in order to act in accordance with them.

Once the institutions exist, the lack of very coherent world
views among individual Sherpas poses no threat to the grid/group
hypothesis. An individual's world view has only to be sufficiently
developed, and sufficiently biased by his social context, for him
not to be tempted to override the automatic pilot. If these minimal
conditions are satisfied then he will be predisposed to grant
credibility to Sherpa institutions and, if he does this, stability
will prevail. Leaving aside for the moment the question of how
the institutions themselves come to exist, it is worth stressing
the immediacy, the practicality and the personal nature of this
minimal world view.

Most descriptions of a people's world view draw heavily upon
their religious beliefs and it may appear almost perverse for me to
develop this discussion of Sherpa world view with scarcely a mention
of the whole complex edifice of Tibetan Buddhism. It is very
tempting to view Tibetan Buddhism as the most perfect and elaborate
statement of the autonomous cosmology: it is certainly very easy
to put forward a convincing argument for this being the case. For
instance, in the Tibetan story of creation, there was, in the
beginning, not primitive communism but private property. The
Tibetan Garden of Eden started off divided into equal individually
owned plots and the fall came with the first theft: one man helping
himself to the fruit from another man's allotment. If egalitarianism and economic individualism are built into the Tibetan Genesis,
the ideal of non-coercion receives expression in the doctrine
relating to the proper use of hidden (Tantric) powers.

> They are most certainly not to be used as mere displays, nor for
> selfish ends, nor even to help others. Until we achieve perfect
> enlightenment we lack perfect wisdom, and lacking perfect wisdom
> we might, in seeking to help others through our power, interfere
> with their Lei (normal course of life) and do them harm. (17)

There are two reasons for exercising caution over this seemingly
perfect fit between Buddhist cosmology and Sherpa social context.
First, individual Sherpas are often surprisingly ignorant of it.
It is the monks who, relieved of the pressing and immediate concerns
with farming, trading and mountaineering, have the time, the
aptitude and the educational facilities that are so essential to
the acquisition of this complex cosmology. The lay Sherpa is
content to go along with this: he grants respect, financial
support and credibility to the monks who for their part concentrate
on their cosmological specialism and perform various religious
services for their lay fellows. In other words, for many Sherpas,
Buddhist cosmology is part of the automatic pilot rather than part
of their personal world view.

Second, one need only cast a glance at Christianity to realise
that complex all-embracing belief systems may incorporate so much
redundancy and latent contradiction that they have the potential
of being all things to all men. They constitute, as it were, a
nature from which, by emphasising this and ignoring that, we may
build up a cosmology to suit whatever our cultural bias happens to
be. I do not claim that Buddhism is totally flexible in this way,

only that it is possible to be Buddhist without being autonomous
and that it is possible to be autonomous without being Buddhist.
    Social scientists are only human and, within the nature that
they study, are as prone to selecting certain data and to discarding
others as is anyone else. Grid/group theory does not release us
from this human handicap but it does provide us with a technique for
recognising our cultural bias and for making some compensation for
it. Students of social change, for instance, have fastened too
superficially on the explicit cosmologies and have, in consequence,
had no option but to regard all changes within these cosmologies as
having equal social significance. Since often there is (or appears
to be) an awful lot of change going on, there is plenty of
opportunity for the observer (despite his best intentions) to
emphasise some specific changes and to ignore others at the largely
unconscious behest of his own cultural bias. The advantage of
grid/group theory is that it allows us to shift our focus from
this almost limitless realm to a deeper source of stability and of
change which, by virtue of its parsimony, should help us to discover
which are the serious changes and which are the changes that we
just think are serious. But, if I am to substantiate this claim,
I will have to give another example.
    As well as the Sherpas of Khumbu, the islanders of Tristan da
Cunha occupy this fifth context and they have established it with
a remarkably minimal cosmology. Munch, (18) their ethnographer,
calls this stable state 'normal social anomie' and he describes how
the founders of the community produced a written constitution in
the hope of guaranteeing its stability. It is clear from this
document that the founders - there were only three of them - had a
shared commitment to equality and independence: 'That in order to
ensure the harmony of the Firm, no member shall assume any
superiority whatever, but all to be considered as equal in every
respect'. (19) Unfortunately, having no Tibetan creation story to
guide them, they chose the wrong institutional means to achieve
their cultural goal.
    According to the original agreement, the settlement was organised
    as a communal enterprise.... However ... the idealistic combina-
    tion of a communal operation with complete freedom from authority
    and control was impossible to realise, and as one of these
    principles had to yield, anarchy prevailed, and the community
    developed into an aggregate of independent households. (20)
Thankful to have survived this crisis, and realising perhaps their
presumption in attempting to manufacture so complex an artefact,
they let Nature and their interaction with her fill in the remaining
clauses of their constitution.
    Like the Sherpas, they found that their environment favoured
exploitation by small family groups and that, since there was little
opportunity for economies of scale, they had nothing to fear from
the socially coercive grid and group threats that such economies
bring with them. At the fringe of this island community opportunitie
for seafaring adventure took the place of trading and mountaineering
among the Sherpas and so helped to keep the exits clear. Over the
years many settlers have entered the community (usually by ship-
wreck) and many have left, either permanently or temporarily, to
seek their fortunes on board the whalers that called at the island

on their way to and from Antarctic waters. Equipped with this
extraordinarily minimal cosmology, the community has stabilised its
predominant social context for more than a century and a half and has
successfully survived two alarming perturbations: the volcanic
eruption of their island home and the evacuation of the entire
community to a disused Air Force camp in England.

The Buddhist efflorescence in Khumbu - the monasteries, the
nunneries and the extensive contacts with their parent institutions
in Tibet - is very recent (the first monastery was founded in 1923)
and was made possible by the arrival of the potato, an event that
transformed the means at the Sherpas' disposal without affecting
their cultural goals. Since many bright young Sherpas, who
previously would have chosen an ecclesiastical career, are now
attracted to work in mountaineering and tourism, these Buddhist
institutions are somewhat in decline and many Western observers have
assumed that this decline heralds the collapse of the Sherpa way
of life. The Tristan da Cunha example provides a corrective to
this tendency to see all change as destructive in this way and
helps us to disentangle the minimal requirements for the stability
of the Sherpas' context from the massive cosmological overkill
that, thanks to this Buddhist efflorescence, they have until
recently enjoyed. (21)

Social and cultural institutions often present an appearance of
massive solidity and, as a result, social scientists have sometimes
tended to invest them with a certain primacy when seeking to understand social behaviour. In the same spirit, they often equate the
unpredictability of certain areas of social life with the absence
of such stabilising institutions. Grid/group theory suggests that
this solidity, whilst often real enough, is not something that is
intrinsic to institutions themselves, but rather is a quality that
is conferred upon (and, under the appropriate conditions, withdrawn
from) them by a grassroots process: the creative interaction
between an individual and his social context. According to whether
individuals are prepared to grant credibility to an institution or
not, so that institution flourishes or withers. Cosmologies are
the soil in which institutions grow and their biases are akin to
the extremes of acidity and alkalinity: if the soil is acid then
only certain plants will grow in it and if, for some reason, it
becomes alkaline then those plants will die and others will
establish themselves. Continuing the analogy, we should expect
grid/group theory, like soil science, to be a very practical and
useful body of knowledge. Not too concerned with the elevated
discussion of how institutions can come to exist, it concentrates
instead on the more down-to-earth problem of why, in any given
situation, we get one kind of possible institution rather than
another.

An institution will only remain stable if people are both willing
and able to support it. The consequence of this is that there are
two very different ways in which an institution can decline:
trivially, when just the means are lacking, and seriously, when the
will is lacking. The solidity of an institution derives ultimately
from the credibility that individuals grant to it, and individuals

grant credibility according to the degree of fit between that
institution and their world view.

If the decline of the Buddhist institutions in Khumbu is the
result of a lack of means, rather than a withdrawal of credibility,
then the Sherpa way of life is not collapsing but simply adjusting
itself to the Chinese occupation of Tibet and the arrival of the
western (and Japanese) tourist. A collapse or, to us a less value-
laden terminology, 'a fundamental change' in the Sherpa way of
life will only occur if, as a result of this adjustment, the fifth
context becomes unstable and there is a progressive shift in
individual social contexts away from zero group/zero grid. This is
the sort of practical contribution that grid/group analysis
promises: a technique for distinguishing between serious and
trivial changes in institutional support.

NOTES

1 The fieldwork in Nepal and the writing of this analysis were
   carried out as part of Mary Douglas's personal research project,
   supported from funds allocated to her by the Russell Sage
   Foundation in respect of her appointment as Director of Research.
2 I should emphasise that it is the fifth flat bit, not the
   presence and position of the two cusp catastrophes, that the
   geometry insists on. It is not possible to complete the
   surface linking the four peripheral flat bits without including
   in it a saddle point. The two cusp catastrophes are just there
   to fit the empirical data, though it may be possible to argue
   (using group and network theories) that they have to be there.
3 Chapter 3 in this volume.
4 No one, least of all the Sherpas, really knows how they got
   there. Oppitz thinks that it is likely that they came over the
   Nangpa La and moved straight through Khumbu to settle in Solu.
   Only later, he suggests, did some of the more marginal Sherpas
   move back to settle in Khumbu. Whichever way they came, their
   name still does not make much geographical sense. Michael
   Oppitz, 'Geschichte und Sozialordnung der Sherpa', Innsbruck
   and Munich, Universitäts-Verlag Wagner, 1968. Sherry B. Ortner,
   'Sherpas Through their Rituals', Cambridge University Press,
   1978.
5 Christoph von Fürer-Haimendorf, 'The Sherpas of Nepal' (1964);
   'Himalayan Traders' (1975), London, Murray.
6 Haimendorf 1975: 286.
7 Ibid.: 287.
8 Ibid.: 288.
9 This perhaps, rather than the cool climate, explains why the
   Rai (who do not have such units) were happy to accept from the
   Sherpas such a low price for the Solu region. To them it was
   not exploitable, to the Sherpas it was. It is now by far the
   most prosperous region of Nepal.
10 These cut-out mechanisms can be natural or man-made and, in the
   Sherpa case, both are present. The mountains that encircle
   Khumbu have, until recently, protected Sherpa autonomy and
   helped to ensure that decisions as to the nature of their

involvement with the outside world remained largely in Sherpa
hands. At the same time other geographical and ecological
constraints have operated in such a way that only a community
prepared to exploit the environment with very small economic
units could make a go of settling there.

11 But they have property significance in Solu where clans own
    valuable grazing lands. Perhaps this provided sufficient
    squeeze for some inhabitants, those without a good claim to
    clan membership, to become marginal and eventually to migrate
    and settle Khumbu?

12 This reflects the gradual process by which Khampas (and others)
    have become 'Sherpaised' and also, perhaps, the marginality of
    the original settlers from Solu. Oppitz maintains that even
    the core clans described by Haimendorf are largely spurious.

13 Haimendorf (1964: 18-19) records that traditions and myths
    relating to the Sherpas' migration to the regions of Solu and
    Khumbu and to the establishment of the present villages are
    almost completely lacking. This he finds all the more surprising
    in view of the high level of Sherpa literacy and of the
    prevalence of myths and traditions concerning the establishment
    of Buddhism in Tibet and of its subsequent arrival in Khumbu.
    He goes on to mention the very vague traditions that members
    of certain clans were the first to settle certain localities
    but that these beliefs find no expression in ritual or social
    behaviour. 'The idea that historical claims should be reflected
    in present-day rights is,' he says, 'foreign to the Sherpas',
    and he suggests that this attitude may account for their lack
    of interest in ethnic history.

    While Haimendorf's observations are perceptive his explanation
    is a shade tautological. Here I would argue that Sherpa social
    contexts are stabilised by a shared commitment to a distinct
    cosmology and that this commitment, by channelling credibility
    to such Sherpa institutions as the cremation and scattering of
    mortal remains, and avoiding mentioning the names of the dead,
    actually prevents such histories from developing. It is not
    so much a lack of interest in the past as a systematic imposition
    of ignorance. Such a systematic truncating of the Sherpa time-
    perspective is consistent with the continued existence of their
    social context.

    To say that an attitude is foreign is not in itself much of
    an explanation for the absence of the sort of behaviour that
    one might expect to find associated with such an attitude.
    The notion of cultural bias, and the hypothesis depicting how
    cultural bias varies with social context, allows us to predict
    in any specific situation which attitudes are likely to be
    'foreign' and which are likely to be 'home-grown'.

    The way in which certain institutions impose ignorance in
    this way is made clear by Clifford Geertz and Hildred Geertz
    (1964), Teknonymy in Bali: parenthood, age-grading and
    genealogical amnesia, 'Journal of the Royal Anthropological
    Institute', vol.94, part II.

14 Haimendorf 1964: 39.

15 The 1978 Women's Annapurna Expedition tried, but failed, to
    recruit high-altitude Sherpinis. Their successful bid put two

American women (using oxygen) and two male Sherpas (without oxygen) on the summit. Though a fine achievement, this does suggest that the expedition was rather inaptly named.

16   The full treatment of what happens to those who move (or are propelled) away from this fifth context is, unfortunately, beyond the scope of this essay but I can, perhaps, draw a very quick sketch of these transformations and give some indication of how the three-dimensional picture relates to them.

Leaving for Kathmandu can be seen as yet another kind of cut-out mechanism. Rows, such as that in which Ang Phu was a central figure, can involve the tightening of loose groupings and the activation of personal networks that, in the normal course of Khumbu life, are but little called upon. Ang Phu, by rushing onto the steeper slopes, is threatening to pull the others with him. If he lets go, they are able to pull back to more level ground. Because of this increasing tension and sudden letting go, it is difficult to say what exactly is happening to Ang Phu's social context, as he leaves for Kathmandu, beyond the fact that it is seriously perturbed. He has left the gentle slopes and is somewhere on the steeper ground that surrounds the col. If the effect of his experiences in Kathmandu is to bring him momentarily to rest somewhere on these steep slopes, then a fairly early return to Khumbu will be the most likely outcome. But his experiences may not bring him to rest; they may carry him ever further away from the fifth context towards one or another of the remaining four. The little fiddle that got Ang Phu onto his first expedition and his rapid subsequent progress suggest that his personal network has become increasingly effective, and the fact that his risk-taking (though now more conscious) has not declined at all tends to confirm that his momentum has carried him up towards the entrepreneurial context. To reach the summit of Everest is still, for both westerner and Sherpa, a great personal achievement; to be sirdar (manager) of an Everest expedition is the Sherpa equivalent of striking gold. In 1978 Ang Phu pulled off the double. (Ang Phu was killed on the West Ridge of Everest in May 1979.)

Some Sherpas are less successful in their networking and, banding together to collectively resist the hostile forces that individually they cannot handle, move towards the bottom right context and adopt the collectivist survival strategy. A few months before Ang Phu's success on Everest, some Sherpas (on a 'safe' tourist trek, not a 'dangerous' mountaineering expedition) were caught in a storm on a high pass. The well-equipped Sahibs and the well-equipped Sherpas survived but several of their local (non-Sherpa) porters, who had only cotton clothing and were carrying heavy loads, died. Some Americans (who also happened to be crossing the pass) did all they could and tried to get the Sherpas to help the exhausted porters. One porter had collapsed in the snow and had been left there by the Sherpas. They refused to go back up to help him, saying, 'he is not a member of the party'!

17   Thubten Jigme Norbu and Colin M. Turnbull, 'Tibet', Harmondsworth, Penguin, 1976: 46.

18   Peter A. Munch, Anarchy and anomie in an atomistic community,
     'Man' (NS), 1974, 2: 243-61.
19   Ibid.: 250.
20   Ibid.: 251. This inevitable contradiction in the islanders'
     constitution is made graphically clear by the three-dimensional
     picture. Freedom from authority and control can only be attained
     when there is no manipulation, and the only stabilisable context
     where this condition is satisfied is zero group/zero grid. A
     communal enterprise inevitably imposes a large positive group
     component on the social contexts of all those individuals who
     are a party to it. The only stabilisable contexts on the
     positive group side of the picture are at strongly positive grid
     and strongly negative grid, both of which entail high (positive
     and negative, respectively) levels of manipulation. If stability
     is to prevail, one or other of the contradictory clauses in the
     constitution must give. Which one?
        The clause insisting on equality and freedom from authority
     and control is a clear expression of a shared commitment to a
     world view; the clause insisting on a communal enterprise does
     not express the shared world view of the founders, rather it is
     included in the mistaken belief that it will provide the
     institutional means that will enable them to achieve and maintain
     their cultural goal. When the contradiction arises, it is this
     tactical, rather than strategic, clause that gets struck out.
21   Another interesting question we should ask is: 'Why should so
     many of us have this tendency?' The answer suggested by grid/
     group theory is that not only are the observations of the
     western student of change (be it social, economic, political or
     ecological) distorted by his own cultural bias but that many
     of these professionals also share the same cultural bias. A
     consequence of this is that, when so many professionals agree
     that every prospect pleases and only western man is vile, we
     should not assume that this near-unanimity among the experts
     indicates that they are right. Though they may be right, such
     a majority verdict suggests simply that many of them occupy the
     same sort of social context.

INDEX

Bloch, M., 256
Bloor, C., 13
Bloor, D., 13
body-symbolism, 279, 280
Bolingbroke, Henry St J., 128
Booger Dance, 173-5
Borges, J.-L., 132-3
boundaries, 117, 202, 206, 246;
  administrative, 151; anomaly
  and, 199; between quadrants, 35;
  classificatory, 196, 197, 201;
  consciousness of, 91; disciplinary, 95; egalitarian groups
  and, 253, 259; external, 4, 8,
  164, 176, 182; in festival, 171,
  173, 174, 187n; geographical
  space and, 265-6; geological, 231;
  identification with, 280;
  institutional, 199; insulating,
  6; lack of, 165; maintenance of,
  175; operational space and, 262;
  penetration of, 293; preservation, 36; professional, 118-19;
  schisms and, 263; transactions
  across, 201-2; unclear, 40, 283;
  weak, 138
bougeois philosophy, 124
Boyer, P., 275-6, 290-7
Brahmin, 21
Britain, 31
Brongniart, Alexandre, 224
Broom, L., 190
Brown, P., 153
Buckland, William, 224, 227, 229,
  230, 231, 232, 236, 237, 238
Buddhism, 309, 320, 321
budget information, 108
budget performance, 107, 109
'Bulletin of the Atomic
  Scientists', 31
Bunyan, John, 249
Burchfield, J.D., 220
bureaucracy, rational, 155
Burridge, K., 249, 250, 267, 268,
  269

Caillois, R., 165, 187
Campaign for Nuclear Disarmament,
  31
Caneva, K.L., 228
Cantor, Georg, 217
capital expenditure, 106
capitalists, primitive, 17

capital resources, 106
Caracas Carnival, 183-4
cargo cults, 249, 250, 253,
  267-70
Cassirer, Ernst, 128
caste relations, 21-3, 45
catastrophe, 12; theory, 42, 47,
  53
category violators, 215n
Cauchy, Augustin, 200, 204, 207
causal explanation, 227, 232,
  238-9
centralism, 21
centrality, 38
centre position, 78-9, 302-27
certainty, 142, 143
Cherokee, the, 173-5
Ch'in, 151, 152
China, 132-59; Chou, 138-44;
  literature, 133; new information on, 136-8
choice, 122
Christianity, 126, 127, 248,
  321-2
Chuang Tzu, 148-51
civic virtues, 166
civilization, march of, 123-4
class differences, 68, 75
classic texts, 133, 146
classification, 20-4, 197-201,
  206; absence of, 164;
  boundaries and, 196, 197;
  constraints, 261; criticism
  of, 148; geological, 226,
  230-1; incoherent, 228; two
  dimensional, 20-4; in witchcraft societies, 278-9, 283,
  285-6, 287-90, 297
Cleverly, G., 103
Cockburn, William, 231-2
Codere, H., 171, 172
coercion, 316, 318, 321
cognitive bias, 8, 44, 49
cognitive economics, 51
cognitive style, 115; in geology,
  219-41; in mathematics,
  191-218
cognitive systems, 256
Cohn, N., 248, 249, 251, 253
collective strategy, 42, 60, 61
colour, 150-1
commitment, 35
Committee for Nuclear Information,
  31